ROD BR

TEA &ME

ONE FOR TEA

VOLUME 1

A country boy becomes a man on an Indian tea estate

ROD BROWN

TEA &ME

ONE FOR TEA

VOLUME 1

A country boy becomes a man on an Indian tea estate

MEREO
Cirencester

Published by Mereo

1A The Market Place Cirencester Gloucestershire GL7 2PR
info@memoirsbooks.co.uk | www.memoirspublishing.com

TEA AND ME

ISBN: 978-1-86151-039-6

Introduction

I wrote this account of my life and work in India in fulfilment of a promise I once made to my mother. Of all the people who ever asked me about my life in tea, Mum was one of the very few who actually listened with genuine interest to what I had to say, to the extent that she made me promise I would write this record for future members of our family to read and enjoy. Whether I have been successful only you, the reader, will be able to say.

Mum always regretted the fact that we were so far away. She once said that had she known how sad and lonely she would feel sometimes, she would have torn the advertisement up before I had a chance to see it. However, I never regretted going to India. It was through her foresight and encouragement that I went and so it is with loving thanks and many fond memories that I dedicate this story to her.

This volume covers my first period in tea, the four years as a young trainee from 1951 to 1955. A later volume, all being well, will cover the years that followed when I returned as a family man.

Gladys Marie Brown (Blackburn)
b. May 1st 1899
d. March 8th 1978

R G Brown
November 2013

Contents

Introduction

Thoughts of India, and preparations for departure

On many occasions over the years I have been asked how I came to go to India to work in tea. Our family had no direct links with the tea industry, and other than the fact that most of the men of my father's generation had fought overseas during the First World War, very few had ever been abroad. In fact, when I was offered the job in 1950 it was almost as though it had been pre-ordained, and the opportunity just occurred instead of being planned.

Although my father did not ill-treat me deliberately and I did not want for the necessities of life, his years in the army, and especially the time he spent in the trenches in France, seemed to have hardened him, and he was a very difficult person to get to know. Born in 1899, he was on the Somme on his 18th birthday, and the memories of the things he saw and experienced during those months must have stayed with him for the rest of his life. In his own rough and ready way I believe he thought he was toughening me up and preparing me for adult life, for he believed that to be tender and considerate was a form of weakness, and that the only way to improve a person was to point out his faults to him. As a result I received very little praise or encouragement from him when I had done well, although my mistakes were always pointed out to me very quickly indeed. He usually came to watch me play football for Coaley Rovers, and afterwards I always heard about the chances I had missed instead of the goals I had managed to score. However in retrospect, I think that had we been closer as father and son, I might have appreciated the fact that at least he did come to watch me play.

I was born on 23rd October, 1928 in the small village of Coaley in Gloucestershire, and after attending the village school until I was 11 years of age, I passed the entrance examination for admission to Dursley Secondary School, where I gained my Oxford School Certificate. After this I could have continued in the sixth form with the hope of going to university, but as so many ex-servicemen were coming home at that time, I decided that if I could do something practical it would be a better plan, so I was accepted by R A Lister, Dursley for a fitting and turning apprenticeship, and for three years everything went fine. I got good results and passed my Ordinary National Certificate. It was not until I completed my apprenticeship and started working full time in the factory that things began to turn really sour.

I began my adult working life as a machine setter/operator in the bar automatic machine shop, and unfortunately this was where Dad worked as well. As a result I could do or say very little that he didn't see or wasn't told about, and gradually things deteriorated. He would tell me about and interfere in things that I considered to be my own personal affairs, and this caused a lot of friction between us. Thinking about it now, I suppose the correct thing to have done would have been to ask for a transfer to another department, but I was stubborn and lacking in experience, and gradually I let things get on top of me until a curtain of silence fell between us and we had very little contact.

On the other hand, Mum was a very much gentler and understanding person who was always ready to help, and it was to her I tended to turn to for help and guidance when things got bad. Gradually I came to the conclusion that the best thing for me to do was to leave home and try to get work elsewhere, but to do this at that time was not as easy as it sounds. Thousands of ex-servicemen were being demobilised and were trying to adjust to life as civilians in a country that was still suffering from the effects of the war, and suitable work and accommodation were very difficult to obtain. However, my work at Listers' had involved me with the setting up of single spindle automatic machines which worked using cams that were made by the BSA Company in Birmingham, and after talking things over with Mum, I decided to travel to Birmingham to see whether there were any jobs going in the field of cam designing.

This is where fate stepped in, and my life changed completely. Mum always read the *Gazette*, our local newspaper, as soon as it was delivered, and one Saturday morning in October 1950 she looked up from the paper and said, 'Here's a good job that would suit you'. Mildly interested, I enquired what it was, and she read out that C A Goodricke and Co., a tea company whose offices were based in Mincing Lane in London, were looking for suitable engineers to go out to work on their tea estates in India and Pakistan.

Before the Second World War the Indian tea industry was very much a closed shop, and in order to be recruited a person

3

had to know someone who was already in tea or be recommended. However, once India had gained her independence things changed completely. The estates and their factories had received very little care and attention during the war, and whole areas of tea had been temporarily abandoned because the labourers who should have been working on them had been taken away to build airfields, roads and bridges, and also work on the Burma Road. In addition buffalo cart transport, by which every item had been carried before the war, was superseded by second-hand army surplus trucks and tractors which were sold off afterwards, and as a result the tea companies needed to recruit lads with a general engineering background who could cope with this new technology and had the ability to become fluent in a completely new language, in addition to learning labour management and the cultivation and manufacture of tea. They needed to be the type who had no preconceived notions of life in tea based on what they had learned of life in the Indian Raj before independence, and also be willing to live a comparatively quiet life up country under the restrictions placed upon foreigners by the new Indian government. In the case of Goodricke's, they decided to advertise in the local papers serving places connected to large engineering works, and because several of their estates were equipped with Lister 16/2 two cylinder electricity generating sets, they tried Dursley, the home of the Lister company, as one of their options, and this was the advertisement that Mum saw.

At first I was extremely dubious. I lacked self-confidence, and could not see how any firm would want to bother with a country rustic like me, but Mum pointed out that maybe this was the type of person they really did require, and if I was interested why not apply and let them tell me that I was unsuitable, rather than pre-judging the issue myself. She was an extremely clever person in her own quiet kind of way, and ultimately she made me see that maybe I did have something to offer them, so I obtained and completed an application form but posted it without much hope.

Imagine my utter surprise when I received a reply asking me to go to London for an interview on the 30th November. Really I had never expected to receive a reply like that, so I was over the moon with delight at having been given the interview without actually worrying about whether I would get the job or not, which seemed to be like something in another world, but from the literature which accompanied the letter the work to be done seemed to be just up my street.

On the eagerly awaited day I cycled over to Stroud railway station and caught the 8.30 am train. As my interview was one of the first I thought this would get me into London in plenty of time for it at 11.45. Imagine my consternation when the train was badly delayed by thick banks of fog and it finally arrived at Paddington at 12 o'clock, over an hour late.

Cursing the slowness of the tube trains I rushed to Mincing Lane, where I arrived at 12.30, out of breath and worried sick that they would not want to see me. To my great relief the young receptionist took it all in her stride, saying that they had guessed that something unexpected must have happened in view of the adverse weather conditions, and that if I wished to wait they would continue the interviews as arranged and then I could go in last of all. Well this suited me fine, so I settled down in the waiting room to get my breath back. She told me that initially there had been over 200 applications, but from these ten suitable applicants had been selected to be interviewed for two jobs, one in India and the other in East Pakistan, and these were being carried out by one of the company directors, Mr J S Graham.

As I waited I talked to a lad who was sitting near me, who told me that he worked as a draughtsman in an engineering works near Brighton, and as I chatted to him my hopes plummeted. He sounded extremely confident, and from what he was saying he was ideally suited for the job and it was only a formality for him to attend the interview. He thought he only had to go in and probably they would offer him the job there and then. This didn't do very much to bolster my ego, and I was quite relieved when his turn came and he passed through the door on his way.

Most of the interviews were taking about half an hour to complete, so you can imagine my surprise when the door opened after about twenty minutes and out he came, face as long as a fiddle and very quiet. It was as much as he could do to say goodbye as he walked out. At this moment I was completely nonplussed, not having any idea as to what had happened. It was only after I had had my own interview that I twigged just what had occurred. The other applicants went and returned, and finally my turn came: 'Mr. Roderick Brown, please'.

Passing through the forbidding door I found myself in a pleasant, airy office with a thick-set elderly gentleman sitting on the edge of a desk. Immediately he put me at my ease by asking me to tell him something about myself, my home life, hobbies, health, upbringing and my general attitude to work. Then he began to ask me practical questions about specific engineering problems. How would I tackle the job of erecting line shafting on a row of vertical columns? If a line shaft bearing was running hot, how would I correct it? What did I know about foundations, and how would I go about putting down floor-mounted machinery powered by the line shaft? How would I scrape in a big end bearing on a diesel engine? What did I know about the operation of steam engines, water turbines and Pelton Wheels?

The list seemed endless, though in reality this part of the interview must have taken no longer than fifteen minutes. Luckily I had done most of this type of work while working in the training school at Listers' or had covered it while working for my ONC at night school, so I was able to answer him with complete assurance. The more we went on the more confident I became, so that by the time he began to ask me what I thought about working odd hours and Sundays, I was completely at ease. I explained that when harvesting and haymaking in the country, you had to take advantage of the weather and keep working until the job was finished, and I presumed that working in tea would be something similar, but little did I realise how right I was. Finally he asked me how I felt about the fact that I would be away from home for five years until my first home leave, and also the fact that it was a condition of service that Assistant Managers could not get married during this period. I replied that I would miss my home and family, but considered the challenge of being in India would compensate for this, and although I did have a girlfriend I had no intention of getting married in the foreseeable future, which seemed to satisfy him.

At last, after about 50 minutes, it came to an end, and after thanking me he asked me to wait outside. As I waited I thought about the interview and how I had done, and wondered about what had happened to the lad from Brighton. In all probability, if he had specialised as a draughtsman and had very little practical working experience, then he would have had no idea of how to answer the practical questions and thus would have been weeded out very early in his interview. In my case it was only my good fortune that I had done this type of work, as working with line shafting etc. was not a part of a normal Fitting and Turning Apprenticeship.

However, it had so happened that in the summer of 1949 I was working in the Diesel Engine Machine Shop operating a helical gear hobbing machine. This consisted of loading ten four-inch-diameter steel blanks on to a central spindle which rotated beneath a hobbing cutter, and this then worked its way along the blanks cutting the teeth until all the gears were cut. Once this was done, the finished gears were taken off and replaced by another ten blanks and the whole routine started again. The operation took about 25 minutes to complete, and other than filing any rough swarf off the gears I had nothing else to do except stand and watch the spindle revolve, which was extremely boring. At this time I was cycling to and from Dursley twice a day, a total of twenty miles, besides working an eight and a half hour day and attending two hours of night school three evenings a week, plus homework, so I felt quite tired.

The afternoon was very hot, and as I stood and watched the blanks go round my eyes got heavier and heavier, until finally I fell asleep leaning on the machine. At this point Nemesis arrived in the form of Frank Lister, one of the Lister brothers, who happened to walk through the shop, and he raised hell the moment he saw me. I was marched up to the Personnel Office so fast that my feet hardly touched the floor, and after a dressing down was asked to explain my actions, which could have resulted in my apprenticeship being terminated. I made a clean breast of things, explained how boring and time-wasting that actual job was, with no capacity for teaching an apprentice anything at all, and the only reason I had not complained about it before was because I was due to move on to another department at the end of the month. As a result I was given a severe warning for my sins and was transferred to the Training School as a punishment.

This was the place where beginners started their training and learned to use tools, gauges and machines while developing their engineering skills, but because I had already had two years' experience in the works the foreman made me his charge-hand (second in command) almost immediately. Thus it turned out that what should have been a punishment proved to be the making of me, because at that time plans were afoot for it to be enlarged and reorganised, and this necessitated making plinths and foundations, uprooting and re-siting the machines and realigning the line shafting which drove them. Subsequently I stayed there for five months, during which time I planned and supervised these operations, learning as the work progressed, and this is how I came to get my practical experience. As I sat and waited I thought about this and was amused to think that Frank Lister probably would never know what a favour he did me that day when he caught me napping. Such is fate.

I didn't see Mr Graham again. I was asked to wait for a while until the receptionist came out from her office to tell me that I needn't wait any longer, but that they would contact me in due course regarding the job. However, if they did decide to offer it to me I would need to pass a general medical examination, so in this eventuality, rather than call me up to London again, would I be willing to go to a local doctor and have it now if I had the time? To this I replied that I had nothing else important planned provided I caught the last train home, and in a few minutes an office junior was leading me through what seemed to me to be a maze of back streets and alleyways to the doctor's where the examination had been arranged.

After a ten-minute walk we entered a very large terraced house with several large gleaming brass plates on the door, and soon I was ushered into a consulting room where the doctor awaited me. He seemed to be a very ordinary little man, but he gave me a very thorough examination and asked about our family's general health, and then it was into the warren of back streets again back to the office where I was given my travelling expenses and told that I would hear from them again in due course. Even though Goodricke's had arranged the medical for me, so they must have been interested, I was so lacking in self-confidence that it just didn't sink in that it was likely that I would get the job, and it didn't surprise me when the days went by without any news.

So you can imagine my surprise and delight when a letter arrived on 14th December offering me the post and saying that if I accepted it I would be sailing for India on the 18th January. When I read this I was absolutely flabbergasted. I also felt quite frightened, with a horrible sinking feeling in the pit of my stomach. Until now it had been like a game. I had been sure I wouldn't be chosen – I was just proceeding step by step to see how far I could go until someone called a halt, but now the chips were down and I had to make a very important decision about something that I knew very little about. Other than for a couple of short holidays I had never been away from home and now I was proposing to cut myself adrift for at least three years, possibly five. I had wanted to leave home, but had never considered making such a decisive cut as this, so I had big decisions to make.

Working a 48-hour week at Listers', my take-home pay was about £7.10s. per week or about £10 if I worked on the night shift because of bonuses and more hours worked. The starting pay of an Assistant in India was not very much better, about £33 per month at the current exchange rate of 13.5 rupees to £1, but considering the fact that I was being paid to learn, and that there was a fixed scale of increments in the years ahead, future prospects looked good compared with staying at Listers'. In addition it appeared that it was cheaper to live in India than it was at home, and then at the end of five years' service I would get eight months' leave on full pay.

What a prospect. It made five years seem like no time at all.

I thought it over for a couple of days and talked to Mum. Although I was not happy at the thought of leaving her for so long, she insisted that I should go if I felt it was the right thing to do, and finally I decided to accept the offer. What I did not realise was that Goodrickes were part of a merger at that time, and Mr Graham was to become the Managing Director of the new company of Walter Duncan & Goodricke, Ltd. when it was incorporated as a Public Company in London on 19th January, 1951, the day after I sailed, so in actual fact I was in at the very start. He had come home from India in 1944, after 31 years in tea, and later became Chairman of the company and President of the Indian Tea Association in London in 1958.

I knew nothing of this at that time and my mind was very disturbed by the speed at which the developments had occurred. However, once I made up my mind to accept the post, despite being rather awed and apprehensive about what I was about to do, it felt as though a great load had been lifted

11

from my shoulders. I accepted the company's offer subject to receiving satisfactory answers to queries about repatriation in the event of anything going wrong, and began to make the necessary arrangements to sail on January 18th, exactly one month ahead.

I handed in my required one week's notice to terminate my employment at Listers', and immediately they offered me a job in their factory in Australia. I was overwhelmed. Why hadn't they offered it before? They say 'Empty vessels make the most noise' but in retrospect it appears that if you work conscientiously and keep your head down you do not get noticed, and everyone assumes you are content to be stuck in your own little corner. It seems it is a good thing to stir the water in the bucket occasionally, because I was asked to reconsider taking the job in tea, but I refused because I was unwilling to let Goodricke's down. In the end Listers' said that if life in tea proved to be unsatisfactory and I couldn't settle down in India, if I let them know they would arrange for me to travel on straight to Australia where a job would be waiting for me. Not too bad for a man who had gone to sleep on the job.

I accepted the compromise and agreed to work to the end of the month so that I could train someone suitable to take over my machines. Then I began to prepare for the journey. Since finishing my apprenticeship I had managed to save £50, quite a substantial sum in those days, and I spent most of this on two steel trunks and a strengthened cabin case to take my luggage which I bought from Bon Marché in Gloucester. I had plenty of ordinary clothes, and the £20 outfit allowance which the company supplied covered the other incidentals which I needed. Goodricke's paid for a first class passage on the *Strathaird*, and I heard that it was normal procedure to 'dress' for dinner while on board, but, when I enquired about this I was told that although a dinner jacket was desirable and I would need one in India, a normal suit and tie was acceptable dress on board ship, so I decided against buying one as it was much cheaper and satisfactory to get one made once I had settled down.

I obtained information about India from a retired army officer, Lt. Col. Pease, who was living at Trenley House in Coaley, and he helped me a great deal. He had served in north-east India for many years, so he was able to give me much good advice regarding suitable clothing, medicines and other necessary items which I would not have considered taking. He told me there was very little in the way of organised western-style entertainment in India, especially away from the cities, but as there was no limit to the amount of personal effects which I could take with me on the ship, I decided to take a box of my favourite books, my records and my trombone as well. My electric record player was unsuitable as the mains current on the estates was 110 volts DC. I packed the books in one of my trunks, but packing the records was much more difficult. I had about 150 of them, mostly old classic jazz discs which I had found in junk shops in company with my old friend Norman 'Punch' Partridge, so I manufactured a customised box to take them. Adapted from an old beer bottle crate, it had dividing slats every 20 records to cushion the shocks and prevent them moving during the journey, and it was tastefully finished in a ghastly shade of brilliant green, the only paint Dad had in his shed. One hundred and fifty 78 rpm vinyl records were very heavy by themselves and by the time the top was securely screwed tight I could hardly lift it. Still I must have done a good job because when they finally arrived at Zurrantee not one was broken, the only drawback was that it was ages before I could afford to buy a gramophone to play them on.

Both the books and the records, together with my two trunks, were to be carried in the hold of the ship as 'Accompanied Luggage Not Required on the Voyage' and as such had to be at the shipping agents' office in London by 10th January so they could be loaded in the hold.

I had had my trombone for two years, and during 1950 had been having lessons from a member of the City of Gloucester Silver Band. Unfortunately, a few months before I had been kicked in the mouth while playing football which caused the loss of three of my front teeth, and the denture with which I had been fitted made trombone playing very difficult. However I thought I should have plenty of spare time to practice in India, so as it had its own case and would travel as cabin baggage I decided to take it with me. Little did I think that the only time I really would blow it in earnest would be to frighten the tea garden labourers, but I'll tell that tale later.

A few days after I had finalised my arrangements another very fortunate thing happened which influenced the rest of my life - I met a girl named Jan, again. I had known her for several years, and we had had a boyfriend and girlfriend relationship during 1951. However the friendship became rather stale, and as Jan thought she was missing out on a lot of fun by being restricted to one partner at dances etc., we parted quite amicably. However we remained friends, and sometimes saw each other at dances and old-time dancing class. On Thursday evening 21st December I had been to the Drill Hall in Bolton Lane where the Dursley Town players did their football training, and as I came down the hill into Silver Street on my bike, I saw

Jan walking along by the old Star Inn. She had visited friends at Fairmead, Cam, on the way home from work in Gloucester, and she was now walking home after spending the evening with them. Although I had had several other girlfriends since we parted she knew I was still very keen on her, and as I wouldn't be able to see her for the next five years, I decided to cycle after her and ask if I could walk home with her, and then tell her about the new job at the same time.

I didn't know it at the time, but much later she told me she had hoped I would follow and catch up with her, and was very pleased when I did so. Of course, she was very surprised at my news, but it seemed to be the catalyst which made our friendship bloom again, and we more or less carried on from where we had left off before. As a result of this I was invited to the family Christmas party, where I met Jan's Uncle Jim Perrin for the first time, who gave me some advice which caused a very humorous incident later, and which made me realise that some of the tales I was told about life in India had to be taken with a large pinch of salt. He had been in the army in India, and amongst other stories he told me was that in the big cities the taxi drivers took advantage of strangers by driving them in a very roundabout way to their destinations so that they could overcharge for a short journey. In all my years in India I never came across this practice at all, but at that time I accepted everything I was told at face value, and this stuck firmly in my mind until I needed a taxi in Bombay one day but was afraid to take one.

To live in India I needed all the usual vaccinations and inoculations, and I got most of these from my doctor. However, I had to cycle 20 miles down to Southmead Hospital in Bristol for the yellow fever injection, which was a horrendous affair. A nurse injected me in the base of the spine with a large syringe and a needle which seemed to be several inches long, and the pain, together with the bruising and swelling which it caused, made the ride home a very long and memorable one indeed, especially as I found out later that I need not have had it in the first place - it wasn't required for India at all.

I finished working at Listers' on 29th December, so my priority in the New Year was to complete my packing so that I could get my heavy luggage away to Escombe McGraths' for loading. My main problem was how to get it over to Stroud Railway Station, but finally I managed to get some help from a neighbour named Reg Woodward who had the use of a lorry, and we managed to deliver it to Stroud without too much difficulty. However the trunks were extremely heavy, especially the one containing my books, and it was as much as Reg and I could do to lift them onto the back of the lorry. Consequently it came as a great surprise to me when I got to Calcutta to see a thin, wiry porter lift a trunk onto his head with only a little bit of help, and then carry it several hundred yards by balancing it on a small cloth ring on the top of his head. The only help he needed was for someone to help him lift it down. Some of the loads the porters carried were absolutely phenomenal, and I once saw two men in Calcutta carrying a grand piano on the tops of their heads, much more efficiently than Laurel and Hardy ever managed to move theirs.

On 4th January I visited the London office again, partly to meet the people with whom I would be involved once I was working in India, but also to be given some information regarding the import and marketing of tea at this end. On this occasion I caught the early train, and as it was a fine, frosty morning I was in London by 9 am. I didn't realise it at that time, but the office staff in London looked on the planters in India as an elite corps, almost like celebrities, and even though I was only just beginning my career I felt a little of this atmosphere as I was shown round the office. For the first time in my life it made me feel as though I really could amount to something, especially when I was introduced to one of the directors of the company, Mr E A Mitchell, whose son John was being groomed to take his place on the board when his father retired, and who was already on an estate in India gaining first-hand knowledge.

Mr Mitchell had also been a director of W S Cresswell and Co, the brokers and tea tasters which handled all Goodricke's teas, and I was taken to their offices where I was shown current tea samples, both good and bad, and the correct way to taste them. Then it was back to the office, where I was shown the general office procedure before being treated to lunch at a local restaurant. All in all it was a very interesting morning, and from what I had seen and heard I thought I should like a life in tea.

The Goodricke's group consisted of four tea companies owning ten estates, all situated in the Dooars area of West Bengal, about 300 miles north of Calcutta. The Dooars occupy a narrow strip of India to the south of the Himalayas, which connects Assam to the rest of India, about 150 miles long and 40 miles wide lying between the Terai in the west, the Brahmaputra River in the east and East Bengal, (now Bangladesh), in the South. The ten estates which made up our group were:

The Aibheel Tea Co. Ltd.	Aibheel	Tea Estate
	Fagu	Tea Estate
The Bagracote Tea Co. Ltd.	Bagracote	Tea Estate
	Baintgoorie	Tea Estate

The Chulsa Tea Co. Ltd.	Chulsa	Tea Estate
	Sam Sing	Tea Estate
	Sathkyah	Tea Estate
	Yong Tong	Tea Estate
	Zurrantee	Tea Estate
The Dangua Jhar Tea Co. Ltd.	Dangua Jhar	Tea Estate

All these were administered locally by a Superintendent, Mr Laurence Tocher, whose office was on Sam Sing. Although the normal procedure was for a new European assistant to stay on an estate for at least two years in order to settle down, in actual fact we could be transferred to any one of the ten gardens at short notice if conditions necessitated. All company business was forwarded to London through him, and each month the estate managers sent a report to London detailing everything that had occurred on the estate during the previous month. I was being shown round by the office manager, a very pleasant middle-aged lady, and unofficially she told me that in all probability I would be going to Zurrantee as my first garden, so wasn't I lucky? Of course this information meant nothing to me, but evidently the manager was a legend named Bill Milne whose deeds were talked about in hushed whispers, and who according to one recent report had shot three tigers in one afternoon.

I was thunderstruck. One tiger a day seemed bad enough, but three in one afternoon was almost beyond belief - surely she was pulling the new boy's leg? But no, it was all true. During the war when many of the male labourers had been taken to aid the war effort, a large area of tea in the northwest corner of the estate on the edge of the Zurrantee river had been temporarily abandoned, and as a result it had grown unrestricted for several years. Without pruning to maintain its artificial shape the tea plant grows naturally into a magnificent tree some 20 to 25 feet high, and so when the time came to reclaim it in 1950 it was a matted mass of tea bushes 12 feet high, in which a family of three tigers had made their home. The tigress, together with her two almost adult cubs, resented the intrusion of the labourers when they came to prune the bushes, and repeatedly chased them to frighten them out. Finally it was decided that the only thing to do was to get rid of them as pests, and Bill organised a shoot. That afternoon all his friends who went shooting gathered in the area, and after setting them out along the edge of the tea, the labourers started beating from the other side. They would have made a terrific noise, blowing whistles and beating gongs, saucepans and anything else that made a noise and for a few minutes all was quiet in the tea, then as it so happened, first one of the youngsters followed later by the tigress and her other cub all burst out of the tea just in front of Bill, all within the space of about forty minutes. I think he was as surprised as everyone else, but he was a magnificent shot, and as each one came out he managed to kill it cleanly on the spot. Afterwards he said they were so close to him that he could hardly miss. What he would have done had they all come out together he never did say, as Bill was already a well-known character in tea, partly due to the fact that he used to tell some terribly tall stories, but this incident made him into a legend overnight. Of course he got his leg pulled unmercifully by the other planters, who told him they couldn't understand why he had called them over to the shoot if he had wanted to shoot all three of them himself.

Another noteworthy thing that had happened to him was that he had been marooned in Darjeeling for several days during the previous year and had to leave his car there. In August 1950, a severe earthquake in the hills east of Assam had caused considerable damage in the Dooars and Darjeeling areas, even though they were about 800 miles away. The railway bridge across the Teesta river had been destroyed, and the tremors, combined with the torrential monsoon rain, had caused severe landslides in Darjeeling town, one of which demolished part of the Planter's Club and carried away whole sections of the two roads which connected Darjeeling to the plains. It so happened that Bill was in Darjeeling at this time, and the damage done to the roads was so bad that he had to leave his car there for several weeks until one was opened again to vehicles. After a couple of days during which the hillside stabilised, he managed to scramble down over the affected area until he reached the other side, several hundred feet below, from where he was able to get transport back to Zurrantee. These were only a couple of the tales she told me, but it seemed the office staff in London lived a vicarious life in India through hearing stories such as these, and they gave me a lot to think about on the return journey that evening.

One thing she didn't tell me though, and what I didn't realise until several years afterwards, was that in the early 1950s the Indian tea industry was in the middle of a catastrophic slump. The Ministry of Food continued to ration tea at the rate of 2 oz per person per week, which suppressed consumption, and also operated a ban on the export of tea from London. The government believed that supplies of tea might not be sufficient to meet demands if the ration allowances were increased, so arrivals proved to be in excess of day to day needs. As a result the nation's consumption was clearly defined, so there was no inducement for the buyers to bid for more than their ration requirements. In fact, in early 1952, up to 50% of the teas in the London auctions failed to attract any bids whatsoever, and it was not until later that year after the ration had been increased and the controls lifted that the off-take improved, and the estates began to make a profit again.

Of course, I didn't know anything about any of this in 1950 and I did wonder afterwards whether I might have reconsidered the Lister offer had I known the state the tea industry was in at that time. Still, they say a little knowledge is a dangerous thing, so I was very pleased that I knew absolutely nothing about it at the time, and as a consequence had nothing to worry about.

I played my last game of football for Dursley Town in the Gloucestershire Northern Senior League at home against Leonard Stanley on 13th January, and at a social held in the King's Head afterwards I was presented with a Parker fountain pen as a farewell gift. We also had a farewell party at Coaley Youth Club where they gave me a book token, and these farewells, together with the fact that I had to go round all my family members and friends to say goodbye, made me realise that my time was running out.

On Monday, 15th January, so that we could spend some time together, I took Jan up to London to see the sights, and we had a lovely day. The weather was mild and dry, and our visit was only marred by the fact that we had to get her shoe repaired in the Imperial War Museum, where a nail had come up through the sole. We persuaded one of the curators to thump it down with a hammer. In the evening we went to the London Jazz Club where we saw Humphrey Lyttelton and his band play, a first for Jan, and we enjoyed it so much that we were late leaving and missed the last train home. After a long, tiring day,

Jan was terribly upset and worried, because she was due to go to work the next morning. However, we made the best of things and did catch the 'milk train' which left Paddington at 12.30 am. Unfortunately this stopped at every halt and station between London and Stroud, so it was 4.30 am when we finally arrived there, tired but happy after a wonderful day. Of course Jan had to go to work at 8.30, but was so tired that her supervisor took pity on her and sent her home to bed.

Regarding our future we talked things over during the day, and decided that as we would not be seeing each other for at least five years we would not get engaged. However we agreed to keep writing to each other, and if we were still friends when I finally came home on leave, we could reconsider things then. In the meantime, if either of us met someone else during the period, then we would be able to make other friends without having any feelings of guilt, and that is how things panned out. Jan wrote to me about three times a week, while I usually managed one in reply, but although we both saw life and made many new friends, our feelings for each other did not change.

The last few days, during which I flew round saying goodbye to all and sundry passed in a whirl, and finally the momentous day arrived. Both Mum and Jan wanted to come to see me off, so Jan came over on the Wednesday night, and I arranged for a taxi to take us and to bring them back. I see from my letters that I left from Stonehouse Station for some reason or other. In those days Stonehouse was at the junction of the Bristol - Gloucester line and the Gloucester - London line via Stroud, so maybe the service was more convenient.

Because we knew we wouldn't have any time in the morning, Jan and I stayed downstairs after Mum and Dad had gone to bed and said our goodbyes, a rather sad but unforgettable experience, because it really brought home to me just what I would be missing. My goodbye from Dad the next morning was just as unforgettable, but in a different way, and partly due to my obstinacy I suppose. As far as I remember I never spoke to Dad about changing my job, and we never discussed my leaving home, although in later years he took the credit for me going to India by saying I never would have gone if he hadn't driven me out, which I suppose is true enough.

It would have been nice if we had said goodbye to each other properly, and I regretted it afterwards, but on the morning of the 18th he got up to go to work as normal and as he left at 7 am he opened the door at the bottom of the stairs and shouted up, 'Cheerio then Rod, I'm off now. I'll see you sometime', and away he went. Strange to say, I didn't think too much of it at the time, and saying 'goodbye' to Mum and Jan was much harder. Still I got away without incident and soon reached Paddington, after which I went to St. Pancras where I left my luggage, then went down to the company's office to pick up some documents before catching the boat train down to Tilbury.

Tilbury, tears and a superb breakfast

JANUARY 18TH 1951

The twenty-five mile journey from St. Pancras to Tilbury was an experience in itself. The special boat train left at 1 pm and arrived at 2.30 absolutely crowded with passengers and luggage, together with family and friends all going down to see them off. Jolly music was being played and there was a holiday atmosphere about it all, almost like a celebration, and when I saw them all enjoying themselves I wished I had known about it beforehand so that Jan and Mum could have shared it with me. Tilbury is on the North bank of the river opposite Gravesend, and we had a lovely view of the docks and ships as the train took us right through into the embarkation area, where after passing through all the formalities, we boarded at 4 pm.

The *Strathaird* was the first really large ship I had ever seen and she looked enormous as I walked up the gangway to the entrance port in her hull. Later I wrote to Mum that she was as long as Coaley football pitch, but in actual fact she was twice as long as that. It is thanks to Mum that I can recall many of these facts, because she kept every letter and piece of paper I ever sent to her in case I ever needed them 'to refresh my memory', so obviously she had something in her mind as early as that.

Built by Vickers Armstrong at Barrow in Furness, the *Strathaird* was commissioned in January 1932 and could carry 1242 Tourist Class passengers from London to Australia via Suez. From 1939 to 1946 she was used as a troop carrier/supply ship, and she rescued civilians, children, gold and 6000 troops from the port of Brest during the evacuation from Dunkirk. Then in 1946 she was completely refitted as a two class ship, and when I sailed in her in 1951 she could carry 573 First Class and 496 Second Class passengers, weighed 22,568 tons gross weight, was 664 feet long, and with her steam turbines had a speed of 17.5 knots, about 22 mph. Later in 1954 she was converted to a single class ship again, but after the widespread use of large, jet propelled passenger aircraft made these ocean beauties obsolete, she was finally scrapped in Hong Kong in 1961, a sad end for a beautiful ship.

Although she looked impressive from the outside, her inside was absolutely bewildering, for she was a maze of corridors, cabins and stairways, all of which seemed identical to the uninitiated, and it was several days before I was able to find my way about without hesitation. The decks were lettered from A to E, A being the top sports deck, from which magnificent views could be had all around the ship, while B deck contained all the public rooms, lounges, bars, shops and reading and games rooms. Below this on C deck were the first class cabins. D deck housed the galleys, dining rooms and more shops and restaurants, while the Tourist Class cabins were below again on E deck, very near the water line. One of the drawbacks with them was that they were very near the engines, which made them extremely noisy. Still, the Tourist Class fare to Australia then was only £40, so I suppose you couldn't expect too much for that amount.

Once aboard I discovered Berth No. 226 with some difficulty, and found that I was in a two-berth cabin which I was to share with a lad named John Duley, who had been recruited by Goodricke's at the same time as I was, although we had not met at the interviews. With his surname starting with D, he had been up at the beginning of the list, and had been in and out while I was still messing about on the train going up to London. He had done an apprenticeship at the Cincinnati Milling Machine Co. in Birmingham, and had been given the job in Pakistan while I got the job in India.

The cabin was nicely furnished with separate beds, a small wardrobe and dressing table each, and also a porthole. All my cabin baggage had been delivered safely, and after unpacking we chatted until we heard over the Tannoy the last call for all those visitors who were not sailing to go ashore or else, so we went up on deck to see our departure. Although it was dark by now, the landing stage was a blaze of lights, and there was pandemonium as we cast off at 5.30 pm amid a bedlam of noise, people shouting, whistling and cheering to each other, klaxons screeching and a suitable march being played over the ship's loudspeakers. However, gradually we edged away from the quay into the January darkness, and within minutes we were in midstream and then started slipping away down river. The journey had begun.

Normally, all the First Class passengers dressed for dinner, which began at 7 pm. If you were part of a group they tried to keep you together, six to a table, and you normally kept your seat for the duration of your voyage. However, because it was the first night and these arrangements still had to be made, dress was casual and we were able to sit anywhere we liked from 6.30 pm until 9, albeit with a restricted menu. I had had very little to eat during the day, I think the excitement had kept me going, so by 6.30 I was ravenous and went straight in. Despite the restricted menu the food was excellent and I thoroughly enjoyed my dinner, especially the pancakes, which was one of my favourite sweets.

I didn't drink in those days, and afterwards, feeling rather lost and depressed and not wanting to stay in the cabin, I decided to go up on the sports deck to have some fresh air, and it was then that the enormity of what I was doing hit me. It was a lovely evening, cold and clear, and as I stood in the darkness watching the distant towns and villages on both sides of the estuary slip by like beads on a string, a sense of absolute desolation and loneliness came over me as I finally realised that I had cut myself off completely from the way of life I had known before. Until now it had been very easy to say 'I shall be away for five years' and it didn't seem very long, but now it sank in that I was just 22 years old and probably would be 28 before I saw my loved ones again, and that seemed to be a hell of a long time.

I had never been away from home before, not even to do my National Service, for although I had passed my medical to join the Royal Navy in the hope of getting into the Fleet Air Arm, I had been told that my age group was not required at the moment but that they would call us when we were needed. Well, I never was called, which was unfortunate, and as a result it took a spell of life in India to make me grow up.

As I stood thinking about all these things and making myself more and more miserable, my eyes filled with tears. I can honestly say that I had never felt so wretched in my life. However I was enough of a realist to appreciate that I now had what I had been looking for, a new and exciting start in life, and if I disliked life in tea so much that I couldn't stick it, then I could always go on to Australia or back home. I suppose I stood there for about an hour, leaning on the rail watching the channel marker buoys gliding by and thinking things over, until finally my misery overcame me and I had a good cry. Then once I got over this and told myself not to be such a baby, I felt so much better that I decided that there was just enough time for me to go back down to the dining room and have some more pancakes before I went to bed, and the great adventure had begun.

During the night we sailed round the Kent coast and morning found us well down the English Channel. The *Strathaird* was very steady and I'd had a good night's sleep, so when the Steward woke us at 7 am with morning tea and fruit, I felt fine and went for a brisk walk around the lifeboat deck before breakfast. We were still in sight of the coast, but in the cold light of day it had lost its ethereal beauty of the previous night, and I was now looking forward to the challenge of a new day and the excitement of the voyage. I was also looking forward to my breakfast, and it turned out that it was one of the most enjoyable meals I have ever had.

Since 1939 all essential foodstuffs except bread, had been severely rationed, and even in 1951, five years after the end of the war, we were still getting only one egg each per week. Sunday breakfast usually consisted of fried bread and tinned tomatoes, so as far as we were concerned, the 'traditional'

English breakfast was just a memory. However, because of the shortages in Britain, the P&O boats did all their revictualling in Australia where there was food aplenty, and their enormous refrigerators and deep freezers were packed with sufficient provisions for the complete 24,000 mile trip to the UK and back, and the only things they picked up during the voyage were fuel and water. As a result of this I was destined to have a breakfast I have never forgotten.

As there was no organised seating plan for this first morning's breakfast I wandered into an almost deserted dining room, where I was greeted by a smiling steward who escorted me to a nearby table and took my order. Beginning with fruit juice and cereal, I then had a full fried breakfast and it was superb. The plate was piled high with rashers of sizzling bacon, juicy sausages, black pudding, mushrooms, fried bread and two eggs, together with fresh toast and butter, and being young and healthy and not having eaten food like that in years I soon cleared the plate, and because the bacon was so good, when the Steward came to see what I would like next, I said I had enjoyed the bacon so much would it be possible for me to have a little more? 'Oh, I should think so' he replied, and off he went, but imagine my surprise when he came back a few minutes later with a rather apologetic look on his face and said, 'I asked the Chief Steward and he said there was to be no bacon on its own, so I've brought you another breakfast. Eat what you want and leave the rest.' He placed another sizzling plateful before me. Needless to say, with food like that there was no way I was going to leave any, and after my second helping I finished off with hot waffles, butter and maple syrup, something I had never eaten before but have loved ever since. Thoughts of it still make my mouth water.

During the first few days of the voyage there was a rather strange atmosphere on the ship, as we were hundreds of complete strangers getting to know each other and trying to discover like-minded people we could be friendly with until we reached our destinations.   As I had never travelled before, at that time I was rather withdrawn and didn't find talking to strangers very easy. Initially when I listened to some of the other passengers talking I was amazed at the number of what I thought were Americans on board. During the war we had had many American troops stationed in Dursley but I had never heard an Australian accent, and it was several days before I could get it into my thick skull that all these 'Americans' I was meeting were really only Australians going back home.

Dinner was at 7 pm each evening and was the one meal for which we had to wear formal clothes. Passengers were allocated permanent seats six to a table, and the Chief Steward tried to arrange for groups of people to sit together if requested. As a result our table consisted mainly of young people, most of them on their first voyage. One of our group was a very pleasant girl from Somerset named Freda who had made it her business to pass among the passengers and introduce herself to anyone who was travelling alone and felt out of things. She then introduced them to the group of people that she had 'collected', and in next to no time about twelve of us were one big happy family sitting at adjacent tables.

Later on when we were in the Mediterranean, I had a very painful reaction from my second series of inoculations and vaccinations, and I felt so ill that I stayed in bed for two days. At this time she looked after me like a mother hen, bringing me drinks, sweets, medicine and sympathy, and after she had disembarked at Port Said, from where she was going on to Teheran to work as a Health Adviser to the Persian Government, we all missed her very much indeed. I often thought about her later and wondered how she had got on in her job, but if her actions on the ship were anything to go by, I'm sure she was a success.

The first part of our voyage was the 1260 miles from Tilbury to Gibraltar, followed by the 2200 mile leg across the Mediterranean until our first stop at Port Said. The weather was good for our 400-mile trip down the Channel, but as we rounded the French coast near Brest and then started to cross the Bay of Biscay, I half expected all sorts of wild things to happen. Once you leave Brittany and head for Cape Finisterre, you have left the comparatively shallow waters of the Continental Shelf behind and are then crossing the depths of the Atlantic Ocean proper. The Bay is noted for its terribly rough seas, and Mum's brother Uncle Joe, who was in the Royal Navy for twenty years, had told me about gigantic waves he had experienced there, 80 feet high to their crests, and 'higher than Coaley church tower', so I didn't know what to expect. As the *Strathaird* did the voyage regularly I knew there was nothing to worry about, but I did expect to see some noteworthy waves, and was a little disappointed when all we got was a bit of a roll from a choppy sea that made us all feel a bit queasy. Uncle Joe always did tell a good tale!

We passed Cape Finisterre, literally 'The end of the Earth' to the Romans, during Saturday night, and Sunday was spent cruising within sight of the Portuguese coast until we reached Cape St. Vincent at teatime. The Cape, with its white lighthouse standing on the edge of its 200 foot-high cliffs, is the South Western extremity of the Portuguese coast, and is the point off which the English fleet under the command of Admiral John Jervis, defeated the combined French and Spanish fleets in 1797. I always loved history at school, and it gave me quite a kick to actually see a place which I had read about, it was almost like living history.

From here we turned East for the 200-mile run to Gibraltar, and our group stayed up in the saloon until we reached the Rock at 2 am on Monday morning. For some reason, but probably for our benefit, Gibraltar was a blaze of lights from top to bottom, with the cliffs and water catchment slopes floodlit, and searchlights playing in the moonlit sky. The Captain took the *Strathaird* in as close as possible as we steamed slowly past, and it was a sight well worth waiting for. From Gibraltar our course took us a little bit north of east along the North African coast until we reached what I believe was the French naval port of Oran, which was also a blaze of lights, but although both these place had been lovely sights, the best was yet to come.

We didn't get to bed until 3 am but the Steward woke us as usual at 7 am, and because it looked like a lovely, sunny morning through the porthole, I hurriedly shaved and dressed and quickly went out on deck, to be met by an absolutely breathtaking sight. The sun was brilliant in a cloudless, deep blue sky while the slightly paler blue Mediterranean was as still as a millpond, and the *Strathaird* was sailing along a few miles out from the North African coast near Algiers. This was a lovely brown and rosy pink colour in the early morning sun, and the cliffs, desert and dry river valleys ran down into the sea without a single dwelling or living thing to alter its colour. This beautiful pink landscape, reflected in the sea as though in a mirror, was suspended between the two shades of blue, a really unforgettable sight, and although I came this way again on three other occasions, it was never the same again. It was one of those never to be forgotten experiences that we treasure for the rest of our lives.

Although we had been blessed with fairly settled weather during the first part of the voyage, there was usually a cold wind which was made worse by the forward motion of the ship, so we wrapped up in coats, scarves and gloves whenever we went up on deck for sightseeing or exercise. However once we were in the Med. it was as though we were in a different world. The days were bright with a hot sun, and most of our time was spent playing games on the sports deck. Most of the older people played deck quoits, a game something similar to bowls played with rope rings, but my favourite was deck tennis, played on a court something similar to a badminton court with a fabric covered ring about six inches in diameter. The scoring was similar to lawn tennis and I got plenty of exercise practising and playing in the various tournaments organised by the Recreations Officer.

We moored in Port Said harbour at 6 am on Saturday, 26th January and it was an absolute revelation to me. The winter sun was already very hot, and from our moorings in the outer harbour I got a good view of the city and the hundreds of ships and boats that were plying their trade around the harbour and the larger vessels that were waiting their turn to pass through the Suez Canal. This was the very first glimpse I had ever had of a foreign city, and I was looking forward to going ashore to see the sights after our formalities had been completed, but while we waited two very favoured '*Gulli-Gulli*' men were allowed on board the ship to entertain the passengers, and these were very clever sleight of hand magicians whom years of practice had made into experts at their craft. They were dressed in long-sleeved, voluminous kaftans which must have been full of hidden pockets, because they were able to make coins, rings, playing cards, cigarettes, bunches of flowers, doves and even small live chicks appear and disappear in the most unexpected places, after which a collection was made by an assistant. It was very entertaining for a while until the novelty wore off and other spectators took our places, but being a country boy I wondered just how long the small chicks managed to live after experiencing such a rough handling, and whether they died and were replaced later in the day.

No other outsiders were allowed on board the liner, so all the other local traders conducted their businesses from countless small 'bum-boats' which thronged around her. They were packed with all sorts of goods and local produce, from leather items, stools, bags, shoes and clothing to Egyptian sweetmeats, postcards, fruit and models of the pyramids. These were sent up for inspection in wicker baskets tied to cords which were tossed up to the upper decks, then after inspection and bargaining they were either returned the same way or the money was sent down. Considering the number of ships which were waiting to pass through the canal, the water in the harbour was remarkably clear, and small boys swam near the stern of the ship to dive for coins which were tossed from the upper decks. They were like eels in the water, and there were very few coins which weren't snapped up by them before they sank too deep to be collected.

Because disembarking passengers were attended to first we had an early breakfast, then went ashore at 8.30. This was the first opportunity I had had to see the *Strathaird* in her entirety without anything near her, and from a small boat at sea level she looked gigantic. Port Said was dirty and smelly, and from the moment we stepped ashore we were besieged by a horde of men and boys who wanted to sell us everything from their sisters to 'cheap' gold rings and 'Feelthy French Postcards'.

There was a lot of anti–British feeling in Egypt at this time, and we had been advised not to go sightseeing alone, so four of us walked along the quay to the statue of Ferdinand de Lesseps at the head of the canal, and then back via the shops without incident, other than that we were spat at and called 'British pigs'. However, another group had walked to the big ANZAC war memorial to commemorate the dead of World War II, and an Arab who cycled by spat in the dust and shouted out, 'Dirty British bastards'. This was quite a shock to me, as at this time this was something that the folks at home knew very little about.

The streets and shops had their own peculiar filth and smells, and after the comparative cleanliness of the shops at home, the dirt and flies in Port Said were also a very big culture shock to me, but it was probably the same in Egypt as I found out in India later, that once you were away from the big towns and cities the people tended to take much more pride in their appearance, and the standards of cleanliness improved considerably once you were out in the country areas.

After the initial element of novelty wore off, we soon tired of wandering through the streets being pestered every few yards with invitations to buy somebody's sister or look at some French postcards, and when we went back to the ship for lunch it was almost like going home. At noon we cast off from the mooring buoys and joined the convoy of ships passing through the canal that afternoon. The speed was restricted to about 5 mph with half a mile between ships to keep wash damage to a minimum, and we proceeded very sedately until we stopped in the late afternoon to allow a convoy of ships which were going the other way to pass us. This passing place was situated in a place where the canal divided for a short distance, and it was fascinating to see these enormous ships passing by as if they were sailing over the surface of the desert. That night, the rest of the canal was negotiated with the help of searchlights mounted on the bridge, and morning found us in the Gulf of Suez.

Although it is roughly 180 miles long, the Gulf of Suez is less than 25 miles wide for most of its length, with desert and mountains on both shores, and as we passed through the southern Straits into the Red Sea we got a clear view of Mount Sinai of Biblical fame and its white monastery. In comparison, the Red Sea is about 150 miles wide, but why it was named the RED Sea was a mystery, for here the water was a brilliant blue. At that time we saw very little of the shoreline, so thought that maybe that consisted of red sandstone or possibly the water turns red after a sandstorm, but at that time I could see no logical reason why it should be named so. However, many years later I came across the theory that it was due to a faulty translation when the bible was translated from the old Hebrew script.

Research has shown that the time of the escape of the Israelites from Egypt coincides with the period when a gigantic volcanic eruption destroyed the island of Thera, or Santorini in the Eastern Mediterranean, and the gigantic tsunami wave it generated was so devastating that the great city of Knossos, many miles inland on the island of Crete was destroyed and the Minoan civilisation was brought to an abrupt end. This could have been one of many such waves, and from Egyptian records it is recorded that the narrow neck of land that connects the Mediterranean with the Gulf of Suez was very low lying in those days, and consisted of swamps and boggy land on which vast beds of reeds grew, and was known as the *Reed Sea.* It was across this swamp that the Israelites would have had to cross to escape from Egypt, and the theory has been formulated that this could have coincided with the retreat of the waters from the land due to the first action of a tsunami, which allowed them to cross safely, and then when the Egyptian army tried to follow them it was destroyed by the resultant tidal wave, as it is evident that a great deal of damage was done all along the Egyptian coast at that time. It has also been proposed that the plume of smoke by day and the light by night which guided them in the right direction could have been that of the remains of the volcano that exploded, which could have been quite clearly visible a few hundred miles away in Egypt. This would all have been construed by the Israelites as acts of God and was recorded accordingly, but the suggestion is that when these were translated originally, Reed Sea did not seem to be right but Red Sea seemed much more suitable, and Red Sea it has remained ever since. It seems logical.

On a large scale map the Red Sea looks quite small, but in actual fact it is about 1300 miles in length, and we didn't reach the Bab el Mandeb, the southern entrance until Monday evening, the 29th. From there it was only another 160 miles to our next stop at Aden, and we moored there at 4 am the next morning. Because of its location at the southern end of the Red Sea, the old Arab port of Aden and its surrounding area were so important that they were annexed by Britain in 1839 and then developed as a ship refuelling station after the opening of the Suez Canal in 1869.

Again we were moored to large buoys out in the harbour, and small tenders ferried us ashore in batches of 40 at a time. There were many large ships moored around us, and as they all had their red, green and white riding lights on, they were a lovely sight as we rounded the stern of the *Strathaird* and threaded our way through them in the darkness. The port of Aden lies in what was once the crater of a volcano which exploded at some time, letting in the sea, and is now surrounded by a semi-circle of jagged, black, volcanic mountains, which in the darkness before the dawn, looked like an extension of the night itself. The shopping and bazaar area is known as Crater, and because there was a large ship in, all the shops were open and the whole area was a blaze of lights.

Although there was to be a great deal of nationalist agitation later before the Aden protectorate gained her independence in the mid 1960s, there was very little of this in 1951, and the attitude in the market towards us was totally different to that which we had experienced in Egypt. In all probability the fact that Aden was a duty free port and we had some money to spend may have sweetened things somewhat. The shops were clean and full of all types of goods at very reasonable prices, but as I had very little cash to spare, all I bought were some pairs of nylon stockings to send home to Jan because I knew they were almost unobtainable in England at that time, and some cotton working shirts. Both John Duley and I had decided to get half a dozen working shirts each, so we went to a likely looking *dukan* (native shop) where the shop keeper opened up a cellophane packet and showed us a very good quality shirt with a collar and a zipped neck for 2/6d. We had been warned about going to some dealers where they took advantage of gullible and inexperienced customers, but this shirt looked fine, so he wrapped it up, together with another five off the pile at the back of the dukan for me, and then another six for John, and once we had paid over our 15 shillings each off we went sight-seeing.

By the time we had looked at all the shops the sky was getting light, and although the Arabs were muffled up in coats, scarves and blankets against the chill of the night, we were wearing just shirts and slacks and thought it was a lovely, balmy morning, so we decided to climb the steps to the top of one of the cliffs overlooking the city. As we climbed we passed some of the water catchment tanks which had been carved out of the solid rock many years before to catch and store the rainwater when it came, the only supply of fresh water at that time, and it made us realise just what a dry place Aden was. In 1951 their water came by pipelines from water catchment areas in the mountains many miles inland, where there were dams which stored the rainwater before it soaked away into the desert, but even with this water Aden looked a dry and arid place. From the top we got a good view of the Crater area and the bay, with its leper colony on a small island in the middle, and just as we were clambering back down the *Strathaird*'s sister ship the *Strathmore* came in, homeward bound from Australia. The two great liners looked a lovely sight moored near each other in the bay, with their gleaming white hulls and superstructures highlighting their buff funnels.

Once back on board we had time to have our breakfast before we cast off at 10 am. Even at this time the sun had got really hot, and it made us realise just how stifling a place Aden must be in the heat of the day, so were very thankful that the P&O ensured that their ships visited at the coolest possible time. For an hour we stood on the sports deck as we slipped away from our moorings and cruised alongside Aden's hostile looking, jagged, black cliffs, and then once we were out in the Indian Ocean, we went back down to our cabins to examine our purchases, and what a surprise we got when we opened up our shirts.

The one 'demonstration' shirt which I had bought was fine, really good quality with a zip fastening neck. However the other eleven, although they looked identical when they were in their cellophane packets, only had two sleeves, the collar and zip fastener and about two inches of shirt below it, and the bottom two thirds of the shirt was completely missing. Although we realised we had been 'had', we laughed like drains when we tried them on because we looked so comical wearing these garments which came down to just above our nipples, but they were so cunningly wrapped around pieces of cardboard and packed so professionally that none of this was visible until they were taken out of their packets. Of course, they were useless to wear and had to be discarded, but they did serve to warn us to be very careful when we were offered 'bargains' in the mystic east. The shopkeeper must have known from experience that with such a short stay in port, we would be very unlikely to open them up before we returned to the ship, and even if we had done so and had taken them back to him, he could have disclaimed all knowledge of it and blamed the factory for sending him a batch of sub–standard goods, and then after apologising would have changed the dud shirts for some good ones. He just couldn't lose. At 15 shillings for one shirt I suppose it was a rather expensive lesson at the time, but it was a good thing that one of the pitfalls of living life abroad was demonstrated to me so early in my career.

The other useless thing I bought at that time was a Remington electric shaver. Because I had been told that double-sided safety razor blades were not available in India, it seemed that an electric shaver would be the answer, but I wasted my money on that as well because it turned out to be something of a white elephant. Later I found out that safety razor blades WERE available in India, but also that it was almost impossible for me to get a really decent shave with the Remington owing to the fact that I usually perspired so much from the heat that I couldn't keep my face dry, so I rarely ever used it while in tea. Such is life.

After our short visit ashore, life on board quickly returned to normal, and we settled down to enjoy the last few days of our voyage. I think one of the most memorable things about the journey was the variety and quantity of food that was provided, for besides the three main meals, refreshments consisting of the usual drinks plus Oxo, Bovril and Vegemite, together with savouries and biscuits which were served at 11 am, and afternoon tea was served at 4 pm, complete with umpteen different varieties of tea, and mounds of sandwiches, cakes and pastries. Ice creams and soft drinks were always available on request, and buffet food was available in the various bars and lounges in the late evenings, just in case anyone felt a bit peckish before they went to bed. After the austerity at home, it was like a wonderland of food, and of course, I made the most of it and put on several pounds during the trip, but I soon shed them once I got to India.

Another thing that remains in the memory was the actual motion of the ship at night in the tropics. It never seemed to be completely dark, for the *Strathaird's* wake, probably about one mile long, together with the white crests of the waves were reflected in what light there was, and were visible a long way from the ship. Her bow wave also stirred up the phosphorescence in the water, and this skittered away in the wave disturbance on both sides of the hull, accompanied only by the hiss of the water as it passed alongside. Most of the evening entertainments on board seemed to finish at about midnight, and usually instead of going straight to bed, I used to go up on the Sports Deck and stand for a while, taking in some fresh air and assimilating this beauty of the night. In good weather the sky was a dark, velvet blue, in which the stars seemed to twinkle and shine much more clearly and brightly than they did at home, and having experienced the mystique of being on a lone ship in the middle of thousands of square miles of empty ocean, I can quite see why some deep-water sailors find it very hard to settle down on shore after a lifetime at sea. I think the almost magical quality of the nights also had something to do with the enhanced sexual activity which seemed to appear once we were in the warmer latitudes.

One humorous incident occurred one night when we met another large passenger liner travelling in the opposite direction. At that time the procedure seemed to be that both the vessels switched on every light they possessed, including playing their searchlights all over their funnels and superstructures, and this made them look like a couple of gigantic nautical Christmas trees as they approached each other. By that time many of the passengers had gathered on the upper decks to cheer, and then as they passed by both ships gave several long blasts on their fog horns, which literally made the air reverberate. Of course I was with them, and was so excited that I decided to run back down to the very small, stern deck that was reserved for First Class passengers so that I could watch her as she gradually disappeared into the balmy night. This was mainly used for sightseeing during the day, and as I preferred the upper sports decks it was a part of the ship I rarely visited, although I had noticed that for some reason it was usually very poorly illuminated at night. As I hurried down the companionways in order to see her before it was too late I didn't give it another thought. Because I had passed from the brightly lit interior onto the dimly illuminated deck, my eyesight had not adjusted properly, and as I hurried over to the rail in the darkness I tripped over something that said, 'Hey, watch where you're going'. In my innocence I said 'Sorry' and took another couple of hasty strides towards the stern rail, whereupon I trod on something else that said, 'Christ, be careful. That's my leg you're standing on', and this was accompanied by a chorus of giggles and chuckles out of the gloom. This made me realise that there was a lot of activity going on in the darkness that I didn't know about, so things were not quite what they appeared to be and the deck must have been littered with couples getting to know each other very much better. Decidedly flustered, and thinking that discretion was the better part of valour, I decided that seeing that ship wasn't all that important after all, especially if I was going to inflict some desperate injury to a couple in the throes of passion by standing on them, so I beat a very careful retreat and went back inside. After that I was always very careful when I moved about the ship after dark, especially if I could see that the lights on the stern deck were missing.

One of the high spots of activity on board came at midday each day, when the distance travelled by the ship during the previous 24 hours was revealed by the Navigating Officer. Depending on the size of the waves and the strength and direction of the wind, an average day's cruising distance was in the region of 500 miles, and each day he gave his estimate as to how far she would travel during the next 24-hour period. Using this information, and taking into account the actual weather conditions we were likely to encounter, the passengers paid five shillings a go to guess what the actual distance covered would be, and this money was then divided amongst the lucky winners who had guessed correctly. The more likely the number, the more people actually selected it and the prize had to be divided among more people if it came up. However, I had one go each day, and in the Indian Ocean had a correct guess which brought me in £12, so actually I was in pocket at the end of the voyage.

Because there was no further sightseeing to be done, the two highlights of the organised entertainment on board, the Fancy Dress Ball and the Race Meeting were reserved for this last 1900 mile leg to Bombay. Owing to the fact that my vaccinations had been playing me up I hadn't taken much interest in organising a fancy dress for myself, but some of the costumes were terrific. Among the passengers was a group of actors who had been in the show 'Oklahoma' in London, and they were now travelling out to Australia to take the show 'Brigadoon' on tour. Two of them, the leading lady and one of the actors, went as 'Sculptor & Creation' and won first prize. She was dressed in a colourful jumper and baggy trousers, with dark glasses, a beret and a spotted neckerchief to complete the effect, and wore a thin moustache and a pointed, black beard. He was supposed to be a white, marble statue of Ganymede, the cup bearer of the gods, and his only dress was a large, white sheet which was draped around him like a robe. He had been whitened all over with stage makeup, and in his right hand, as a waiter carries a tray; he carried a white, china chamber pot as a wine vessel. His eyes were closed, and other than moving his feet slightly when he went past the judges he was statuesque, staying absolutely motionless, while she darted around him chipping small, imaginary bits off him with a mallet and chisel. They were worthy winners.

Very few of the entrants were dressed in prepared costumes they had brought with them, and it was very entertaining to see what some of them had concocted out of all sorts of bits and pieces. Many of the more difficult items had been supplied by members of the crew, and I remembered some of the ideas and what was required when Jan and I entered and won a prize on a later voyage.

The race meeting was held on the last night, February 2nd, and was very well organised. There were six races with six runners in each, and the winner of each race went forward into the 7th race for the 'Strathaird Cup'. During the previous week the horses in each race were auctioned out to the highest bidders, and the cash paid went towards the race prize money. An Indian gentleman who sat at our table for dinner bought four of them, and we had great fun naming them. There was a deadline for giving all the horses' names because the race-cards had to be printed, and some of them were excellent. 'Turkish Delight' by Giggles out of Harem, 'Disaster', by Elastic out of Panties and 'Haggis', (Pedigree Unknown) were typical, and because 'Jockeying' the horses turned out to be quite strenuous, the owner asked me to ride one of his. The course was laid out in a straight line from one end of the Main Saloon to the other, and the 'Jockeys' sat at one end on a seat with a winding handle attached to a small diameter roller in front of it. The horses were made of wood, and were fastened to the central roller by a long length of cord. For the start of the race they were positioned at the far end of the course with the cord fully extended, and then, when the race started, the jockeys turned their handles as fast as they could to wind their horse across the floor. Because one revolution of the handle only advanced the horse about three inches it was quite a tiring business to wind the horse in about 60 feet. My horse, 'Swift Work' by Lover out of Desperation won the second race, The Baksheesh Hurdle, without too much difficulty, making me one of the favourites to win the seventh race, and seeing the others I felt so confident that I actually placed a bet on myself, but as they say, 'Pride comes before a fall'! Midway through the race I was going well, winding very fluently and slightly in the lead when I suddenly felt something grasp my tie that pulled me into the winding roller. I had wound several revolutions and my face was pressed right up to the wooden framework when I realised that, in the excitement and the exertion of winding, the tie I was wearing had been caught up between the roller and the cord, and as it rotated it took my tie in as well until I couldn't go any more. Once I realised what had happened I stopped winding and pulled my tie out, but this meant I had to re-roll all the loose cord before I could start winding in again, and by this time the other five horses were past me and away, much to my annoyance. At the time I felt really devastated that such a stupid accident should wreck my chance like this, and as I had been quite heavily backed I wondered what the other people would say. However I needn't have worried, for most of them were laughing like drains at the memory of me with my face pressed hard up against the horse's head on the wooden winding frame, trying to release my tartan tie. Still it made the last night on board a very memorable one for me.

While crossing the Indian Ocean the weather was superb, with just a heavy swell which made the *Strathaird* roll at times. Her air-conditioning and forced ventilation were fine, so we had no difficulty in doing all our packing in order to be ready for going ashore the next day. However, it was hot enough to make us realise that without these artificial aids it would have been unbearably hot inside the ship, and brought home to us the old story, that in the days when this voyage took weeks instead of days with only the wind for ventilation, the people with money always booked the cabins on the shady side of the ship, hence the word 'posh', from 'Port Out, Starboard Home' that the booking agents used to write on the ticketing documents.

My last bit of glory on board was that I was beaten in the final of the Table Tennis Singles Final by an Australian, and this was one of the more difficult games to play owing to the motion of the ship, even though the table was positioned in the centre of the saloon to keep deck movement to a minimum. It was quite amusing at times trying to go one way while the roll of the ship pushed you the other and you were chasing a ball that was almost but never quite within reach.

On a later voyage when Jan and I were going back to India on the *Orsova*, we experienced some really bad weather in this patch of sea, and both of us felt so queasy and seasick that we could only stay in the cabin and do our packing for about 30 minutes at a time before we felt so ill that we had to go up on deck and get some fresh air. The best place to be when you felt like this was right on the top deck with the wind and spray whipping into our faces, so we took it in turns to do a spell in the cabin packing and then recover on the top deck. During the same period we were dancing the Gay Gordons one evening during the Gala Ball, and the boat was rolling so much that all the dancers went tottering down the deck to the one side, and then as she righted herself and heeled over they all went skittering down the other side, and finished up in a heap against the wall, rather like a flock of sheep in a pen without being able to do anything to stop themselves. It really was hilarious.

However, this was all very much in the future, and I went to bed that night regretting that this part of my journey was over, but knowing that the following morning I would get my first glimpse of India, and that my new career would begin in earnest. After all the fun and excitement, I was looking forward to it with a lot of interest but with a certain amount of uncertainty as well.

The Gateway of India, and a memorable train journey

The moment I woke the next morning I sensed that something was wrong and I knew something was missing, so for a few seconds I lay there gathering my thoughts. Then I realised what it was. The engines had stopped, and for the first time in two weeks the *Strathaird* was as silent and steady as a hotel. For the first time since we had left Tilbury I was lying in my bed without the movement and vibrations of a ship at sea, so we must have sailed quietly into our berth and moored up without making enough noise to wake me, and it was a very strange feeling to be back to normality.

I was so excited that I woke John Duley, and then, not waiting to have my fruit and morning tea, I jumped into my clothes and rushed up on deck to get my first view of India, only to be greeted by the sight of Bombay docks. There to my intense disappointment we were moored at a quay alongside large dock buildings and slab sided, corrugated iron warehouses, which hid any view I might have got of the city or the Malabar Gardens, and although there was a lot of bustle and activity on the quay, this was not quite what I had had in mind.

When we visited Port Said and Aden, the views of them from the sea had been superb, and in my innocence I had thought my first sight of the mystic east would be even better, probably an unforgettable view of the Gateway of India as we steamed in. This was a large, marble arch on the waterfront near the Taj Mahal Hotel, which was erected to commemorate the landing of King George V in 1911, and was the spot where visiting dignitaries and royalty always stepped ashore when they visited India. I knew this honour was not for me, but I did think I might see it as my introduction to India. As it turned out, it was 1956 before I saw it for the first time and it was not until 1961 that I heard the story of why the docks looked like they did.

At that time I visited Bombay to meet my sister Marion who was coming from New Zealand to visit us, and while there I met one of the Port Authority ship pilots who told me that on 14th April 1944, a 7400 gross ton Canadian freighter named the *Fort Stikine* which was being unloaded at the quay accidentally caught fire, and in addition to her cargo of cotton bales, spitfire fighters, gold and ammunition she was also carrying 1400 tons of explosives. This resulted in two catastrophic explosions later in the day that devastated two square miles of the dock area, sank or badly damaged 27 other vessels moored nearby, and also killed 740 people and injured 1800 more. He also said that when it was realised that the ship was likely to explode at any moment, his office staff were told to run away from the area as quickly as possible and then take cover, so two girls who were friends and worked in the same office were running a few yards apart up a street about half a mile away, one a few yards in front of the other when the ship disintegrated. The one in front heard the tremendous noise of the explosion and when the searing rush of hot air from the blast reached them she also heard a jagged sheet of corrugated iron whirr by as well, but didn't think anything of it as it clattered on up the street, and just kept running frantically until she reached comparative safety. It was at that time that she realised that her friend was no longer with her, and retracing her steps she found her friend's headless body lying in the road at the point where she had almost been hit by the flying iron, with her head lying several feet away. She had had a close brush with death, but her friend had not been so fortunate.

It took the Emergency Control teams three days to bring the hundreds of fires that raged all over the devastated area under control, and then as the war in the Far East was still in the balance at that time, it was essential to get the harbour working again as quickly as possible. Although this was done, it took 8000 men seven months to clear the 500,000 tons of debris away from the area and then repair or replace all the warehouses and offices which had been destroyed, a really mammoth task, and with the Japanese knocking on the Indian door, one which left no time for frills or fancy buildings. When he told me all this I realised I had been unjustly critical of the docks at that time, and had I known the story then I think I would have looked at the scene with a lot more interest, considering that the area had been a devastated wasteland only six years before.

One other item of cargo the *Fort Stikine* was carrying were crates of gold bullion bars to the value of between one and two million pounds sterling which were being sent to Indian Banks to help prop up the Indian exchange rate. Unfortunately, these were blown up with the ship, with the result that gold bars rained down all over the area and although many were found and handed in, probably some found their way into the local bazaar to be cut up and melted down into jewellery over the years. Some of them are still found accidentally at regular intervals, the last time being in 2011 when two bars were recovered by a dredger from the dock area where what was left of the *Fort Stikine* sank.

Although we had docked at 6.30 am there was a large number of passengers disembarking, and it was 9.30 by the time they had unloaded our luggage from the hold and the Customs Officials were ready for us. Our travel arrangements were being handled by Balmer Lawries in Calcutta, and after breakfast their representative came on board and we were called down to the saloon. We had made lists of the things we were carrying with us, and the only one which seemed to cause him any concern was my box of gramophone records which I had valued at £15, about 200 rupees. He thought I might have difficulty getting them through, but when my turn came and I was called down to the customs shed, I found him waiting there with all my luggage and he asked me whether I was willing to settle for paying 100 rupees to get my stuff through. Of course I agreed straight away, and he instructed me to give him the 100 rupees and then open any case for inspection when asked to do so, and that's all there was to it. I gave him the money, and when my turn came I opened my suitcase, which was given a very casual inspection. The chalk crosses went on, and I was through.

I had already passed through Immigration Control before I left the ship, so once I had passed through Customs I was free to go, and the Agent told me he would attend to all my baggage, so all I had to do was to be at the Central Station at 7 pm that evening to catch the Calcutta mail train, which left at 7.30 pm. The rest of the day was my own because he would see to everything else. He would meet me there at that time with the tickets and see me safely aboard, and with that comforting assurance he said goodbye and walked off to deal with someone else's baggage.

Being on my own, and stupidly not having made any arrangements to accompany someone who knew what they were doing, I decided to make my way to the Central Station straight away so that I would know where it was, and then do a little sightseeing from there. I had brought all my hand luggage with me from the ship, so I walked out of the main doors of the customs hall to be assailed by the heat, smells, hustle, bustle and bedlam of an Indian street. I was absolutely thunderstruck. The moment I appeared I was surrounded by a group of about a dozen men and boys, all yelling at the tops of their voices, and all offering various services. Did I want a rickshaw? A taxi? My shoes cleaned? My money changed? Did I want to buy gold? Have my fortune told? My finger nails manicured? Buy some socks? Give money to a beggar? The list seemed endless, and the more I dithered the more vociferous they became. I hadn't prepared myself for anything like this, and as their hands plucked at my clothing and they became more insistent, I panicked, my nerve gave way, and I turned and rushed back inside the customs shed where they couldn't follow. I was shaking with relief at having escaped from them, but I realised that it was only a matter of time before I would have to go out there and face them again. What was I to do?

I hung around the customs hall for a while collecting my thoughts, and then as nobody seemed to take the slightest bit of notice of me, I decided to go back on board the *Strathaird* for a while until I decided what I should do, so as I sat in the deserted lounge for a couple of hours and drank several cups of coffee, the silence was like heaven after the chaos outside, and it enabled me to think. It was something I had to face, but forewarned is forearmed, and I decided I would walk straight through them, forcing my way through if necessary, and then walk straight on to the station without taking any notice of them. Balmer Lawries had given us a map of the area so finding the way should not be difficult, and I finally took the bull by the horns, left the *Strathaird* quite sadly, rather like deserting an old friend, then walked through the deserted customs shed and out into the street ready to do battle with anyone and everyone.

As I burst out through the door determined to stop for nothing or nobody I came to an abrupt halt. To my surprise and utter relief, the area in front of the shed was deserted. Everyone had gone, and there wasn't a rickshaw or a beggar in sight. I suppose they had waited until the last passengers had passed through and then had decided to call it a day and go and look for richer pickings. Reconsidering my plan I thought I should take a taxi, but then Uncle Jim Perrin's dire warning about the devious Indian taxi drivers came into my brain and I thought that after my previous experience it would not be wise to tempt providence, so I decided to walk after all. Oh dear, what a green, callow youth I was then.

By this time the sun was hot and I was perspiring freely, but I made good progress as I picked my way through the paper, tin cans, coconut husks and assorted rubbish which littered the dirty pavements. After a while I stopped to check my progress against my map and became aware of a small boy in a shirt and a ragged pair of shorts who had been quietly following me, and who was now watching me intently with a pair of big, brown eyes. When I put my map away and began to walk again, he spoke.

'Where you go, Sahib?' he said.

Pretending I had not heard him and ignoring him completely, I walked on. He tagged along behind me. 'Where you go Sahib?

'Go away'.

'Nai Sahib. Where you go? I take'.

In desperation I said, 'Central Station'. His face lit up.

'Ah, Central Eestayshun. Come Sahib, I take', and away he went.

Checking the map to see that he was guiding me in the right direction, I followed along behind and he padded along at a merry pace, until finally with a broad grin on his face, he stopped at a pair of wrought iron gates and said proudly, 'There Sahib. Central Eestayshun'.

Many times since then I have wished I had rewarded that boy properly, because he had walked about one and a half miles and guided me to my destination, but at that time I was so hot, flustered and so relieved to reach the station that I took the first coin I came across in my pocket, and put it into his hand as I passed through into the station yard. It must have been something very small, probably a two anna piece, and not worth him spending the time with me, for the disgust and disappointment showed on his face, but at that time I thought very little of it. Probably once he had got over his initial disappointment he forgot all about it, but I never have.

Once inside the station I was greeted by what appeared to be a scene of absolute chaos and pandemonium. There were people everywhere, standing, squatting and lying down, surrounded by their children, boxes, bedding rolls, luggage and livestock, all waiting for their trains. Through this throng the chai-wallas, pani-wallas and other vendors threaded their way, selling everything from hot tea and cold water to fruit, sweetmeats, bread and biscuits. Sweepers wandered around with their brushes searching for a bit of unoccupied platform to sweep, and in one corner a group of professional letter writers squatted. These were quite learned people, well versed in many of the languages and dialects of India, who could write and post a letter home for any illiterate person for a few annas.

Because of the heat, very few passengers boarded the carriages until the last moment, but once the departure of a local train was announced, there was a concerted surge of people all determined to get on board. Those who could not get a seat inside scrambled up on the roofs of the carriages, where it was much cooler and they didn't have to pay, or stood on the outside foot boards clinging on desperately, and some of the trains seemed to have more passengers plastered on the outside than they did inside. As each departing train cleared an area of platform, the waiting sweepers moved in and gave it a quick flick with their brushes before it was inundated again by all the new arrivals waiting for the next one.

I had been told that there was a First Class waiting area inside the station, and although it was still hot and oppressive inside, I found it to be much quieter and pleasant to wait in rather than wander about outside, so still hot and bothered after my walk, I sat on a seat having a look round and getting my breath back. I had been there for a while and had just decided to go back outside into the street to while away some of the time when I heard a cheery voice calling to me from somewhere above. Looking up, I recognised two fellow passengers from the *Strathaird* leaning over a first floor balcony, a Mr Campbell and his wife. He was the manager of a tea estate in Assam just returning from home furlough, and as they had done this journey many times before they knew the ropes. Above the First Class waiting area were some apartments which consisted of a sitting room, a sleeping alcove with two beds and a shower room and toilet, together with access to a balcony which overlooked the platform. These could be rented at the time of ticket purchase, and knowing they had a long wait, they had booked one of them so that they could spend the day in some comfort. While on board the ship I had talked to them about life in tea, and when they were standing on the balcony and saw me sitting alone they realised I might be feeling a bit lost, so they called out to me and invited me up. Their help and kindness at that time is something I have never forgotten, and afterwards I always tried to do the same thing for 'new boys' coming out to India whenever we came across them on our travels.

After a cup of tea with them, a cold shower and a change of clothes I felt a new man, and things didn't seem so bad after all. While we sat and chatted they told me that although the cooked food and hot tea which was available on the train would be safe to eat and drink, the cold food and water were not, and as the amount of cooked food available was limited, they advised me to carry enough extra food and drinking water with me to last until we reached Calcutta on Monday afternoon. As a result of this I went out and bought a large milk can in which to carry some boiled drinking water, together with cream cracker biscuits, pasteurised cheese, tinned meat and corned beef, and also some chocolate, bananas and oranges, as fruit which had to be peeled was also safe to eat.

When I got back from my shopping expedition I found that Mr Campbell had ordered a meal for us from the station restaurant, and it was here that I experienced the first curry I had ever eaten, and golly was it hot. The sweat poured off my nose and chin as I ate it, which amused them no end, but I cut up a couple of bananas in it and ate plenty of rice, and thoroughly enjoyed it. Afterwards we had some excellent coffee, and once I had filled my can with boiled water from the kettle, we had nothing more to do until 7 pm, so as we were unlikely to get very much sleep on the train that night, the Campbells went and rested in the bed space, while I stretched out on one of the long chairs.

At 7 pm we found the Agent waiting for us, and I found I was sharing a four berth compartment with John Duley and a European businessman. The beds folded down out of the wall on top of the seats, and the windows were fitted with both glass panes and slatted fly-screen sliders which were adjusted to control the ventilation inside, while in the centre of the floor was a big aluminium box in which sat a large block of ice, which was intended to lower the temperature slightly as it melted gradually during the journey. True to our agent's promise, our main baggage had already been loaded into the luggage van, so we quickly made ourselves at home and settled in until we pulled out on time at 7.30. We had been given a menu on which we had to indicate what food we wanted for breakfast and lunch the next day, and this was collected before we left. These orders were then telegraphed up the line and were collected for us when the train stopped in the morning, and the empties were dropped off at the next stop. Surprisingly, it was quite an efficient way of supplying us with food without having a dining car, and the actual meals were excellent.

The journey from Bombay to Calcutta via Allahabad was about 1300 miles and took 42 hours to complete, so we didn't reach Calcutta until 2 pm on Monday. For the first few hours we travelled through the fertile country North East of Bombay, but as it was quite dark by this time, and we could see very little of the scenery through which we were passing, it was not long before we decided to have our supper from the food we were carrying and then make our beds. With the noise and motion of the train we didn't get much sleep, and early morning found us well into the plains of Northern India on the way to Allahabad, and what sights we were when we woke up. Everything inside the compartment was covered with a thick layer of red dust, which had infiltrated through all the cracks and holes in the compartment during the night. Our bedclothes, faces, hair and all our belongings looked as though they had been coated with red, drinking chocolate powder, and it was not until we made our stop to pick up our breakfasts that we three 'Red Indians' were able to go to the station waiting room to clean ourselves up.

When we got back to our compartment we found four sweepers gathered outside, all clamouring and arguing amongst themselves as to which one would attend to ours. Of course, the big attraction was the tip they expected after sweeping it out, but the one we selected, much to the annoyance of the other three, did a very good job and seemed happy with what we gave him. Once it was all reasonably clean we adjusted the air vents to allow as much clean, fresh air as possible to come in, so that the compartment was pressurised and kept the dust out, and once we knew what we were doing, this turned out to be very successful.

The scenery across the plains of Central and Northern

India turned out to be very dull and boring. Sun-baked wastes of land, with patches of thorn and shrub jungle disappeared into the distance, where we sometimes saw the shapes of low, rounded hills, and occasionally saw flocks of goats, scrawny cattle and camels grazing on the parched vegetation. Coming out from England's green and pleasant land we wondered how on earth they got enough food to keep themselves alive, but I suppose harsh conditions result in a very hardy breed of animals. Seeing this arid landscape made John Duley and me very depressed, especially if we were going to have to endure six years of it, but Mr Campbell reassured us by saying we were seeing these areas at the worst time of the year, and that the tea areas of West Bengal and Assam were nothing like them, and how right he was.

Every three hours or so the train stopped at a station, a small oasis of green in the midst of the dusty, brown plain, to collect our food or postal packages, or to take on water. We usually stopped for about fifteen minutes, during which time our compartment was cleaned and we were allowed to alight from the train and walk around to stretch our legs. The Europeans tended to group together at this time to pass on bits and pieces of information which had been gathered, or just to chat and answer queries. There were three English language daily newspapers in India at that time. The *Times of India* was the upmarket one, *The Statesman*, (or the *Tetesman* as it was known to the newsvendors) and the *Hindustan Standard*. On board the *Strathaird* we had had a daily news sheet, issued by the ship's wireless room to give us the news, but we soon came to rely on the *Statesman* to keep us abreast of developments, although they were usually a couple of days late with the news.

The two things that did impress me during this journey

across the plains were the sunrises and sunsets. Because India is so near the equator, sunrise and sunset varied very little from 6 am and 6 pm summer and winter, and there was hardly any twilight. The sun would go down, there would be about 15 minutes of dusk, and then bang, night had fallen. However, at dawn and sunset the sun was like a large orange ball, and its slanting rays penetrated the swirling clouds of dust, turning the earth to a beautiful violet or rose-red. At daybreak, the sky changed from dark blue to golden red and electric blue as the sun rose, and all the houses, hills, valleys and trees etc. took on a delicate pink tinge, which tended to conceal the harshness of the landscape, and made it look nothing like the baked, parched countryside which we saw later in the day.

However, once we were past Allahabad and got nearer to Calcutta, things changed. Thorny scrub and bush were replaced by mango trees and plantains, there were many more rivers and streams even though it was the cold weather, and the people and cattle didn't look anything like so tired and worn out. As we stood at the window looking out over the landscape this cheered us up no end, and as we rattled into Howrah Station on Monday afternoon we began to think that this long and uncomfortable journey might have a satisfactory ending after all.

In the 1940s, Howrah Station was completely closed all night from 11 pm until six the next morning, but the guide books record that as many as 10,000 platform tickets were sold on a busy day. I can quite believe this, for I think there must have been at least 9999 people there when we rolled in at 1 pm. Our train was inundated with porters, all smartly dressed in white shirts and dhoties, and wearing red turbans, together with their registered licence numbers engraved on polished brass, oval badges. Everything that wasn't grabbed and held tightly, including my trombone, disappeared immediately they stormed the compartment, and I wondered if I would ever see any of it again. However Mr Brown, the contact from Duncan Brothers' office who met us, assured us that everything would be safe. He had arranged for our hand luggage to be transferred to the Grand Hotel where our rooms had been booked, while my heavy luggage was to be taken direct to Dum Dum airport by Balmer Lawries, where it would be held until I flew up to the Dooars later in the week. The organisation was really efficient and the porters were even more amazing. None of them were very big men, but the loads they were able to carry were astounding, and it was quite common to see a man with two large suitcases balanced on his head. Even my gramophone record box, which took two of us to lift at home, was carried easily by one man.

Howrah Station is linked to the city of Calcutta by the new Howrah Bridge which spans the River Hoogly, and which was completed in 1941 to replace the old, floating pontoon bridge built in 1874. From a distance it looked as though some giant's child had knocked it up from his Meccano set one day before breakfast, but it carried four lanes of traffic in each direction, and for pedestrians there was a fifteen feet wide pavement on each side. Many years later the bridge was the scene of a very amusing happening which was reported in *The Statesman* newspaper at the time. According to reports, large numbers of small children were disappearing from the streets of Calcutta at night, and there were various theories that either they were being taken by jackals and hyenas, or they were being stolen by professional child stealers to be brought up as beggars. There was a feeling of hysteria in the bazaars at that time, and one morning a rather suspicious looking character was seen walking across the bridge with a bulging sack on his back, in which something could be seen alive and moving. Very soon some public spirited citizen who saw this movement put two and two together, and assuming he had caught a kidnapper in the act, began shouting for the people in front to stop the man with the sack because he was a child stealer, and immediately gave chase. Hearing the hubbub and seeing a crowd chasing him, the man took to his heels over the middle of the bridge, but because of the heavy sack bouncing on his back he wasn't able to run very fast, and just when the badly frightened man was about to be grabbed by his pursuers, he dropped the sack and disappeared into the crowd, leaving the leaders of the jubilant posse to open it and release the poor children. Imagine their surprise when they emptied the sack and a couple of dozen frightened and angry cobras shot out, which the snake catcher was taking home. As the angry snakes started striking out at the people nearest to them and they turned round to run away, they were pushed back onto the snakes by the people in the back of the crowd who were still shouting 'Stop him. Stop him'. It was a classic case of 'Those behind cried 'Forward' while those in front cried 'Back'', and for a few minutes there was absolute chaos in the middle of the footpath as the frightened people tried to avoid the even more frightened and angry snakes. It was not until they had all been caught and thrown into the river that normality returned, and I don't think they ever did discover what had been happening to the children.

We didn't see any snakes as our taxi crossed the bridge en route to the Grand Hotel, but it was a very exciting journey nevertheless. Most Calcutta taxis were and still are, old Hindustan Ambassador cars with a black body and a yellow roof. After the old Morris Isis model became obsolete in Britain, all the jigs and tools were shipped out to India for the cars to be made under licence by Hindustan Motors, and these were named Ambassadors. They were the only large cars made in India during my time out there, and became immensely popular. When I came home in 1967, three models of cars were being made in India, the Triumph Herald and the Fiat 1000, both of which had a waiting time of six years from the time of placing the order, and the Ambassador, for which you waited ten years. At the time of placing the order you had to pay a percentage of the cost price as earnest money, together with a bank guarantee which certified that you were able to pay the rest, and many fathers who intended to give their sons a car as a wedding present when they got married were placing their orders when they were a few years old to ensure they got it in time.

The streets of Calcutta were absolutely crowded with tramcars, buses, lorries, cars, cattle, cycles, pedestrians and bullock carts, and the taxi drivers threaded their way through this mass of humanity and machinery with great abandon, often taking risks to make their way through gaps that no sane driver would dream of attempting. Although I became a very competent driver while in India, I would never have attempted to drive in Calcutta because the rules of the road there differ from any other place I know. If you are behind another vehicle and wish to overtake you have to give him a blast on your horn, at which he will do one of three things. He will either indicate with his driver's side indicator, which means he is ready for you to pass him on that side, or signal with his near side indicator so that you can pass on his inside, or he will do nothing which means it is not safe for you to pass or he doesn't know where he is going and he may be turning left or right. If he himself is going to turn anywhere he will either stick his arm out of the window and signal or simply not bother, and I never did find another place in India that was as frightening to drive in as Calcutta was. On one occasion I was in a taxi that was rammed by another because neither driver would give way, and when a violent argument ensued and my driver tried to place the blame for the accident on the other by saying he had a Sahib in his taxi who would know it wasn't his fault, they both came round to me for confirmation. Needless to say I wasn't going to get involved in anything like that, and got out of it by saying I never saw anything of the incident because I was half asleep at the time and had my eyes shut! A likely story because there was no way in which I would be able to go to sleep in a Calcutta taxi, the ride was too much of a nightmare.

Situated on Chowringhee Road, one of Calcutta's main thoroughfares and overlooking the Maidan, the Grand Hotel was Calcutta's largest hotel, with over 500 rooms and a ball room large enough to take 2000 people. My room was the largest I had ever slept in, with 15-foot-high ceilings, lovely cold marble floors, and two pendant fans which squeaked away to themselves all night as they shook and pirouetted and stirred the air. The two windows which overlooked a rather dirty yard at the back of the hotel were fitted with both fly-screens and shutters, and I found that the best way to keep the room cool when I went out was by closing it all up and drawing the curtains. The one thing that didn't come up to standard was the food. I even remarked on this to Mum when I wrote home, but this could have been due to my taste buds having been spoiled by the superb food we had had on the *Strathaird*.

John Duley had a room adjacent to mine, so we were able to get acquainted with Calcutta together. We went to the Sir

Stuart Hogg Market, or the New Market as it was called to buy the other goods we needed, including some more working shirts to replace those we had almost bought in Aden. The New Market is situated on Lindsey Street at the rear of the Grand Hotel, and it was a revelation to me, for it was possible to buy literally anything there all under one roof. The only drawback was that all the shops selling a certain type of goods were in a block somewhere in the market, and as all the alleyways looked the same, it was almost impossible to find what you were looking for unless you had been in several times. However, the moment I entered the building I was 'adopted' by a guide who steered me to the areas of shops which sold the goods I required, for which I haggled with the shopkeepers. He was accompanied by a coolie with a basket on his head who carried all my purchases as I made them, and he followed on at our heels like a little dog and grinned a crooked, yellow-toothed smile every time I looked at him. No doubt they got a commission from the shops at which I bought things, but their charges were not excessive, so once I grew to trust them they were a great help. Many of the Calcutta Mem-Sahibs had their own, favourite 'guides' whenever they visited the market, and there was a lot of rivalry between them if one tried to poach another's customer.

The Maidan in Calcutta covers about 1400 acres in the very heart of the city, and was once the area around the new Fort William which was cleared for defensive purposes and never built on, so that any attackers would be unable to find any cover from the defender's fire. Fort William is situated with its back to the River Hoogly, and the site was especially selected by Lord Clive to replace the old Fort William which was destroyed after the siege in 1756. In the late 1600s, Job

Charnock, a merchant adventurer employed by the East India Company landed on the mud flats on the banks of the Hoogly, and obtained permission from the local ruling Prince to build a thatched hut and trade there. By 1756, the Company by the use of strategy, avarice and good luck controlled most of India. It made its own laws, mustered its own armies, marshalled its own police, and though it existed and traded only by the sufferance of India's great potentates its presence was so profitable that in all but name it was the ruler of India. In time however, it became so successful that it became extremely arrogant, and this annoyed and made enemies of the ruling Nabobs, who were Muslims. Things finally came to a head when the Governor of Calcutta interfered in a case of succession after the old Nabob had died, and when one of the contenders, a man named Kissendass was given refuge by the British, his rival Siraj-Uddaula decided that this was the ideal time to seize the throne and drive the hated foreigners out of his country once and for all. At this time, the city of Calcutta covered almost a square mile with the Company's fort in the centre, and although some defences had deteriorated through neglect, it should have been strong enough to cope with any opposing army. Unfortunately however, although the garrison had sufficient food and powder to withstand a siege for an indefinite period, in actual fact, through a combination of stupidity, arrogance, cowardice, treachery and sheer incompetence, it held out for only six days against the Nabob's army, after which many survivors were treacherously massacred, despite being assured that they would be spared if they surrendered. Subsequently 146 were taken prisoner, and on the night of Sunday, 20th June 1756, 145 men and one woman were crammed into the notorious 'Black Hole of Calcutta', a room beneath the ramparts 18 feet long by 15 feet wide, with two small, barred windows. During the long night the conditions and heat in the tiny room must have been appalling, and the next morning when the door was opened, only 22 men and the woman staggered out, leaving 123 dead behind.

Retribution was swift. The Company sent an army from Madras to retake Calcutta, which it did in January 1757, and on 23rd June the famous battle of Plassey was fought, in which 800 Europeans and 2200 Indian troops under Lord Clive routed the Nabob's army of 50,000 men. The Nabob managed to escape but was assassinated shortly afterwards, and the Company, determined that this catastrophe should never occur again, decided to build a new Fort William on open land south of the old one. The foundation stone of the new fort was laid in October 1757 and completed in 1781, at a cost of £200,000, and is now considered to be one of the finest of its kind in the world. The ruins of the original fort later became the site of the new General Post Office, which was completed in 1868, and brass lines let into the pavements and courtyards defined the boundaries of the vanished stronghold. When I was there in 1951 and 1955, there was a black marble tablet near the North East corner of the Post Office which marked the actual site of the Black Hole, but this was moved later when structural alterations were made.

Nowadays, the Maidan is Calcutta's playground, and is used for games and sports of all types, including kite fighting. This is very popular on Sunday mornings. The top five feet of the kite strings are coated with glue and powdered glass, and competitors try to 'kill' their opponents' kites by cutting their strings. All the leading sports clubs have their grounds on the Maidan, including the Indian Test Cricket Ground, Eden

Gardens, and also the Calcutta Football Club ground, supposedly the finest in the East, where I played several times for the Dooars team against the CFC. It also contains the racecourse, and Red Road, which crosses the Maidan, was used as a runway for Spitfire fighters defending Calcutta against Japanese air attack during WWII.

The other notorious place which we visited was the 'Chhor Bazaar' or Thieves Market, where most things stolen in Calcutta were sold. Everyone knew the traders there sold stolen goods, and it was known for people to go and buy their own goods back, without being able to prove it was once theirs. One very common commodity for theft was car parts, especially hub-caps and windscreen wiper blades. Most of the car owners I knew in Calcutta kept their wiper blades in the glove box, and only fitted them when it started raining. It was very amusing to see all the cars stopping and the drivers fitting their wiper blades at the start of a downpour.

However, during my first few days in Calcutta I saw very little of this, because when I visited Duncan Brothers office where they attended to Goodricke's affairs in Calcutta, I was told I would be flying up to Bagdogra in the Dooars, on Thursday morning, but I saw enough to realise that it was a lovely city with an extremely interesting history, and I hoped I would be able to explore it more fully at some time in the future.

Welcome to Calcutta, diarrhoea and Dracula

One of our group on board the *Strathaird* had been a man who worked for one of the Agency Houses in Calcutta. He was returning from home leave, and instead of coming over from Bombay by train like the rest of us, he knew what he was doing and had flown over on Saturday. When we arrived at the Grand on Monday, we had found a message from him waiting for us, saying he felt rather 'fatherly' towards us new boys, and in order to introduce us to Calcutta, he wanted to show us the sights on Tuesday evening if we had nothing else on.

Of course we jumped at the chance, and after tea on Tuesday he picked us up in his car and gave us a chauffeured tour of the city. After seeing the sights, he then took us to several of the very exclusive clubs which existed in Calcutta at that time, although most of them disappeared over the years as more and more Europeans left India. It was very expensive to join these clubs, let alone have a meal there, but we did the rounds, and he wouldn't take a penny from us, saying the treat was on him.

We visited the Royal Calcutta Turf Club, the Three Hundred Club and the Saturday Club, in addition to Prince's and Spencer's restaurants, where we had shellfish starters, followed by tandoori fish accompanied by champagne, whisky and cherry brandy, although I didn't normally drink at that time. After a most memorable evening he delivered us back to the Grand at about midnight, where we jumped into bed and were soon fast asleep.

Not for long, though. It could have been something we had eaten, or it may have been some doubtful water, but both John Duley and I woke at about 1 am with terrible pains in the stomach and diarrhoea, although of course, at that time, neither of us knew the other was ill. For the first few times, going to the toilet seemed to ease the stomach cramps a little, and I would jump back into bed thinking I could go back to sleep. However, after a while the amount of time I spent in bed between visits got less and less, until finally it was a waste of time, and I went and sat on the toilet from about 2.30 to 7 am. Oh dear, I did feel ill. Luckily, in the afternoon I had bought a paperback edition of Bram Stoker's 'Dracula', and between bouts of stomach cramp and passing a lot of watery fluid, I read it from cover to cover to pass the time. The pains in my stomach were intense, and the frightening thing was that it was the first time I had ever been ill on my own. At one time I debated whether to try to go to get some medicine or some help, but I knew I wouldn't be able to leave the toilet long enough to do any good.

Gradually the night dragged by on leaden feet, hour by hour, and my eyelids drooped wearily over Dracula as the pages turned and the explosions shook the pan. Finally morning came, thankfully the cramps in my stomach eased, and although I felt absolutely worn out and exhausted I felt able to go along to John Duley's room to see if he could help me at all. What a hope! If anything, he was worse than me. He had been up all night with diarrhoea AND sickness - at least I hadn't been sick, and he had quite a high temperature. Like me, he had lost count of the times he had been to the toilet, and as he felt so ill that all he wanted to do was lie in bed, I realised he needed a doctor and decided I would wait until 9 am when Duncan Brothers' office opened, then I would phone and ask them to arrange for a doctor to come to the Grand.

In the meantime, I decided to visit the chemist's shop in the hotel arcade, in the hope that someone could prescribe something to settle my stomach until the doctor arrived. This I did, and the manager in Frank Ross the Chemists was very helpful, saying that if I cared to wait he would mix me up a potion that would tighten me up and stop me going to the loo. From what I remember of the taste, it was probably Kaomorph, a mixture of Kaolin and Morphine, which we still use today, and probably it would have worked had I been able to keep it down. Unfortunately, soon after I had swallowed it, and as I was waiting for him to bring me my change, I felt myself breaking out in a cold sweat. Perspiration dripped from the end of my nose, hot and cold waves of nausea came in the pit of my stomach, and to my horror I realised that I was going to vomit there and then – which of course was probably the best thing that could happen.

Without waiting for my change I rushed through the door, and I had just managed to reach the corner of the building when I was most horribly sick. Up came everything I had eaten the night before, and I leaned against the wall with my shoulders heaving, feeling as though the end of the world had come. Looking back on it, it was a pity I had not vomited before, for in all probability I rid myself of whatever had affected me, but seeing the looks of disgust on the faces of the passers-by, I felt as though I wanted the ground to open and swallow me up. Probably they thought I was just another European who had been out on the town all night, who couldn't handle his liquor and was making a nuisance of himself - little did they know. Finally, when I was empty and had finished retching, I gathered my strength and went back to my room where I lay down until it was time to ring Duncans.

They were very good, and by 11 am a doctor had come and given us some suitable medicine, after which we both spent the rest of the day in bed, but I recovered quickly enough to be able to visit John that evening without too much discomfort. However, that was the last time I was able to speak to him, because when I left the hotel early the next morning and looked in on him to say goodbye, he was in such a deep sleep that I was unable to wake him, probably something to do with a sedative that he had been given, so I never did say cheerio. Afterwards I always hoped our paths would cross again at some time in the future, but it was not to be. Unofficially, I did hear later that he made it to Sylhet, but something about the life there compared to Birmingham made him decide to resign, and he went home after a couple of years.

Of course, I have never forgotten that night in the Grand, and I don't think I have ever read any book under more traumatic conditions, so Dracula has a special place in my favourite reading, and very often when I see the name on a book or on the TV, old memories come flooding back to me and I think, 'Thank God for Bram Stoker'.

The next morning the airline bus picked me up at 6.15, and

after a roundabout journey, during which we collected several other sleepy passengers from other parts of the city, it delivered us to Dum Dum Airport, about ten miles away. I had been instructed to be waiting outside the Grand at 6 am, and as I was anxious not to miss the transport, I was out with my baggage at 5.45 - no wonder John Duley wasn't awake! I still had to learn that in India times were only approximate, and just an indication of when things should happen.

In reality, because Indian Airlines flew the scheduled internal flights on a standard timetable, 6 am was a very civilised time to travel out to Dum Dum, as the aircraft wasn't due to leave until eight. Once I reached the Dooars I found out that most of the tea areas were served by a much smaller combined freight cum passenger company named JAMAIR. This ran a much more informal and convenient service, and because they tried to keep their aircraft busy by doing two journeys each day, they usually left Dum Dum at 5 am to ensure that they arrived at their destination upcountry at first light. This meant leaving Calcutta at 3.30 am and it was a horrible time to be travelling, when most of Calcutta was silent and hundreds of people lay on the pavements and in shop doorways swathed from head to foot in thin white blankets, like a lot of corpses. Usually the only signs of life at that time in the morning were the occasional car or taxi, and the ubiquitous pie-dogs, which rummaged in the piles of rubbish in the gutters searching for their early breakfasts.

However, by 6.30 the city had come to life in the warmth of the early morning sun, and it took us 50 minutes to bump and rattle our way over the ten miles out to the airport. The streets teemed with people and all sorts of transport, from cycle rickshaws to buffalo carts, and country labourers carrying their goods to market slung from bamboo poles over their shoulders were forced to thread their way through the local people performing their early morning ablutions in the roadside drains. The journey was usually very interesting because the route took us through an area of Calcutta that the casual visitor did not normally see, but the one which always comes to mind whenever I think of Dum Dum was when I flew back to Calcutta by myself in 1966 after my home leave. After an uneventful flight out from Heathrow, we were held up for a good two hours on the outskirts of Calcutta by an enormous crowd which choked the whole area. Nothing was moving on Serampore Road as far as the eye could see, pedestrians were mixed up with vehicles in one seething mass, so we weren't able to turn round and go another way, and no one seemed to know the reason for the hold up.

At last, when we were all heartily sick and tired of sitting in the smells and the sweltering heat of the bus, the crowd gradually thinned as if by magic, the traffic started moving, and we were able to complete our journey to the Great Eastern Hotel with absolutely no indication of what had caused the hold-up in the first place. It was a complete mystery until the next morning when I read in the paper that it had been caused by two buffaloes which had fought in the street for 90 minutes. This was quite a spectacle, so people had gathered round to watch the entertainment with the inevitable consequences, and it was not until someone managed to tie a rope round the back leg of one of the combatants that they were able to drag it away, and the fight came to an end. According to the morning paper, a copy of which I still have, the contest was declared to be a draw.

Calcutta had two airports, Barrackpore, the military airbase, and Dum Dum, the civil one. Besides the airport, Dum Dum was noted for two other things, the Government Arms and Ammunition Factory which gave its name to the infamous, expanding, lead nosed, Dum Dum rifle bullet and which also made the greased cartridges which were used as a reason for starting the Indian Mutiny in 1857. It was also the home of the HMV gramophone record factory, which manufactured millions of records for sale all over Asia. During the war it turned out large quantities of all types of records for the Allied Armed Forces in the Far East, and one day when I was in a small music shop in the local bazaar, I asked the owner if he had any western style records. It turned out that he did, and from beneath a pile of rubbish he produced a very dusty box of HMV jazz and swing music records, together with a stack of V-Discs, which had been produced exclusively for the American Forces during the war. What a find they were, for they were extremely hard to come by, and the very last thing I would have expected to find in an Indian bazaar. On enquiring how he came to have them, he said that the previous owner of the shop had bought them during the war, and after he had taken over, as no one had been interested in them, he had despaired of ever selling them, and finally forgot all about them! Naturally, I took most of them off his hands at a very reasonable price - I think he was as pleased to dispose of them as I was to buy them - and I spent many happy hours listening to them on my old wind-up gramophone. Had I kept them in mint condition and brought them home with me they would have fetched a tidy sum, for mint V-Discs were extremely rare, but playing them on my gram with steel needles didn't do them any good, and I left them behind with the rest of my 78rpm records when I came home from India in 1967.

Although this was a scheduled internal flight on Indian Airlines, there were very few frills on the service, and as there was no departure lounge or anything like that, once we reached the airport we were given a cup of coffee and then waited in a small office at the side of the hangar until it was time to board the aircraft. Our destination was Bagdogra, a small airfield situated in the Terai, about ten miles west of Siliguri, and about 300 miles north of Calcutta. The service was mainly used by Indian businessmen and tourists visiting Darjeeling and Kalimpong, and as a result we had an air hostess who distributed various drinks and newspapers on the flight. Even though our aircraft was an old ex-military Douglas DC3 Dakota which took just under two hours for the flight, I was in heaven once I got aboard, and despite the incessant engine noise, I enjoyed every minute of it. It was wonderful as I had always longed to fly, I didn't feel apprehensive at all, and as we winged our way north on that memorable February morning, little did I think that that journey was only the first of dozens of flights I would make in these delightful old aircraft.

The Dakota cruised at about 7000 feet, and we got a good view of the countryside below. For the first 200 miles we flew over the valley of the River Ganges, which is very flat and only a few feet above sea level, and in the monsoon, because thousands of acres are inundated with flood water, from the air the whole area looks like one gigantic lake studded with millions of tiny islands. However, because we were nearing the end of the dry, winter season, it looked like a dusty patchwork of dried up river beds, desiccated paddy fields and clusters of small, thatched houses. These were perched on man-made. rectangular platforms about six feet high, which were made by digging quite broad, deep drains on all four sides, and piling the excavated earth in the centre. This ensured that the houses stood above the floods during the monsoons, while the drains acted as water storage tanks during the dry season.

As we neared Bagdogra, the Captain invited me up to the flight deck to get my first view of the Himalayas, and the sight was superb. Before us, as far as the eye could see, mountain ridges rose up through the clouds like a jagged barrier between us and Tibet, and individual peaks, such as Everest and Kanchenjunga were clearly visible, mantled in snow. From a modern jet-liner, cruising at an altitude of 39,000 feet, mountains seem rather distant and insignificant as you pass over them, rather like a rumpled bed sheet, but because we were flying so low and so close to them, the Himalayas looked awe-inspiring as they dominated the horizon, a most memorable sight.

Other than this, my first flight was uneventful, and the only fright I had was when we landed at Bagdogra. Nowadays it has excellent airfield facilities, with concrete runways and modern beacons and navigational aids, and is used by the Indian Air Force jets as well as civil aircraft. However, in 1951 it consisted of a small office, a couple of storage sheds, and a runway made out of slotted and perforated steel sheets connected by interlocking joints. Because they could be assembled and dismantled very quickly, they were used extensively during the war for making temporary runways, and as we bumped down and landed they made the most frightening noise and clatter, as though the bottom was falling out the aircraft. Dakotas aren't the quietest of planes at the best of times, but this sudden noise was appalling, and for a moment I thought the undercarriage had collapsed, but I took a quick look round at the 'regulars' who seemed to be completely unconcerned, and as our speed dropped and the clatter subsided, I realised that all was well. Later, when these steel sheets were replaced, they were sold locally and used extensively as fencing material, and I wouldn't wonder that some of them are there still in Siliguri. I had been told someone would meet me at the airfield, but there was no one there, and after the other passengers had left and the aircraft had loaded up and disappeared on its way back to Calcutta, I found I was the only one left.

What to do? I felt rather worried, especially when the office clerk told me that Zurrantee was about seventy miles away, but he said, as near as I can write it, 'Donut worree Sur, they weel com', so I settled down to wait. I soon found out that cultivating the ability to settle down and wait patiently was essential if I wanted to be successful in India.

My heavy trunks had been brought up by air freight the day before, so I spent the time getting them out of the godown (storehouse) so that they would be ready when someone did arrive, and finally, as per the forecast, they did 'com'. At about noon, an old American Ford three-ton truck, painted in the green and black company livery and with ZURRANTEE T.E. painted along its sides rolled up and came to rest in a choking cloud of red dust. Down stepped two Europeans who introduced themselves and then apologised for being late - evidently an overloaded buffalo cart had shed a wheel on a narrow bridge, completely blocking it, and it had to be unloaded and moved before they could cross. Ian Munro was a big, bronzed, round-faced Scot, a little older than me, who had joined the company about eight months before and was the actual Assistant Manager on the estate. The other lad, John Mitchell, was the complete opposite to Ian, and had only come to the garden the week before. He was slightly built, with a thin face and spectacles, and I remembered that I had met his father, Mr E A Mitchell, when I had visited the London office in January. Although very quiet, he had a cultured accent and possessed a devilish sense of humour, often coming out with very witty and pithy remarks. As it was planned that he would become a Director of the Company when his father retired, he had been sent out to India to gain some first-hand knowledge about the country and the tea industry before doing so. Although we were as different as chalk and cheese, and had very few interests in common, I shared a bedroom with him for several months, and by making the necessary adjustments to our ways of life, we got on well together.

CHAPTER FIVE

Journey's end -
Zurrantee at last

We stopped for a curry lunch in Siliguri bazaar, and then after collecting several items from the local garage and hardware store, we set off on the journey back to the estate with me sitting in the seat of honour in the cab. For the first ten miles the road ran almost straight through the sal tree forest north of the town until we reached the valley of the River Teesta, but here it began to twist and turn as it climbed up the valley to the Sevoke Coronation Bridge, where we crossed to the east bank. At times the road seemed to have been carved out of the solid hillside, clinging to the almost vertical slope with only a small stone wall separating us from a fall of 200 feet into the river. Once on the east bank we travelled down river until we reached the plain again, almost opposite the place where we had entered the valley, and then struck off east through some more forest towards the tea areas.

From the Teesta, the main trunk road ran parallel to the foothills of the Himalayas, and it was quite a surprise to see the tree-clad 'hills' some 5000 feet high rising up from the plain within a couple of miles of us. They were rather indistinct as they were veiled in a blue mist of dust and smoke haze from forest fires, but I could see enough of them to make me think that, in comparison with the other parts of India that I had seen so far, the Dooars scenery was going to be something special, and I wasn't disappointed. At Chulsa Station we branched off up Chulsa hill to make our way to Matelli, the local bazaar, then took the dirt and gravel road to Zurrantee, another three miles further on, where we arrived at about 5 pm.

As Ian Munro showed me into the office, the legendary Bill Milne met me at the door, and said, 'Hello, so you're Rod Brown, welcome to Zurrantee. Did you have a good trip? I hear you're a good footballer.' He then started talking to the other two about the whale of a time that they had spent at the club the previous evening. Evidently, with John Mitchell there it had turned into a bit of a celebration, and the drink had flowed! By this time quite a group of clerks and labourers had gathered round, all wanting to get a gawk at the new 'boy', and when Bill introduced me to the Head Clerk he grinned and said, 'We have been waiting for you Mr Brown. We have heard you are a veree good footballer'!

I never did find out where this information had come from, although I had been asked whether I played football when I visited Duncan's office in Calcutta, but it was obvious that being a good soccer player was of paramount importance on Zurrantee, and I hoped I would not let them down. Evidently Bill was a first class goalkeeper, but neither Ian or John Mitchell played, so it was third time lucky so far as they were concerned and they could but hope.

There were three bungalows on Zurrantee, but at that time only two were habitable. The Engineer Assistant's bungalow, sited on the hillside above the factory, which should have been mine, had not been used since the war, and although it had a steel frame and a corrugated iron sheet roof, the walls and floors were made of wood and the termites had had a field day, steadily chewing away at the planks until it was unsafe. Repair work was in progress, but until this was complete it was planned that I should live in the Garden Assistant's bungalow with Ian and John.

I had no real idea of what the bungalow would be like, but in the back of my mind I had a vision of a type of thatch and bamboo shack, rather like something out of a Tarzan film, so I was pleasantly surprised when we reached the bungalow that night to find that, other than the fact that the kitchen was detached at the rear of the building, it would not have seemed very much out of place on an estate in the UK. It is an interesting point to note that, although the name 'bungalow' has been adopted in the West to indicate a house with only one storey, in actual fact the word was derived from the Hindustani word 'Bangla', meaning 'Of Bengal' and was used for a house built in the Bengali style, usually raised on stilts, with a large veranda, irrespective of the number of floors. This meant that a bungalow in tea could have one, two, or sometimes even three storeys.

The Garden Assistant's bungalow was a single-storeyed, brick-built building with concrete floors, which had a very large living room and two large bedrooms, all of which opened out onto a wide, shady veranda which ran along the entire front of the building. At the rear of the living room was a smaller dining room and its connected 'bottle *khana*' or scullery, flanked by two bathrooms complete with flush toilets, one for each bedroom, while the cookhouse, which contained the solid fuel cooking range and hot water boiler was about ten yards from the bottle khana at the end of a paved walk. It was situated on the edge of a small, wooded valley in a clearing in the tea, with a lovely view over the plains below, and although the grass was crisp and brown underfoot, the compound was a riot of colour, with cannas, cosmos, bougainvilleas, hibiscus and frangipani bushes, all in full bloom.

The cold weather in the Bengal Dooars was like a sunny autumn at home, with a warm sun during the day and cold nights. Although we never had a frost, the evenings were cold enough for us to need a fire, and we often had thick mists with a heavy dew which made the early mornings very cold. That first evening, as I entered the bungalow, I was greeted by a bright fire burning in the fireplace, a small centre table laid for tea, upon which the bearer soon placed hot toast, butter, cheese and tea, and the remains of a very large, iced Christmas cake. I was amazed, especially at the sight of the cake, and thought to myself, 'This is just like being at home. If being in tea is all like this, then I think I am going to like it.' I had yet to learn that there were always plenty of Christmas cakes around at that time of year, but more about them later on

Because he had the benefit of seniority as well as possession, Ian had the smaller bedroom as his personal room, while John and I shared the larger one. Evidently it had been stressed that, because his father wished him to experience the day-to-day life of an ordinary planter at first hand, he was not to be given any preferential treatment, otherwise he could have had accommodation in Bill's bungalow, so he got me instead. The room was large enough to take four single beds, so there was enough space in there to accommodate our two, together with all our unwanted trunks and cases as well.

I believe John had been educated at one of the big universities and was a very studious fellow indeed, but considering the differences in our backgrounds, in most things we got on with each other very well indeed. I can recall only one occasion when he had to put me in my place, and I learned that lesson well. We had had some kippers brought up on the cold store plane from Calcutta, and when we had them for tea that evening I noticed we had an extra plate each, but as we had always done at home, I went and got a piece of newspaper and put it on the table to put the skin and bones on. When he saw it John exploded. 'What are you doing with that newspaper?' and when I explained that this was always the way we did it at home, he said ' Well, you're not at home now. Use that spare plate and act like a gentleman. We're not having newspaper here', and like a lamb I obeyed. Then he laughed and said 'Right, now we've got that out of the way, eat up your kipper like a good boy', which I did, and we remained the best of friends.

Regarding servants, it was the normal practice for a planter to have his own servants such as a bearer, cook, driver and, if he had children, an ayah, and pay for them out of his own pay and allowances. These moved with him whenever he was transferred to another estate, and they lived in estate houses near the bungalow which were kept especially for their use, known as the 'servants' line'. The other bungalow servants were supplied and paid for by the estate, and were permanent residents on the garden.

The bearer was the Sahib's own personal servant and was head of the household, rather like the butler in 19th century British society. He looked after all his clothes and personal belongings, prepared the table for meals and served all the food, allocated the jobs for the other servants and checked that they were done properly, and ensured that life in the bungalow ran smoothly. The relationship between the two of them was built on trust and mutual regard, and was something special which developed over the years, not like the idea which normally springs to mind when the terms 'master' and 'servant' are used, and many of them grew old in each other's company. They became accustomed to each other's ways, and the most common occurrence which upset the relationship was when the Master took a wife. This meant that an outside person, often unable to speak the language and with very little knowledge of the way of life in India, moved in as head of the household, and insisted on such sweeping changes that the bearer was unable to cope. Thus the Sahib was left to find a suitable trustworthy bearer, often an older man, who was not averse to having a Memsahib in the house, and this was not an easy thing to do. Fortunately, I recruited my bearer, Kancha, in 1951, not long after I arrived on Zurrantee, and he was able to accept the change and remained our trusty bearer until we came home for good in 1967, which was rather a feather in Jan's cap.

The cooks, most of whom got rolling drunk at regular intervals for some reason, were precisely that, and only prepared the meals, although some assistants, in order to save money, employed a dual cook and bearer who did both jobs at an enhanced rate of pay. Later on we had one cook who didn't actually drink while he was working, but every 10 or 12 weeks or so, he would come and ask for leave to 'go and see his family, because they thought his grandmother was dying and he wanted to see her'! Of course, after the first time we both knew what he wanted, but we played the game and off he would go for several days. When he came back he was like death warmed up, with red eyes and looking as though he had all the troubles of the world on his shoulders, but when we asked him how his grandmother was, he would reply that fortunately she was very much better, so he felt better too, and we knew that after a binge like that we would have no more trouble from him for several weeks.

Of the garden-based servants, the most important was the 'pani wallah' or water boy, who did all the jobs in the kitchen other than the actual cooking, although most of them knew enough about it to stand in in an emergency. He helped prepare the vegetables, did the washing up, stoked the hot water boiler, and kept the kitchen and bottle khana clean and tidy. Good ones also helped the bearer, in an effort to learn the job in the hope of being taken on as a new bearer if the opportunity arose.

The actual cleaning of the bungalow was done by two younger boys called 'polish chokras' or polish boys. They swept and cleaned the floors, polished the windows and cleaned the bathrooms, and in bungalows which had polished timber or tile floors, it was quite common to see the two boys with polishing rags tied to their feet, skating round buffing up the floors as though they were on an ice rink. Understandably, this was one of their more popular jobs.

The estate also supplied two gardeners, or 'malis', who kept the compound and garden in order, and they were usually assisted by an older woman or nursing mother who swept up the leaves and rubbish, and also watered the plants in the dry season. Some of the malis were excellent gardeners, and provided they were given help and encouragement by their Sahibs, could produce an abundant supply of first class fruit and vegetables during the cold weather, and there was always a lot of good natured rivalry for the 'Malis' Cup' at the annual, local horticultural show.

Most estates also supplied two 'chowkidhars' or watchmen who were responsible for the security of the bungalow, especially when the Sahib was away at night. Usually they worked as a pair, and theoretically took it in turns to sleep so that there should always have been one awake - but very often theories didn't work in India. One Sunday night when we were on Chulsa, we had been to the film at Nagakata Club and arrived back home to find the compound gates chained, and the bungalow a blaze of lights with all the doors open. Our usual night chowkidhar had been given leave, and had been replaced by two usually reliable garden men, who had been told to keep the gates shut and stay awake until we got home at about midnight, after which they would be able to go home. Despite repeated blasts on the car horn, no one appeared to unchain the gates, so finally we climbed the fence and went inside, where we found both men asleep on the living room floor. Goodness knows what they had been doing during the day, but they were absolutely out to the wide, sleeping so soundly that shouts and repeated nudges with the foot failed to wake them. Whenever we travelled through the forest at night, I always carried my rifle and shotgun with me in case we saw a wild pig or deer, and having brought my rifle in with me, I decided I would startle them awake, so opening one of the dining room windows, I poked the rifle through, pointed the muzzle skyward, and pulled the trigger. It was a 250/3000 underlever Winchester rifle, and in the confined space of the room the report was deafening, with the noise echoing and reverberating round enough to wake the dead - or so we thought, for it didn't make a scrap of difference to them, and they continued to sleep like two children. Finally, in desperation, I took a bottle of cold water out of the fridge, and poured it over their heads until I got a response. As though coming out of a coma, one of them opened his eyes, and saw Jan's feet alongside his head. Gradually his gaze travelled up her legs, then her body and then up to her face, and it was hilarious to see the realization of what had happened gradually creeping into his consciousness. Finally, when he had gathered his wits together, he scrambled to his feet and started kicking his mate all the while shouting, 'The Sahib has come! The Sahib has come! Utao! Utao! [Get up].' Once they were fully awake they were full of apologies.

Of course they hadn't intended to sleep, and if any thieves HAD come, they would have been up and at them like tigers, etc, and they HAD locked the gates behind us as instructed. As it was, no harm had been done, but although I was bursting with laughter inside, I put on a straight face and gave them a right dressing down, telling them how disappointed I was that they had let me down, etc etc, and then let them go home. As they disappeared down the path that led back to the labour lines across the river, we could still hear them arguing about who should have been asleep and who should have stayed awake.

Later on I realised that the expression 'to sleep like a child' was not so far off the mark for them, for when we had our own two children, there were so many strange noises in and around the bungalow that we decided they would have to get used to them and sleep through them, and they did so with no trouble at all. In fact, Viv would sleep soundly through the loudest jazz music on our record player, which I played even though he was fast asleep, and he never stirred. No doubt this accounts for his present day love (or dislike?) of Dixieland jazz.

Two other people connected with the bungalow who were

not actually bungalow servants were the *Dhobi walla,* or laundryman, and the *nappet,* or *nappie walla,* the barber. The dhobi lived in quite a large house on the bank of the river so that he had a supply of good, clean water for the whole of the year, and besides doing the washing for the managerial staff, he also washed the clothes for the Bengali office clerks as well. Each Monday morning the bearer would gather together all the items to be washed and make a list of them in a special book, and then later the dhobi would bring back the previous week's washing, which would all be checked and marked off. Every item was meticulously ironed and folded and then bundled up in a sheet which he carried on the top of his head, and considering that most of his work was carried out in the open air on the river bank, with no artificial aids other than a big block of washing soap and some large, flat stones to rub and beat them on, it was remarkable that the clothes and sheets were always spotlessly white. The only drawback was that shirts and bedding etc. didn't take kindly to that kind of treatment, so they tended to wear out very quickly and had to be patched and darned. As a result, any garments that needed a bit of careful attention had to be done by ourselves in the bungalow, but other than this all the dhobis we ever had were excellent, and I never did find out how they managed to dry the clothes in the middle of the monsoon when it poured with rain every day, because none of ours ever smelt of smoke. I suppose it was a trade secret.

The nappet lived in the labour lines, and as many of our workers liked to be short haired in the heat he was always busy. However one unusual thing was that no matter how short the rest of our labourer's heads were shaved, he always left a small tuft of hair on the top of their scalps which they usually oiled and tied in a knot. When I enquired one day as to why this was done, the man said that when he died this tuft was what his God would grasp when he pulled him up to heaven.

Whenever I needed a haircut I would send a message down for the nappet to come to the bungalow at lunchtime, and he would be there waiting for me whenever I came in. He was an excellent barber and I never had any complaints about his work, but it was disconcerting that he did most of his work, including all the procedures a modern barber would carry out, with a large cut-throat razor. It was such a disturbing experience to have it flashing around my throat that I never quite got to grips with it, and I was always glad when he was finished.

That night, after dinner, we sat down to consider what we should do regarding the servants, as three Sahibs sharing a bungalow was quite an unusual event. Both Ian and John had their own bearers, but were sharing the cook, and as there were no more quarters available in the servant's line, it was decided that, provided they were willing to accept the added work for an increase in pay, I would share John's bearer, and also pay one third of the cook's pay until the situation changed, and in the event the arrangement worked out very well indeed until John transferred to Fagu Estate later in the year.

This gave me the opportunity to look around and gain some idea of the attributes I would look for in a bearer, and when the time came, I was approached by the then pani-wallah in the bungalow, a young Nepalese youth named Kancha Rai, who asked whether I would be willing to take him on for a trial period. He wasn't able to speak any English, but I considered this to be an advantage, and as Bill told me he came from a very good family who lived on Zurrantee, I took him on and he stayed with me for the rest of my time in tea.

There were two schools of thought regarding the desirability of a bearer to be able to speak good English or not. I thought it defeated the object if you were trying to learn Hindustani yourself, but one assistant with whom I discussed the matter had a bearer who could read and speak fluent English, and he declared that it was a distinct advantage, as it was almost like having a permanent tutor in the bungalow. However, that was until he returned to his bungalow VERY unexpectedly one day from what should have been an afternoon trip to Siliguri. He had only travelled a couple of miles down the road when his car broke down, so he had to walk back to the bungalow, and as he walked up the veranda steps everything seemed quiet and in order. However, as he entered his bedroom he heard a noise in the bathroom, and walked in to discover his bearer lying in a hot bath drinking a glass of his whisky, and reading the letters his fiancée had sent him from the UK! As he told me later, the sight of him chasing his naked bearer out of the bungalow and through the tea must have been very funny indeed.

Because they are affected by both the south west and north east monsoons in season, on the estates in Ceylon and South India the winters stay wet and warm enough for tea production to continue all the year round. However, in North East India and Darjeeling the working year fell into two quite distinct periods, the cold, dry winter from October to February, and the very hot wet weather caused by the South West Monsoon from May to September. The weather during March, April and May was very hot and oppressive, and it was at this time, immediately before the monsoon, that we got very severe hail and electrical storms.

The labourers called the hail 'donga pani', or 'stone water', and as it was quite common for individual stones to be solid balls of ice larger than golf balls, it was the one weather condition in which they refused to work, and we could hardly blame them. Hailstorms in India had their own distinctive, bilious colour, and once they saw the dirty, yellowish grey clouds forming and coming their way, they would leave their work and run for the nearest shelter, and they were very rarely wrong. During these storms it was quite a common occurrence for goats and cattle to be killed, windows broken and holes punched through old corrugated iron sheets, and I once saw a car that was dented all over where it had been peppered with large stones. Hail damage could be so severe that the estates in Goodricke's group had Hail Damage Insurance Policies to cover the loss of crop and repair the damage caused by these storms. This was assessed on a scale from one to ten, ranging from bruising and slight damage at number one up to a maximum where all the branches had been stripped from the bushes and they would die. Tea bushes damaged as severely as this rarely survived, so they had to be uprooted and replanted, a very expensive business indeed.

Electrical discharges during thunderstorms also caused long-term widespread damage to the tea. The rows of bushes were inter-planted with large, permanent shade trees at 40 x 40 foot-square planting, and when these were struck by lightning, the charge travelled down the tree trunk into the earth and affected the roots of the surrounding bushes. Although the shade tree usually survived, the affected bushes seemed fine for a while, until quite suddenly, several weeks later, most of the bushes within a thirty-foot radius of the tree would die within a matter of days, so one of the most important jobs during the cold weather was the uprooting and replanting of these areas.

Another fascinating natural phenomenon which occurred at this time were the electrical storms. No rain would fall, but heavy banks of cloud would build up and the air would become charged with static electricity, so much so that it almost made the hairs on the head stand erect. In one bungalow in which we lived the pendant lights had metal shades and were so placed that a static charge would build up gradually from the surrounding air until there would be a snapping 'crack' and a bolt of electricity would leap from one shade to the next, leaving a smell of ozone in the air. No damage was ever done, but nevertheless, it was a very memorable experience.

As the days became hotter and more oppressive, people longed for the monsoon to arrive to cool things down for a while, and each evening we listened to the All India Radio to hear the latest weather reports. It was a great day when we heard it had reached Bombay at last, for we knew that within two weeks it should reach us. Usually it reached the Dooars during the third week in May, and as the first of the storms were not unduly heavy, they came as a blessed relief after the long, dry spell, as they cleaned the atmosphere and laid the dust. However, the real rains soon arrived, and in the four months from mid-May to mid-September, our area received between 250 and 350 inches of rain. It would pour down out of leaden, grey skies, everything and everywhere became sodden, and streams which had been stony, dried-up rivulets during the cold weather became thundering, flooded rivers, foaming from bank to bank. For 12 inches of rain to fall over a 24-hour period was common place, and as the temperature was usually in the upper 80s Fahrenheit with over 90% humidity, conditions quickly became very tedious again and we looked forward to the cold weather once more. The most rain which I ever experienced in my time in tea was 36 inches of rain in nine hours but this really was exceptional, and it carried away just about every road and rail bridge from one end of the Dooars to the other.

During the 1965 monsoon, the rain fell for day after day from a dull, grey sky, with hardly a let up, and when the clouds finally lifted and the rain stopped, we checked the records and found that we had not seen the sun for 62 days. Naturally, everything in the bungalow was damp. The curtains hung like rags, and at times it was possible to wring the moisture out of them, while books and papers became damp and smelt musty. Even the thicker clothes such as suits, jackets and dresses had to be taken out of the wardrobes and dried out in front of the fire at regular intervals, otherwise they became green with mould, and a casual visitor would have been dumbfounded had he seen the fire blazing in the living room grate with the temperature at 90 degrees F while the clothes dried out.

My stamp collection also suffered badly, especially the mint ones, which stuck together and spoilt the gum, until finally I was forced to buy a small, wooden cabinet. Into this I fitted a low powered electric bulb, and by keeping this switched on whenever we had power in the bungalow, I managed to dry out my albums and prevent any further damage, although many of the mint stamps were spoilt.

During the cold weather, the tea bushes were pruned to remove last year's growth, and once the weather had warmed up in March, the leaf started to grow once more. The bushes were allowed to put on five to 10 inches of new growth above the pruning height, in order to bring them up to waist height, after which they were tipped and plucking began in earnest. The good thing about the heat and humidity was that they were ideal for tea growth, and the leaf developed so quickly that we could almost see it growing. A small bud left on the bush one day developed into two large leaves and a bud within a week, and it was at this time that the bulk of the crop was made. Seven-day leaf, or two leaves and a bud were essential to make the best tea, and we always endeavoured to pluck the same area of the garden on the same day each week. The Indian Tea Association (ITA) and the labour unions had come to an agreement regarding the size of the labour force, whereby each estate should standardise on a ratio of one labourer for every acre of mature tea it had, and by carefully recruiting good workers and monitoring absenteeism this was sufficient for most normal purposes. However, if very severe weather or sickness disrupted the work, it was possible for the plucking round to rise up to 10, 12 or even 14 days, and if this occurred you were in trouble. The fine, tender leaf quickly became hard and stalky, and lost its flavour, the manufactured tea became reddish with bits of dried stalk in it, instead of being, a glossy black, and the blenders and brokers refused to buy it, one of the worst crimes in the tea planter's book. Once an estate lost its reputation for making good quality teas it proved to be extremely difficult to recover it.

Once the monsoon finished during September the temperatures fell quite abruptly, and with the colder nights the leaf buds became dormant and the bushes stopped growing. This was the beginning of the cold weather which lasted for five months until February. During that time we could almost guarantee that there would be no rain, and all the tennis, cricket and golf tournaments, together with picnics and other outdoor events could be organised, secure in the knowledge that the days would be fine, something different to our climate.

During this period the garden labourers did all the other jobs which we were unable to do during the plucking season. The tea bushes were pruned, the entire tea area was cultivated and manured, drains were cleaned out, the areas planted with bamboos were cleaned and burnt out to eradicate ants nests, houses, roads, bridges and water supplies were all repaired, new labour quarters were built, firewood was cut and collected, tea seed nurseries were planted for the next year and the old tea was uprooted and other areas were replanted.

During the plucking season, the working day was from 7 am to 3 pm for six days, with Sunday off to visit the bazaar, but during the cold weather these hours were relaxed, and because the mornings were chilly, most of the garden labour worked from about 7.45 am until about 1 pm on a task basis for a fixed, standard wage. The harder they worked, and the sooner they completed the allotted task satisfactorily, the quicker they could go home. The fixed wage consisted of the 'hazree', which also entitled the worker to concessional rations and other benefits, and the 'dubli', extra pay which was added to the hazree for extra work done, and most labourers were able to complete a normal hazree/dubli well within the allotted time. The amount of work required to complete the task was based on the difficulty and quality of the work to be done, and was usually decided after reference to similar work done previously and discussion with the supervisory staff.

Because the labourers had the afternoon off, they were able to harvest their *dhan* (unhusked rice) from the paddy fields they had planted during the monsoon, and also dry and husk it. They also gathered firewood from the forest and river valleys, and cultivated their gardens. They grew maize, tobacco, cucumbers, melons and pineapples, with a variety of leaf vegetables, all of which matured in the cold weather, for very little grew in the rains as the soil quickly became waterlogged.

For the factory labourers, the working pattern was slightly different. During the monsoon, when the factory often worked 24 hours a day, seven days a week, extra men were drafted in from the garden labour force to make up three eight hour shifts, and these returned to work in the garden during the cold weather. The permanent factory labour force on Zurrantee, which was usually about 120 men, was needed to work in the factory for the whole of the period. All the machines were dismantled, cleaned and repaired, line shafting, steam engines, diesel engines, water pumps and generators were serviced, and all the factory buildings were cleaned, repaired and painted. In addition to this, most of the workers had to take their annual leave. They were all entitled to one day's paid holiday for every 25 days worked, and this was normally taken in the cold weather, although they could take it at other times by arrangement.

This, then, was the situation when I arrived at the beginning of February, with most of the cold weather work complete, and the labour force filling in with smaller, odd jobs until the plucking started.

On my first morning, John's bearer woke us up at 6 am with 'Palang ka char', or 'bed tea', which consisted of tea, toast and a banana, and by 7 am we had walked down the dusty road to the office, which was sited in the factory compound. On the way we met a great number of the garden labourers all going out to the working areas, or 'melas', all of whom had a good look at the new boy. Initially I felt very self-conscious, because they all, without exception, raised their right hand to their forehead and greeted me with 'Salaam, Sahib' to which I had to respond in the same way, rather like an army officer being saluted by his men. I had been warned that, because the left hand was used for toilet purposes, to be salaamed with it was an unforgivable insult, so I had to remember to use the right one only. It was used as a greeting or farewell at any time of the day or night, rather as we use our Good Morning, Good Night, and Good Evening etc. so I quickly got used to it, but I did feel a bit of a wally that morning.

The sun was breaking through the early morning mist when we reached the office, where we found Bill already there discussing the day's work with some of the supervisory staff. Afterwards we had a chat in his office, and he explained that, although the office and factory clerical staff were educated Bengalis, or Babus, who could speak English, all the rest of the practical work was carried out by using a type of generally understood Hindustani, colloquially known as 'Garden Baht', so there was very little actual work I could do until I could converse a little. Of course, it was accepted that all beginners were there to adapt and learn, but I was instructed to learn at least a smattering of Hindi as quickly as possible. In the meantime I was to divide my time between the factory and the garden, acclimatising myself and getting used to being with the labourers, and it was agreed that I would work in the factory from 7 am to 9 am each morning, when I could learn about the machinery and check the work being done with one of the Babus. After breakfast I was to spend the rest of the morning finding my way about the garden and watching the labourers at work. Finally, I was not to interfere with anything I saw, but was to make notes of anything I didn't understand or which I wished to query so that I could ask Bill about it afterwards.

Once this was all settled, his next question was, 'Are you able to drive a car'?. He seemed genuinely surprised when I told him that the only transport I had ever had was a pushbike. 'Well' he added, 'An assistant who can't drive is no use to me. You'll have to learn', and straightaway he asked Ian what work the garden vehicles were doing that morning. It appeared that one lorry was visiting Sam Sing Workshops to collect repaired factory machinery, the other was carrying gravel from the river bed to repair the roads, and the tractor was delivering building materials to the labour lines where houses were being built and repaired. 'Cancel the gravel', instructed Bill, 'Put the lorry on to house repairs, and tell Somra to have the tractor on the football field at half past nine so he can teach Rod how to drive'. For a tractor driver, who couldn't speak any English to teach his boss, who couldn't speak any Hindustani, how to drive in one morning, seemed to me to be a rather tall order, but nevertheless, after breakfast I drove it round and round the football field next to the factory for three and a half hours until I felt I knew every blade of grass on it. I zig-zagged and reversed in and out of boulders that Somra craftily placed in my way and which he designated 'goats', 'cows', 'carts' and 'admies' (people), and by lunch time I had knocked down enough goats and killed enough imaginary admies to become a fully-fledged tractor driver. Actually this story has a sting in the tail, inasmuch as Jan says it is easy to see how I learned to drive, because I am extremely heavy handed and have driven our car like a tractor ever since.

There was another sting in the tail, because Bill, unbeknown to me, had an ulterior motive in teaching me to drive. A few days later on a Sunday afternoon, he arrived at the bungalow and asked me if I would like to go down to

Chulsa Club for a game of tennis. The other two had already gone out for the day, so feeling a bit lonely I jumped at the chance. Now Bill was the proud owner of a very sleek and sporty SS Jaguar saloon which he had brought out from the UK about 18 months before. It was a beautiful car, glossy black with red upholstery, walnut fascia and trims and 'knock on' wire wheels, for which there was a special hide mallet in the boot. The only drawback was that he kept wiping the exhaust box off on the very high ridges which formed in the middle of the roads, and so for most of the time it sounded like an old motorbike instead of a swish sports car. There were several other planters there that afternoon, so we had some good tennis followed by tea and some games of snooker, but afterwards most of the others left as they were going to the weekly film at Nagrakata Club, about 25 miles away. Soon there were just three of us left, me, Bill and one of his cronies, and because I didn't drink alcohol in those days, I had numerous Coca Colas while the other two got stuck into the hard stuff.

I sat and listened with rapture while they discussed all aspects of tea, shooting, fishing, labour welfare, cars, and seemingly a thousand other subjects until finally, at about midnight, Bill had had enough and went to sleep sitting at the bar.

'Right', said the other planter, 'You'd better get him home, where is your driver'?

'We didn't bring one with us' I replied,' Bill drove down this afternoon'.

'Well', he said, 'He's in no fit state to drive, so you'll have to drive him back unless you want to stay here all night'!

So it came to pass that, after three hours' tuition on a Fordson Major tractor, the first car I ever drove was an SS Jaguar. Inside I was petrified, for I didn't know where any of the controls were, and it was about four miles back to the bungalows along dark estate roads. However we half carried Bill out to the car, where he slumped in the front seat and went straight off to sleep again while the other man explained the gear shifts, light switches and other controls to me, then off I went. For the first half mile the road was fairly straight, but I crept along in first gear until we reached the Chulsa factory hill. This was not very steep, but it did have a very sharp, hairpin bend in the middle of it, and it was at this point that I learned that the rear wheels of a car have a much smaller turning circle than the front ones. I thought I was safely in the middle of the road and in the darkness it was not until I heard a metallic, scraping sound from the nearside back wing that I realised I had cut the corner too sharply and had damaged it on the wall on the inside of the road. Bill never moved while this was going on, but a sick, empty feeling came up in the pit of my stomach and I wondered what on earth I was going to do.

From Chulsa, the main road ran through the local Matelli bazaar, then on through Nagaisuree and onto the Zurrantee roads, and as I knew these slightly better, I did get her into 3rd gear. Finally I reached Bill's bungalow on the top of the hill, and the two night watchmen came out and took him inside, where we put him to bed after which I took the car back down to our bungalow, where I spent a sleepless night while I worried about what Bill would say about the damage to his car. I had dented and scraped all the paint off the top of the wheel arch, and while I thought it was repairable, I knew no one would be happy having damage like that done to his car. Finally, at 6 am I could endure the suspense of waiting no longer, and I decided to take it up to the bungalow and wait there for Bill to finally 'surface' after his binge, when I would make a clean confession of what had happened.

After leaving him at 1 am I didn't expect him to be around for several hours, and it was not until later that I found out that, although Bill was, like so many other planters, quite a hard drinker, he never let this interfere with his work. So you can imagine my surprise when I walked round the front of his bungalow at 6.30 and found him sitting on the veranda having his breakfast.

'Hullo Rod, come on in and have a cup of coffee' he said. 'That was a good night we had last night, wasn't it?' Looking at him you wouldn't have thought he had had a drink for a month, but with my heart in my plimsolls I told him I had a confession to make and told him all about it.

He was wonderful. After listening he told me he thought I had done very well to get us home at all, and as for the damage to the car, well, that was repairable and if that was all that ever happened to it, then it would do very well. As far as he was concerned, I could forget all about it, and that was that. He never mentioned it again.

Later on I drove the Jag quite regularly, and improved my driving skills on the two garden lorries. Both of these, an American Ford and an old Dodge truck had been bought in India as Army Surplus after the war, and it was on the Ford I passed my driving test a few weeks later. Harry Duncan, the Manager of Chalouni Tea Estate about six miles away, had been appointed as the local Driving Test Examiner by the District Commissioner in Jalpaiguri, so on the Sunday morning I drove it up to his bungalow and round the compound, then backed it into a space, and got out and went up the veranda steps. Harry was sitting there in an easy chair drinking a coffee, so I joined him, and as we were both very keen on football we drank our coffees and chatted about soccer at home until he said, 'Well laddie, do you fancy a gin and tonic?' Well, I told him I would like a gin with orange as the tonic was too bitter for my taste, but didn't he think I should take my test before we started drinking? At this he laughed and said 'Get away laddie. You drove the truck up here and backed it into that space, didn't you? What more do you want? No, you've passed, so come and have your gin' and that was that, and it wasn't until almost 20 years later that I failed my UK driving test at the first attempt because the tester said I was 'too confident!' Our tractor was very much newer as it was one of ten Fordson Majors that had been brought up the Brahmaputra from Calcutta by river steamer, a journey that took about two weeks. On arrival in the Eastern Dooars they were landed at Dhubri Ghat, where ten assistants, one from each of our gardens collected them and drove them back, a road journey of about 200 miles which took them two days. The Fordson Major tractor was not the fastest of vehicles, but it must have made a very impressive sight to see ten of them in convoy, charging along the road at top speed in a cloud of dust.

After learning how to drive on the tractor that first morning, I did my first proper engineering job that afternoon, although this was a bit more by luck than judgement. The Manager's and Assistant's bungalows were built on two hills separated by a very steep sided valley, in the bottom of which ran a small stream. About a mile upstream this had been dammed, and water was piped down to a small surge pump below the bungalows, which used the power generated by a large quantity of water running down the pipe to force a much smaller quantity up the small delivery pipes to the bungalow storage tanks. The pump consisted of a central chamber which contained two valves, one large, mushroom-shaped one which normally hung open and allowed the water to flow away through it, and a smaller one which was kept on its seat by external springs. The working was simple. Provided the main supply pipe was full, the water ran out of the large valve faster and faster until its velocity was great enough to force it shut and then forced the smaller valve off its seat and allowed a small amount of water to flow through and up the delivery pipe, until the pressure fell sufficiently for the large valve to fall open again. Theoretically this process was repeated indefinitely as long as there was water running down the supply pipe. As there were really no working parts as such, these pumps normally ran trouble-free year after year with the minimum of maintenance, and it was just my luck that the darned thing had started giving trouble a few weeks before. As the only other way of getting water to the bungalows was by tanks on the back of the tractor, they had been waiting impatiently for me to arrive so that could put it right, like an engineering guardian angel. Such faith!

Although I had covered hydraulics while studying for my Engineering ONC and knew the theory of how these things worked, I had never seen one in real life, and I was absolutely amazed when I scrambled down the steep side of the jhora and reached the rusty, corrugated iron shed in which the thing lived. It looked so old and so battered, where countless numbers of enraged engineers had thrashed hell out of it because it wouldn't work, that it looked as though it could have been made at the beginning of the Industrial Revolution, and probably that wasn't far wrong. In place of the two coil springs which originally kept the small valve seated, it was festooned with replacement 'springs' made out of sections of old car inner tubes, rather like thick rubber bands.

When it was working properly, the pump went 'click - CLACK, click - CLACK', every few seconds as the valves opened and shut, so on the garden it was known as the 'clack pump'. When Bill asked me to look at it he had arranged for the head factory engineer, a Munda tribesman named Lopo, to help me. He was a middle-aged man, very dark for an Indian, with a round face and a very engaging smile, and as we squatted by the dratted article considering what to do, I asked him what he thought was wrong with it. For a few moments he gazed at it in silence, then he grinned at me and said, '*Uske clack nai hai, Sahib*', (It hasn't got a clack, Sahib), and even I was able to understand that. Finally we took it apart, and I soon realised that the valve stems and seats were so worn that they didn't seat properly, and new ones would have to be made at Sam Sing and fitted before it would perform efficiently. Still, after reading the instruction book which they still had, and consulting my hydraulics textbook which I had taken with me, we finally managed to get it going, and much to everyone's obvious enjoyment water reached the bungalow tanks for the first time in a month, and everyone could have a shower. Later, as I sat by the living room fire that night, eating my Christmas cake after my first proper day in tea, I felt a bit of a hero.

CHAPTER SIX

Settling in

Zurrantee was a medium-sized tea estate with a total grant area of about 1800 acres, of which just over 1100 acres were planted with tea. The remaining 700 acres were made up of land used for the factory site, roads and river valleys, hillsides planted with bamboo and firewood trees, thatch barries, grazing areas, rice fields, which were allocated for the use of the labourers, tea nurseries and the labour house lines which were usually built on the river banks or near some other convenient water supply.

Tea planting in North East India started in Assam in the 1830s, but it was not until the 1870s and 80s, after the planting up of suitable areas in Assam and Darjeeling was almost complete, that forest clearing and planting up began in our area, the Bengal Dooars. With satisfactory pruning, a young tea plant begins to produce useful quantities of leaf after about six years, and it was generally accepted that tea bushes were in their prime from 20 to 40 years old. After that, both quantity and quality of leaf were supposed to fall, but in spite of this, we had areas on Zurrantee that had been planted in 1894 that were still cropping satisfactorily, almost 60 years later.

When the estates were planted out, whole tracts of virgin forest were felled, cleared and burnt by a specialised labour force of young men who travelled on the job. Later, when the bushes matured and needed continual plucking and upkeep, there was no pool of local labourers who were available to do the work, so the tea companies arranged for labour contractors, or sirdars, to recruit workers from villages in the states of Bihar and Orissa, west of Calcutta, to come and work on a temporary basis. Their return railway fares were paid for by the estate, and this arrangement was fine as long as there was an adequate supply of suitable workers. However, as the gardens grew and the demand for workers exceeded the supply, the companies realised that the only way to ensure they were guaranteed a plentiful supply of good labourers was to keep them on the estate as a permanent labour force, and the first labour lines were built. The sirdars recruited whole families for whom they were personally responsible, and to ensure that they brought good workers, the sirdar was paid a daily commission for every day one of his recruits worked. As a result of this, sirdars tended to recruit from one village or area they knew, many of the families were connected and had mutual relatives back home, and as the young people took their parent's sirdari when they started work, the commission was still being paid when I left tea in 1967. In 1951 there were very few of the old people left who could remember the early days, and most of the labourers thought of themselves as Zurrantee people, as they had been born and lived their lives there, although there were many who used their annual leave to visit the areas around Ranchi in the state of Bihar, which was their ancestral home and the place where many of their tribal relations still lived.

As they were from a variety of different tribes who practised a type of animism as a religion, they were not really strict Hindus. They believed that although natural objects such as mountains and rocks have no life in themselves, they can be the abode of dead people, spirits and gods, and as such were worth worshipping. They were very superstitious, and were very involved with a type of witchcraft and spells, and the local 'Pahan' (village priest) or 'Bhagat' (witch-finder) was often called in to lift a curse or purify something or someone who had been defiled, all for a suitable fee, of course. Still, more about that later.

In accordance with an agreement which had been worked out between the labour unions and the Indian Tea Association, we had about 1100 permanent labourers, men, women and children, together with about 140 supervisory and security staff, in addition to the factory staff. The garden supervisors were called Daffadars, while the head man was called the Munshi. He was usually an older man who had grown old in the service of the company, and he formed the link between the managerial staff and the garden labour force. In addition to these workers there were about 2500 other family members living on the garden, and they were all housed in approximately 800 labour houses built in different parts of the garden. In the old days these would have been made from bamboo with a thatch roof, but in 1951 most of them were constructed with steel frames, corrugated iron roofs and wooden batten and plank walls, although new quarters built with hollow, concrete block walls and asbestos cement roofs were beginning to make their appearance.

On a map, Zurrantee looked like a very long, inverted triangle, about 1.5 miles wide at its widest point, and nearly three miles long, North to South. The straight top edge was a common boundary with two other estates, a small Indian-owned garden named Engo TE on the west, and the much larger Chalouni TE on the east, which belonged to Messrs. Duncan Brothers, our Agents in Calcutta. The two sides of the estate were demarcated by two rivers, the Nagaisuree river down the eastern side, and the Naura river down the west, and these two met at the most southerly point on the estate. On the western side of the Naura was the Naura forest, a large block of jungle connected to the wild Himalayan foothills about six miles distant, and it was from this forest that most of the animal visitors to the estate originated.

I had a map of the garden, which was divided into numbered blocks of tea, each about 50 acres in area, so most of the time I wandered around on my own, finding the work areas and seeing what was being done. Sometimes I accompanied Bill or one of the other assistants, especially when there was some new work being started, and although things were a little frustrating at first, as I wasn't able to express myself or understand what was being said, by and large the labourers were very friendly, and my introduction to tea was not as worrying or traumatic as I had once feared it would be. However, I soon realised that what Bill had said was true, and until I could converse with them I was virtually useless, so I bought myself a 'Teach Yourself' Hindi primer from which I learned a list of nouns and verbs and the numbers 1 to 100. By using these, together with some English and sign language, I learned to express myself, and some of the labourers actually took an interest in trying to teach me some common expressions. At first I felt rather self-conscious about making mistakes, but once I lost my inhibitions rarely a day passed without I made significant progress. At first I thought in

English and then translated into Hindi, and I was well into my second year before I actually thought and spoke in Hindi. However, once I reached this stage progress was swift, and by conversing socially with the labourers on all types of subjects I became very fluent and never lost the ability.

One amusing thing which happened at this time occurred one Sunday afternoon when I was lying on the grass at the side of the bungalow, reading my Hindi primer. The afternoon sun was warm, and gradually my eyes closed, until I was almost asleep. Suddenly my rest was disturbed by a dry, rustling sound which I realised was coming closer and closer, and I opened my eyes to look into the face of a large monitor lizard about two feet away. At first I thought it was a snake, and a shiver of horror ran down my spine, then it gave a hiss and ran off as quickly as its legs would carry it. From nose to tail it was about three feet long, and the noise I had heard was the sound of its long tail being dragged over the crisped, brown grass as it ran along. In reality I think it had not noticed me lying there, and was as surprised as much as I was when I came to life and opened my eyes.

The first time I was able to pick up the use of a Hindi verb was one day when I was out with Bill. We were out on the mela talking to the Daffadars, and the words '*sakega*' and '*nai sakega*' kept coming into the conversation. As usual, I stood and listened, not understanding any of it, but afterwards I asked Bill what all the talk was about regarding sucking eggs. He laughed and explained that it was the future tense of the verb '*sakna*', to be able; '*sakega*' would they be able to do something, '*nai sakega*', no, they wouldn't be able to do it, and I never forgot.

Of course, there were many apocryphal tales about young

assistants learning the language which did the rounds. One new lad wanted to buy a small, cane stool for his bedroom, and someone told him to ask his bearer to bring him a chokhi from the bazaar. This he did, and after going out for the day, thought it would be waiting for him in his bedroom when he got home. Looking round and not seeing it, he called his bearer and asked him where it was? 'Oh, she's waiting for you in the cookhouse' the Bearer answered, and to his utter amazement he walked out and soon came back with one of the young prostitutes from the bazaar that his bearer had brought back for him. Colloquially these were known as 'chokries', literally young women, and this is what his bearer had thought he had asked for. Being very new to the country he was so embarrassed that he gave her some money for her trouble, then sent her back to the bazaar with a big sigh of relief.

There is another very amusing tale regarding a Sahib and his bearer which I believe is true, and to understand it you have to know that the Hindi word for hard is 'sakut'. He was very keen to learn the language, and asked his bearer to tell him the Hindi translation of any words he did not know. One day his bearer brought him in some very hard, dry toast, and not knowing what the correct word was, he waved a piece under the bearer's nose and said, 'Hard, bearer, hard'. 'Sakut, Sahib, sakut' replied the bearer, whereupon the Sahib retorted, 'Suck it your bloody self. It's much too hard for me to do anything with'.

One other misunderstanding which could have had very serious consequences occurred in 1967 when the Indian Government was laying a gas and oil pipeline from Upper Assam through the Dooars down to Calcutta. The work was being done under contract by a consortium of foreign firms, and I was quite friendly with a young Canadian lad who was working on the project. He had a Jeep and a driver allocated to him for transport, but had only learned a few Hindi words, two of which were 'sala', which is a very derogatory insult, and 'roko', which means stop. One morning he was being driven along the main highway in the open Jeep with the windshield down, when a big lorry forced his Jeep off the road, and his driver had to take to the grass verge to avoid a head on collision. Absolutely incensed, Tony leaped to his feet in the front of the Jeep, shook his fist at the offending truck driver, and shouted '*roko!*' at the top of his voice. Taken completely by surprise, his own driver banged his foot onto the brake pedal, did a magnificent emergency stop, and in a whirl of arms and legs, Tony was catapulted over the front of the Jeep, slid over the bonnet and finally finished up on hands and knees on the grass. Luckily the Jeep was not travelling very fast, and as he continued to roll when he hit the ground, he was not badly injured, just severely shaken up and bruised. However, he did learn a very valuable lesson, and as he told me later, 'I shall make sure I never get my salas and my rokos mixed up again.'

The distance from Calcutta to the Dooars was about 300 miles as the crow flies, and in all that distance the ground level only rose to about 350 feet above sea level. However, once the plains reached the foothills things quickly changed, and three miles south of Zurrantee was the edge of a plateau some 400 feet high on which the gardens of the Chulsa area were situated. On the very edge was Sathkyah, and north of that was Aibheel, where I was later Manager. Then came Zurrantee, and at the very northern edge were Chalouni and Sam Sing. From Sathkyah to Sam Sing was about eight miles and in that distance the altitude went from about 650 feet up to nearly 1000 at the Sam Sing top garden. North of Sam Sing the 'hillsides' started, covered with forest and native jungle, and rising up to peaks 6000 feet high, and it seems to be a bit incongruous to be talking about 'hills' which are several thousand feet higher than our highest mountains.

On a clear day in winter, it was possible to see the mountains surrounding the Nathu La Pass shining in the sunlight. This was the main pass on the frontier between India and Chinese Tibet, and at one time was the main trade route over which all the pack mule trains carried all the goods into and out of Tibet, but once hostilities flared up between the countries it was closed, and it has only been reopened in the past few years. To reach the pass from Zurrantee entailed a semi-circular road journey of about 150 miles up the Teesta River Valley and through the mountains, but in reality it was only about 22 miles away at an altitude of about 11,000 feet, and these snow-clad peaks made an unforgettable sight.

Actually, although the cause of the Chinese-Indian conflict of the 1960s was mainly political and ideological, and went much deeper, the actual reason given by the Chinese was that they wanted to recover territory south of the Himalayas in the Dooars, which at one time had been claimed by them as part of Tibet. In fact many of the place names in our area, such as Sam Sing, Indong and Yong Tong had Tibetan and Bhutanese origins and were retained after the Anglo-Bhutanese wars of the 1860s, so there may have been some truth in this.

When I arrived on Zurrantee, although these 5000 foot high hills were only eight miles away, they were completely invisible, owing to the pall of dust and smoke which hung in the atmosphere, reducing visibility to a couple of miles. After five months without any rain the dust was everywhere, and every vehicle which passed along any of the dirt roads left a dust trail a hundred yards long behind it. The labourers raised little puffs of dust when they walked along, all the plants and bushes were dust covered and it penetrated into all the houses. The smoke came from the forest fires which were lit during each period of cold weather to burn out all the dead wood and shrub jungle from the forests. Because the undergrowth still had plenty of moisture left in it after the monsoon the fires were not fierce, and were easily controlled, but they did clear up all the dead rubbish and killed many of the insect pests, and all the areas soon greened up again once the next monsoon arrived.

Looking north from our bungalow it was hard to believe that the hills existed, for the only evidence was the glow of the fire fronts at night as they steadily crept along the hillsides like thin snakes in the darkness, and it was not until late in March, when we got our first heavy rainstorm that most of the filth was washed out of the air. It rained heavily all night, and when we rose in the morning what a transformation had taken place, for there they were, rank upon rank of glistening, green, forest-clad slopes rising for thousands of feet into the sparkling morning air. As it was a new experience for me and they looked so superb, I kept stopping and looking up at them, almost as though they would be hidden again before I could commit the sight to memory. I never did forget that first view of the hills, but what was especially nice and one of the unforgettable things about our life in India was that it was repeated year after year, rather like hearing the first cuckoo in spring.

Regarding the labourer's religious beliefs and taboos, it was at this time that I made my first, unintentional mistake, although I didn't realise it at the time. Because all the tribes and castes would normally only eat or drink anything that had been given to them by their own kind, they would have been deemed to be corrupted if they consumed anything that had been tainted by someone else. However, there was always a way out of these things, and there was a special caste of people who were specially exempted from this taboo, and they were employed as tea makers and water carriers for the use of the labourers while working. They were usually older women who provided drinking water during the monsoon and made tea during the cold weather, and usually they did this in large, earthenware vessels called ghilas which they heated over a small fire in the tea. They received a small ration of tea from the factory each day to do this. Usually it was drunk without milk or sugar but with the addition of salt instead.

During the morning I had visited one of the melas where the ground beneath the tea bushes was being hoed, and in my wanderings I had passed by some of these tea makers. When I went down to the factory in the afternoon, Bill called me to one side and asked me if I had visited the work being done on No.8 in the morning, and I confirmed that I had.

'Well' he said, 'You owe me two rupees, eight annas. I shall take it out of the safe and you can pay me when you get your pay'.

I was rather taken aback, and couldn't see what I had done to warrant a fine until he explained to me. He thought it was a tremendous joke, and was laughing fit to burst as he told me that when I had walked close by the tea maker's fire, my shadow had passed over the ghila and defiled it. This meant that the tea in it could not be used and that the vessel had to be smashed and replaced, hence my payment went to buy another one. It wasn't a serious matter at all, and Bill could have paid from the petty cash, but he always felt that we should all learn from our mistakes. He thought paying the cash would teach me to be more careful in future, and more thoughtful when dealing with the labour, and he wasn't far wrong, for this was another lesson which I never forgot.

I had never thought about my shadow being unclean or unlucky, but later I found out that most of the Indians thought the Europeans were a little 'unclean' or tainted because we took a bath sometimes instead of always showering. It doesn't matter how clean or how dirty the actual water is, to a strict Hindu, static water becomes polluted once it comes into contact with the human body, so in order to become properly cleansed it was essential to bathe in moving water such as a shower, or a river or large water tank. It appeared that large amounts of water didn't become impure, as long as it was moving, but our preference for soaking in a nice, hot bath, especially at the end of a day's work in the cold weather made us a bit suspect. Of course, nothing was ever actually said, and being Westerners and not 'of the country' gave us something of an exceptional status, and the Indians accepted that our behaviour was a little unusual sometimes.

One thing which astounded the labourers, and which marked us out as being a little beyond the pale, was the fact that when we had a party we danced with other men's wives, very closely, and what was worse, even kissed them sometimes. Now at this time, kissing on Indian films was completely taboo, so for us to be doing this when we had a party at any time drew a tremendous audience of the labourers from our local labour lines who came and hid out in the tea and trees that edged the compound, and watched everything that was going on with avid interest. They called western style dancing '*pagla nautch*' or crazy dancing, and very often if we had had a small party at Christmas or some other celebration some of the labourers would ask me questions about it the next morning, to find out what we were actually doing and whether we really did do these things back in England. I don't think they really did understand us at times.

Religiously, the cleanest and most holy river in India was the River Ganges, even though it was usually a dirty brown and filled with all sorts of rubbish, including the remains of the funeral pyres which had been built on the banks of the river at the burning ghats. Because the cost of actually incinerating a body completely was beyond the purse of most people, a token cremation was carried out by the priests and then the remains were placed in the holy river for Mother Ganges to carry them away. As a result, this supposedly 'clean' water was used by hundreds of thousands each year for both bathing and drinking. Another place where running water was highly desirable was in the streets of Calcutta, where the fire hydrants at the side of the street were often broken. Whether this was done accidentally, or deliberately to obtain a water supply, we never did find out, but from each broken fire hydrant a jet of none-too-clean water from the River Hooghly shot out several feet high, enabling hundreds of people to have a daily shower.

One of the most surprising things we ever saw was when were on holiday in East Pakistan, now Bangladesh, in 1957. We were on a visit to stay with a friend who worked for the Indian Steam Navigation Company which ran vessels through the Brahmaputra-Ganges delta and up the river into Assam. We travelled on one of their stern-wheelers, which was very similar to a Mississippi river boat, and one morning we had tied up at the landing stage of Narayangunj, one of the delta towns. Jan and I were leaning over the side rail admiring the view in the cool of the morning, prior to going into the saloon for breakfast, and we noticed a man sitting in the shallows at the side of the river washing himself and cleaning his teeth etc. and having a really good bathe. A few yards upstream there was a house built on stilts on the bank of the river, the veranda of which projected over the water and which the owner obviously used as his toilet! By using a small hole over which he squatted, he was able to complete his full business and deposit all his 'goodies' into the river without being observed from the ground, but from our vantage point on the upper deck of the boat he was clearly visible, and we have often wondered whether this was a regular occurrence, and whether the unfortunate man downstream ever did find out what riches the man on the veranda was sending down to him on the current each morning.

The Bhutan Dooars, as they were once known, filled the area between the Bhutanese mountain range in the north and the frontier of the predominantly Muslim area of East Bengal, later named East Pakistan and Bangladesh, in the south. The area also acted as a land bridge between the main body of India in the west and Assam in the east. In fact, the narrow corridor of territory between Bangladesh and Nepal, west of Siliguri, where Bagdogra airfield was situated was only about 12 miles wide, yet through it ran the main trunk road and three railway lines which connected the Dooars and Assam to India proper.

The western boundary of the Dooars was the River Teesta, which rises in the mountains in the Kanchenjunga mountain range, then flows south through the independent state of Sikkim until it disgorges into the Bengal plain near Siliguri. West of the Teesta lies a very damp belt of wild, marshy forest, situated between the lower foothills of the Himalayas and the plains, named the Terai. which has given its name to a wide-brimmed felt hat with a double crown and special ventilation which is especially favoured by Europeans in the tropics. In more recent times, because of its wildness and inaccessibility, it became the home of numerous bands of murderous dacoits, or bandits, who sallied out at night to rob and pillage isolated homesteads, and molest travellers on the roads and rivers, before returning to their lairs in the morning. Because of the inhospitable terrain and their detailed knowledge of the area, the local police had very little success in tracking them, rather like the outlaw gangs of the old American west.

On a map, the Dooars look like the head of a large garden rake, with the mountains making the tee bar of the head in the north, and the tines being made by a series of large rivers which rise in the Himalayas and then flow south through the independent state of Bhutan. until they reach the plains. Because the monsoon rainfall in the mountains is very heavy, the river valleys run so full, that once they reach the plains they spread out over vast areas, and many of the river beds are over a mile across.

Once the Teesta leaves the mountains its course gradually curves eastwards, then runs south east, flowing away from the mountains until it becomes a tributary of the River Brahmaputra some 150 miles to the east. As a result of this, all the rivers flowing through the Dooars split the area into a number of natural districts, which were divided from each other by the large rivers which were virtually impassable during the monsoon. On some of the more isolated estates, the only means of communication with the outside world at this time was by large elephants which were used to wade across the foaming torrents, and in the local Christian burial ground there were several tombstones which recorded that the person had been accidentally drowned in one of the rivers. Usually this occurred when their ponies were swept away while they were trying to cross them when they were in spate.

Before the 1939-45 war, because of the lack of roads and bridges, there was very little motorised transport, and the West Bengal Railway line, which ran the length of the Dooars, was the essential means of transport. Everything needed by everyone in the district was brought in to the local railway station and then carried to the estates or the local bazaars by hundreds of buffalo carts, the owners of which carried on a lucrative business. All the tea manufactured by the estates was carried out by rail, either direct to Calcutta or to the nearest steamer ghat for onward shipment down the Brahmaputra, and most of the estates had their own collection of buffalo carts. Subsequently this caused a lot of trouble on some of the estates when tractors and lorries made their appearance as the carters were forced to accept other employment.

Because of this enforced isolation, each district had to become self-sufficient so far as organised, western-type entertainment was concerned, and although conditions had improved by the early 1950s, things were still very primitive compared with entertainment at home. Each district had its own Planter's Club, usually built in a central location on land owned by one of the estates, and most of them had several grass tennis courts, a squash court, a large 'maidan' which was used for cricket, soccer and rugby football, and a nine hole golf course.

The maidan and the golf course were usually laid out on what was normally grazing land, which was used by the labourers for their cattle and goats etc, and as a result the grass on them was usually kept very short. The cricket square and the golf greens were fenced off to protect them, and the fairways were kept mowed, but other than this, maintenance work was kept to a minimum. On the golf course, the 'rough' really was that, very rough, and consisted of patches of short grass overgrown with masses of rank vegetation and small shrubs, which made life in the rough very interesting indeed, especially if there were snakes around. The stronger boys on the estate vied with each other to become caddies, and through this many of them became excellent golfers in their own right, although most of them played with home-made clubs which they carved out of bamboo stems with the root still attached. If they showed real promise, many of the planters gave them some of their old clubs to play with, and although they usually played with just a couple of clubs, some of them could have given many of the regular golfers a very good game. Each cold weather during the Dooars Golf Championship, which was held at one of the courses, a 'Caddy's Championship' was also held, and some of the play was of a very high standard indeed.

With rough like this, lost balls were very commonplace, and as they were all imported and very expensive, it was common practice to buy them back from the small boys, or 'chokras' who found them on the course. At eight annas for a good one and four for a 'tatty', some of these lads made a lot of ready cash - until it was discovered that some were actually hiding out on the course behind bushes etc. and stealing any they could lay their hands on. As a result of this, sales of 'ownerless' balls were banned and the stealing stopped, only to be superseded by a host of small boys who hung about in the rough near the more difficult holes. They usually chose a good lookout point, such as a tree stump or termite mound, from where they had a good view of where an errant ball was likely to land, and would sit there like little vultures waiting for the next victim. When a mishit drive finally arrived and disappeared into the rough, they would sit like statues while the luckless player searched and scratched around in the jungle to find it, until he finally gave up in disgust. While he was looking, although they knew exactly where the ball was, they wouldn't give the slightest clue as to whether he was near or not, and it wasn't until he gave up and finally said, 'All right, show me where it is', that their faces would break into smiles and they would lead him straight to it and get their reward.

The planters differed in their attitude to lost balls, and most of us would have a look round for a few minutes until we decided we were wasting good playing time and gave up, thinking a few annas were not too high a price to pay for making a poor shot. However, one or two absolutely hated losing their balls, and considered it a point of personal pride to hack and scrub around in the jungle until they found them, and it was these that the chokras watched with alarm, hoping against hope that the Sahib would finally give up and they wouldn't lose their money.

Because these courses were very primitive and not smoothed and mown like more civilised ones, what we lacked in amenities we made up for in interest on the course. One hole on Chulsa ran along the edge of the Jaldakha river in the shape of a crescent moon, with a 30-foot drop into the boulder-studded water on the left hand side. Most of us played it safe and went round the long way, but it was a great temptation to go over the water for a direct shot to the green on the other side, and on many occasions I saw the ball curve down into the river, only for it to hit a boulder and fly off, never to be seen again. Not even the chokras could help us with those. However, if you were very fortunate it was known for the ball to hit a boulder and fly off the other way back onto the fairway again, but these incidents were few and far between. On another course one of the main hazards was a 25-foot high cliff, with the approach at the bottom and the green on the top. From beneath, it looked at least 100 feet high, and the secret of playing it was not to get in too close, otherwise it was impossible to lift the ball vertically enough for it to clear the lip. However, if you didn't get near enough, you were too far away to gain the required height and distance to clear the top, and the ball ran down the face of the cliff into the rubbish at the bottom, a very interesting hole indeed.

The Chulsa club building was typical of those in the Dooars, with one very large room and a veranda at the front covered by a corrugated iron roof. At one end was a large stage which was used for dances and celebrations during the cold weather, and for performances by the CADS (Chulsa Amateur Dramatic Society). These were organised and run by our old friend Martin Hawes, our Company's Accountant in the Superintendent's office at Sam Sing, and the plays he turned out were of a very high standard indeed. However, stories about the CADS could fill a chapter in their own right, so more of this anon.

Inside the club we had two billiard tables on which we played a variation of snooker which we called 'slosh', the main difference being that the colours could only be potted in their own pockets, a table tennis table, the NOVEM Book Club with quite a large library of books which had been built up over the years after it had been started by its NINE original members, and of course the bar. The main thing we didn't have was a film show, and for this we either had to go to Mal Club on a Saturday night, or to Nagrakata on the Sunday. The films shown were selected by the Club Secretaries from a list of the ones that were available in Calcutta, and each Friday the selected film came up to Mal by air, then went back to Calcutta from Grassmore airstrip in Nagrakata on Monday morning. A visit to either place involved a round trip of some 40 miles, but on many occasions, when there was an exceptionally good film, we would see it on successive nights and still enjoy it the second time. Because most of the Assistants were unmarried, and there was a distinct shortage of any suitable available females, films showing nubile young maidens and comely Hollywood starlets were always popular, and were often responsible for some quite spontaneous, unintentional humour. In one classic, biblical film which I think starred Victor Mature, he found one of the Princess's very beautiful handmaidens straying in the garden at night, where she had no right to be. 'You shouldn't be here', said Victor, in his own inimitable style, 'You should be in bed' whereupon a great bellow of spontaneous laughter went up from the audience, because most of the lads were thinking the same thing, albeit for a very different reason!

By 1951, because of the availability of motor vehicles and the escalating cost of feeding and keeping horses, very few planters kept ponies for work or playing polo, but before the war this was the main form of transport for work and play. Most of the planters belonged to the NBMR, the North Bengal Mounted Rifles, which was the local volunteer defence force, and during each cold weather all the members were expected to attend various camps where they honed their skills at rifle and pistol shooting, and competed against other units at cross-country horse riding, tracking, pig sticking, 'tent pegging' a similar sort of thing where the lances were used to pierce tent pegs stuck in the ground instead of real pigs and other similar military skills. Of course polo was also played, and most of the clubs had a field marked out on the maidan.

When discussing planters in India, very much is often made of the amount of alcohol which they drank and which usually portrayed them as gin-sodden drunks whose only interest in life was to drink as much and as often as possible. In reality, although they did drink a lot of alcohol, a lot of it was for medicinal purposes. Before the war, virtually the only prophylactic or cure against malaria was quinine, which is a vile-tasting medicine at the best of times. The old planters needed to take quite large quantities to keep them fit, and they found that the best way of taking their daily dose and enjoying it was as 'gin and tonic'. Luckily, by the time I got out there, by spraying breeding grounds with chemicals and killing the malarial mosquitoes at source, malaria in the tea areas had been almost eliminated, and by taking one Paludrine tablet twice a week we never suffered from it at all, so most of the drinking we ever did out there was for pleasure.

Other than on special occasions there was no organised entertainment, so after a hard day's work in the heat it was very relaxing to sit and have a couple of drinks in the evening, which did no harm at all. Of course, as in all aspects of society, some planters had drink problems and made a proper mess of their lives, but the vast majority of the people we knew kept their drinking under control and lived normal lives, mainly because like us, they were sensible folks and couldn't afford to do otherwise if they wished to have a decent standard of living when they finished their time in tea.

Although most of the Europeans were employed by 'sterling' companies which had their head offices in London, the Managerial Staff were paid monthly in rupees, and the Indian government allowed us to transfer only a percentage of this to the UK in sterling. We all knew that sooner or later our life in India would come to an end, and at that time we would need every penny we could scrape together in order to start a completely new life elsewhere, so most of us tried to live sensibly and stay out of debt so that we were able to send the maximum allowed home each month.

Unfortunately, the one rather unsatisfactory aspect of our style of life was that we hardly ever carried money with us when we were out, and rarely ever paid cash for anything in the local shops. Bread, petrol, liquor, medicines, groceries, hardware, drinks at the club, just about everything we needed could be obtained by signing a 'chit', and then these, together with a bill were sent for settlement at the end of the month when we received our pay. In many ways this was a very satisfactory arrangement, as the shopkeepers knew that we were very good customers and allowed us a certain amount of credit, but for many of the Assistants, especially those who were new to the life, the temptation to live beyond their means became too great, and before they had time to realise it they were up to their necks in debt.

Usually this was kept on a personal level between the shopkeepers and the customer, but the dukhanwallas knew that the companies would never allow any member of their staff to get away with an unpaid debt, and the ultimate insult was for the creditors to complain to the Agency office in Calcutta, or in our case to the Superintendent in Sam Sing. This action was only used as a last resort because it tended to give the shopkeeper a bad name with the other assistants, but they knew the debt would be paid without more ado from the garden safe and the debtor would get a monumental rocket and have the money stopped from his wages until the debt was repaid.

The first period of work in India was usually for about five years, and an assistant went home on his first UK furlough during his second three-year contract with the Company. At this time it was quite common for a lad to have to sell his radio, shotgun, rifle, motorcycle or even his car in order to realise sufficient cash to clear his debts before he could leave. However, in the meantime he had probably had a whale of a time, and in most cases, once he had had to do this it acted as a very useful lesson, and he usually came back a much more mature and reliable planter. I suppose it was all a part of growing up.

One amusing story about this concerned one of the young lads in our Company who owed a fair amount of money to the local shops. Although he was making efforts to reduce his debts, he wasn't having much success, and he owed quite a large sum to the local petrol station. Finally the owner's patience ran out, and he sent him a rather businesslike letter in which he told him that if he didn't pay off the outstanding sum in the very near future he would be forced to report him to the Superintendent. Evidently this put the lad's back up, and his reply went something like this!

'Dear Sir, With reference to the sum of money which I owe you, I see from your letter that you intend to complain to my Superintendent about the debt. Each month I put the names of all my creditors in a hat, and draw out the names of all the lucky people who are to be paid this month. However, in view of your very unhelpful attitude, I regret to inform you that I have decided not to include your name in this month's draw, and consequently you have no hope of being paid. Yours faithfully'.

Evidently this letter was successful, as the Kayah didn't complain to the Superintendent and ultimately got paid without any more ill feeling, but it was a rather unusual way of going about it.

CHAPTER SEVEN

Snakes... and more snakes

Ever since I slipped and fell on top of what was probably a grass snake when I was a boy, I have had a completely irrational fear of snakes. One summer I was on holiday with my aunt at Tytherington and had gone up onto the top of the hill to play football with some of the local lads. The hilltop was pitted with small, shallow depressions, and when I followed the ball down into one of these, my shoes slipped on the short, dry grass, and I slid on top of a snake which was asleep in the hot sun. To my terror it hissed and rolled beneath me as I slid my hand over it, and I don't know which of us was the most frightened, but Mr Snake quickly recovered and disappeared into some long grass, while I sat and shivered in an absolute funk. My knees had turned to jelly and I had a horribly sick feeling in the pit of my stomach. For many years after that, so far as I was concerned, the only good snake was a dead one, and that is how I felt in 1951.

The Dooars, in common with the rest of India, was absolutely full of snakes, and rarely a day went by when I didn't see at least one. We always carried a thick, bamboo walking stick with us which was used for all sorts of things, but for me its prime use was for killing snakes, and initially whenever I saw one, large or small, I gave it the full treatment. However as they say, familiarity breeds contempt, and after a while I overcame my fear, so much so that provided it looked as though they wanted to escape, which of course most of them did, I gave them the benefit of the doubt and let them go. However, it wasn't until much later that I was introduced to the Curator of Darjeeling Natural History Museum who was a keen Herpetologist.

When he knew I was from the Dooars we had a long talk about snakes, during which I told him of my fear, and when I said that we very often came across dead ones he was very interested. He was of the opinion that my phobia stemmed from lack of knowledge about them, and as there were very few specimens of snakes from the Dooars area in the museum collection, he asked me whether I would be willing to collect as many different ones as possible and let him have them. He thought that the more I knew about them, the less fearful I would be, so he gave me some bottles of Formalin (formaldehyde) to preserve them in, together with a book on snakes, and we arranged for me to let him have as many as possible. Once the labourers knew I was collecting snakes they brought them to the office, usually dead but sometimes still alive, and ultimately I built up quite a collection which in time found its way to the museum, although some of them were thrown out by an Acting Manager who couldn't stand the look of them. I stored them in glass jars in the office, and some of the labourers loved to bring their children to see the 'sanps' and were quite interested to see any new ones I had acquired.

Because of variations in habitat, it is possible for two snakes of the same species to be totally different in appearance, and depending on the habitat in which they are living, most snakes vary in their colour and pattern shades. There are a few that are totally unmistakable, like the black and yellow rings of the banded krait, but for most snakes the only really reliable way of identifying them is by counting the under body scales beneath the chin, the body and the tail. Each member of a species, irrespective of its colour, has the same ratio between these three body scale counts, and by counting these and then referring to a master chart, it was possible to make an accurate identification. Of course, usually this could only be done with a dead snake, so if we were ever in any doubt we never gave it a chance to bite us, but gave it a thump and identified it afterwards. However, as I gained knowledge over the years, by the time I left tea in 1967, I had collected several hundred specimens and was able to pick up and hold the harmless ones in my hands, something I had never thought I would be able to do.

There were 76 known species of snakes in our area, and of these, only 15 were poisonous. None of these were particularly common, and some were very rare, so it seems likely that very few of the snakes I ever encountered were dangerous. In retrospect, I am very pleased that I saw the light and the error of my ways, and let the innocent live. All our venomous snakes belonged to three distinct groups, namely the cobras, the kraits, of which there were five species in our area, all deadly, and the members of the viper family. Most people, when asked to name the most poisonous Indian snake, plump for the cobra, and assume that this species is responsible for the majority of deaths that occur from snakebite each year. In actual fact, most deaths from snake bite in India are caused by members of the krait family. These are usually quite small, usually less than three to four feet in length, and normally their food is principally other snakes, small mammals, lizards and eggs. However, cobras feed principally on rats and mice, and because food is scarce in India, very little of it is wasted, and the rats tend to frequent the places where it is easier to come by. In addition, like the rattlesnake, the cobra is a gentleman, and always hisses a warning before it strikes, which it can only do once it has reared up. Actually the cobras are quite shy snakes, and will only attack if they are frightened or feel threatened.

On the other hand, the kraits, although they keep mainly to the ground, frequently crawl into lofts and thatched roofs after small vermin, and as they are nocturnal, a glossy black in colour and strike without warning, they are an absolute menace to any barefooted person walking outside at night. They are not normally aggressive, but krait anti-venin is extremely hard to prepare, and their bite is usually lethal, with death occurring within a few hours of being bitten. When alive, all the ones I saw were a lustrous, glossy black with a beautiful purplish-blue sheen on the scales, but once it was dead this soon disappeared, the colour dulled and gradually faded to a muddy brown when preserved in Formalin.

Knowing about these snakes and the danger made us extremely careful whenever we walked outside at night, and we usually wore something substantial on our feet and carried a stick and torch whenever possible. Very often nowadays, when I walk outside at night to go up the garden or out to the shed in my slippers, as I walk in the darkness it crosses my mind just how lucky we are to live in such a lovely, safe country where lethal serpents are virtually non-existent, and the only painful thing on which we are likely to tread is a hedgehog.

I think I was so conditioned to beware of snakes while in India that even now a tremor of fear runs up my spine if I tread on something that rolls beneath my feet accidentally, and this was exploited by two of my friends later in my life when I was working at Berkeley Nuclear Laboratories. Ray and Richard knew of my reaction to snakes, and this day when I was bending over a rig concentrating on a particularly intricate item of work, they took the compressed air hose down from the wall of the room next door, and carefully pushed it round the doorpost until it lay on the floor behind me. In time I finished what I was doing, stepped back and trod on the nozzle, which rolled beneath my feet and hissed at me. Ray and Richard were peering round the door frame to enjoy my reaction, and they said afterwards that I jumped at least three feet in the air and my legs were already running when they touched the floor again. Of course, they were convulsed with laughter at my antics, and it took me a long time to live the incident down.

Of the five species of kraits in our area, the only one which wasn't black was the banded krait, and this was a very spectacular looking snake. It was quite thick, up to 6½ feet in length, with quite a pronounced, angular ridge along its back, and alternating bands of black and bright yellow, varying from half an inch to an inch and a half wide, encircled the whole of the body and tail. Because it too was nocturnal and very sluggish, it was often run over by vehicles on the roads, because one of its favourite habits was to lie on still warm roads and paths after the sun had gone down to enjoy the warmth. It was not an aggressive snake, and its food was other non-poisonous snakes, but by doing this it put itself into a position where it could be stepped on very easily by unwary, barefooted walkers, and once this happened it struck hard.

Its venom acted on both the central nervous system and

also clotted the blood, so the time of death depended on which was affected the most, varying from up to a week with the former, or down to a few hours if the blood was seriously affected. Instead of having a long, pointed tail like most other snakes, the banded krait's tail was very short and blunt at the tip, rather like a thumb, and this gave rise to a widespread myth among the natives that they had a head at each end, thus making them doubly dangerous. The local Bengali name for this snake was the 'sankhani', and there was a Sunkani Tea Estate in Mal district, so called because of the number of banded kraits which lived there. I'm very glad it wasn't one of our gardens!

Because of the fear which the labourers had of this unmistakable snake, whenever they saw one they killed it as quickly as possible, and one of the first large snakes which I ever saw was one they killed on the way to work one morning and draped over the roadside fence. Looking at the old photo which I took of it, it must have been about six feet in length. The staple food of the banded krait is other non-venomous snakes, the larger the better, and because a snake is virtually one large stomach for most of its length and its fangs do not allow it to let go, once it has started swallowing its prey, it has to keep working up its body and enveloping it until it has gone down. It has been recorded that two banded kraits started to eat the same snake one at each end, and they kept swallowing until they met in the middle. As there was no going back for either of them, the larger one finally opened up its mouth a little more and then took in the other banded krait with the first snake still inside it as well. Rather a case of two for the price of one or a double whammy. Quite a substantial meal.

Finally an amusing story about the banded krait goes as

follows: During World War II an army major was touring various units in India giving lectures on fighting and survival in the jungle. At one unit he visited in the backwoods of Bengal he finished his lecture in the usual way by describing the danger of the banded krait and said, 'The most dangerous snake you are likely to see is the banded krait, because it likes to lie on a warm path in the cool of the evening and you may step on it. If you see one it will be unmistakable, because it is covered with rings, black, yellow, black, yellow all down its length. But if you see one, don't panic. The first thing to do is orientate it, that is, find out which is its head and which is its tail. Once you have found out which is its head and which is its tail, grasp it firmly behind the head with your thumb and forefinger, give it a quick flick of the wrist, and hey presto, you've broken its neck.' Then speaking to a man in the front row, he said, 'Right gunner, what do you do if you see a banded krait?'. 'Well Sir', the man replied, 'First of all I orientate it, that is, I find out which is the head and which is the tail. Once I have done this I grasp it firmly behind the head with my thumb and forefinger, give a quick flick of my wrist, and hey presto, I've broken its neck'. 'Well done' said the Major. 'I can see you will have no trouble with snakes in the jungle', and finished his talk.

A few days later he called in again on his return journey, and during an inspection of the hospital found one patient in a terrible state, completely swathed in splints and bandages from head to foot. However, he did recognise him, and said, 'Aren't you the gunner who answered my question on the banded krait when I was here before?'. 'Yes sir' said the man,' and it's because of you that I am here'. 'Oh, why is that' replied the Major. 'Well sir, I was walking down the path to the toilets the other night minding my own business, when suddenly, there it was, a banded krait, all black and yellow, lying across the path. However, I didn't panic sir. First of all I orientated it, that is, I found out which was its head and which was its tail. Then, once I had done that, I grasped it firmly behind the head with my thumb and forefinger, gave it a quick flick of the wrist, and hey presto, I'd shoved my thumb up the ass of one of the biggest tigers in West Bengal.'

In our area, the only true viper was the Russell's Viper, an extremely venomous snake, the bite of which was usually fatal after about 24 hours. However, although it is quite plentiful in some of the hotter parts of India and Burma, it was very rare in the Dooars, and luckily I never saw one. There were also seven species of pit vipers, so named because they possess a sensory depression, or pit, between the nostril and the eye which is thought to help them detect and catch their warm-blooded prey at night. All these pit vipers had a poisonous bite which was not deadly to a normal healthy man, but it could be extremely painful nevertheless. I once saw one man in Sam Sing hospital who had been bitten on the calf by one. His leg ballooned up to twice its normal size from his ankle right up to his groin, and the venom caused the flesh around the bite marks to blacken and decay until he had a suppurating ulcer about two inches across and he was in agony for several weeks. Finally, after several months it healed and the skin grew again, but the decayed flesh was never replaced and he always had a deep hollow in his leg where the bite had been.

In appearance, the pit vipers were thickish snakes with a clearly defined neck and an 'ace of spades' head, usually a beautiful shade of lime green, and when they were ensconced in the top of a tea bush, entwined among the leaves and twigs, they were very difficult to see, so the labourers kept a very keen lookout.

The other deadly snakes which we had were the two species of cobra. Unlike the kraits and vipers, which actually inject their venom through hollow fangs, the cobras have small, grooved fangs down which the venom trickles into the wound, so as a result they have to get a good grip on their victim, rather like a dog, and then chew it in. All the cobras are able to rear up vertically with about one third of their length off the ground, and they are only able to strike from this position. Of all the cobras, the common Indian cobra had the best developed hood and looked very spectacular when roused to strike, but because the rats and mice on which they usually fed were quite scarce on the estates, we saw very few wild ones, and the ones we did see usually tried to slide away.

The other member of the cobra family, the king cobra, or hamadryad, is the largest poisonous snake in the world, being about two and a half inches in diameter and up to 15 feet long. The hood is not as pronounced as in the common cobra, being much smaller and flatter, but it is much more frightening when roused, and one observer described it as, 'rearing four feet high and standing motionless, like a great candlestick, staring fixedly at its victim'. Its food is almost exclusively other snakes, and there is a record of a 10-foot-long python being swallowed by a 12-foot long hamadryad. Because it has extremely small fangs compared to its size, it has to strike hard and hold on viciously in order to chew the venom into its victim, and in one recorded case a king cobra held on to its victim for eight minutes before it let go. Although records of death after being bitten by this snake are rare, it would appear that death in man, after a full, lethal dose, appears to follow in about 20 minutes.

Hamadryads are essentially snakes of the forest, and the female lays about 25 eggs in a rough, mounded nest of leaves and rubbish. It is thought that both the parents stay in the vicinity of the nest to guard the eggs and young from predators, and it is at this time that they are supposed to attack anything which appears to be a threat without warning, even man. When roused they move very swiftly over the ground, and are supposed to be able to catch a running man from a standing start quite easily, especially if he is running downhill, as they tend to float over the surface of the ground. They are very intelligent, and because they are quite fearless and very aggressive, they were the snakes most feared by the labourers on the estates which bordered the forest areas. Because they tended to live in pairs, the story grew up that if one was killed, its mate would come looking for its killer afterwards in order to get revenge, and it was a fact that when I had to kill one on Sam Sing in 1960, another was killed in the labour lines a short distance away the following afternoon, but this was probably a coincidence.

That morning I visited a section of the Sam Sing tea where 250 women were supposed to be plucking, only to find them all massed in groups on the road which ran along the edge of the tea. As I approached my heart sank, as I thought they were refusing to pluck because of some union trouble we had been having, but when I stopped and asked the Daffadars I soon found out otherwise. Evidently some of the women had discovered a very large 'kala naag' (black cobra), their name for a Hamadryad, sleeping in the tea, and because they were all frightened of what it could do to them or their children, they refused to go in and pluck until it had either been killed or driven out of the section. I tried to get them to see reason by saying it probably wasn't a king cobra anyway, and even if it was, if it was asleep it had probably eaten and wouldn't wake up if we left the small area where it was asleep unplucked. They listened while I spoke then said that it was definitely a kala naag, and who would know if it suddenly woke up and attacked them, so it was all to no avail. Rather reluctantly I took my stick and walked through the tea to where the snake was asleep in a natural hole between four large boulders, and sure enough it was a BIG king cobra. Its head was completely hidden within its coils, but its side was stretched where it had eaten something quite large, and I could see its dull, black skin with its dirty white cross bands through a gap between the stones. Seeing how large it was I would gladly have let it sleep on undisturbed, but I realised that no work would be done until it was disposed of, and the only person to do it was me, which was all part of the job. I didn't possess a shotgun at this time, but in the bungalow I had an old, unlicensed Spanish, single barrelled-12 bore which I was 'looking after' while its owner was on home leave. I had never fired it, and didn't even know whether it was in complete working order, but it was any port in a storm, so I hurried up to the bungalow and collected it without telling Jan what I wanted it for.

Soon I was on my hands and knees looking through the small gap in the boulders again, and seeing it again it looked absolutely enormous, at least eight inches in diameter. Knowing that I had just the one shot before all hell broke loose, I put the muzzle close up to the snake's side, somewhere near where I hoped its head would be, pulled the trigger and ran like mad for the comparative safety of a large, concrete water flume which ran through the tea while trying to put another cartridge in. Behind me the tea bushes heaved and boiled as the wounded snake shot out of its hole and thrashed around, but gradually things quietened down and there was silence.

Not knowing if the thing was dead or craftily slithering up to attack us at any moment, I waited for a while, then as nothing else happened I took three of the braver daffadars with me to see what had happened. With our hearts in our mouths we worked our way carefully through the tea without incident until we reached the boulders, where we found all the jungle flattened and sprayed with blood, but the snake had gone. Its trail finished at a three-foot-deep drainage ditch into which it had fallen, and this ran straight through the tea until it exited into a dry stream bed about 150 yards away, so while the daffadars trailed it down the drain, I ran around the block of tea until I reached the spot where it emptied into the stream. I knew I would only have time for the one shot, and my mouth was dry as I checked that I had a good cartridge in and that the safety catch was off, then waited anxiously as the trackers shouted, 'It's coming. It's coming'. After what seemed to be an eternity it was suddenly all action as the snake boiled out into the stream bed with an angry hiss and then rose up into the vertical strike position about six feet away. Its head, almost five feet from the ground was level with my face, and it stared at me with an angry, baleful glare for a split second before I took careful aim and blew its head off.

When I examined it later I found the reason why I had thought it was so large, and why it had travelled so slowly along the drain. A short while before it had killed and eaten a large monitor lizard about three feet long, and was digesting it while it slept, so the pluckers would not have been in any real danger. However, where the lizard was inside its stomach its outside skin had stretched to accommodate it, thus giving the impression that it was much larger than it really was, and it was at this point that I had shot it. The wound had split its side, and luckily the lizard's tail and one back leg had protruded through the gap and dragged along the side of the drain, thus acting as a brake. When I measured it at the office later it turned out to be 13 feet four inches long, and though I felt sorry that I had been forced to shoot it, and would have preferred to let it live, for several nights afterwards I had cold sweats at night as I lay awake and thought of how different things might have been had something gone wrong with that last shot. And as for its mate? Well, the following afternoon another very large hamadryad entered the labour lines a short distance away, and was killed quite near our bungalow, so of course, the labourers said it was looking for me. I'm very glad it didn't find me.

On the other hand, there were some planters who kept the occasional snake as a pet. I once had tea with a planter who had a large wooden coffee table in the centre of his living room with plate glass sides and top, inside which he kept a collection of live snakes. We sat and had afternoon tea while we watched his little friends slithering around inside trying to get at our sandwiches. Still, strange as he seemed to be, he had a friend who had been in the Metropolitan Police before he decided to try tea, and he was morbidly fascinated with dead bodies and forensic evidence. He had several books containing photographs and text on how to identify bodies, wounds, weapons, time after death and other technical details, and it seemed he would read these for pleasure as we would read a popular book. I met both these men soon after I arrived in India, but I never saw them again, so probably they decided that tea was not for them.

However, there were some planters who did keep the occasional snake at home, because on one occasion we were at a friend's bungalow for the evening, and when Jan rose to go to the toilet he said to her, 'Don't worry about the bath'. She didn't realise what he meant until she was sitting on the loo and looked into the bath, where to her surprise she saw a large python lying in a pool of water watching her. It turned out that it was quite tame and completely harmless, but Jan said afterwards that it was one of the quickest pennies she had ever spent.

Pythons were quite common in the Dooars, and because they were excellent to eat and their skins were used for making fancy shoes and leather handbags, the labourers killed them whenever they could. Usually this was done by hitting them on the head with a stick, so that the body would not be damaged, but it was possible to do this and stun them, only for the snake to recover and come back fighting shortly afterwards.

On one occasion an Assistant was checking the work in the tea when he found that the men had killed a very large python. He had promised his fiancée at home that he would try to get her some snakeskin shoes and a handbag, so he agreed to buy the snake from them and told them to put it in the boot of his car. When he reached his bungalow at lunchtime he instructed his bearer to call one of the experienced shikaris (hunters) from the lines to come and skin it, and thought that was the end of the matter. It was while he was eating his lunch that the bearer came and said that they couldn't get the snake out because it was too fierce, and would he come and see to it. Evidently it had only been stunned, and when they opened the boot lid, they were met by several feet of infuriated python with a headache, hell bent on attacking anything that moved.

Not being able to get near enough to grab it, they finally managed to drop a rope noose over its head and tried to pull it out, but it had got a good grip on the spare wheel inside, and even with four men on the end of the rope, each time they stretched it out the snake retaliated and it pulled them in again. Finally, in desperation, he backed the car up to one of the 12 inch posts which supported the roof of the garage and tied the free end of the rope to it. Thinking there was no way the snake could resist the power of the car he slipped it into first gear and started to drive away, hoping that it would be pulled out of the boot, only to find that it stretched longer and longer until there was a twang and the snake broke in two, the front third still attached to the post and the rest tightly coiled round in the back of the car, where it still refused to let go. After they finally managed to get it out and measured it they found that it was almost 14 feet long, and I think his fiancée did in time have her shoes, but I wonder if he ever told her what he had done to get them. Had he done so she probably wouldn't have worn them. Regarding eating snake flesh, the natives considered most large snakes to be a delicacy, especially python meat, and when I was invited to the labour lines to a wedding party one evening, I was given some and found it quite edible, rather like chicken.

One rather intriguing fact about most snakes was that their nervous systems seemed to respond long after the rest of their bodies were lifeless, and in some cases their muscles would jerk and twitch for several hours after they were killed. However, there was one thing that would kill a snake completely in double quick time, and that was tobacco, so smokers beware. Because the labourers hated the poisonous snakes so much, especially the kraits, they tortured them to death whenever they had the opportunity to do so. Many families grew tobacco plants in their gardens, and most of the men carried small tins of dried, crushed and powdered tobacco dust which they chewed while working. This was tobacco leaf pure and simple, with no other chemicals or additives, but it was lethal. Once a snake was caught, it was held by the thumb and forefinger just behind the head, so that it couldn't bite, until the man had a large gobbet of chewed tobacco spit in his mouth. He would then squeeze it and force its jaws open, spit into its mouth, and then hold it until it had swallowed. Once it had done this it was finished. He would place the snake carefully on the ground, then step back and watch it die. Because a snake's digestive system is extremely efficient, the nicotine in the tobacco spit began to be absorbed almost immediately and acted as a poison, and within a few seconds the snake would begin to writhe and coil, tying itself up in knots, until finally after a few minutes of agony, it would give up the struggle and lie absolutely lifeless. No doubt the amount of nicotine in the chewing tobacco was much more concentrated than that in the smoke of twenty cigarettes, but after seeing what it did to those snakes, it made me wonder what harm heavy smokers are doing to themselves. It was a fact that many of our labourers suffered from a form of mouth cancer in later life.

Sometimes snakes were used by itinerant beggars and fakirs to frighten the local people into giving them handouts of food and money, and there was something sinister and creepy about the way these dirty, near-naked characters operated. They would creep quietly from house to house, and as the labourers were very superstitious, it must have been very worrying to find one of them peering into the doorway completely unannounced. Other than for a filthy loincloth they were usually completely naked, their hair being matted with filth and coloured pigments and their skins coated with dirt, ashes and paint. They usually carried some snakes round with them which they would produce if the householder was not inclined to give them some alms, and I was told that if anyone refused to pay, the beggar would threaten them by saying that he would send his little 'friends' into the house to visit him that night, and that was usually sufficient to bring him round. In all probability the snakes were harmless, but nevertheless, the implied threat was there, and whenever we heard that there was one of these beggars on the estate we would get some of the security staff 'chowkidhars' to see him off.

Finally, to finish this chapter on snakes on a humorous note, I'll relate an occurrence that happened to me when I was on Bagracote in 1954. One Sunday I was out in the garage pit working beneath the car when I saw a pair of dirty bare legs appear by the side of it which turned out to belong to a snake charmer. I didn't like these characters at the best of times, and as I didn't want to be disturbed the conversation went something like this:

'Sahib, would you like to see my snakes?'

'No. Go away.'

'No Sahib. Please see my snakes.'

'No, I don't want to see your snakes. Take them away.'

'Sahib, if you come and see my snakes I will make them dance,'

'Look, if I have to come out from beneath this car, I will make your snakes dance because I shall get my gun and shoot them! So CLEAR OFF!'

'Sir, You are my mother and my father, I shall die if you don't see my snakes and give me some money'.

At this point I heard a swishing sound and a howl of pain as Birbahadur, an ex Gurkha and a staunch company man who worked as the day watchman for the bungalow, brought his thick, five foot-long bamboo lathi down across the man's shoulders and sent him reeling. He had been standing nearby, listening to the conversation, and bellowed, 'If the Sahib says he doesn't want to see your snakes dance, he doesn't want to, so clear off unless you want some more of this' and without any more ado he fetched him another couple of whacks with his wire bound lathi which almost fetched him to his knees. This was completely unexpected, and the last I saw of him and his snakes was as he was being chased out of the compound gate holding his head in one hand and his snake basket with the other. I very much doubt if he ever considered sending his 'little friends' in to see me that night. One thing was certain, after that welcome he must have passed the word around because no more snake charmers ever visited the bungalow while I was there.

CHAPTER EIGHT

'That's only my uncle, just drive over him'

Once I had settled in, life on Zurrantee became a completely irregular routine, if such a thing exists, because although the six working days were always basically the same, inasmuch as the actual hours worked varied very little, each day presented its own completely new problems and occurrences. Every aspect of life, both indoors and out, was a new experience, and on many occasions I almost had to pinch myself to make sure I was actually in India and not dreaming. There was something almost mystical and magical, and very hard to imagine, about walking down to the factory in the early morning, with the dew still on the roadside bushes and the first rays of the rising sun making the hazy clouds of dust glow with a diffused pink light. Very common roadside weeds were the evergreen Lantana shrubs which seemed to thrive on the dry, dusty verges, and thrust their dense, yellow-pink flower heads through the coating of dust, brightening the roadsides. It wasn't until much later that I recognised a variant of it as a prized plant in Dad's garden, and was able to tell him, quite proudly, that we had them as weeds out in India. As you can imagine, he was not very happy about this.

One thing that did strike me as strange at this time was the fact that we got so little actual dawn light and twilight. On the equator, sunrise and sunset are at 6 am and 6 every day, with about half an hour of half-light between day and night, and they don't vary with the seasons as they do in Britain. Because we were about 25 degrees north of the equator the change was not quite as abrupt as that, but it varied very little and it was always dark by 7 pm. Novelists usually portray night in the tropics as being something velvety-blue, warm and sensual, and although most of ours were spoilt either by monsoon clouds or cold weather dust, nights in October and November were often like this and were really beautiful. Born late on October 23rd, I am partly a Scorpio in my birth sign, and because it is a southern winter constellation it isn't visible from Britain. However, later on in 1951 I was walking back home at about 9 pm, and in the brilliantly starlit sky I noticed an absolutely superb group of stars hanging immediately over the bungalow. I didn't recognise them at first, but then, when I saw the pincers and the raised tail of the scorpion I realised with a thrill that I was getting my first real sight of something I had seen before only in books. I thought it must surely be a good omen to welcome me into tea.

I have always been interested in astronomy and the heavens, and because the autumn nights were so good for star watching, I bought myself a book which illustrated all the constellations, and on suitable evenings would take it, together with my binoculars and lie on an old mattress out on the lawn and identify them. Normally, this didn't attract any attention, presumably because the servants accepted that this was something that some of the more eccentric Sahibs did, but on Bagracote in 1954 some of the permanent bungalow servants, not my personal ones, had more enquiring minds. I suppose they thought no one would lie out on the lawn in this manner unless there was an ulterior motive and a bit of hanky-panky going on with one of the garden girls, so every so often one of them would creep onto the veranda and peer round one of the pillars to see what I was doing. Gradually I noticed the movements from the corner of my eye and realised that I was under surveillance, so finally when they began to annoy me, I walked over and asked the watchman what he was looking for. 'Oh Sahib', he said,' I am just making sure that everything is all right and you are not in any trouble'. 'Oh well', I told him, 'In that case you'd better come out onto the lawn with me and sit down, and then you can look after me properly while I look at the stars'

This seemed to take the wind completely out of his sails, because he suddenly remembered a job he had to do and disappeared, and I never had any trouble with them after that.

By the end of February, all the essential cold weather work such as planting, pruning, draining and cultivation had been completed, so the labourers were filling in time doing other small, secondary jobs which were always done at the end of the period if time permitted. This was the easy time of the year, when the pressure was off before plucking started. Wells were cleaned out, ripe bamboos were cut and stored ready for use later in the year, chemical manures were applied to the tea, roads and bridges were built and repaired, and a thousand and one other small jobs were found for the labourers to do.

Despite the abundance of tea bushes and shade trees, the firewood which all the labourers needed for their day to day living was always in short supply, so to deter them from cutting the garden trees, which was an offence for which the penalty could be dismissal, each household received an annual ration of firewood from the estate. This consisted of a mixture of uprooted old tea bushes and wood from the afforested areas on the estate, but because this was never enough for their needs, the estates always purchased additional supplies of proper firewood from the West Bengal Forestry Service to make up the deficit. In Zurrantee's case, this came from the Naura forest, just across the river, and it was one of my favourite jobs to cross over and walk through the forest to the cleared area to check the work. The forest was full of unusual sounds and strange bird and animal life, and I always made these trips last as long as possible, because although I wasn't actually homesick, it was the nearest I could get to wandering over the village fields at home.

The arrangements for clearing the firewood areas and actually felling the trees were usually done by a contractor, but we often used garden men to cut and stack the firewood prior to collection. The amount of firewood was measured in 'peels'; one peel was a flat packed stack of wood five foot by five face area by two and a half feet deep. These were made by sinking two stakes into the ground five feet apart and then filling them up to the required height with pieces of cut wood 2½ feet long, but the actual amount of wood in a stack could vary considerably, depending on whether the wood was very densely packed inside, or whether plenty of 'air-holes' were left. As the contractors were paid on the quantity of peels of wood that they produced from a given area, and they could always make extra cash by selling firewood that they had 'saved', there was always a certain amount of friendly competition between them and us as to just how much they could get away with without losing the contract, and it was my job to wander around the cleared area examining the peels to make sure that they were reasonably stacked and then report back to Bill. It took the best part of a morning scrambling around to look at a couple of hundred stacks of wood, but as I didn't need to talk to anyone I enjoyed every minute of it.

In the factory, my work consisted mainly of wandering round looking at all the machinery and repairs that had been done, usually alone, but sometimes accompanied by one of the factory babus. The manufacturing machinery was virtually ready for a test run prior to the first leaf coming in, so I tended to get the instruction books from the office and read up all the details of what the various machines were used for. One thing that wasn't operating properly was a humidifying plant of a type that was used originally to maintain the humidity in the cotton factories in Lancashire, but which was now used to maintain it during the hot, dry period in the run up to the monsoon.

The rolled and crushed leaf needed a cool, moist atmosphere in which to ferment, without actually getting wet, and what had worked very well in Lancashire didn't seem to do so well in India. A large, belt-driven piston pump supplied water at a very high pressure to a series of sprayers slung from the roof, where it was atomised in nozzles and sprayed onto flat metal plates which propelled it into the atmosphere. Because the pump was driven by a belt drive from the line shafting, which in turn was driven by an old horizontal steam engine, it was almost impossible to raise the water pressure high enough to make a fine enough mist, so there seemed to be streams of water everywhere when it operated. I spent many happy hours on the system tinkering with the atomisers and trying to improve the pump efficiency, but I never did get it to work properly, and the next cold weather we threw it out and built a 'mist chamber' instead. In this, two large fans drew air through a large chamber in which there was a curtain of spray made by the atomiser nozzles that we had cannibalised from the humidifier setup, and this worked fine, as all the excess moisture dropped out of the incoming air before it reached the fermentation room. This was the first real engineering project that I designed and completed in tea.

The factory was powered by an old, twin cylinder, horizontal steam engine with an enormous twelve-foot diameter flywheel, and as a backup there was also a smaller single cylinder steamer which could carry the essential factory load if anything happened to the prime mover. During the day, when neither of these engines were working, electricity was generated by an ancient twin cylinder Petter diesel engine which coughed and spluttered away by itself for most of the time with the minimum of attention. This seemed to be a very good thing, because, from the way all the corners of its nuts had been rounded off by a variety of spanners, it looked as though once it did give up the ghost it could never be repaired. However, run it did, until one day it ran so well that it nearly disintegrated. It had been giving trouble and one of the younger 'kaulwallas' (Engineers) had dismantled the governor and failed to reassemble it correctly. I was sitting in the office at the time, and heard the engine start and run up, expecting the governor to cut in and stabilise the speed at any moment, but nothing happened. Gradually the speed increased while the sound of the engine rose to a high pitched whine, and to my horror I realised that it had run away, and if it wasn't stopped it was possible for the speed to rise to a point where the centrifugal forces would cause the flywheel to disintegrate.

I had been at Listers' when I had heard about an engine that had run away while on test, and after the flywheel had exploded, pieces of it had gone through three walls before they were stopped, rather like pieces of shrapnel. Luckily at that time there were no casualties, but realising what could happen if something was not done quickly, I rushed over to the engine house, where I found the kaulwalla rooted to the spot gazing at the blurred flywheel in absolute amazement. I was in such a panic and desperate to stop the engine that I didn't wait to think about looking for decompression levers or cutting off the main fuel supply at the tank, which would probably have stopped it before any real damage was done, but simply picked up the largest spanner which came to hand and hammered the fuel supply pipes out of the injectors by brute force. To my utter relief it did the trick, the high-pitched whine started to fall and the flywheel gradually slowed until it finally came to rest.

As though coming out of a deep sleep the kaulwalla gradually roused himself and came back to life, grinning self-consciously at the crowd that had gathered, while I stood with hands trembling feeling completely drained of energy. As I looked at the mangled pipes I thought, 'Fool, why did you do that? Now someone will have to repair it', but it was not as bad as I had thought. I found some spare pipes in the factory store, and after I had stripped and reassembled the governor myself and replaced all the manky nuts with new ones, the old girl started straight away and worked like a dream from then on.

The Zurrantee electricity supply was even more antiquated. The current was 110 volts DC and power was generated for the factory, the offices and the two bungalows whenever any of the engines were operating. At other times it was supplied by a storage battery of 120 cells, each supplying one volt, which were housed in a battery house in the factory compound. These cells were charged twice weekly, and every six months we had a visit from the Chloride and Exide Engineer from Calcutta, who toured the estates giving the cells a prolonged charge to clean up the plates, and carry out any essential servicing that was required. In his report he never failed to advise that they should always be charged until they were 'gassing freely,' and that was how he came to get his nickname. He was never referred to as anything other than 'gassing freely'.

All the wiring consisted of two insulated wires running an inch apart through porcelain conductor plates screwed to the walls, and all the other fittings, such as light switches, junction boxes, and ceiling roses etc. were very bulky and made from the same material. Throughout southeast Asia lizards abound in all the dwellings, and in the Dooars we had very small ones called 'tik tiks' which used the ceiling roses as nests in which to lay their tiny eggs. Fully-grown adults were usually about two inches long from nose to tail tip, and their almost transparent eggs were minute, about half the size of a pea but perfectly formed. They were found in all the bungalows, and local tradition had it that if there was a bungalow in which there were no tik tiks, it was an unlucky place and likely to be destroyed by fire, so we were quite pleased when we saw some in our bungalow chasing each other across the ceilings and uttering their distinctive cry of 'chik-chik-chik-chik'. They were completely harmless, but nevertheless, some planters hated them and tried to get rid of them, because it was quite a common occurrence for an overhead tik tik to lose his foothold on the ceiling during an exciting encounter and plummet down to hit the tea table or the newspaper held in front of them. I suppose they were so light that they never seemed to hurt themselves, but it did come as rather a shock when one fell on you unexpectedly.

One aspect of work which I disliked intensely and never got used to was the fortnightly ration issue, which was usually done on the second and fourth Saturdays in the month. Because the labourers were unable to grow enough *dhan* (unhusked rice) to last them for the year, arrangements were made between the ITA and the West Bengal Government for the estates to make bulk purchases of rice from their stocks, which were then sold to the labourers, together with a kind of wheat flour named atta, mustard oil and kerosene oil at concessional rates.

On ration day, all the labourers gathered in a large lean-to shed at the back of the factory where the bags of rice etc. were stacked and where we sat at desks accompanied by an office babu each. Provided they were not wilfully absent more than two days during the period they were allowed a full ration, and as the babu read out their names and stated how much they were to receive, they came forward to me to pay for it. The actual distribution was done by selected men who squatted by the great piles of rice and measured the quantities in specially made boxes into which the grain was loosely tipped and then levelled off across the top of the box with a wooden scraper. If this was done properly, these were extremely accurate, but it was possible to cheat a little by pressing it down when filling the box for family members or other favourites, and if it was done on a large scale over several thousand boxes, the loss in takings and rice could be quite substantial, so we were always looking out for the crafty 'presser'. What I disliked about it was that the grain was always very dusty, and as the sacks were emptied onto the piles, and the boxes were filled and emptied into the cloths in which the labourers took it home, great clouds of smelly dust filled the atmosphere, and it was often difficult to see from one end of the shed to the other. At times like these Bill very sensibly kept out of the way most of the time, as he had three, able assistants to do the work, but we would go back to the bungalow after it was all over looking as though we had just climbed out of a bag of flour and with our lungs full of irritating dust. It was a good job that it only occurred once a fortnight.

Because the labourers disliked keeping large quantities of cash at home, on a ration day they were allowed to take advances against their monthly pay to buy their rations, and also any other goods that they required, so the local traders usually brought their stalls and set them up just outside the compound, which made a very colourful scene indeed.

The monthly payday was very similar, except that we each sat with a babu who called out the amount to be paid to each worker while we paid the cash over, and this was a very much cleaner job. However, the scent of pay always brought the outside money lenders, the Kabuliwallas, who always charged an exorbitant rate of interest, so much so that very often people who got caught were only able to pay off the monthly interest and never cleared the debt. Whenever possible, we helped good workers who needed money for any reason by allowing them to take an interest free advance against future pay, which was paid back at an agreed amount each month. By doing this we were able to keep many of our labourers out of their clutches, but they still did a roaring trade in the bazaar and made sure that they took their share of a man's pay within minutes of us giving it to him, or else.

Because just about everybody went to the bazaar on Sunday

to do their week's shopping, we usually paid out on the first Saturday after the end of the month. Unfortunately this meant that the drinkers had money in their pockets to spend at the local liquor shop, and it was known for some of them to spend their whole time there drinking until late on Sunday night. For alcoholic drink, most of the workers made *haria*, a type of home-brewed white beer made from fermented rice, which was not too unpleasant a drink. However, *darhu*, a really evil smelling spirit made by distilling a mash of millet seeds was legally only available for sale from licensed liquor shops called 'ghadikhanas', but there were many illicit stills in the area which produced a wide variety of brews. It all probability the illicit stuff was of a better quality than the legal liquor, because when supplies got short in the shops after the district paydays at the end of the month, the ghadiwallas tended to adulterate their existing stocks with all sorts of rubbish from oil to methylated spirits in order to have enough to fulfil the demand, sometimes with disastrous results. They could do this because, when a man got drunk on darhu he tended to lose all sense of reason, and probably wouldn't have realised what he was drinking anyway. On one occasion in a local bazaar, the gaddiwalla adulterated the drink with some rubbish he had picked up and a large number of his customers were severely ill as a result. Three died and several went blind, but nothing could be proved, and it didn't seem to have much effect on the drinking habits of the others. The spirit seemed to leave the drinker with a horrible hangover, and the Monday morning after a Saturday payday was always conspicuous by the shortage of men who turned out for work, and many of the ones that did had bloodshot eyes and reeked of booze.

To illustrate how it affected them, one Saturday afternoon

in 1961, not long after I had taken over the management of Aibheel, one man had got horribly drunk on darhu and was standing outside the office, shouting insults about the office staff. I stood it for a while, hoping that he would go away, until finally I called the office watchman and told him to find out what he was shouting about, and to tell him to go back to his house otherwise he would be in trouble.

When he came back he told me that he was shouting that all the Bengali office staff were thieves, that the Head Clerk had stolen his pay and he wasn't going to go until he was sacked. Of course, there wasn't a scrap of truth in it, but he was making such a noise that I thought that the sooner I dealt with him the better it would be, so I went out and confronted him. Standing before him I said, 'Look, you are drunk, what you are saying is all lies, so go back to your house before you get into trouble'.

I think he was so drunk that he didn't recognise me, because he fixed his bleary eyes on me with difficulty, and said', 'Who are you to tell me to go back to my house? If I want to stay here I shall please myself'.

Now, it was an unwritten rule that you never laid hands on any of the labourers, whatever the provocation, because of possible repercussions from the labour unions, but if you had to hit them, never punch them but give them a slap. When he said this I realised that, with a large group of labourers gathered round and with my authority being directly challenged, I had to do something fast, so without more ado I fetched him a slap on the side of his jaw that must have rattled his teeth, because he tottered backwards over the grass until he collapsed in a heap, where he lay moaning gently. I was thunderstruck, because I didn't think that I had hit him very hard, and was absolutely amazed that one small slap would have such an effect, so I had to think quickly what I could do. I remembered that he was one of the garden Munshi's men and lived in the same line, and as he happened to be at the office as well, I called him over and said, 'Look Munshi, this man has been telling lies about the Head Clerk, he has insulted me, and now I have punished him. Arrange for some of your men to carry him back to his house before he gets into more trouble and I decide to sack him' then turned and walked back into the office. At this there was a murmur from the assembled labourers, but I took no notice, and the next time I looked out of the window he had gone.

That evening I thought about the wisdom of what I had done, the only time I had ever hit one of my labourers, and what action the labour force would take about it, so I went to bed that night in a disturbed frame of mind. Imagine my thoughts the next day when Kancha awoke us with our morning tea and said, 'Sahib, there is a man waiting at the compound gate who wants to speak to you'. When I asked him who he was, he said, 'It is the man that you hit at the office yesterday afternoon, and he has something to say to you'. Thinking all sorts of dark thoughts and ready for just about anything, I dressed quickly, and carrying my stick walked down to see him, appearing confident on the outside but with an empty feeling in the pit of my stomach. Thinking that the best thing to do was to take the initiative, I said to him, 'Well Budhoo, that was a terrible rumpus you kicked up in the office compound yesterday afternoon, what have you got to say for yourself'? Whereupon he gave me a most abject salaam with his head bowed and both hands raised to his forehead, and said, 'Yes Sahib, I was very evil yesterday, but I had had too much to drink and a devil got inside me and I didn't know what I was saying. When I awoke in my house, the Munshi told me just how bad I had been, and said that I should come and apologise to you before I could go to work tomorrow, so I have been waiting to see you'.

This approach was completely unexpected, but I was very relieved at the development, so I told him that I was very pleased that he had come to see me because I was thinking of sacking him anyway. However, because he realised that he had done wrong, and had come to see me, provided he went and apologised to the Head Clerk as well, I would consider that he had been punished enough and he could go back to work. And that is what he did. He worked the next day after making his apologies, and although he didn't actually give up drinking, I never had any more trouble with him while I was on Aibheel.

On another occasion we were going to Nagrakata to the cinema one Sunday evening, and as we were travelling through the Sathkyah tea, we came upon what looked like two bodies lying in the road. This was only slightly wider than the car, with deep ditches on both sides, so I stopped with the headlights still on to see what had happened. As I got near one of the 'bodies' roused itself and sat up, blinking owlishly in the lights, and told me they had been drinking at the guddikhana and were on their way home when they felt sleepy. When I explained that I couldn't get the car past he immediately staggered to his feet, asked me to wait while he tottered over and collected a full bottle of hooch that the other man had been carrying. Then he scrambled into the tea with the bottle cradled in his arms and said, 'It's all right now Sahib. You can drive on.' When I pointed out that the other man was still lying in the road, he said, 'Oh, don't worry about him, Sahib. That's only my uncle, just drive over him.' Finally, when he realised that I wouldn't do this, he put the bottle down carefully in the tea, weaved his way over to his uncle, and taking a firm grip on his arm, gave one enormous heave which, instead of moving him, pulled himself over the top of his uncle until he disappeared headfirst into the roadside drain. I waited for a few moments to see what would happen, then walked over to where he had fallen, and to my astonishment found him lying stretched out in the bottom with his eyes closed, snoring, so I pushed his uncle in on top of him and left them there, both sleeping like babes. When we returned from the club later that night I diverted along the same road to see if they were still there, but the ditch was empty and the full bottle was gone, so obviously they had recovered enough to make their way home.

One rather interesting fact that intrigued me when I started working with the garden registers was that many of the labourers had the same or very similar names. Many of them were quite strange, although they seemed vaguely familiar, until I realised that they were based on the days of the week. When I enquired about it, it turned out that it was considered lucky to name the baby after the day on which it was born, rather like us naming girls born during the Christmas period Noelle, Carol, Holly and Ivy. The Hindi name for Monday was Somvar, so many of the girls were named Somri, Somari, Somni, Somti, Somi and Sumi, while the boys had names like Somra, Soma, Somnath and Somrath. Tuesday was Mangalvar, which gave us Mangri, Mangni. Mangti, Mango, Mangoo and Mani for the girls, and Mangra, Mangna and Mangloo for the boys, and so on through the days of the week. There were some other names which were used, but the main exceptions to this custom were the children of the Christian workers who adopted biblical names such as Sarah, Ruth, Mary, Lucas and Matthew when they were accepted into the local Roman Catholic church, but on most estates these were in a minority.

In 1964 we had 28 Somaries and 22 Budhnies on the Aibheel books, who were only distinguishable by the fact that they worked for different Sirdars, so we composed a list of about 200 different names, from which newly recruited labourers could choose a name under which they would work on the estate, irrespective of what their name was at home. As a result, Aibheel had its first Nancy, Lulu, April, Judy etc., and because we made them all as short as possible, the labour of writing out repetitive long names in the labour registers was reduced considerably. Such is progress.

Pigs and chilli juice

Another thing I found completely strange when I joined Zurrantee, yet took to like a duck to water, was shikar (hunting and shooting). In the cold weather, many of the labourers had most of their afternoons free, and parties of them took their dogs and weapons across the river into the Naura forest whenever possible, hunting for all types of game, from jungle fowl to deer. In the early spring the river was easy to cross, the grass was brown and crisp, which ensured that there were no leeches, and as the jungle was at its least dense, visibility inside the forest was at its best, and this made any game which was shot easier to see and track. Because Bill Milne was absolutely fearless and a first class shot, the garden shikariwallas (hunters) tried to get him to go with them at least once a week, and for this big hunt even the factory men were given the afternoon off to take part.

The most popular game was pig or deer, and in the early morning a couple of the best trackers would go over into the forest to find out what animals were around and where they were likely to be that afternoon. These shoots were very popular with the labourers because they were a very valuable source of meat. Anything up to 120 men would gather in the factory compound in the early afternoon, and then, accompanied by Bill, would walk the two or three miles into the selected area of forest. In 1951, because neither Ian Munro nor John Mitchell were very interested in shooting, Bill usually went alone, which was a distinct disadvantage, as he could only shoot at a percentage of the animals raised by the beaters. He was very disappointed when I told him that owing to the fact that I had never been called to do my National Service, I had never handled firearms of any kind, but he brightened up considerably when I added that I was pretty good with an air rifle! Actually, this was only an airgun that Auntie Toby and Uncle Jim had given me as a combined birthday and Christmas present one year, but I had learned to use it properly and became quite proficient at target shooting, so when he asked if I would like to go out with them I jumped at the opportunity.

At first I used his 12-bore shotgun so that he could see how I handled it, but once he was satisfied, he allowed me to use his second rifle, a .375 Mannlicher, whenever we went out together, and because we had doubled our firepower, our bag increased accordingly. The labourers were armed with spears, which had five-foot-long bamboo shafts tipped with razor-sharp steel heads about six inches long, or bows and arrows. The bows were made from split bamboo, thick in the middle but tapered down at each end and then hung in the smoke of a cooking fire for several weeks to mature and increase their elasticity, while the arrows, which were also made of split bamboo, had flat wooden tips like corks when used for killing birds, or barbed, steel heads about two inches long when used for animals. These bows were extremely powerful, and it was not uncommon for one of the stronger men to drive an arrow completely through the body of a small pig or deer from one side to the other.

The forest was divided into blocks by wide paths every 400 yards or so, and normally the guns and the best archers went ahead and waited at the next path, while the rest of the beaters spread out along the opposite boundary and beat their way towards them. If they knew that a big cat was in the vicinity, they made as much noise as possible, but the rest of the time they walked through the trees making very little disturbance, as this was enough to keep the game moving in front of them without causing any panic. However, they did have a code by which they could tell us what kind of animal might appear before us, for if they knew they were driving deer they would whistle, while for pigs they would knock on the tree trunks with their spears. No noise meant either that there was nothing there, or they didn't know what they had in front of them.

Deep in the forest, because of the policy of annual burning and the thickness of the shade canopy, the undergrowth was not very thick, but where the blocks bordered the river and were flooded each year many of the trees died and were replaced by a type of thatch grass which was known locally as 'Bhabni jungle'. This was about six feet tall and extremely thick, and the pigs loved to lie up in this during the day, using clearly defined tracks that they made through it to move about. On one occasion, a very large pig was disturbed and made its way out to the edge of the block using one of these well-worn tracks. I had positioned myself in the thatch right on the edge of the track, so that although I was not directly in view to anything coming along it, I could get a reasonable view of anything on the path. For large animals wild pigs can move extremely silently, and suddenly as I waited, although I heard nothing, I sensed that something was coming and raised my rifle into the ready to fire position, with the sight trained on the middle of the track. The pig was obviously very suspicious, and although it hadn't seen me and couldn't smell me, it sensed that something was wrong, and was inching its way towards the mouth of the track before charging across, when I saw it. I didn't have to correct my aim, for as I was peering down the sights, I realised that what I had seen as an absolutely empty path a few seconds before, had been transmuted into the face of an enormous pig which had magically appeared about four feet away, and was looking directly at me through the thatch. For a moment I gathered my senses as I tried to assimilate how it had managed to creep up on me without me hearing it, and then as I was already aiming right between its eyes, I squeezed the trigger just as it began to move. For one moment it was just as though everything was happening in slow motion, then the boar gave one grunt and pitched over on its side without moving another step, and I breathed a sigh of relief. When I examined it closely I was very pleased to find that I had shot it through the brain, as it was a very large boar with vicious looking six inch long tusks protruding from its top jaw, which could have caused a lot of damage if I had only wounded it. When injured, a pig of this size tends to try to knock its assailant down and then savage its soft stomach and underbelly with its tusks, and can cause horrendous injuries.

Wild pigs were always very clever and crafty, and when being hunted, one of the tricks the sows used to confuse the hunters was to shoo their sounder of piglets out into the road before them to draw any fire, and then charge across at a point a few yards away while the hunter's attention was distracted by the horde of small, squeaking piglets bolting across the road.

Another very crafty boar which gave us a lot of trouble on another shoot had discovered that instead of being driven along in front of the beaters, it was better to hide in the undergrowth until they reached him, and then break back through the line into the area from which they had come. This one afternoon it had done this three times, breaking back and scattering the line of beaters on each occasion, so finally I suggested to Bill that if he stayed on the path to shoot it if it kept going, I could go in at the back of the beaters, and maybe get a shot at it while it was breaking back because it wouldn't be expecting me to be there. He wasn't very keen at first, because it would be coming at me from the direction of the beaters, but when I assured him that I would not shoot at it unless I had a clear view of it with a side on shot, he agreed, and it worked like a dream. Once again the beaters walked through the area while I followed along some 30 yards behind until I reached the thick patch of jungle where it usually hid, and then suddenly, to the accompaniment of shouts and whistles, I heard it coming towards me through the undergrowth like an express train. I couldn't see it, but I could gauge its progress by the agitation of the vegetation, and estimated that if it kept on the same track it would pass by me about 20 yards away, so I followed him with my rifle until I got a good side view of him, then let him have it. It must have thought that as on the other times, once it was through the beaters it was safe, because it slowed down to a trot just as it reached me, which enabled me to get in a good shot just behind his shoulder. This would normally have killed a lesser animal outright, but he raced on for another 30 yards before he slid to a dead stop and keeled over, and he was so big that it took four men to carry him out of the forest suspended from a bamboo pole over their shoulders. As it so happened, this was the only thing we shot all the afternoon, but nevertheless it was big enough to give everyone a large ration of meat.

Although shooting like this was a sport, with hunters on foot pitting their wits and their skills against the animals, nothing was ever killed purely for the sake of killing, and everything we shot was eaten. Our normal rule was that if we couldn't eat it, we didn't shoot it. On these garden shoots, all the bag was carried back to the factory compound for the big share-out under the security lights, and it was done with scrupulous fairness. Because it was quite possible for an animal to be wounded by one person and then actually killed by someone else later, under the generally accepted rules of shikar, a dead animal was actually claimed by the first person to wound it and draw blood on its body or head. By this rule, he would say which portions of his animal he wished to keep for himself, which in the case of leopards and tigers were the skins, but because most of our game was shot by our guns, usually we got a leg or a cut of meat, irrespective of who had actually shot it. Once ours was put to one side, all the rest of the animals were cut up into portions and placed in small heaps on the ground on plantain leaves, one for each of the men who had been in the hunt, and all identical as far as possible. Nothing was thrown away, and all the skins, bones and flesh were cut up and added to the piles. All the men participated in this, and while they were butchering and cutting up the meat. they chatted and laughed, reliving and describing incidents that had occurred during the shoot, especially those in which any of the men present had made fools of themselves. Once all the piles were complete, the head shikari checked them and asked if anyone was not satisfied with his allocation, after which any complaints were sorted out and everyone went home, usually with several pounds of assorted meat.

Sometimes, if the hunt had not been successful and the share out was small, several men of the same family would pool their allocations so that the most needy of them would have something worthwhile to take home, so it was all settled very amicably.

Of course, because I was the new boy and an unknown quantity, everyone kept an eye on me to see what I was doing and how I measured up, and I was very fortunate in gaining a reputation amongst the labourers for being quite fearless and a very cool customer when it came to facing wild animals. And how did this happen? Well, it was by mistake actually, during an afternoon shoot a few weeks after I had arrived on Zurrantee, but of course they never knew. Because the trackers had found signs of several pigs in a scrub covered river bed near Sam Sing, Bill had been invited by his friend John Adams, who was the Assistant Manager there, to bring some of his best men over to join the shoot and increase the firepower, and I went with them. Bill had lent me his shotgun loaded with birdshot so that I could have a go at any jungle fowl I saw, but not to shoot at anything else. There were plenty of pig tracks all over the area, so to give me an idea of how these shoots operated, I was told to go up the stream into the middle of the scrub and wait until the beaters came by me. It was a lovely afternoon, and I took the shotgun and picked my way up the boulder-covered river bed until I reached a fallen tree trunk in the middle of the jungle which looked quite comfortable and settled myself down to wait. Other than the occasional shouts and whistles from the beaters, nothing much seemed to happen, until there was quite a commotion and I heard something heavy crashing through the jungle a few yards behind me. I didn't see anything as the animal crossed the stream, but as I had never heard the grunts and growls before that it was making as it ran, I thought that they were the normal sounds that a large pig would make. As I didn't intend to shoot at it I was not worried and just sat tight and admired the scenery until John whistled out and told me to come back down. I strolled back to where he was standing with a rather incredulous expression on his face, and he said, 'Did you see it?' so I told him that it had crashed over the stream a few yards from where I had been sitting, but I didn't actually see it, to which he responded, 'You know what it was, don't you?'. At this point I began to think that there might be something not quite normal going on, but said, 'Well, it was a big pig, wasn't it?' at which he burst out laughing. Evidently the beaters had disturbed a very large tiger which had charged them and then leapt the stream a few yards from where I was sitting. As I was armed with a gun loaded only with birdshot, all the watching shikaris on the edge of the jungle had expected me to be absolutely panic stricken when I saw it, so the fact that I had just continued to sit there quite nonchalantly had impressed them no end, and as I sauntered out afterwards without a care in the world, I got a somewhat undeserved reputation for being an ice-cold shikari with nerves of steel who was not scared of the occasional tiger ! This was one of the regular stories that were repeated whenever the beaters gathered together during a shoot, and many years afterwards, when I was actually working on Sam Sing, some of the labourers told me that they had been there on that memorable day when I had gone after the tiger with the bird gun!

Other than the ones which concerned me directly, the incident I remember best was one afternoon when, because the beaters had to travel farther than the guns before they started beating, we had to wait for half an hour or so in a clearing in the forest before things started to happen. Because their eyes and ears were attuned to the jungle, and they knew the forest sounds, we usually took a shikari with us, and on this day he sat on one side of a fallen log while I sat alongside him facing the other way. The secret of waiting successfully was to make as little noise and commotion as possible. We had been sitting absolutely motionless for about ten minutes, when suddenly he gave a terrified yelp and a strangled scream and, without getting out of his sitting position, cart wheeled backwards over the log and finished up on his hands and knees in front of me. 'Sanp, Sahib. Sanp!' he said, and as I quickly jumped up and looked over the log, I saw quite a large snake retreating into the undergrowth. As he told it afterwards, it must have been sleeping in a hollow beneath the tree trunk immediately beneath him, and as he rested with his arms on his knees looking down between his legs, suddenly this great snake materialised as if by magic between his feet. It was probably a large rat snake, and quite harmless, but as he was very surprised and wasn't waiting to find out, he simply threw himself backwards. Naturally this made a good story which was repeated many times afterwards, but I do think the snake got larger and more ferocious at each telling.

Another humorous thing that happened occurred during another of these afternoon shoots. After walking through the dry and dusty forest for several hours, we broke out of the jungle feeling very hot and tired and found ourselves on the riverbank. I was feeling very thirsty, and when I asked Bill if the river water was safe to drink, he replied that it wasn't , but then added that the local villagers grew a type of fruit that was extremely good for quenching a thirst. On the bank a short distance away was a small village where some of the forest employees lived, and in one of their gardens he showed me some small bushes which were absolutely covered with dozens of fat, shiny red and green fruits which looked very inviting and which I had never seen before. Being very new and trusting, I examined them closely and asked him which ones were the best, and Bill, ever the joker, said that the green ones were quite sweet, but the red ones were the juiciest, so I quickly picked two of the largest, juiciest red ones that I could find. Without stopping to think I popped them into my mouth and bit into them, making the juice squish over my lips, and for a few moments everything was fine, until suddenly I thought my whole head was on fire, inside and out. Of course they were chillis. Spitting them out I rushed over to the river, and oblivious to the fact that I might get an upset stomach, I washed my mouth and face with copious quantities of cold water until the fire subsided and the feeling came back. While all this was going on, Bill had been translating our conversation to the beaters, and they had all been waiting to see what I would do, so when I squawked and jumped into the river they were all creased up with laughter, which made another good story to tell everyone. In fact, the raw chilli juice blistered my lips, and I realised that I had been had, but as no real harm had been done I knew that it would do no good to lose my temper, so I just grinned at my mistake and marked it down as another lesson learned on the road to settling down in tea.

I had only been on the estate two weeks when I saw my first tiger, during a big shoot for wild pigs in the river valley between Zurrantee and Nagaisuree tea estates, which Bill Milne had organised for Sunday, February 24th. The area, which covered several acres and was smothered with a tangled mass of dense undergrowth, creepers and thorn trees, had become the home of numerous pigs which had come across from the Naura forest to feast on the ripe dhan which the labourers had grown in their khets. Earlier in the week, shikaris had reported that there were up to 50 pigs living there in the dense undergrowth, so Bill had arranged for several of the local planters to come to the shoot, including his friend John Adams from Sam Sing, Sandy Frain from Sathkyah and Noel Barker from Matelli, and as I had never been to a big shoot, he invited me to go as well.

On that day about 150 workers from Zurrantee and the adjoining estates gathered at the head of the valley and started beating at 9 am, but despite their best efforts, by midday after two beats, no pigs had been seen, although tracks were there in abundance. It seemed as though they had all disappeared quite suddenly without trace. However, when we started the third and last beat all was revealed. This covered the southern end of the area, where the valley narrowed and the Nagaisuree river ran close under the Zurrantee tea beneath a cliff about 25 feet high. Within a few minutes of the beat starting, we heard the roars of what seemed like several tigers in the block, and as some sounded quite near and I was armed only with Bill's gun loaded with shot in case I saw any jungle fowl or small pigs, I quickly made my way over the rocks in the river bed to where John Adams was waiting. We were soon joined by Noel Barker and several beaters who had had to scatter when a tiger charged them, injuring one of the men. It was at this point that we heard three shots from upstream where Bill had gone, so we scrambled up over the rocks until we met Sandy Frain, who told us that Bill had fired the shots at a large tiger which had emerged from the jungle in front of him. The first had hit it in the shoulder, which caused it to roll down the bank into the undergrowth, and as he had not seen any further movement, he thought that he had killed it, but although he was unable to see it, he fired another two with his rifle and shotgun at the spot where he thought it was lying in the hope of making sure. How wrong he was.

Just as we arrived near the spot we heard it regain consciousness and start growling about 20 yards away, and soon after Bill had slid down the bank and joined us, there was a roar and it shot out of the undergrowth and charged. Absolute pandemonium broke loose. My lasting impression was of a terrible head with wide open jaws and gleaming teeth, followed by a brownish black mass charging at an incredible speed only about 50 feet away. With absolute clarity I realised that my small shot was virtually useless against it, so decided to hold my fire until it was almost on us, when I would blast it in the face with both barrels in the hope of blinding it. Bill was actually sideways on to it talking to us when it emerged, and it was only about ten yards away when he fired his first shot backwards over his left shoulder. The bullet hit it in the mouth, luckily causing it to veer off the path and crash into a large boulder about 20 feet away, before it scrambled back onto the path and tried to reach us. This gave the others time to fire at it, and as I judged that it was now too close for comfort, and there was a chance that it would roll into the river bottom amongst us, I carefully aimed the shot gun and fired both barrels into its face. It was still frantically struggling to reach us, when with several more shots in it it finally collapsed and rolled over about 10 feet away.

It was then that we realised just how lucky we had been and how close we had come to disaster. If the first bullet had missed or caught it a couple of seconds later, nothing could have stopped it from rolling down into the jhora amongst us, and the result would have been mayhem, as it still had plenty of fight left in it. In the confines of the narrow river bed it would have been difficult to shoot it, as besides us four Europeans there were about a dozen beaters, all of whom had stood firm with weapons ready, except for two who had tried to climb the cliff and scramble through the tea at the top. In their panic they made very little progress, and repeatedly scrambled up a few feet before they rolled down again in a shower of earth and stones, and in their blind terror they were still doing this even after the tiger was dead, much to their colleagues' amusement.

Nine shots were fired in all in about 10 seconds, five by Bill and two each by John Adams and Noel Barker, plus my contribution, and later, when I told Bill of what I had done, I think he accepted my story with a pinch of salt. However, the next morning after it had been skinned, he saw me at the office, handed me a match box and said, 'This is for you. It was the best thing you could have done in the circumstances, and you hit her exactly right. Well done'. Inside were about 50 small shotgun pellets that the skinners had found embedded in the tiger's face and eyes when they skinned it, and although Bill had the skin preserved and the head mounted afterwards, when he retired from tea in 1962 he presented it to me and said. 'There you are Rod, that was your first tiger, so keep it safe'. And even though it was not in too good condition and looked a little bit battered and chewed where his dogs had played with it when it was on the floor of his bungalow in Zurrantee, I treasure it still.

When we examined the beast it turned out to be large tigress, 9'4' long from her nose to the tip of her tail, three feet in height at the shoulder and weighing 320 lbs. She had been accompanied by three almost fully-grown cubs, and these had made their getaway in the confusion and weren't seen again. Tigers regularly prey on pigs, and I suppose in their wanderings they had come across the river and found what they must have thought was the promised land until the pigs ran away. Unfortunately, tigers and tea garden labourers do not mix, and even if we had not killed her that day, they would have had to have been driven out in the near future as soon as they had started killing goats and cattle. Afterwards, although I was rather sad when I saw her lying there, I realised that it was a necessary evil, and as she was eaten by the labourers, they were quite happy.

As a sequel to this, the next day Bill sent us down some venison which he said he had had left from our previous shoot. He had hung it for several days to improve the taste and wanted to know how we liked it, so we had it roasted for our evening meal. In fact it didn't taste very good at all and was rather stringy and had quite a strong flavour, so the next day when he asked us how we had liked it we told him that although it was all right we really didn't like it very much. At this he said, 'Well, never mind, now you can tell all your friends that you have actually eaten tiger meat', and he creased up with laughter. As he told it afterwards, when the labourers were skinning the tigress that day they talked among themselves and wondered whether we would like it or not, so he suggested that they sent some down to find out as a joke, and that is what he did. All I can say is that compared with pork or lamb it leaves a lot to be desired.

There were two more sequels to this shoot. For a long time Bill and Noel Barker had had an ongoing friendly argument about the right kind of firearm to use when hunting dangerous game. Noel used an ex-US Army self-loading carbine, which theoretically enabled him to fire twice as fast as Bill was able to with his old five-shot, bolt action, .375 calibre Mannlicher rifle. Bill's contention was that you rarely fired more than two shots quickly in succession, so the added speed of the carbine made very little difference. As it emerged in the inquest afterwards, Bill had fired his five shots in a few seconds, at least four of which had hit, while Noel's carbine had jammed after he had fired twice. In his haste he hadn't been able to clear it, which could have been really dangerous had he been on his own, and as far as I know he never used it for dangerous game again.

The other rather humorous sequel concerned me. The whole incident made a deep impact on me, and that evening after I had got back to the bungalow, I thought very deeply about what had occurred, and I realised that we had been within a cat's whisker, well, a tiger's whisker actually, of disaster. Had it reached us in the jhora any one of us could have been killed, and I thought how futile it would have been for me to die so young and so soon after having reached India.

At that time one of our favourite monologues on the wireless at home was one performed by an entertainer named Stanley Holloway entitled The Lion and Albert', which recounted what happened when the Ramsbottom family made a trip to Blackpool Zoo. During their visit, their little son Albert annoyed an old lion named Wallace by poking his stick 'with the horse's head handle, the finest that Woolworth's could sell' into the lion's ear, which prompted the lion to drag Albert inside the cage and gobble him up. When the keeper asked what was wrong his Mother answered. 'Yon lion's ate Albert, and 'im in his Sunday best too.,' As I sat and thought about what I had experienced that afternoon, the vision of this enraged tigress charging down the path to kill us kept coming into my head, and it occurred to me that if Goodricke's had had to send a message to Mum along the lines of 'Sorry Mrs Brown, yon tiger's ate Roderick, and 'im in his Sunday best too', then I hadn't made a will, nor did I have any life insurance in case of accidents, so she would have lost everything. I had been told that it was company policy for all the managerial staff to make wills, and arrangements were being made for me to visit Jalpaiguri 100 miles away to make the necessary arrangements as soon as possible, but taking out a life insurance policy was something I had never considered and didn't know how to do. However the afternoon had been so traumatic that I felt I needed to do something and decided to make some enquiries.

Now, as if fate had planned it an Anglo-Indian who had acted as agent for the Sun Life Assurance Company of Canada happened to come to our bungalow the next day. As we sat on our veranda eating our lunch we heard the sound of his old two-stroke motor cycle, (normally known by the labourers as a 'Phut Phuttia') labouring up the hill road beneath the bungalow, and soon he cruised up to the veranda steps in a cloud of dust. He was dressed in an old, white cassock, rather like a Catholic priest, and wore a battered old sola topi (pith helmet) and a dusty pair of goggles. Having received all sorts of welcomes and rebuffs during his lengthy career as an insurance salesman, and knowing that we were having our lunch, I believe he thought that we would kick him out as quickly as he had arrived and send him on his merry way. You can imagine his surprise then, when without any pressurisation or sales talk from him, I told him that I was very keen to take out a life assurance policy, and would like to get on with it straight away. Immediately his attitude changed and he went onto the defensive, for I am sure he thought that I must be on my last legs and likely to pass away that very afternoon, and it took several minutes for me to persuade him to sell me a policy. How times have changed.

Finally I bought a 30-year policy which would pay £1000 to my dependants in the event of my death, and that amount plus profits at the end of that time if I lived to claim it. For this I agreed to pay £9.1.3d per quarter over the next 30 years, and as £1000 would have bought several cars or a really up market house in 1951, I thought this was a sound investment, and called it my 'Tiger Insurance'.

In 1981 it matured for the princely sum of £1800, which was not even enough to enable me to change the car we had at that time, let alone buy a new one, and our local Sun Life agent laughed like a drain when I recounted how I had come to buy it. He was so impressed that he told me he would write a small item about it in their house magazine and send me a copy, but it never materialised, so I don't know whether he did or not.

It does illustrate how inflation took over during those 30 years. Mum and Dad had bought their house for £390 in 1952, while a letter cost 2d (1p) to send. By 1981, the value of their house had risen to about £20,000, while the cost of a letter was 13p, quite an increase.

After the shoot I wrote a three-page account of it complete with all the gory details, and sent it home to Mum in my next letter, thinking that she would like to know what her son was doing, and completely disregarding the fact that the knowledge that he was being involved with ravening tigers probably worried her sick. She must have shown it to someone who told the *Dursley Gazette*, and an abridged account of it appeared in the next issue. In it I was referred to as an 'Old Dursleyan', and other than the fact that they had described me as working at Mawdsleys' instead of Listers', at that time it seemed to be a pretty fair account. However, on reading it now, I feel that it gives the impression of having leapt straight out of the *Boy's Own Paper*.

It was after this tiger incident that I remembered what I had been told in the London office about Bill, and began to think that life on Zurrantee revolved around big cats, because a couple of weeks later we shot a leopard in the tea a few yards from our bungalow. When prowling at night, both leopards and tigers make a very loud purring noise which actually sounds like someone sawing wood, and on several nights we had been woken by the Prrr-aah, prrr-aah of a leopard as it had prowled down the jhora at the back of the bungalow. It was a regular visitor to the labour lines, where it had become a pest by killing and carrying away goats, dogs and even a calf over the previous few weeks, and the labourer's big worry was that one night it might take a child if nothing else was available.

On that day we were sitting down to lunch when we were surprised to hear Bill's Jaguar coming up our drive through the tea, because we had only left him at the office a few minutes before. Quickly he told us that a large leopard had been seen by some of the labourers entering a patch of scrub jungle on the edge of the valley, about 200 yards north of our bungalow, and as they were convinced that it was the one causing the trouble in the lines, a couple stayed on guard to make sure it didn't leave while the others notified Bill. Giving me his shotgun, which was loaded with solid 3/16' diameter LG shot, he took his rifle and we headed to the top of the jhora, where the labourers who had gathered tried to drive the leopard out in front of us. However, it was very stubborn and refused to move, even though they beat the undergrowth and threw stones into it, and it was not until they set fire to the edge of it in an attempt to burn it out that it suddenly charged out on the other side, leapt the stream and began scrambling up the side of the valley about 100 yards away. Sighting carefully, Bill waited until it had reached the top of the slope and he could see it clearly, then fired several shots, one of which brought it down on the edge of the tea, where it disappeared from view. Hurrying around the head of the valley, we walked carefully, side by side along the edge of the tea until we reached the place where it had disappeared, expecting it to charge at any moment, but a few yards further on we discovered it lying just inside the tea, stone dead. One of Bill's shots had broken one of its back legs, and had then passed up through its lower abdomen into its chest cavity, which had killed it instantly. It was an old male leopard, 6'2' from nose to tail tip, and it didn't seem to have any major physical disabilities, but when we examined it closely, we found that all its teeth and claws were very badly worn with age, which probably explained why it had abandoned hunting its natural prey and had taken to living the 'easy life' in the lines each night. When I saw it lying there, I felt rather sorry that it had been necessary to shoot it, but Bill had explained to me that it took the labourers a long time to save up to buy their animals etc., and if they lost one to the leopard it was like a car being stolen in the UK, with no insurance forthcoming with which to buy a new one. It was a total loss. So, provided they lived where they belonged, in the forest on the other side of the river, we left them alone, even the occasional kill in the tea being accepted as an act of

God or a bit of bad luck, and it was only when they became a serious pest that steps were taken to get rid of them. So, sad as it was, I realised that it was a fact of life that the labourers relied on their Sahibs to protect them from the dangers that they were unable to deal with themselves, and when I saw the look of relief on the faces of the women and children as they gathered around it afterwards, I thought how lucky we all were back in England that the largest carnivores that we had wandering around our houses at night were foxes and badgers, or the next door neighbour's cat.

In contrast to some of the rural parts of India, where man-eaters were quite common, we had very few of them in the tea areas, and this policy probably had something to do with it. The only one that I had personal knowledge of was much later when I was the Manager of Aibheel. I had given one of my workers leave to visit a sick relative on Baradighi Tea Estate, about six miles away, and part of his journey took him through a section of the Nagrakata forest. There was some talk of a man-eater being in the district at that time, but as the bus service was erratic, on his return journey he decided to walk back and he disappeared in broad daylight. Had he been travelling at night, or if he had been carrying something of value, then there could have been some other reason for his non-arrival, but despite a frantic search by his relatives over several days, nothing was ever seen of him again. If he did meet the tiger, then travelling alone he was easy prey for it, and he didn't stand any chance of escape.

At about the same time in roughly the same area another kill took place, and in this case they did see what happened. A young gaywala was out with his herd of cows in the grazing land on the edge of the forest, when he heard some of his friends shouting that they had seen a tiger prowling through the undergrowth. His cows, sensing that there was a tiger in the vicinity bunched together for safety, and the cowherd, not wanting to leave them, pushed his way through until he was in the middle of the herd. Normally if a tiger was hungry enough, it would try to kill one of the smaller cows, but once a man-eater has lost its natural fear of man, it becomes very crafty and absolutely fearless. And so it was with this one. With bated breath the onlookers saw it charge out of the forest like a large cat, leap up onto the back of a cow, and then run over the others, from back to back, until it reached the boy in the middle. Frantically he fell to the ground in the hope that it would be unable to reach him, but the cows scattered in panic, the tiger leapt down and gathered him in its jaws, probably killing him instantly, and within seconds it had vanished back into the jungle with its kill.

Once his friends had recovered from their shock they organised a search party to try to rescue him, but although they managed to track the animal, when they found him several hours later, all that was left of him were some of his torn clothes that the tiger had ripped off, together with his head and legs. It had eaten all the rest. Although, to the best of my knowledge, the animal was not shot in our area, it did disappear after this, so it could possibly have been shot elsewhere or died of natural causes. It could have been ill when it took the boy, because, for it to do what it did in broad daylight in front of other humans, was not natural behaviour, and it must have been extremely desperate and hungry for it to eat him so quickly. Still, that was very little consolation for him and his relatives when they brought his sad remains home, and I feel that we were very fortunate that we didn't have more of them in our neck of the woods.

CHAPTER TEN

The Land of Umbrellas

On March 20th we had the first rain since my arrival in India six weeks before, but although it was very welcome and laid the dust for a few days it wasn't enough to clear the atmosphere. The nights were still cool and we had a fire in the bungalow each evening, but the day temperatures rose steadily until by the end of March they were in the upper seventies. Neither of us new boys were used to working in such constant high temperatures as these and as a result we both developed severe attacks of prickly heat. This is caused by large amounts of perspiration trying to pass through pores which are unable to cope with the amount of liquid produced, and as a result stale sweat clogs them and builds up in rashes of small pimples beneath the skin. These developed on the back, chest and upper arms, and itched unbearably as soon as we got hot or excited and it was self-propagating. The more we scratched, the more the rashes irritated and the more we had to scratch them, so it was absolutely horrible.

This was a very common ailment for Europeans in the tropics and our doctor recommended frequent cold showers and liberal applications of talcum powder, but as the shower water from our outside steel water tank was usually lukewarm they didn't seem to do much good. A really cold, invigorating shower with a massage was what was required but this was not available, and how we suffered. Through April and early May we had one good storm and several light showers which wetted the grass and very little else, and as the temperatures soared into the 80s day after day our prickly heat got steadily worse. Depending on what we were doing, it either itched unbearably or burned as though we were coated with liquid fire, and the doc could do very little for us

Finally, on the evening of May 25th, we got what we had longed for. For several days thunder had been rumbling round without producing any rain, but the clouds had gradually built up until quite suddenly the heavens opened up and we had an absolute downpour which lasted all night. The torrential rain hammered down onto the parched earth, washing the dust, rubbish, leaves and blades of withered grass into the drains around the bungalow, and within an hour they were choked with debris and the compound was awash with dirty brown water. For a while we stood on the bungalow veranda and watched amazed as the pelting rain raised small fountains of spray.

Then John had the idea that here was a heaven-sent opportunity for us to have the ice-cold shower we so badly needed. Stripping down to our underpants we rushed out and cavorted in the downpour, allowing the stinging water to massage and pummel our rashes and stimulate our circulations.

Then I noticed that one of the gutters at the side of the bungalow was broken and from this a solid jet of water was falling as though from a fire hose - this was the icing on the cake. Slipping and sliding in the ankle deep water we stood beneath it and allowed it to hammer our bodies until they were almost numb, while the servants looked on in disbelief. I don't think that they had ever seen sahibs behave with such abandon, but they got used to it and it did the trick.

To our delight our prickly heat was very much better by the next morning and we 'danced in the rain' at every opportunity afterwards. The result was that by the end of June it had cleared up completely, never to return. The only thing on the debit side was that while he was capering around, Ian Munro lost one of his teeth. A few nights previously when we were fooling about I had accidentally hit him in the mouth and loosened a crowned tooth, and when he towelled himself after the 'shower,' he found that it had come out in the excitement. However the wonder of it was that the following morning we sent all the bungalow servants out to search for it and one of them discovered it in a drain, so he was able to put it back in and it all ended well.

This was the storm that washed all the smoke and dust out of the atmosphere, and after a perfect night's sleep we awoke to find the air smelling clean and fresh, and the sun rising in a cloudless blue sky. A few miles to the north beyond Sam Sing, the forest-clad foothills of the Himalayas rose thousands of feet into the sparkling, morning air, and it was then that I first realised just how beautiful this part of India could be and how fortunate I was that I was not working in Calcutta.

I suppose the main social amenity we lacked in the Dooars were swimming pools, but owing to the shortage of water in the cold weather very few estates had them. One that did was Killcott about three miles away, a very simple affair where a shallow valley had been dammed and the bottom cemented to make a small pool about six yards wide and 30 yards long. The water that supplied it originated from a spring which ran during the monsoon, and as it was in the middle of the tea and there were no houses nearby it was quite clean and clear, so we took every opportunity to go and swim to allow the cold water to continue our cures. However one Sunday morning I was swimming a length when out of the corner of my eye I noticed that someone was moving alongside me. This was fine and I took no notice until I realised that the 'someone' was the head of a large snake which was keeping pace with me a few feet away. I was absolutely petrified. Never a strong swimmer and completely surprised, I opened my mouth to give a cry of alarm, which filled it with water and made me cough and splutter, whereupon I stopped swimming and sank like a stone while the terror-stricken snake made its getaway. After that, although I did go back for the occasional swim even after my prickly heat had healed, the place didn't have the same attraction for me and I never went in without examining my bathing companions very closely.

Although I had been warned about mosquitoes and advised to buy a net to sleep under, because I had been short of cash and hadn't seen any mossies since I had arrived it was something I had omitted to do. However once the rain came I soon had a rude awakening, because I hadn't realised that they required small pools of stagnant water in which to breed, and once some rain fell it only took about two weeks for the eggs to hatch out and the mossies to appear. Through a very successful anti-malarial campaign in which all stagnant pools were covered with a thin film of light oil which prevented the larvae from breathing, and the walls of all the houses were sprayed with DDT, the malaria carrying Anopheles mosquitoes had been almost wiped out in our part of India, and by taking two Paludrine tablets per week I never suffered from it.

Unfortunately this operation had not wiped out the less dangerous but equally irritating common mosquitoes, and one night a couple of weeks after the storm I suffered the tortures of hell. While it was light they had stayed away but as soon as I put the light out to go to sleep I heard the high pitched whine of a mosquito's wings as it homed in on the side of my face, and the only thing I could do was wait until it stopped, which indicated that it had landed, then slap the place where I thought it was. This was quite effective against individual females but was absolutely useless against the hordes of demons that attacked me that night. There seemed to be millions of them, and as the electricity had been shut down I tried to sleep by covering my head up completely with my sheet, but this wasn't very successful. It foiled the mosquitoes but made me quite hot which irritated my prickly heat, and I couldn't really decide which was worse.

Finally at about 3 am in the cool of the morning, I was completely exhausted and fell into a fitful sleep, from which even the mossies were unable to wake me, only to wake up at 7 am with a face like a balloon, and it was enormous. The whole of my face was puffed up and red as the result of dozens of bites, my eyes looked blearily out of two slits and I wondered what I was going to do. Bill seemed to be the best bet, so I walked up to his bungalow and explained what had happened and he was superb. He advised me to bathe my face with chilled water from the fridge, then soothe it with some antiseptic cream, which worked a treat. In the meantime he lent me an old net until the one I had ordered arrived from Calcutta, and by tying this up to a framework of bamboo poles lashed to the bed legs I was able to sleep undisturbed. This was such bliss that I always made absolutely sure I had a net with me when I needed one. Actually I need never have suffered as much as I did because our bedroom was equipped with inner secondary doors and windows fitted with fine wire mesh, which if they had been closed at sundown would have kept the mossies out anyway. However neither John nor I knew what to expect so they were left open, and as he already had a net I was the one to suffer through my inexperience. Still we learned fast and thereafter all the doors and windows were closed at 4 pm, the bearer sprayed our bedroom with a Flit gun which we bought from the local store, and by tucking the nets in when the beds were made we had a three-way line of defence which worked a treat. The only drawback was that the Flit made the room smell awful for a couple of hours, but this was a small price to pay to keep it pest free.

Because we didn't have large areas of standing water in which the mosquitoes could breed I wondered where they had all come from, until it was explained to me that they bred wherever there were large bamboos. Bamboos are members of the grass family and their stems consist of solid sections where the leaves develop, named nodes, and the hollow sections between them are named internodes. The simplest way to cut a bamboo is by slicing through the inter node, but by doing this a natural cup is left which is completely watertight, and can often hold several ounces of liquid. As the rain falls it trickles down the inside of the cut stem until it is caught in this natural cup, and it was in these small, stagnant pools that the larvae developed until they emerged as fully grown adults two weeks later. As a result, if you lived near a bamboo barrie you got plenty of mosquitoes, and we had bamboos in their thousands.

One rather comical device that many of the *Mem-Sahibs* (ladies) used when they were sitting outside in the evening and the mossies were biting were pillow cases. Because they were very poor fliers, they needed an inert, dimly lit target to attack, and as long as you moved your head, arms and legs regularly they stayed away. However in the dark under the table they came into their own, and it was a common sight to see several 'mems' sitting with their legs in pillow cases, with the tops pulled up over their knees to protect them. Many of them carried their pillow cases with them, and although they realised that they looked amusing they didn't mind as long as they kept the fiends at bay.

Because of the thick layer of cold weather dust which coated the tea bushes, attacks by a pest called the red spider mite were always a problem, especially if the previous year's foliage was left on. The mites tended to breed very successfully in the dust beneath the old leaves, and then attacked the soft, fresh, green buds and leaves as soon as they appeared by injecting a solvent chemical into the cells of the leaves which dissolved them. Once this occurred they were able to suck out the solution and digest it, taking the cell structure with it. Unfortunately, although the mites moved on to another spot to inject some more, the old solvent still left in the leaf continued to work on the cells, and gradually the surfaces of the affected leaves turned red, withered and died. Badly-affected areas turned almost completely red with very little fresh green leaf to be seen, and tea affected to this extent took weeks and even months to recover. Consequently every effort was made to ensure that mite infestations were kept to a minimum and infected areas were sprayed with chemicals as soon as they were detected, which was a very time-consuming and expensive business indeed. In view of this it was far better if they didn't start in the first place, so when time permitted all the pruned areas were defoliated and the old leaves removed before the end of the cold weather. As a result these areas looked as though the tea had died, with all the bushes cut down and bare, and not a trace of green to be seen.

However within a few days of the first rain falling, fresh green buds appeared on the twigs, and as these could grow at anything up to three inches per week, by the end of April they had reached the tipping height and plucking could begin. This period leading up to the start of the season was filled with a sense of suppressed excitement as all the necessary preparations were made. Garden tools such as hoes, axes, saws and pruning knives, which had been issued to the labourers to enable them to do their work, were brought back and returned to the stores, while each labourer was issued with two plucking cloths, known as *rhumals* or *jhulies*. A rhumal could be a square of material of any size from a handkerchief upwards, but in this instance it was a piece of loosely-woven hessian cloth about four feet square, the corners of which were tied and then worn suspended at the back with the corners passing over the worker's forehead. By doing this the plucker was able to pick the young leaf with both hands and then toss it back over the shoulder into the cloth. On many of the estates in other parts of India such as Assam and Darjeeling where top quality, withered teas were made, woven baskets made of split bamboo were used instead, but in the Dooars where the leaf was kept as fresh as possible prior to manufacture, these cloths were found to be the most satisfactory. They were also issued with a waterproof tarpaulin, popularly known as a *tirpal'*, which was worn as a kind of apron to keep them dry and protect their clothes as they walked through the waist high tea bushes, and also a black umbrella to keep the rain off. Just about everyone in West Bengal used a *chattri* or *chatta,* from the highest to the lowest, and it was quite amusing to see a block of tea being plucked in the monsoon. The pluckers tucked the handles down through their rhumals and then inside their aprons, so that they were firmly fixed, leaving both hands free to pluck, and from a distance the tea looked as though it had sprouted a crop of large, black mushrooms. In order to identify their own umbrellas, many of the labourers wrote and painted pictures on them in white paint.

When my sister visited us on holiday in 1961 I asked her what she would remember most about India. I thought she would choose something like the squalor in Calcutta or the views of the mountains from Darjeeling, but not a bit of it. 'I shall always think of India as the land of umbrellas', she said, 'Plucking tea, riding bicycles, walking in Calcutta, driving buffalo carts, everybody, but everybody has an umbrella, and I think it's lovely.'

The other thing that had to be ready on time was the factory, and long before any leaf appeared we had to have a trial run. The main boiler had been checked by the Government Boiler Inspector and passed with flying colours, so it was fired up and the old Marshall's steam engine clanked into action. For several hours the line shafting was run at full speed to weed out any bearings that were running hot. The rollers ground round and round, and old chaff cutters, which were exactly like those on the farms at home, were used to shred the leaf, clanking and whirring as the razor-sharp blades flashed around. In the drying room the large, overhead fans hummed as they sucked hot air from the furnaces and blew it through the trays in the endless chain dryers, while in the sorting room all the sifting machines jiggled and vibrated as though they were about to break free from their foundations. These were the sights and sounds I was going to become very accustomed to in the next seventeen years, but that day as I wandered round seeing how it all operated, I was very impressed when I thought that all these machines had just been heaps of parts when I had arrived on the estate ten weeks before.

There was always a certain amount of friendly rivalry between the managers on our estates to see who had their factories ready to take the very first leaf. Because the initial quantities gathered were quite small it was found to be uneconomic to manufacture them in individual factories, so to solve this problem it was arranged for several of our estates to pluck on the same day, and then the leaf was carried in lorries to one selected factory for manufacture, with an equivalent amount being returned later in the season as payment. At first glance this seemed to be a very fair way of doing it, but the drawback was that this very early first flush leaf which had taken two or three weeks to grow was usually of exceptional quality and made excellent tea, while mid-season leaf tended to grow more quickly and lose its character. This early season first flush tea was always in great demand at the tea auctions in Mincing Lane, and immediately after manufacture samples were sent to our Agents in Calcutta who forwarded them to the tea brokers and tasters in London. Contrary to advertisements and popular belief, very few of the tea blending and packaging companies owned their own estates, so they had to buy all the teas they needed to make their popular blends in the London auctions. To enable them to do this, samples from each invoice of tea were sent to them as soon as it was packed, so that they could see exactly what quality of tea would be available, and then chests were opened and further samples were taken as soon as the ship reached London Docks to ensure that the contents were what was expected. Although it was not a common occurrence, when the quality of the tea produced fell during the rains, when it often became very stalky and coarse, it was known for the samples to be 'doctored' on the estate before they were sent by having the stalk etc removed by hand, and this meant that they bore no resemblance whatsoever to what was in the chests. I suppose the persons concerned did it in the hope that the differences would not be noted, but the blenders were masters of their craft and I don't think that anyone got away with it over a long period.

Depending on the quality of the leaf and the amount of moisture it contained, it took between four and five pounds of green leaf to make one pound of unsorted black tea, and a close check was always kept on this ratio to ensure that the quality of the leaf being plucked was maintained and that it was being weighed properly. These weighments were done several times a day on spring scales fitted with large, brass dials which were suspended from bamboo tripods, and very often during the monsoon the rainwater streamed from the bottoms of the rhumals as soon as they were lifted onto the scale hook. It was accepted at times such as these that a fixed amount was deducted from each total recorded to compensate for this excess water, but at other times it was possible for a crafty plucker to cheat by dunking the rhumal in the water in the roadside ditch to make it heavier, just before being weighed. However the vast majority of the labourers were usually honest, and provided that the weighments were supervised properly and the pluckers trusted us and could see that they were not being exploited, incidents like this were not common.

Holidays, tennis and cricket

The one thing that did interfere with the preparations for the plucking season was the *Holi* Festival or *Puja*. In Chamber's dictionary this is defined as 'A Hindu spring festival characterised by boisterous revelry', but this rather bald description gives very little idea of how colourful it was or just how much fun was had by everybody. Holi is the festival of fertility and must be the Hindu equivalent of the ancient Saxon festival worshipping the fertility Goddess Eastre, which was held annually at the Spring equinox, and it appears that as with many other old pagan festivals this was taken over by the ancient Christian church and called Easter in an attempt to win over the followers of the old religion. The egg and the red of menstrual blood have always been symbols of fertility and there is still a tradition of colouring and painting eggs at Easter, but whereas the English painted eggs, the Hindus went the whole hog and coloured themselves and just about everything else, and how they enjoyed it.

All the Bengali clerks on the estate were Hindus, but as explained previously the majority of the garden labourers were recruited from tribes such as the Mundas, Santals, Oraons and

Kharias which had lived for centuries in the states of Bihar and Orissa that lie to the west of Bengal. The areas they lived in were very isolated and because they had very little written history, not much was known about them until after the mutiny in 1857 when the British Raj began, and even now there are doubts as to where they came from originally. Their religions were based on a clearly defined structure of gods and spirits, like a Christmas tree. At the very top rather like the fairy, was the supreme God or Deity, who was responsible for making the universe and everything in it. He was all-powerful and kept the world in order, and it was to him they prayed if help was needed. Below him were the 'village gods', who looked after all the communal affairs such as crops and harvests, hunting expeditions and water supplies, etc. while beneath them came numerous personal household gods who were believed to be the spirits of deceased family members. All these gods had to be worshipped to ensure good fortune.

At the bottom of the tree came the evil and malevolent spirits who brought bad luck and misfortune, and these had to be appeased or exorcised with offerings or sacrifices. The tribals believed that they were the earthbound spirits of people who had died a violent or unnatural death, rather like some people's ideas of evil spirits or ghosts, and they had to be dealt with by a *najos*, or ghost finder. In addition to the above they also believed in the 'elemental spirits' or nature gods, and they all had their own personal 'Guardian Angels' or totems, rather like the Indians of North America. However, because most of the families had lived on Zurrantee for three or four generations, it appeared that some of the old beliefs had lost their importance and over the years many of the workers had been converted to a kind of Hinduism, though this didn't prevent them celebrating all the other religious festivals whenever they came along.

Because Holi was a National Festival everybody got a paid holiday, including us. However on Zurrantee it was the custom for all the garden supervisory staff to visit both the managerial bungalows for a drink before we went down to the office to distribute cigarettes and cash to the labourers and then visit the football field to see the celebrations. Once we had done this the rest of the time was our own and we planned to go to the club afterwards. Knowing this, we bought in several large containers filled with haria, a rather sharp tasting white beer made from fermented rice which many of the labourers made at home, and also some large bottles of darhu, the foul-tasting, evil-smelling spirit distilled from millet seed. I suppose the idea was to include us in the fertility celebrations and for us to join the garden staff in ensuring that we had a fruitful and profitable season in the year ahead, but in all probability it was just to get a free drink.

Anyway, dead on 8 am they all appeared in the bungalow compound, led by the Munshi dressed in his 'Bazaar best'. It was obvious that many of them had been celebrating previously and were rather the worse for wear, so they were very pleased to use the chairs which had been taken out by the bungalow servants and arranged in a circle on the grass. They were all in very good spirits. It was explained to us that after they left us they would go up to Bill's bungalow to see him, and then go to change their clothes so that they could really get into the swing of things. Later we realised the reason why. I was amazed at their capacity for knocking back the booze, for they drank both kinds in big, satisfying gulps rather like drinking lemonade, and in next to no time all our stock was gone. This was the signal for them to get to their feet and approach us to say their thanks and farewells, standing in a long line for each one to approach us individually to give us a salaam, with both hands raised to the forehead. By nine o'clock they had gone.

After breakfast we went down to the office as arranged and to us it looked as though the world had gone mad, for dozens of private battles were being fought as people and children chased each other to shower them with colour. The powder was probably a type of poster paint that would wash off, and everybody was plastered. Bright magenta red, yellow, blue and green were the favourite colours, and many of the participants looked like animated rainbows from the tops of their heads to the tips of their toes.

Some of the more enterprising youths had armed themselves with bicycle pumps or Flit guns and with these they sprayed all and sundry with jets of coloured dye. This caused little rivulets of colour to run down their clothes, and when these combined with the powders already plastered there they produced an even more lurid effect.

The other things that caused a lot of consternation and fun were small 'water bombs' made out of folded sheets of paper about the size of a tennis ball. When they were filled with dye, either liquid or powder, and lobbed into the midst of the crowd they spattered all and sundry when they hit. Besides the humans all the animals were 'encouraged' to join in the fun as well, and bright red goats ran round with yellow pigs, while multi-coloured dogs and puppies trotted excitedly through the crowds.

Although several of the Bengali clerks came to the office with us, it was obvious from the state of their clothes that they had been well and truly pasted by their children before they left home, but they had washed the colour from their faces in an attempt to appear a little dignified, and when we passed their '*bashas*', (Dwelling houses) a little later, from the colour that was splashed all over the walls and trees it was evident that they too had entered into the spirit of things. In fact when we came to leave it was apparent that we four Europeans were the only ones who had not been given the full treatment; obviously care had been taken to ensure that we were not hit directly. Probably this was due to our rank and to the fact that we didn't really 'belong', but when we got back to the bungalow I found that in addition to some general colouring, I had two red, powdery palm prints on the back of my tee shirt, so someone had been determined that I should not escape unscathed. I think most of the powders were water soluble, because the hand prints certainly washed out of my shirt, but it is possible that some weren't because many of the labourers wore clothes that were still a faded rainbow colour at the end of the rains.

There were two other big pujas when the garden closed during the working year, and luckily these both occurred during the cold weather. The first was the *Durga* puja which was held in October, during which the Goddess Durga was worshipped, and the other was *Diwali,* also called the 'Festival of Lights', which was the equivalent of our Halloween, when the spirits were abroad and all the houses were lit up with thousands of tiny, clay oil lamps to keep them away. However besides these there were many other smaller festivals during the year, when various groups worshipped individual deities with whom they were connected, similar to the old Saints' Days in the Christian church. As shoemakers had Saint Crispin's day as a holiday and musicians venerated Saint

Cecilia, so the Hindu schoolchildren worshipped Saraswati as the patroness of speech, writing and learning and of the arts and sciences. On her feast day the Zurrantee school was closed for lessons after having been thoroughly cleaned throughout, and pictures and effigies of the goddess were garlanded with marigold flowers and presented with token offerings of food and drink. The teachers were also garlanded and led the students in their worship, and it was obvious that they were held in very high regard by their pupils. I suppose when something is not available to the masses as a whole, it is especially valued by the ones who do possess it.

Being an engineer, the puja which did interest me very much indeed was the craftsmen's festival, in which all the tools and items a craftsman needed to do his work were worshipped. No proper work was done on this day, but all the workplaces were cleaned and rubbish removed, all the tools were cleaned and polished, and broken tools were repaired before they were all laid out to be garlanded with flowers. Lathes, presses, benches, welding sets, drills, anything and everything a man depended on for his livelihood were painted with festive symbols, garlanded and offered small plates of food, in the hope that they would give him good service and bring him good luck in the year ahead. Even people who owned buffalo carts or taxis entered into the spirit of the thing and many of the carts and taxis were cleaned and painted, while the bullocks and buffaloes were decorated with good luck designs and fed a special meal. After the religious ceremony in the morning the men spent the rest of the day celebrating, but all the workshops etc opened as usual the next day and work went on for another year in the sure knowledge that all the tools realised how much they were valued, and how much their owners needed them to make a living. Perhaps this is a sentiment that is unfortunately lacking in the 'easy come, easy go' disposable society in which we live today.

After returning to the bungalow and changing our messy clothes, Bill picked us up and we went down to Chulsa Club for some tennis. Because he had injured his back quite severely in an incident during the war he usually played golf, but because I played quite a good game of tennis and our styles were compatible, we had taken to playing together and had actually won a doubles competition. I had learned my game on the vicarage lawn at Coaley, where the Vicar's wife had taken all the members of the junior church in hand and taught us to play. Because there was a large group of us we only played doubles. As I never developed a really good serve I didn't ever get very far playing singles, but doubles was a much craftier game. She was a very aggressive player, whose favourite position on the court was to be as close over the net as possible, and she drummed it into us that if you could dominate the net then the match was half won. This was quite true until one fine day when we were both playing up at the net on opposing sides and I felled her with my racket. It was a complete accident, because when I went to hit a fast ball which was just clearing the net, I accidentally let go of my racket and it flew through the air and hit her in the chest, whereupon she fell to the ground like a pole axed steer. Luckily she was only shocked and winded, but ever after that she treated me with a certain amount of respect whenever I was playing at the net, and I realised that what she had said was right. Dominate the net and the game is half won.

Because she was such a good player at the net we had to devise ways of passing her, and through this I discovered that

I could do a very fast, flat, topspin return which just skimmed the top of the net and then died and ran along the court once it landed, which made it very difficult to return. When we started playing tennis at the club, Bill told me that Dewars, the whisky distillers had donated a cup to Chulsa Polo Club, to be played for by pairs from each estate on a knockout basis every year. The favourites, Baradighi, had two excellent players and had won it for several years in succession, but after we had played a few games together Bill was delighted to find that our styles seemed to complement each other, and he decided to enter us to represent Zurrantee. We had a bye in the first round, and in our second round match against the Aibheel manager and his wife we took a while to settle down and lost the first set 4-6, but by imagining that Mrs Rand was the vicar's wife and getting my secret weapon into play, we won the next two 6-2, 6-4.

A week later came the semi-final, when we beat Bill's friend, Noel Barker, and his wife from Matelli in straight sets 6-4, 6-3, which put us into the final on the following Wednesday against the favourites, Wright and Patterson from Baradighi. Frankly I didn't think we had very much of a chance, because as individual tennis players there was no comparison between us and them, but Bill was quite happy. Because of his age and old injury he was not a very energetic player, but what he lacked in speed and agility he more than made up for in craft and cunning at the back of the court while I prowled the net, and to our great delight we managed to beat them 6-4, 4-6, 6-3 and put Zurrantee's name on the Dewar's Cup for the first time. He was absolutely ecstatic and insisted on filling the trophy several times so that everyone could celebrate with us, and as we both had several celebratory drinks in addition to this, we were soon as Bill would say, 'pootled.' Still it was an unforgettable evening, and as he had brought his driver to take us home I made the most of it. In theory, in addition to the trophy which we kept for one year we should have had small replicas presented to us for us to keep, but I don't know what happened to them for they never appeared.

All the courts in the Western Dooars, at Chulsa, Nagrakata and Mal, were grass, lush and green at the end of the monsoon and parched and dry at the end of the cold weather. It was always difficult to keep them watered, so to avoid this some of the courts in the Eastern Dooars were made of a type of clay and repaired each year. Each cold weather period the Dooars Tennis Championships were held at a different venue, and one year when I went over to play in the East, I was told that when the local club courts had been made, elephants were used to trample and consolidate the clay until an even, firm surface was obtained. According to my informant this had taken several days, but the courts were absolutely first class, and if they were made in this way then the elephants are to be congratulated.

On Sundays and Wednesdays when we played golf and tennis, small boys known as *chokras* presented themselves at the club to act as ball-boys and caddies. Because it was a more manly job and paid more, most of the older, stronger lads who were interested in making a bit of cash on the side went with the golfers, which left the younger, smaller ones for us. Most of these were very fast and wiry, scuttling around the back of the court and picking up the balls and feeding them to us whenever it was our turn to serve, but whereas these are now just shadows in the mists of time, the one which we will never forget was at Chulsa in the late 1950s. He was very small and painfully thin and looked like Dopey from *Snow White and the Seven Dwarfs*. He was probably an orphan and because he moved very slowly and never quite learned what he was supposed to be doing, he was only selected when the other, more capable boys were not available, usually on a bazaar day. As a ballboy he was virtually useless, because he was slow and couldn't throw the balls straight. He ambled around the back of the court working out what he was going to do next, but what he did have was the glorious name of Bhijli, which meant lightning or electricity. Anything less like lightning was hard to imagine, but because of his name, his 'little boy lost' appearance and winsome smile, all the Mem Sahibs felt they would like to mother him and we would accept abysmal service from him which we would never have tolerated from any of the other chokras. He must have made a real impact on us, because even now as Jan and I watch Wimbledon and see the extremely efficient ball boys and girls operating one of us says, 'Do you remember Bhijli on Chulsa? I wonder what happened to him?' Now I have included him in this story, his name will live for evermore.

The end of the cold weather also signalled the end of the cricket season in the Dooars. Most of the representative matches had been played by the time I reached India, but after playing in a couple of local club games I was selected to play in the last big match against the Darjeeling planters. This was played over the weekend of May 5th/6th and on the Friday morning, after having received special permission from our Superintendent to play, another member of our team named Dick Knights took me up in his car. The first part of the journey was the 50 miles back to Siliguri that I had covered on the day I had arrived, but from then on it was all new and wonderful. The first ten miles out of Siliguri ran alongside the narrow-gauge railway, almost dead straight towards the mountains dominating the northern horizon, but once the climb began it was like no journey I had ever made before. Because the road took the more direct route up the side of the mountain spur until it reached Tindarhia, it was crossed and re-crossed by the railway dozens of times as it took the less steep path. There were no level crossing gates or warnings that there could be a train across the road other than the shrill sound of its whistle, and all a driver could do was to take very great care whenever he heard the sound of a train, because by law the train always had the right of way. Naturally that made everyone extremely careful, especially when you saw the drop that awaited you if you went off the road.

Tindarhia was the home of the railway, for it was here that the engines and rolling stock were serviced and repaired, and where most of the operating staff had their homes. From Tindarhia the road zigzagged on up the mountainside, passing by waterfalls and streams thundering down ravines and the debris from the last landslides, until it reached the town of Kurseong about 30 miles from Siliguri.

At about 5000 feet above sea level Kurseong was a typical Nepalese hill village, and it was fascinating to see how the whole character of the people, the houses, and the landscape had changed from the plains of Bengal. From the road the view was absolutely magnificent, and I only wish I had the talent to describe it adequately, but from Kurseong up to the village of Ghum, at 7400 feet the highest part of the journey, the whole of the North Bengal plain was spread out below us. Rivers twisted and turned like glittering ribbons until they disappeared over the distant horizon, and thousand-acre tea estates and blocks of forest looked like accidental green smudges on an artist's canvas. I was absolutely spellbound at the wonder and beauty of the view, for I had never seen anything like it, but Dick had seen it all before and said, 'Wait until you get your first view of Kanchenjunga from the Ghum Saddle'

From Ghum the road began to descend to Darjeeling and about a mile out from the bazaar it ran round a corner and I got my first view of the town with the Kanchenjunga range in the sky beyond. It was absolutely breathtaking to see these magnificent mountains almost hanging in the sky, rather like a theatrical backdrop, with the town in the foreground clinging to the mountainside like a child's toy village. I was very fortunate that I saw the mountains like this on my first visit, because quite often they were obscured by mist and clouds, but whenever we made the journey afterwards we always looked for our first view of the snows with a sense of anticipation, and even if we only got a fleeting glimpse of them they never disappointed.

From Ghum it was all downhill and we finally rolled into Darjeeling in the late afternoon, having taken three hours to cover the 50 miles from Siliguri that the 'Toy train' normally takes about nine hours to complete. Arrangements had been made for us to stay with members of the Darjeeling Cricket Club, so after a very welcome cup of tea and sandwiches at the Planter's Club we followed our hosts home, where I saw some of the damage that had been caused by the landslides in 1950. This was the time that Bill had been marooned in Darjeeling, and one wing of the club had been completely carried away when the bank above it slipped down the slope in a mud slide. The people with whom I stayed had also suffered when part of their house had been carried away, and they had lost many of their belongings, but they had repaired the damage and now made me very welcome, especially when they realised that I was so new to tea. They only lived a few minutes' walk from the Mall, the main street in the town, but as we spent the next two days playing cricket I saw very little of Darjeeling itself, so I will describe my impressions of it later.

Because flat land was at a premium all the houses were built on small platforms carved out of the hillsides, and the only places where cricket or football could he played were on the recreation fields of the two Darjeeling Colleges, St. Joseph's and St. Paul's. These were situated considerably higher up than the town and had been levelled out of the crest of the ridge with great difficulty, so both were completely grassless with quick draining, sandy surfaces and high wire fences strung along the outer edge of the playing area to stop the balls disappearing into the wide blue yonder. The hillsides below them were so steep that a six hit over the boundary fence would fall down a couple of hundred feet before the ball hit the ground far below, probably resulting in a lost ball and possibly causing quite severe injuries if it hit someone. For cricket we played on a matting wicket and the flat, sandy surface was excellent for fielding, but when playing football it was almost impossible for us to tackle or fall on the abrasive surface without inflicting quite severe friction burns on ourselves, which made us rather careful. The other drawback at playing sport at 7500 feet was the rarefied atmosphere, which made us pant and gasp for breath if we broke into anything more than a dignified trot. Not being used to it, running for any length of time was completely out of the question for us, and several years later when I played football at 8400 feet on the St. Paul's ground I could hardly get my breath at all. At the end of the match my throat and lungs were sore. Because the Darjeeling planters were used to it they gave us quite a beating, but we always got our own back when they came down and played us in the middle of the monsoon, because they weren't able to cope with the long grass, temperatures in the nineties and a humidity of over 90 per cent.

I would like to be able to record that we won the match that weekend, but my records show that it was only the rain that saved us, because they scored 294, while we made 157 and 40 for four wickets before rain stopped play. This was mainly due to an innings of 164 by one of the Emmett brothers, Bill I think, who was the manager of an estate near Darjeeling. There were several of them from a well-known West Country family, some of whom had played for Gloucestershire, and as they were all excellent cricketers Bill was no exception. For a long time we could do very little with him and he hit our bowlers all over the field with gay abandon, which was a delight to see but horrible to field against. However the wire netting defences did their work, and even he was unable to clear them in order to send one down over the side of the *khud* (hill side).

The rain which stopped the match had also brought very low-lying thick cloud, so after tea we decided to start for home as soon as possible and it was a good thing that we did, as the 40 miles from Darjeeling down to the plains were shrouded in a thick blanket of fog. We didn't have to worry about the trains as they didn't normally run after dark, but with the twists and turns in the road, no cat's eyes or white road markings and visibility at about 10 yards, the journey was horrendous. On several stretches where the edges of the road had been damaged by landslides, I had to walk along in front of Dick to show him where the road was. What should have been a pleasant three-hour roll down out of the hills, with the lights of the plains sparkling below us, turned into a five-hour torture trip where we peered into the fog trying to keep the car on the road. This was my first experience of the road from Darjeeling and one which I never forgot, but it was also one I was to repeat many times in the years ahead.

CHAPTER TWELVE

Prelude to the rains

When India and Ceylon gained self-government in the late 1940s, they followed different policies regarding the futures of their tea estates. In Ceylon all the foreign-owned companies were nationalised, and after their former owners had been compensated they were sold to new Sinhalese owners. Many of these were financiers pure and simple, who knew very little about the tea industry but did know a lot about asset stripping and making quick profits, so labour forces were reduced and unessential works such as cultivation, replanting and manuring were kept to a minimum. Shade trees were cut down and sold as firewood, leaf quality was sacrificed so that larger crops of inferior tea were produced and then sold locally, and all methods of cutting costs and maximizing profits were used. This went on for several years until the labourers started agitating and the Sri Lankan government realised that if things continued in this manner for very much longer, the island's tea industry would be only a memory and had to legislate to bring order to the chaos.

Because the Indian tea industry was run mainly by companies based in London who sold the bulk of their tea in

Mincing Lane, thus bringing in large sums of much needed 'hard' currencies, the Indian Government decided to adopt a much more 'softly, softly' approach to the problem. When any small privately-owned estates were disposed of they were sold to new Indian owners, but other than having to obey some new regulations regarding finance, labour welfare and trades unions which were brought in, the large tea companies were allowed to continue to operate more or less as normal. However in order to bring in a gradual 'Indianisation' of the industry, in the 1950s the companies were instructed that for every new European assistant who was recruited they had to recruit two Indian ones. Ultimately this scheme worked so successfully that by the end of the 1970s there were hardly any Europeans left in tea.

The main drawback to this plan, which delayed things and which was unforeseen at the time, was that in order to be capable of doing the work it was essential that the applicant had a top-class education. In reality there was no shortage of these, but the trouble was that most of them were university graduates from quite prosperous families who had been used to the bright lights and city life all their lives. Coming to live and work in tea, with its practical work, long hours, often quite primitive living conditions and lack of conventional entertainment often proved to be so much of a culture shock to some of them that they were unable to settle down, and many left after completing their first contract. This meant that the handover did not proceed quite as swiftly as had been planned, but the Indian lads who did stay were excellent, and it is to their credit that the transfer to Indian management was finally completed with the minimum of fuss and animosity.

On our estates, provided a profit was made in any year, an

allocation was made in the following year's financial estimates for labour, welfare and entertainment. While some of this was used for garden projects which benefited the labour force as a whole, there was always some cash set aside for general entertainment for them to use as they wished. Magic shows, circuses and traditional dance troupes were always popular, and on Zurrantee, because of Bill's excellent relationship with the labourers, he often paid for these shows out of his own pocket as a personal 'thank you' to them. As a result of this, at the end of the cold weather we had two of these shows within a month, both of which were entertaining in their own way.

At the end of April we had a visit from a travelling Chinese circus which gave a three-hour show one evening on the football field. They carried all their equipment, which included a couple of almost fully-grown leopard cubs and some horses in three old ex-US Army lorries, and because they only performed during the cold weather when there was no rain, they lived and slept in the open air beneath the trucks. They arrived in the morning and then spent the rest of the day setting up their ring in the middle of a dense crowd of onlookers, which must have been quite a problem.

The ring was made from a rough circle of wooden benches with a steel wire six feet off the ground stretched between two posts diagonally across it, and the fifteen performers had a small tent in which to change. That night Bill picked us up in the Jag at 7 pm and we arrived to find that there were basket chairs waiting for us and the show was ready to start. Most of the men were superb athletes, acrobats and jugglers, but the three girls were not so skilled and the show opened with one of them who must have been learning the trade, because she tried to balance on a roller board mounted on a table while she attempted to juggle with plates and balls which she kept dropping. Despite her best efforts she was not very successful, and when she finally fell off the table she gave up and ran off in tears. She was followed by the other two, who kept falling off the tightrope, and soon they too decided that enough was enough and disappeared into the tent as well. However the men were all excellent athletes and whole sections of the show consisted of them doing tricks while balancing on roller boards and the wire, which were much better than many I had seen at home. There was also a knife thrower who was good enough to pierce the ace of spades on a playing card at a distance of 12 feet. He was followed by a trick cyclist, who was very skilful on his smaller cycles, but once he started to ride his seven-foot high unicycle he was in trouble. The football field had quite a steep slope on it, and as it became very heavy with dew at that time of the evening it made the grass very slippery, so each time he attempted to circle the ring, the moment he reached the slippery area at the bottom his wheel would slip sideways and he would have to leap off. Nevertheless he was very game. He made four attempts to go round 'Tattenham Corner' as we laughingly named it, but on his fourth attempt he dived headlong into the crowd, and was so shaken that he too decided to call it a day, and he limped off accompanied by wild applause from the labourers. We couldn't really decide whether they really appreciated his efforts, or whether they were just happy that he had finished.

The two things the labourers really did enjoy were some performing horses which chased two clowns around the ring and gradually tore their clothes off, and as a grand finale two leopards which played with a girl just like a couple of cats. After the show we went round to see them, and the owner told us that they had been caught in Bhutan when they were very small cubs and their mother had been killed. Later he had bought them and his wife had brought them up as pets, so as a result she was able to do virtually anything with them. However, now that they were almost fully grown they were getting to be a bit unreliable with other people, so they had decided very reluctantly to send them to a circus in Europe, our show being one of the last that she would be doing with them. It was obvious that she was very attached to them and extremely sorry that she was going to have to let them go. The feedback from the labourers on the work melas the next morning was that they had enjoyed it immensely, and the clowns and the horses that had chased them made such a lasting impression on them that they were talked about for weeks afterwards.

On the other hand, Major Massey's Mammoth Circus, which visited us a month later, was a very different kettle of fish, because the owner, 'Major' Massey, was a very strange character indeed, as it seems that he told different stories about himself on each estate he visited. When John Mitchell chanced to meet him in Matelli Bazaar, he told him he had been an officer in the Royal Canadian Mounted Police, while John Adams was told that he had been in the Bombay Police. When Bill and I met him on the afternoon of the show, he regaled us with a story of how he had been in the American Texas Rangers and had chased outlaws down on the Mexican border. As he spoke with a Western or Canadian drawl this sounded quite authentic, but as we knew that his title varied between Major, Colonel and Captain depending on where he was, nothing seemed to be quite as it should be, and his circus was no exception. Whereas the Chinese circus had been purely professional and slickly produced, Major Massey's outfit was one of the funniest for unintentional laughs that I have ever seen. When they were organizing the ring in the afternoon he asked for a bench for the 'band' to sit on, and this turned out to be a drummer and a battered old man trying to strangle a battered old cornet which he played completely out of tune. Their ring was made out of old wooden benches and the performers used a small tent similar to the Chinese to change in, but they had a cracked bell which tinkled to announce the entrance of each new turn. It appeared that the circus was a very personal 'family' affair, with the Major being the star turn, supported by his son dressed as a western cowboy, who tried to do fire-eating and tricks with knives, revolvers and a lasso. The son's wife, who was dressed as an American Indian squaw, who did gymnastics and contortions, and the old man who tortured the cornet also appeared to be a relative. Unfortunately the son was absolutely awful, as he dropped his knives on several occasions and got his feet caught up in the lasso until he was booed from the ring. The girl stood as a target for the Major to throw knives at her while he was blindfolded, and he was very good at it until he threw a murderous looking flaming knife too near to her costume and she almost went up in flames, much to the audience's amusement.

One good thing was that he was an excellent shot with both a rifle and revolvers. He shot a candle out with a rifle through a ring which I held on top of a man's head with my thumb and forefinger, and he also shot out two candles simultaneously, one on each side of a man's head with his pistols while lying on his back. Unfortunately the skill needed to do this was lost on the labourers, who much preferred to see some clowns being chased by a horse. Long before he had finished they began to leave, and the show was brought to an abrupt end by the arrival of an absolutely torrential rainstorm which drenched everyone.

When we talked about it with the labourers the next morning it was evident that they enjoyed 'slapstick' comedy and action entertainment much more than they did skill, and they thought that it was so bad that Bill should not pay him. However the Major did get his money, because Bill said that at least they had tried, but the labourers talked in the bazaar afterwards and it seems that the bad publicity got around so much that they got very few subsequent bookings. In fact although we did see the Chinese circus for several years after that, to the best of my knowledge the Major's circus never visited Chulsa district again.

All these shows and the festival entertainments took place on the football field, a large patch of flat grazing land west of the factory. As no rain had fallen since the previous October, the ground was parched and the grass was burnt to a short, crisp mat, but after we got our first rain in March it all started to shoot, and in next to no time there was a carpet of fresh, new grass, ideal as a playing surface. It was kept nice and short by an army of small goats which nibbled away at it each day.

Football was extremely popular on most of the estates and each evening after work, from about 5 pm until it got dark at 6.15, a very energetic game took place with everybody playing, often 17 or 18 players a side. In these games everybody seemed to run after the ball like a pack of hounds chasing a fox, and although very few of them had boots and played with their bare feet, they were able to hit the ball with surprising force. Once we were able to separate the proper footballers from the chasers, a couple of times a week I selected two teams and proper games were played in order to prepare them for the inter-garden matches which started once the monsoon came.

I really enjoyed these. I was never a really fast mover, and in those days 'stepovers' and other crafty tricks which are commonplace nowadays were almost nonexistent, but we played a kind of direct, hard football with the one aim of scoring goals, and this was the one thing I could do well. Before going to India I played for Coaley Rovers for three seasons, and we broke the Stroud League record for the fastest first 100 goals to be scored in a season when we completed it on January 15th.

The clerical staff usually organised the matches with other estate teams, and once the rains came and the ground softened we played most weeks. Work on the plucking areas finished promptly at 3 pm and everyone hurried in to the factory to get the leaf weighed. This took about 45 minutes, and then if we were playing away about 150 of our supporters would cram into the backs of our two lorries and the tractor trailer and off we would go. Chulsa district was a very compact area and most of the estates were only two or three miles apart, so usually the journey did not take too long and we were usually playing by 4 pm, so it was possible to get in a full match provided it wasn't raining too hard. Bill Milne was an excellent goalkeeper, but the back injury he had suffered in Burma during the war caused him a lot of pain, so our tractor driver, Somra, the lad who had taught me to drive, was our regular goalkeeper. In addition to being a first-class goalie, he was a very good-natured lad from the Uraon tribe in the state of Bihar and was well built and very fit. However, one evening we were on opposite sides in a practice match, and as a bouncing ball came to me in the penalty area, I hit it on the turn for what I think was the best shot I have ever struck. It went like a rocket and as he was unable to move out of the way, he stuck out his hands in desperation and parried it over the bar before collapsing in a heap clutching his forearm. Luckily the Doctor Babu lived nearby, and he quickly diagnosed that he had badly cracked the bones in his forearm, which meant he was unable to drive the tractor or play football for several weeks. I still have a photograph of him accompanied by his wife and daughter, with his arm in a grubby sling and a smile all over his face.

Because the post of Clerk on the estates was an excellent job and very sought after, vacancies were very often filled by the relatives or acquaintances of Babus who were already working for the company and had a good record. Many of our clerks originated from a small town named Makliganj, which was on the bank of the Teesta river a few miles south of Jalpaiguri. The town had quite a good football team which was entered in the local football tournament, and hearing of my goal-scoring prowess, the Head Clerk asked Bill whether he would allow me to travel to Makliganj to play for them in the competition as a guest player. He was very pleased that I had been invited so I went, and I would like to record that I scored several goals for them and covered myself in glory, but unfortunately it was not to be. The kind of football they played just did not gel with my style, and although I did score one goal, most of the time I floundered round like a fish out of water and we lost 3–1.

The one thing that I do remember with real affection was the absolutely superb curry they had prepared for me when I arrived and the sweet afterwards. When I had finished the curry I was asked if I would like a sugar sandwich, and never having come across this before I said yes. You can imagine my surprise when I was given a slice of bread with butter on both sides and then dipped in sugar on both sides, a sugar sandwich, which was rather crunchy to eat and which I can safely say that I have never had since.

The one thing the football was not allowed to interfere with was the Wednesday afternoon shoot over in the Naura forest, which continued until the monsoon arrived at the end of May. Most weeks Bill came as well, and on these occasions I used his spare rifle, but when he was absent I used a bow and arrows which Lopo, the Chief Engineer in the factory, had made for me. He was a Santal from the country west of Calcutta, and he was the one who had looked at the 'clack pump' with me when I arrived. As I had been hunting with them I think he took a bit of a shine to me, and one day he arrived with a beautiful bow and five hunting arrows which he had made for me as a gift and would take nothing for them. It is one of my regrets that I didn't bring them back with me when I retired from tea.

I had always messed about with bows and arrows when I was a boy, and it wasn't very long before I became quite proficient with them. I practised regularly in the compound trying to hit a small cardboard box, and on the day I managed to put an arrow into a barking deer in the forest I don't know who was the most pleased, Lopo or myself. Unfortunately this was the only thing I ever hit while out shooting as I bought a rifle for myself before the next cold weather, but I did use it later on during my time in tea for a very different purpose, and I shall always remember that bow with affection.

It was at this time that I saw my first live tiger (other than the ones that had been shot) close up in the wild by myself. It had been reported to Bill that a buffalo had been killed by a large tiger while it was grazing on the edge of the forest on the other side of the Naura river, and as this represented a considerable loss to the owner Bill was asked if he would go and try to shoot it. Tigers in the wild are normally nocturnal creatures, and do most of their hunting at night while roaming over vast tracts of territory, travelling as much as 30 miles at a time and hoping to bag a wild pig or deer. Then during the day they normally lie up and sleep until the late afternoon, when they rouse and move on again looking for food, so in most instances cattle that grazed in the forest until mid-afternoon and were then herded back to the labour lines were usually safe, but this one was unlucky. The cost of a buffalo was in the region of 400 rupees, which represented several months' wages, and as there was no insurance its loss was a severe blow to the owner.

When the owner explained what had happened Bill listened intently, but as he was a true sportsman he did not like killing any of the big cats unless it was absolutely necessary, and as he felt that it was partly the owner's own fault for having let the buffalo roam in the forest anyway, he told him that as he was busy elsewhere he would be unable to do anything about it. He did suggest that it would be an excellent bit of experience for me to sit up and see it even if nothing else happened, and said he would lend me his rifle 'just in case', although I was not to shoot at it at all unless I had a clear side view of it which would enable me to kill it with one shot. If I didn't get this I was to leave it alone. He also said that if the tiger was coming back to feed it should reappear at about sundown, so at 3.30 pm after the leaf had been weighed, I dressed in long trousers with the legs tucked into my socks, and a long sleeved shirt and a cloth cap to protect me from the mossies, and then walked down to the forest with the owner and three of his friends. The buffalo was lying on the edge of a small clearing surrounded by low bushes and some small trees, so the men cut some bamboos and made a small platform which they lashed onto the branches of one of them about 10 feet off the ground for me to sit on. Then I scrambled up onto my seat and they handed up my rifle and torch and walked off back to their homes, leaving me to the sounds of the forest.

Bill had told me that the secret of sitting up over a kill was to sit absolutely still and keep all unnecessary noise and movement to an absolute minimum, because the big cats moved absolutely silently and you could never tell whether the animal was 12 miles or 12 feet away, so it could quite possibly be watching you from the shadow of the jungle. It was about 4.45 pm and I had another hour to wait for sunset, so I sat back against the trunk of the tree and tried to wait without moving. The mosquitoes hummed and whined around me, but I resisted moving to slap them and tried to identify the calls of the various animals and birds as I waited. I had a clear view of the kill about 15 feet away, but as I watched I noticed a small movement in the adjacent tree from the corner of my eye and was petrified as I realised that I could see a green tree snake about 10 feet long with a one inch thick body coming to visit me. It looked like a very long piece of green rope as it moved very smoothly through the branches, In all probability it was hunting for small birds or lizards amongst the branches, so I remained motionless as it passed by about five feet away without it taking the slightest bit of notice of me and finally melted away into the next tree, much to my relief. This shook me up, but it had been a real experience for me even if the tiger didn't come.

As the minutes ticked away the jungle creatures became more and more vociferous as the sun dipped towards the tops of the trees, but then I was suddenly aware that all the noise had stopped and the forest was strangely silent for several minutes, until a troop of monkeys began chattering and a deer barked twice before it became silent again. The light was still good in the clearing, but then as I gazed at the kill I realised that a magnificent gold and black head and shoulders had silently materialised from the bushes behind it, and I knew that I was looking at a ten-foot-long tiger about 20 feet away.

With a small frisson of fear I also realised that as my machan was only about ten feet up off the ground, it could rear up on its hind legs and get to me with no difficulty at all if it so wished, so I stayed motionless and hardly breathed at all as I gazed at it in all its wild beauty. I think it must have realised I was there, because it stood and looked straight up at me for what seemed an age, though it was probably only about 30 seconds. Then completely undisturbed, as though it had decided that, although the machan hadn't been there when it killed the buffalo it was nothing to worry about, it walked forward to the buffalo, bent over and got a good grip in the centre of its backbone with its jaws. It lifted its head and dragged the 300-pound carcass straight out of the clearing and into the jungle out of my sight.

I was absolutely amazed with what had happened. It was so beautiful and majestic that I had forgotten all about trying to shoot it, so I sat up in my tree as darkness fell and listened to it tearing its supper apart while I thought what a superb creature it was and what a wonderful sight it had been. As it ate it made all sorts of grunts and satisfying noises, and as I didn't want to be part of its supper I stayed in the tree for a couple of hours until all was silent and I was reasonably sure that it had gone on its merry way before I scrambled down and walked home after a truly memorable experience.

It was experiences like that that brought home to me just how fortunate and privileged I had been to be selected to work in India. They also helped me to cope with the periodic attacks of homesickness which I experienced during my first year.

I had felt very sad and despondent when I boarded the *Strathaird* at Tilbury and also a bit lonely at times during the passage, but once I reached Bombay and the adventure of a new life I didn't feel very homesick, although at times I did have some 'blue' periods when I thought of Jan, Mum and the things I had left behind me, especially when the *dakwalla* (post carrier) brought letters from home. Every day was so filled to the brim with new and exciting things that I rarely had time to mope and feel I was homesick. In fact it wasn't until the beginning of May that I experienced my first tinge of regret when I remembered that the next Saturday was Cup Final Day at Wembley, and for some reason I felt terribly sad.

Then Ian said he was going to the club to see the film that evening and gave me permission to use his radio, so as it began at 3 pm British time, at 8 pm I went into his bedroom and tuned in. It was on the Overseas Service of the BBC on the short wave, and the reception was terrible owing to terrific electrical storms in the Himalayas, but as the set hissed and crackled with static I sat entranced as the crowd sang 'Abide with me', which brought tears to my eyes. Then I settled down to hear Newcastle beat Blackpool 2-0 with two goals by Jackie Milburn and enjoyed every minute of it. In retrospect it was just a small thing at the time, but it put my world to rights and afterwards life didn't seem to be so bad for a while.

My next incident like that was six months later, when I heard the remembrance service and march past from the Cenotaph at 11 am on Armistice Sunday in London. This corresponded to 4.30 pm in India, and the setting sun was a crimson ball in a golden haze as it sank behind the trees in the Naura forest and Big Ben struck the hour to start the two-minute silence that made me think of home. As I listened to the music and the description of the march past, it all seemed to be more poignant to me than it had when Dad had listened to it on his old wireless, so I was very sad for the rest of the evening, but fortunately these feelings of self pity didn't last very long and the next day I was back to my old self once again.

CHAPTER THIRTEEN

And the rains came…

Earlier in my story I recorded that although I had brought my trombone with me to India, because I had been fitted with a dental plate after a football accident I was unable to play it properly and only did so on only one more occasion at the end of the cold weather.

Our bungalow was built on a small hill about half a mile from the factory, and the main road to the top garden wound around its base. Normally it was very quiet and the labourers didn't make a lot of noise. The main exception to this was in the evening after a pay day, when many of them who lived near the factory visited a labour line in the top garden which was occupied by Nepalese families, many of which specialised in making haria and darhu, the wicked spirit that was distilled from fermented millet seeds, the same grain that we feed to our budgerigars. There was a Government ban on the making of unlicensed, illicit darhu, but we turned a blind eye to it as we knew that the hooch that was brewed in the top garden was a lot cleaner and more wholesome than the contaminated rubbish that was sold in the liquor shop in Batabari bazaar. This was sometimes adulterated with ethylene glycol and other noxious chemicals by some of the more dubious suppliers, and in the past had been the cause of several fatalities, so Bill thought that if they were intent on drinking, it was better for them to do it where we could keep an eye on them rather than in the bazaar.

Consequently every month after receiving their pay, some twenty or thirty factory men would walk up to the top garden and then get tanked up until they were really merry and had to walk back home. We hardly ever heard them walking up there, but going home at midnight was a very different matter as many of them were quite afraid of the dark, and they plucked up Dutch courage by yelling, whistling and making a hell of a din all the way back to the factory. After one particularly noisy night I spoke to Lopo, who confessed that he was one of the culprits, and when I asked him why they made so much noise he said that it was to drive away the evil spirits that were abroad at night and also to frighten any leopards and tigers that might be wanting to eat them. I told him that if a tiger really wanted to eat them, in my opinion it would be attracted to them by the noise instead of being frightened away, and after thinking about it he agreed that this was probably so and would ensure that there would be no more noise. Well as we know, talk is cheap, and I took that promise with a pinch of salt.

It so happened that on the next pay day we had invited some friends over for drinks and an evening meal, and at 11.45 pm we were still sitting and talking when the inebriated gang started their noisy ramble home. We could hear them from a half a mile away and one of our friends said 'Do you always have to put up with that noise? Can't you do anything about it?'.

Suddenly I had an idea. Rushing into the bedroom, I grabbed my trombone from its case, then ran for 200 yards down a path through the tea until I reached the edge of a steep, 12 foot-high bank which bordered the road and waited for them to come. After 10 minutes or so I heard them coming round the corner about 100 yards away, so I lay down on my back in the tea with my feet resting on a tea bush and the trombone pointing into the air. After a few minutes they reached my spot, and without showing myself I kicked the tea bushes with both feet making them shake violently, and at the same time blew several rasping calls on the trombone. For a moment everyone stopped and there was a deathly hush, then pandemonium reigned as they shouted 'Tiger! Tiger!' at the tops of their voices and then rushed headlong down the road to the lines as though all the hounds of hell were after them.

When I got back everyone thought it was great fun and John said, 'Well, that's that. Probably that was the last we will hear of them' and we all agreed, so first thing on Monday morning I called Lopo over to the office and asked him what all the commotion was up by our bungalow on Saturday night. 'Oh Sahib' he said, 'You were quite right. We were chased by a monstrous tiger and we were nearly killed.' When I asked him if he had actually seen it he grinned and rolled his eyes and said 'Oh yes Sahib, we did. It was this big', and with his hand he indicated that it was about three feet high at the shoulder 'and it had flashing red eyes and a great gaping mouth and it chased us all the way to the factory, so we've all decided that we are never going up there to drink again.'

Well this sounded too good to be true and actually it was, because the very next pay day they were up there again making as much noise as usual, just as though they had never seen this monstrous, man-eating tiger, so I didn't win after all, but I never did think that my trombone playing was much good anyway. Maybe if I had played them a bit of 'Tiger Rag' it might have had more effect.

In the previous chapter I described how I had one or two blue days during my first few months in Zurrantee, and in retrospect I think that not having any transport of my own by which I could get out and about a bit under my own steam had a lot to do with it. The estates were widely scattered all over Chulsa district and the club was four miles away, so I was completely dependent on someone to give me a lift wherever I went. Normally when Ian and John were in the bungalow everything was fine as I had someone to converse with in English, and Ian normally took us to Mal Club to the cinema on a Saturday night in his Jeep. However Sunday, which was our day off, was a different matter, because at those times he tended to go out by himself to see his own friends, and John, being the son of a Company Director, was usually invited out at weekends, which meant I was in the bungalow by myself all day. I could have gone down to the club with Bill when he went down to play golf, but he usually stayed on drinking and yarning with his pals and came home late, and as I had never drunk very much alcohol and didn't play golf either, I found it was better for me to stay at home and write letters or learn Hindi.

Martin Hawes, the Superintendent's Accountant, lived on Sam Sing, and always tried to help the new assistants until they could find their feet, so he would always take me to the film at Nagrakata Club on a Sunday evening if I asked him, but when the other two were out Sunday was usually a long, lonely day.

It was not always like this though, because sometimes I had a visit from some of the other assistants in our company to see how I was getting on. One Sunday afternoon a car climbed up the hill and turned into the bungalow compound in a cloud of dust. In it were 'Wee' Mackenzie, Pete Barr and two more of our assistants, and they said that as they were going into Siliguri bazaar for a Chinese meal would I like to go with them? Well I had never had Chinese food and had no idea of what to expect, but I was so overjoyed to see them that I grabbed my money, jumped into the car and off we went in another cloud of dust. The journey into Siliguri took about an hour, and the Chinese restaurant turned out to be a large timber building built on thick log piles about 12 feet high on the other side of the main roadside drain, with the Chinaman's goats, pigs, ducks and chickens all living beneath it. A flight of wooden steps took us up into the living accommodation, where we were greeted by the Chinaman and his wife. As there only seemed to be the two of them, presumably the husband was the waiter and looked after the guests while his wife prepared the meal. On the tea estates all the Chinese carpenters were known as John the Chinaman, presumably because their own proper names were too complicated to remember, and even the labourers knew who John was. Very courteously he conducted us into the dining room and seated us at a large oval table, and then after serving our drinks came to take our orders. Pete Barr was the first to order, and knowing that many Chinese and Japanese have trouble in pronouncing the Western letter 'R' which they pronounce as an 'L,' he decided to have a bit of fun with the Chinaman and said, 'Well John, I think I will have Plawn Cully and Flied Lice please.' Then to our absolute amazement, from being a small, quiet man John went absolutely ballistic. He must have been having a bad hair day or something, because he brought his hand down on the table with a tremendous smack and shouted, 'You no make fun of John. If you in my countly I kill you. You no say 'PLAWN

CULLY AND FLIED LICE!" His voice dropped. "You must say, Plawn Cully and Flied Lice.'

At that Pete smiled engagingly at him and said, 'Oh, so solly John. In that case I will have Plawn Cully and Flied Lice.'

'Yes. That bettel' said John, and without turning a hair he got on with taking the orders and we finally finished up with a lovely meal. I am unable to recall what dishes we had, but it was an absolutely magnificent repast of authentic Cantonese food cooked by someone who had been doing it all her life, and as it was some of the best Chinese food I have ever tasted I have loved it ever since.

Once we got our first rain in March with regular storms afterwards, I was quite surprised how quickly the leaf grew once the temperatures rose. On May 19th we plucked in earnest for the first time for which all the women were used, and a total of 9020 lbs of green leaf was gathered, which was manufactured into about 2000 lbs of black tea. During the previous month we had had a succession of electrical and hail storms with temperatures in the upper eighties, and it was to our great relief when we got the downpour we danced in on May 25th, followed by a 'storm' which delivered two inches of rain in two hours the next day. I was absolutely amazed at the quantity and power of the deluge as it fell, for large spots of water as big as small grapes hammered down into the standing puddles on the ground and sent up splashes six inches high. Having seen it all before Bill was quite amused at my surprise and said, 'You think this is bad. Just wait until we get some proper monsoon rain and that will really open your eyes'. I thought he was pulling my leg until we reached the middle of the rains, when it was commonplace for 12 inches of rain to fall over a 24 hour period. That was real rain, but there again it did not compare with the rain which fell on Cherrapunji in Assam in July 1861, when 366 inches of rain fell during the month, giving it the highest recorded rainfall on earth. That must have been something to experience.

The advent of the rains brought the three things which I hated most about the wildlife in India, and these were leeches, mimosas and batchikeras. Once we had daily rain with temperatures in the upper eighties and a humidity to match, several species of leeches appeared as if from nowhere and lay in wait on the undergrowth or bushes alongside the paths for any warm-blooded creatures to pass by. The tiger leeches got their name because they had black and yellow stripes all along the length of their bodies, and as their prey passed by they would stretch out and attach themselves by their mouth suckers to the skin, usually quite unnoticed, and then get to work. So that it wouldn't hurt the victim the leech would exude a local anaesthetic which numbed the spot, then after using small rasp-like teeth to perforate the skin it would inject an anti-coagulant to stop the blood from clotting and then drink its fill. This could be quite a long business and often went on for a couple of hours if the leech was not spotted, but finally, once it was completely bloated and swollen with blood, it would detach itself from its host and very slowly make its way to some damp refuge where it could digest its meal. A hungry tiger leech was about two inches long and as thick as a drinking straw, whereas a fully bloated one was only just over an inch long and about a half an inch in diameter. Once a leech was firmly attached to the skin it was very difficult to remove because it was very slippery to grip and stretched like rubber, so they had to be persuaded to detach themselves either by burning them with the lighted end of a cigarette, or by rubbing them with either tobacco or salt. As I didn't smoke and it was very difficult to keep salt dry, I experimented a little and found that they didn't like neat Dettol either, so most mornings I rubbed my legs all over with it before I went out into the tea and also carried a small bottle with me for topping up the coating when required. This seemed to do the trick as they tended to avoid me. Probably they didn't like its bitter taste.

The main trouble with them was that once the leech had been removed, because of the anti-coagulant the wound would not stop bleeding for a couple of hours, and sometimes my socks were a horrible mess. I never found out where they lived during the cold weather because they had to have moisture on their skins to survive, so presumably they must have overwintered in the soil either as eggs or young because we never came across a winter nest of adults. Once the rains came though there they were, and on several occasions I saw a bush further along the path that looked as though it was cloaked in a shimmering greyish brown mass, and I realised that it was covered with thousands of common brown leeches all twisting and turning and waiting for me to pass by. Naturally there was nothing I could do about them, so I just played chicken and avoided them as much as possible.

One that did give me a bit of a shock craftily attached itself to me while I was playing football one Sunday afternoon and as I didn't feel it at all, after the game I went back to the bungalow, had a bath and dinner and then went to bed at about 10 pm where I fell into a sound sleep almost immediately. All this time the leech had fixed itself firmly up in my groin and it sucked away there to its heart's content. As long as it stayed there it was nice and moist and must have enjoyed itself, but once it was fully bloated it detached itself and began an attempt to leave the bed by looping itself over the sheets. Unfortunately these were hot and dry, a lethal combination for a leech, and as it wandered about the bed looking for a way out it gradually dried out until finally it reached the stage where it was forced to expel the blood it was carrying. Goodness knows how much it had taken from me, because when I woke up in the morning it looked as though a murder had been committed during the night. The sheets were covered with blood trails and large circular bloodstains where it had rested during its wanderings until it had finally died. When I first saw the bloody mess I was quite worried, because not knowing where the blood had come from I thought I was bleeding to death for some reason. Then I looked around and found the culprit lying near the bottom of the bed, all limp and shrivelled up. I sighed with relief and wasn't sorry at all, although it took me ages to find out where it had bitten me.

Another kind of leech which didn't affect us directly but which I really disliked was what we called the buffalo leech. These were very large, about four inches long, and they would wait on the vegetation at the sides of the drinking pools until a buffalo came down to drink. As it did so the leech would reach out and attach itself to it and then make its way up into its nostril where it would settle down and suck contentedly. Of course this interfered with the buffalo's breathing, especially if it had one up each nostril, but there was nothing it could do until it had gorged itself, when it came out by itself or the buffalo snorted it out. Still if I ever saw one and was able to catch it I made certain that it would never drink buffalo blood again.

The second pet hate of mine was a type of mimosa, or sensitive plant. The cultivated variety is a useful ground cover plant with a low, spreading habit, tough stalks, small, dusky pink, ball-shaped flowers and like other sensitive plants, when their leaves are touched they fold in on themselves. Although its cousin that grew wild in India was very similar to this, in addition its stalks were equipped with very hard hooked thorns with wicked points which inflicted deep scratches on the legs of anyone that got tangled up in it. Normally a scratch of this size would have been a bit painful but nothing to worry about, rather like a bramble scratch, but these thorns had a chemical poison on them which usually caused the scratches to go septic and prevented them from healing for several weeks, so when they finally did they would leave white wheal marks all across the skin, even on the labourer's brown legs. Because these plants grew very quickly beneath the tea bushes, I often walked into one of them before I realised it and got scratched, and during my first few weeks my legs suffered badly. Then I discovered that once I began to rub them with neat Dettol against the leeches I found out that it also worked against the mimosa poison. Although I still got scratched, the wounds did not go septic and soon healed, so I got a double benefit from my bottle of disinfectant. In fact I think I must have been one of the firm's best customers in those days.

The third of my pet hates was not quite as commonplace as the previous two, but was still noteworthy in its own way. The *batchikera* was the name given by the labourers to any one of a whole family of small, flat, stinging insects which lived beneath the mature leaves on tea bushes. I never discovered their true scientific name, but they were normally very flat and oval in shape, coloured very tastefully in various shades of mottled green and brown, and were equipped with what seemed like hundreds of small stinging hairs or fibres which inflicted a very painful wheal or burn the moment they brushed against the skin. There was never any warning, and when pushing my way through the bushes in a tee shirt and shorts while checking the work I must have passed by thousands without knowing, but when I did get stung it felt as though I had been scalded with boiling water. The affected skin would swell up in seconds once the poison took effect, and with an immediate reaction like this it was very easy to examine the adjacent bushes to find the culprit and then tear off the leaf and throw it away. Before I did so I usually examined it closely because they were all very delicately marked and little jewels of nature's art in their own way, but I am glad we do not have them over here. Here again the effect of the poison took a day or so for the swelling to subside and the pain to ease, but unfortunately my little bottle of Dettol was useless against these little jiggers, so I just had to avoid them whenever possible.

The other thing that made a lasting impression when I came across it in 1951 was rabies. This terrible disease is permanently established in India, but for some reason it seems to disappear in the cold weather, only to reappear as soon as the hot, wet weather comes. Possibly the virus which causes it cannot stand the cold, because although it is quite common in European countries as far north as France, Germany and Poland, it seems to be almost non-existent in Norway and Sweden. It was common in Britain until 1902, when steps were taken to eradicate it by shutting up all dogs and pets for a period while infected wildlife was systematically culled, and luckily for us it has never re-established itself. However Zurrantee in 1951 was not so fortunate.

Rabies, or hydrophobia as it is known in humans, is a viral disease of the central nervous system which can afflict all warm-blooded creatures. It is usually transmitted by a bite from an infected animal, and is almost invariably fatal once the symptoms have shown themselves after an incubation period which can vary from as little as ten days up to several months. Death is usual within five days from the onset of the symptoms, which result in the victim developing a terrifying fear of water and an agonizing death. In 1951 the only thing that could save a person who had been bitten by a rabid animal was a course of rabies vaccine and anti-serum as soon after the bite as possible. In the 50 years that have elapsed since then medicine has made tremendous strides and modern techniques may not be so painful, but in those days it was a terrible affair and absolutely dreaded by everybody. The course consisted of 21 very large and very painful daily injections which were injected into the patient's abdomen in a circular pattern that resulted in very large, painful swellings, and although the first seven were not too bad as they were injected in a circle into unbruised flesh and the second week's were also reasonable as they went into the gaps between the first seven, the third week's went into the bumps and swollen flesh made by the previous ones and by all accounts they really hurt.

Rabies vaccine and anti-serum were always kept in a refrigerator in the hospital, and if infection was suspected the treatment began immediately because everyone knew that delay could be fatal. In the meantime the suspect animal was killed and decapitated if possible and its head was sent down to the laboratories in Calcutta by post for its brain to be examined to see if it was rabid or not. The answer normally took a week or ten days to come back, so during that time the patient had a very worrying and exceedingly painful wait before he found whether he could stop the treatment, or whether he had another two weeks of purgatory to endure.

The disease was carried onto the estates by infected jackals which came out of the forests and tea at night to visit the labour lines to scavenge for food, and while doing so would fight with the unwanted line dogs which roamed free at night and thus pass on the infected saliva to them. To see a dying animal in the last throes of rabies was pitiful to behold, for they foamed at the mouth and roamed aimlessly around, shaking their heads and whining piteously. They snapped and bit at anything and everything that came in their way, including cats, dogs, goats, cows, horses and humans, and the only thing that brought them any relief was death.

Actually it was not essential to be bitten to be infected, because if a person had a cut, sore or an open wound on his body and he was licked by the infected animal and some of the saliva entered the wound, it was possible for the virus to enter his body without him knowing. A few years ago a local woman from Stroud went on a foreign holiday and developed rabies after she had returned. She said that although she had petted local stray dogs while she was on holiday, she was quite adamant that she had never been bitten by any of them, so the first thing she knew about it was when she began to feel sick. Unfortunately, although she was admitted to hospital, by then it was too late to save her and she died a few days later.

Luckily, neither Jan nor I ever needed to have this treatment, but I did come very close to it one day in 1957 when I was on Fagu Tea Estate. Our bungalow was on the hillside about 500 feet above the factory, and as I was walking home up a secluded path which was a short cut home I saw a dog running down the path. It had froth around its mouth and from the way it was staggering along and the sounds it was making I could see it was rabid, so when it suddenly altered direction and ran straight for me I realised I was in trouble. Luckily it was not a large dog, only about a year old, and I was holding a four-foot-long bamboo stave or *lathi,* which I always took with me when I was walking in the tea, so when it came within range and made a lunge for me I brought the lathi down on its neck just behind its head, and knocked it to its knees. As it lay there yelping and whining I felt really sorry for it and for a moment I considered giving it the benefit of the doubt and leaving it there, but then I realised that I would be condemning it to a slow and agonizing death and the best thing I could do would be to kill it, so I gave it several more thumps on the head and put it out of its misery. Although later on I shot many more infected and unwanted dogs in the labour lines in an effort to reduce the incidence of rabies, I think that beating that little fellow to death that day affected me the most.

Later on Jan became involved with rabies when we were living on Sam Sing after the young son of one of our friends had been in contact with a suspect dog. Although he had not actually been bitten, it was decided to kill the dog and send his head to Calcutta and then begin the boy's treatment 'just in case,' but once he had received his first jab he was absolutely terrified and as soon as he saw the Doctor Babu walking in through the compound gate each morning he went completely berserk, and his mum was so distressed that she was unable to hold him. As a result she asked Jan if she would do it for her, so each morning Jan would go down to the bungalow, sit him on her lap and clamp his two legs between hers, then hold him tightly around his upper body so that he was unable to move and the doctor could administer the injection. Naturally the lad was terrified and struggled violently to get away, and as he screamed all the time Jan absolutely hated it, so you can imagine how glad and relieved she was when the news finally came back from Calcutta that the dog had not been rabid and the treatment was stopped. Unfortunately it didn't help the dog at all.

The one humorous thing that did come out of this was that when the Doctor Babu came to give the dog the lethal injection so that its brain could be examined he was asked to give one to the cat as well, as it had always played with the dog and might have been infected accidentally. However as he tried to do this it was almost as though the cat sensed what was about to happen, and it bit, kicked and scratched the boy that was holding it so violently that he was forced to let it go and it shot out of the window, over the veranda rail and disappeared, inadvertently saving its own life. It was away for several weeks, and then one day long after it was found that the dog had not been rabid and need not have been put down, the cat walked in just as though it had never been away, so it must have used up several of its nine lives that day.

Lastly, the other two things that came in with the rains and left a lasting impression were two species of cuckoo that drove everybody mad. Unlike the European cuckoo, which calls intermittently, the Indian versions would sit in the top of a tree and call monotonously for minutes at a time. In the ornithological books they must have had proper names, but because of their calls they were known to us as the 'make more pekoe' bird and the 'brain fever' bird. Pekoe was the name given to a grade of tea, and the four notes of the pekoe bird's call sounded exactly as though it was singing the words 'make more pek-oe' to the first notes of the old popular song 'My heart belongs to daddy', but repeated over and over and over again without ever getting to the last part of the melody. This was extremely frustrating to listen to, and as the monotonous call went on and on, I always hoped that at some time one of them would actually finish the line, but it was never to be.

Bad as this was to listen to, it was nothing compared to the call of the brain fever bird. Its three-note call sounded exactly like 'brain fe-ver, brain fe-ver, brain fe-ver' repeated over and over again, but unlike the pekoe bird, instead of calling the same three notes continuously, it would start in a low key and then gradually work its way up the scale, going higher and higher until finally it could go no further, when it would drop back to the bottom and begin its vocal climb again. Lying in bed in the stifling heat and listening to it for hour after hour, wondering just how much higher it could go before starting again, strained the listener's nerves to breaking point, and it was enough to give anybody brain fever! Indeed they were two amazing little birds, but we were all very thankful when the monsoon ended and they cleared off to wherever they went to for their winter holidays.

CHAPTER FOURTEEN

Monsoon highlights

Most planters in India kept dogs partly for companionship and partly from the security angle, but because we had always had cats at home and I knew very little about dogs I was never a 'doggy' person. Then one day when I was chatting to Bill he sucked on his empty pipe, which was always a sign that he was thinking deeply, then he suggested that it could be a good idea if I got myself a pup to share my life. He followed this up with the news that Joyce and Noel Barker on Matelli bred golden cocker spaniels, and as they had a litter of pups that were almost ready to leave their mother, why didn't he take me over there on Sunday morning to have a look at them? At first I didn't feel very easy about the idea, but Bill could be very persuasive when he wished to be and after a while I agreed that a look wouldn't do any harm, so he picked me up on Sunday and off we went. Well of course, once I saw those little golden bundles of fluff romping and rolling around I lost my heart completely and on June 5th I became the proud owner of Rufus.

Being pure bred and registered with the Kennel Club he had a pedigree name that was almost unpronounceable, but Rufus was in it and Rufus he became, although the servants had a bit of difficulty pronouncing this and tended to call him Buster, for some reason. After an initial difficult spell during which he took a while to become house-trained and weed all over the bungalow, he became a faithful and loving companion and went everywhere with me, even sleeping in a basket in the corner of the bathroom. Unfortunately in my ignorance I didn't realise that in the hot climate and quite primitive living conditions we had in India, pure bred animals were liable to pick up all sorts of obscure illnesses and ailments which would have had very little effect on a country-born mongrel, and Rufus was no exception. He was fine for the first few months and grew into a beautiful little dog which everyone adored, but then in the middle of 1952 he contracted some sort of unknown stomach illness from somewhere, which nothing seemed to cure. The nearest vet was in Jalpaiguri, 50 miles away, and I did manage to take him there, but despite trying all sorts of medicines he was unable to do anything and I lost him. It was a very sad affair. Now with hindsight I realise I would have been much better off with a half-breed mongrel, but nevertheless I loved Rufus and was very grateful for the time we had together, as he gave me something else to think about and helped me settle down in tea.

Another thing I bought in June 1951 was a rifle. I think Bill was quite impressed with my shooting ability and was very keen that I bought my own rifle so that I would be ready for the shooting in the next cold weather, so he suggested I took a company loan to purchase one, with the repayments to be deducted out of my monthly pay. Here again he had heard that one of the lads who was going home on leave had had to put his rifle up for sale to raise funds to clear his debts, quite a common occurrence in those days, and as he knew the rifle and pronounced it a good one I decided to go for it. It was a .375 calibre Mauser five shot, bolt action rifle which I bought for Rs. 600 (45 pounds sterling) and for this I got a quantity of cartridges as well. Most of these were lead nosed, which spread out when they hit the target, and as these were always used against soft-skinned game such as pigs, leopards or deer I was well set up for shooting. After being vetted by the local Chief of Police in Matelli I received my rifle licence from the Firearms Department in Jalpaiguri on June 17th.

Despite all my grand thoughts of shikar and shooting big game, in actual fact the very first thing I shot with the rifle was the *Munshi's* horse. In Hindustani a Munshi is a language teacher, but on Zurrantee Monbahadur Munshi was the Head Foreman or Supervisor on the garden, and acted as a buffer between the Manager and the labour force. If Bill had some instruction or information that he wanted the whole of the labour force to know, then Monbahadur was the man who made sure everyone was informed. Conversely, if there was any dissatisfaction or unrest on the estate, then it was his duty to bring it to Bill's notice so that he could do something about it, and the arrangement seemed to work very well indeed.

Monbahadur was a very old Nepalese man who wore a large *pagri*, or turban, which set off his big moustache and long white beard, and he lived in a *basha* down in the factory labour line. As a symbol of his importance he owned a smart grey pony which he often rode to the Sunday bazaar, and I often saw it grazing near the factory compound. On August 9th Bill had gone to visit the Superintendent's office at Sam Sing and I was sitting in the office waiting to sign a report which was due to be sent in the morning's post when Ian Munro walked in and asked where Bill was. When I told him he said, 'Ah well, I've got a job for you. The Munshi wants you to shoot his horse!'

At first I thought he was pulling my leg, but then he told me the full story. It appeared that the pony had suddenly gone absolutely crazy, probably through being in contact with a rabid dog, and in its agonies it had forced its way into his house and then broken its leg when it fell. Not wanting to see it suffer, Monbahadur had asked him to find Bill or me and ask us to shoot it for him, so it was my job. As we walked down to his house I was not really very happy about doing it, but once I saw it lying on the floor, writhing in agony and making strange noises, I knew that the sooner I did it the better for everyone concerned. I knew that I had to be careful, because the Munshi's basha was surrounded by other houses and a large number of his neighbours were all out waiting to see the fun, but luckily I was able to avoid its flailing hooves and got round behind it, which enabled me to put the muzzle right up against the back of its skull, where one shot was sufficient to put it out of its misery without making too much mess.

After that the problem was that they had to move it away from the house and carry it out to the open grazing field several hundred yards away where it could be eaten by scavengers, but unfortunately as it was quite a large pony this was easier said than done. While I was still there they tried to drag it away by its legs without any success. Afterwards I heard that finally they had had to dismember it and carry it away in pieces, so the vultures had to wait for their dinner that day.

Thinking back on it, it seems that life plays some strange tricks on us sometimes, because although I had only had the rifle for a couple of months the second thing I shot with it on

August 29th also belonged to the Munshi, his pig! Evidently he was a bit of a businessman and had fattened up a specially big pig in order to sell its meat to his customers, but when he came to kill it that day it seemed the pig had taken exception to being stabbed with a spear, and instead of lying down like a good little piggy it had broken free, crashed straight through the basha gate like a runaway Sherman tank and out across the football field into a large patch of scrub jungle near the hospital. Here it had stayed all the afternoon, resisting all efforts to move it. We were having tea after work when a messenger came up asking me to go down and shoot it, because they feared that if it was left there overnight it might run away and escape in the darkness. I think I might have done that if I was the pig. John didn't like having very much to do with animals, but Ian and I went down and found about 150 people gathered round the spot, shouting and cheering like a crowd at a football match, and I got a special cheer when I arrived with the rifle.

Although the pig was an absolute monster, I wasn't too worried about shooting it because it had had its tushes (tusks) removed, so about the worst it could have done to me was knock me down, but with all the spectators gathered around I would have liked to have had a shotgun. In addition one of the line pye dogs had got excited and started harrying the pig, which made it keep moving inside the jungle, and as the spectators started cheering whenever they saw it this agitated it even more, so that it made it even more difficult for me to get a clean shot at it. Finally, as a bit of an anticlimax, it came docilely out in front of me about ten yards away and one shot was sufficient to do the job.

I think some of the crowd were a bit disappointed at this as they would have liked to have seen a bit more excitement, but the Munshi was delighted, and insisted that both Ian and I should go along to his basha to celebrate with a thank you drink. We weren't very keen at first but didn't quite know how to refuse without offending him, so finally we agreed and were shown to a bench which had been brought out especially for us.

As it so happened the crowd got some more entertainment after all. The dog that had harried the pig must have been so worked up that it attacked the next dog it saw and a tremendous dog fight broke out, with bits of fur and blood flying everywhere, so this kept them entertained for several minutes. Then once this was over we were quickly surrounded by a large crowd of the Munshi's family, friends, relatives, neighbours and people who had come to buy his meat, and they watched us avidly as we each drank a glass of darhu and two glasses of Carew's brandy, a rather fiery spirit which was distilled in India. What made it memorable for us though was that we got our entertainment as well, because in front of us about five yards away, a man disembowelled the pig on a sheet of corrugated iron and cut it up into healthy looking chunks ready for sale. We tried to ignore this butchery as much as possible, but finally Ian couldn't endure any more of it and said to me, 'Two years ago, if anyone had told me that I would be sitting here drinking native liquor while watching somebody pulling out a pig's insides onto a piece of corrugated iron I wouldn't have believed him' and I agreed with him wholeheartedly.

These highlights of the monsoon were little patches of brightness in what developed into a three-month grind, during which the weather didn't help as the rain pelted down out of leaden skies and we tried to cope with all the leaf. With the heat and the humidity it was almost possible to see it growing from day to day, and as it was imperative that only the most tender, seven-day-old leaf was harvested, it became essential that all our resources and manpower were used to their maximum efficiency. Each morning we would rise at 6 am and while the other two went out to the areas being plucked to ensure that everyone was on time, I went down to the factory to check on the machinery and taste the previous day's manufactured tea samples with Bill in order to check whether any changes to the manufacture were needed and to teach me what was required. Normally the factory ran for most of the night and finished manufacture at about 5 am, but even if there was some of the previous day's leaf still untouched the manufacture was closed down at 6 am so that all the machinery could be thoroughly cleaned. If this was not done the juice and bits of shredded leaf which had been left after manufacture would gradually ferment and affect the good tea, so it was essential that all this was removed, all the rollers, cutters, shredders and fermenting trays were power-washed and scrubbed down or sometimes steam-cleaned to kill any bacterial action and then manufacture started again when the next shift came on at 7 am.

The blocks of tea were laid out in ten-acre sections wherever possible with vehicle roads between them. By beginning at one side at 7.30 am the pluckers were able to work across the section so that by 9.30 am they were near the next road for the first leaf weighment to take place, and this was repeated for the second garden weighment at about midday. On Zurrantee we had two ex-US military three-ton trucks, one Ford and one Dodge, together with a Fordson Major tractor, and all these were used to bring the leaf in. The actual weighments were done by the junior office staff or the garden Daffadars, while the Assistants checked the quality of the leaf whenever possible, and as all the good pluckers were well known this usually entailed nothing more than a glance over the contents of the plucking cloth. However the few more crafty, unreliable workers were often marked down for much closer attention, and their rhumals were checked very closely. If sub-standard leaf was found on a regular basis, or if they had done some other mischief such as dipping their rhumal in the roadside drain in order to soak the bottom and increase the weight, they were either given a verbal or a written warning. After two written warnings they got a suspension, then after another two they could be dismissed under the Labour Relations Rules, but it rarely came to that. Once they realised that we were strict but fair and wouldn't tolerate any tricks, very few people wanted to jeopardise their job on the estate as they were in great demand, and we had very few habitual trouble makers.

Had the tea areas remained clean and weed-free during these months we could have coped with the crop without any great difficulty, but unfortunately the creeper and coarse jungle grew just as quickly as the tea and it was a continual battle trying to stop it smothering the tea bushes in some areas. This work was usually done by the younger boys and girls, who were adept at scrambling round beneath the bushes, and also by the pensioners, which meant that they weren't available to pluck, so at the height of the plucking season when we had great difficulty in maintaining the seven day round we had to import outside pluckers in order to cope. These came from the country villages or *busties* anything up to 15 or 20 miles away, and each morning our two lorries left the garden at 5.30 am to pick up as many of the *bustiwallas* who wanted to work that day. All the estates in Chulsa did this and depending on how they were treated they had their favourite estates to work for, so there was always a lot of rivalry in getting the better workers. Many of them liked Zurrantee so our lorries usually had a full load, and those of them who had relatives on the garden sometimes stayed with them when the work was available. Because they were not permanent workers they were paid at a fixed rate for the amount of leaf they plucked, which was not entirely suitable for us as it was in their short-term interest to rip off as much leaf as they could, but by paying them a fair wage for good leaf and by telling the habitual poor pluckers not to come back, Bill had built up a solid corps of good workers who came back year after year and were invaluable.

Once the weighment was complete the leaf was carried back to the factory and unloaded as quickly as possible to keep it fresh. Then it was carried to the upper floors of the factory building into what had been the old withering lofts. Before the war the standard system of manufacture was for the leaf to be spread out on wire mesh racks for anything up to twelve hours in order to remove as much moisture as possible, and this kind of manufacture was still employed in Assam in 1951. However because our tea bushes had to be hardy enough to cope with drought during the cold weather and virtually being drowned during the rains, which were conditions which did not exist in Assam, our bushes were of inferior quality when it came to making withered tea, and as withering was very expensive it was decided that it would be much more beneficial to stop it and concentrate on producing good-quality, fresh-leaf black tea. Now the object was to keep the leaf fresh and undamaged and manufacture it as soon as possible, so it was spread loosely in a four-inch thick layer all over the floors of the withering lofts so that it could be kept cool. Then when it was time for it to be processed it was sent down chutes to the cutting and rolling room, where it was cut into small fragments, then rolled in special machines to break up all the cells in the leaves and release the essential juices. In Zurrantee in 1951 the leaf was shredded by old-fashioned five-bladed chaff cutters, exactly as used on the farms at home, but later these were superseded by much more efficient Legg cutters in all our company gardens. These cutters were designed originally for shredding tobacco but they were adapted to cutting tea very successfully. By making one cut and then turning the cut leaf through ninety degrees, then cutting it in another machine, very fine and even particles could be produced, just right for the tea packets of today, but we had to ensure that it was of the exact size so that a quarter pound of tea would fit exactly into a quarter-pound packet, otherwise the blenders would not buy it. To do this we had glass measuring cylinders with two marks on the side, into which a quarter of freshly-manufactured tea was poured and then it was given a sharp tap on the desk. If the surface of the tea was between the marks then everything was satisfactory, but if not the cut had to be altered.

The chopped leaf or 'rung mal' as it was called was then spread in a two-inch thick layer on trolleys or trays and allowed to ferment for about 30 minutes, after which it was transferred to the drying room where it was passed through large, endless chain-drying chambers with perforated trays until virtually all the moisture had been extracted. Once this was complete it was taken into the sorting room, where the dry mal was passed over a succession of perforated or wire mesh trays, all of which extracted a certain size or grade of tea. These were removed to the packing room, where they were stored in large heaps on the floor until there was sufficient to be packed.

The normal tea chest was made of a soft wood frame onto which plywood panels were nailed, then the sides and corners were strengthened by nailing on aluminium strips and corners and the whole interior was lined with sheets of foil and tissue paper to ensure that it was moisture proof. On some estates the chests were assembled by the labourers as a normal job, but on Zurrantee the Chinaman had the box-making contract, and on Sundays and many evenings during the plucking season his whole family could be seen assembling tea chests like an army of ants. John ran the whole operation like a military exercise and each member, including his smallest children, had their own jobs to do, from carrying panels and fittings to assembling and carrying the completed chests to the 'ready' store, and very few sub-standard ones were ever found. Nowadays tea chests are a thing of the past and the tea is packed in aluminium coated plastic bags inside toughened cardboard boxes. I wonder what has happened to the dozens of plywood mills which existed in India to make the parts for the millions of tea chests that were used over all the years.

Normal-sized chests of first-class tea for export to the UK contained 120lbs of tea per chest, and were made up into 'breaks' containing 30 or 36 chests. Usually three breaks of the same grade of tea made up an 'invoice', or about four and a half tons of tea, while the smaller grades of tea and dusts were packed in 90lb chests. At the height of the season rarely a day went by without an invoice of some type being dispatched. This was usually done in empty railway wagons from the railway station at Sathkyah about three miles away, although some were sent from the local airstrip at Grassmore in

Nagrakata district in order to give them some return freight when other goods or passengers weren't available. The airline that ran the daily service from Calcutta to the Dooars was JAMAIR, which flew a fleet of about six aging DC3 aircraft up to the local airstrips. It was a common occurrence when flying down to Calcutta to be accompanied by a load of oranges, mangoes, vegetables or tea chests, all covered over with a freight net to keep them safe. Of course it did work the other way as well, and after we had been down to Calcutta for the weekend to play the local sides at football or rugby, it was quite a common sight to see some of the team members who had celebrated the trip a little too well and not too wisely stretched out on the top of the freight fast asleep. Usually they only woke up once we touched down upcountry.

Servants and transport

It was also in July that I decided to take on Kancha as my personal bearer. At that time I was still sharing the second bedroom with John Mitchell, but I knew he was due to move from Zurrantee to another of our estates at the end of the monsoon and that he would take his bearer with him, so rather than share Ian's until I was forced to get one of my own, I decided that I would try to recruit one as soon as possible.

The Engineer's bungalow was built on the hillside just above the factory and had a steel frame, but it had been unoccupied and used as a store during the war, so some sections of the wooden floors and walls had been eaten away by termites. Plans were in hand for it to be refurbished during the next cold weather, but it appeared that it would not be ready for occupation until early 1952 and until then I would have to share the other bungalow with Ian. Knowing this I was in no desperate hurry to employ a bearer, but nevertheless I made a few enquiries and also asked Ian's lad to tell me if he ever heard of a reliable one becoming available, so you can imagine my surprise when the bungalow *paniwalla* asked to speak to me a few days later.

Kancha was a clean and tidy Nepalese lad about the same age as myself, the son of one of the garden *chowkidhars* or security staff, who didn't smoke or drink, which was unusual at that time. He told me he had heard I needed a bearer, and although he had never worked in that capacity before it was his ambition to become one, so he had always taken an interest in the bungalow work and had a good idea of what was required. In addition he said the other two bearers were willing to help him and teach him as much as possible, so if I would give him the opportunity to show me what he could do he would endeavour to be a loyal and trustworthy servant.

I knew Kancha's work in the kitchen was excellent and was quite impressed by him, but rather than make a hasty decision I decided to ask Bill's advice. Bill said he knew both him and his family very well and thought it was an excellent idea. His opinion was that the best master/servant relationships occurred when they were both of a similar age, and he felt that if they were both starting off from scratch they were more likely to accept and adjust to each other's habits and ways. As a result I decided to take him on, and he remained our bearer for the whole of the seventeen years we were in India.

He was a very quick learner and was willing to try his hand at anything, although we did have the occasional mishap. On one occasion he came and asked me to get him some darning wool so that he could mend the holes in my socks, so as the local wool was of very poor quality I got Mum to send some darning needles and wool to me wrapped up in our home newspapers. Kancha was absolutely delighted when they arrived and using an old light bulb as a 'mushroom' support inside the socks he got busy darning in his spare time. Actually my socks were not in good condition, because the *dhobie* tended to beat them to death on the rocks in the river every time he got his hands on them, but one day I came in from the garden to find all my neatly darned socks laid out in a line on my bed ready for inspection. Unfortunately, either he was slightly colour blind or he had used a bit of artistic licence, because when I examined them he had darned all the brown socks with blue wool and vice versa. Obviously he had been very proud of his efforts and was a little crestfallen when I showed him what was wrong, but he didn't turn a hair and just took them away again. Once I had shown him what he should have done I forgot all about it and I was quite happy to wear the two tone socks, so I was very pleasantly surprised when I came in from work again some weeks later to find all my socks laid out on the bed again, and all darned to perfection. Evidently he had removed all the faulty wool and then done a marvellous job in darning them all over again in the correct colours. Such was his devotion to duty and he had a grin from ear to ear when I told him what an excellent job he had done.

As my bearer Kancha was responsible for looking after all my clothing and personal belongings, as well as dealing with all the other aspects of day to day life, and later when we were in our own bungalow he was in charge of all the other servants with the exception of the cook, who was another personal servant. He made sure that the bungalow was kept clean and tidy and that each room was thoroughly cleaned at least once a month. Usually this was done in the morning after breakfast when I was out on the estate, but I could usually tell when it had been done because the polish chokras would take the pictures down to dust them and then replace some of them upside down - it appeared that pictures such as seascapes and landscapes meant nothing to them. Kancha never seemed to twig how I knew which room had been cleaned that morning without being told. Maybe it was something to do with his eyes again!

After reading what I have written in the past two chapters, I realise now that it was at this time that I changed gradually from being the very inexperienced, callow youth that I had been when I came to tea, into a more mature and adventurous person who had gained a bit of confidence and liked the experience enough to be determined to make a career out of it. As a result it was not long after this that I decided that I needed some transport of my own in order to give myself some independence, but because I knew very little about cars I didn't quite know how to go about it. Our company paid a monthly transport allowance to anyone who had his own transport, which varied in amount depending whether this was for a car, motorcycle, scooter or pony and was designed to defray petrol and running costs, or to feed the pony. We were also allowed to take a company loan to finance the purchase of the vehicle in the first place. This was paid back by fixed monthly deductions from our pay, but the main drawback was that because new cars were not made in India nor officially imported from abroad, good reliable cars were very hard to come by and usually the only ones available were those that had been imported privately by other planters, and they normally only sold them when they went home on leave.

I puzzled over this for a while, then one Sunday when I went to Nagrakata club with our Accountant Martin Hawes to see the weekly film I asked his advice. His opinion was that I should have no difficulty in obtaining a loan but he thought I might have trouble in finding a suitable car. They took a terrific pounding on the rough roads in India, and as reliable garages were very few and far between, the nearest one to us being 50 miles away in Siliguri, and imported spare parts were not readily available, most of the servicing and repairs were done on a DIY basis. In view of this he thought it would be unwise for me to buy a car straight away, and that it would be more sensible if I bought a motor cycle or scooter. This would give me a comparatively cheap form of transport with the minimum of upkeep. Once I had gained a bit more experience about motors and driving I could change over to a car when a suitable vehicle became available. This seemed to be very sound advice, especially as the monsoon was coming to an end and I could look forward to six months of dry weather, so I kept my ears open and when a motorcycle was advertised for sale a few weeks later I took the plunge. It had been imported by an Assistant who worked on another estate in the Chulsa area and he had used it regularly, but he had been forced to sell it because he was being transferred to the Darjeeling district where it would be of little use to him on the steep dirt roads, so it was very reasonably priced because he wanted a quick sale.

The bike was a dark maroon Triumph 500 cc Speed Twin, very similar to those used by the London police at that time and in spotless condition. Martin knew both the owner and the history of the bike and confirmed that it was in excellent condition, so although I had never ridden a motorcycle I decided to buy it. I had no difficulty in getting a loan to pay for it, and I soon realised the benefits of a machine doing 60 miles to the gallon when I compared it to Ian's Jeep, which did about 25.

Most of the garden roads were made of beaten earth and shale while the main roads were very little better, so high-speed travel was out of the question most of the time and the bike proved to be an excellent first time buy for me. It added a whole new dimension to my life, for I was able to go out when and where I wanted to without being dependent on other people, and the more I used it the more confident I became. My previous contacts with cars and motorcycles had been minimal, and initially it was a source of wonder to me how they could run, day after day, week after week, with the minimum of attention without breaking down. At first, whenever I was riding through the forest miles from anywhere, I always had it in the back of my mind that this would be an awful place for it to break down, so I was very meticulous in carrying out the servicing detailed in the handbook and this paid handsome dividends. Then gradually as I became more experienced and undertook longer journeys I lost this feeling, and soon I was able to leave Zurrantee at first light on a Sunday morning, ride up to Darjeeling and spend Sunday night there at the Planter's Club, then ride back at first light on Monday morning ready to start the day's work at 7 am as usual.

I used to cover the 100 miles from the garden to Darjeeling in about three hours, partly because the last 50 were all uphill and also because the little Mountain Railway trains were active by the time I got up there. The lines crossed and re-crossed the road about 40 times during the climb, and as there were no level crossing barriers the only warning you got that a train was about to shoot across the road in front of you was a strangled whistle sounding from somewhere in the surrounding forest. Then the next thing you knew, this 'Puffing Billy' would launch itself out of the roadside bushes, and woe betide you if you hit it. The law decreed that the train had to run on tracks so it was unable to take any avoiding action whereas a motor vehicle was controlled by the driver, so it made no difference whether you hit the train or whether it hit you, it was always your fault. Even if you were at death's door your insurance didn't cover you, although you still had to pay for any damage you had done to the train.

I know of one instance where a planter's car was hit by a train and pushed over the edge of the road, after which it fell and rolled down the mountainside. Luckily it only went down a short way before it was stopped by some trees, but it was a complete write off, and the planter, his two daughters and their ayah were all seriously injured. It was very fortunate that they had not been killed.

One humorous thing was that although it was usually quite warm when I left the estate and I wore my normal shorts, once I got about half way up the climb into the mountains it got extremely cold, which tended to numb my nether regions, so I always carried a pair of thick, long trousers which I would don as soon as the going got chilly. This always seemed to amuse the locals who gathered round to enjoy the show as soon as I stopped. Of course I always wore them when I left Darjeeling to come home, and this paid dividends one morning when I had my first spill from the bike. The weather was dry and the road conditions were good until I heeled the bike over to come round a sharp, right-handed curve where the railway line crossed it, and we parted company. I hadn't realised that the morning dew had condensed on the cold rails and the oil between the tracks, making them very slippery, and the next thing I knew the bike had slipped sideways from under me and I finished up lying in the middle of the road while it clattered down the railway lines on its side. I wasn't travelling very fast and my trousers took most of the abrasion from the slide, but the bike hadn't fared so well as the lines had torn off the right hand silencer and exhaust pipe. Not having any tools with me I couldn't repair it, but I managed to bind them roughly back into place with a piece of wire which I discovered by the roadside and I rode back down the hill with flames coming out of the exhaust port and sounding like a demented traction engine. Still it got me home on time and as no real damage had been done I was able to replace the pipe and exhaust box, and after painting up the small scratches and abrasions it was soon as good as new.

Of course riding it round the garden roads in the rain was not really satisfactory as I soon became absolutely soaked, but I did discover that I was able to tuck the handle of my umbrella down the front of my shirt and shorts and was able to ride and keep fairly dry like that. Whenever we walked through the tea we used our brollies to keep our top half dry, and one day I was in the middle of a block when I fell into a deep drain. One moment I was thrusting through the tea and the next thing I knew I had lost my footing and was lying in the bottom of a drain with the wind knocked out of me and my umbrella still resting on the tops of the tea bushes above. As a result it took me a while to recover and scramble out of the drain and up through the tea, rather like a deep sea diver surfacing, so as I was covered with wet mud and had a broken umbrella as well I must have looked an awful sight that the pluckers thought was as good as a circus. It took a long time for them to let me forget that one.

It was also at this time that I saw my first really big snakes. Normally they hid up in holes and crevices in the bridges, walls and roadsides and only came out at night or when they were hungry, but it seemed that if there was exceptionally heavy rain and their nests got flooded then they had no alternative but to come out, and this was rather hazardous for them. The labourers hated snakes and killed them straight away if they had the chance, whether they were poisonous or not and one morning when I went out to the mela I saw two large snakes draped over the roadside fence after they had been attended to by some workers. Both were about six feet long, one a delicate pink with black markings on it, and the other was a banded krait about two inches in diameter, probably one of the largest I have ever seen, but obviously they hadn't stood a chance that morning.

Another thing that appeared towards the end of the monsoon which I had never seen before were the fireflies. Millions of them seemed to gather in the trees and bushes at dusk and then treat us to an absolutely fabulous display of flashing lights, presumably to attract the opposite sex. It wasn't a haphazard affair either, as all the insects on one bush would flash their lights simultaneously so that it was lit up like a Christmas tree, and then a couple of seconds later they would all be extinguished, only to be repeated time and time again. All the different trees had their own individual timescales, so when their display was at its peak it seemed as though they had been decorated with millions of tiny light bulbs and then switched on and off repeatedly. It really was a magical thing to see.

The other things that were always featured in jungle films and came at that same time, and lasted for the duration of the cold weather were the cicadas. They were very small and extremely difficult to see, but it appeared that the sound they made was much larger than their bodies, for every night they would make an absolute orchestral din of sound, cheeping, whistling and humming until the early hours of the morning.

Because there was very little artificial light in India the tropical nights possessed an almost ethereal quality, as the stars shone brilliantly out of a very dark velvety sky much clearer than they ever do here, and this together with the sound of the cicadas made many of the nights absolutely magical and unforgettable.

Old Donald Mackenzie

June, July and August were terrible months as the rain beat down out of a leaden sky, and with the humidity and the high temperatures it was almost possible to see the tea shoots and the weeds growing. However once September came and the monsoon ended, weather conditions became very much more bearable as the rainfall became more intermittent with most of it falling at night and the day temperatures fell from the mid-nineties to the lower eighties. Although we had had about 300 inches of rain over the four months, once we reached October and the nights cooled down we knew we would not have any more rain until February. It was amazing how cold it became at night with a very heavy dew, and quite often we woke to a thick mist which gradually dispersed as the sun came up, but as a result of the low temperatures the tea bushes became dormant, which stopped the fresh leaf from growing and we were able to start the cold weather work in earnest.

Once the last leaf was manufactured all the factory machinery from the prime movers to the forced air fans was dismantled, and either replacements were ordered for worn out items or the originals were sent away to the Central Workshops at Sam Sing for repair. Because all our ten gardens used the workshops and the work was done on a 'first come, first repaired' basis, it was in our own interests to get them up there as quickly as possible, so I spent most of my days in the factory at this time.

If the tea was plucked properly during the season the bushes gained about six inches in height over the four months, so after two years of plucking, what had been a comfortable height for the women labourers to pluck at the start became a much more difficult task when the bushes were 12 inches higher. As a result about 60% of the mature tea was pruned to a reasonable height each year, while the rest was 'skiffed' with long knives to reduce the height slightly and level the bushes off until they were pruned the next year. Because the pruning was a highly-skilled job only the most reliable of the workers were employed on it, with the men doing the heavier pruning while the women did the lighter work, and razor sharp, numbered pruning knives were issued to them from the stores. Many of the labourers marked their knives to make sure that they got the same one each year and they took a great pride in keeping them so sharp that they could almost have shaved with them. Meanwhile the rest of the garden labourers were employed in a multitude of different jobs, from hoeing, weeding, applying chemical manure and uprooting creeper to repairing drains and roads, and when time permitted replanting the young tea plants in the uprooted areas.

In the cold weather most of the labourers worked for about six hours a day and returned to their homes at about 1 pm after completing their tasks, but for us assistants our afternoon job was to visit the labour lines with the Labour Housing Registers to check on the condition of the houses and arrange repairs where necessary, and also conduct a census of all the occupants of the houses so that we knew who lived where and whether any strangers had moved in. This gave us an opportunity to practise our Hindi, while it was also invaluable for us newcomers to know how the labourers lived and who their family members were and it also gave them the opportunity to get to know us.

Under the terms and conditions of their employment, because the labourers spent most of their time working on the estate and did not have time to be self-supporting with their gardens and rice fields, provided that they worked a set minimum of days during the month they were allowed to purchase rations of rice, wheat flour and other foodstuffs at concessional prices for themselves and their dependants. These rations were distributed every two weeks to the people who were recorded in the Labour Registers, so it was essential that they were brought up to date each year, and each afternoon the people in the labour line that we were going to visit were warned to be in their houses that afternoon so that we could check them against the record. If for some reason anyone was unable to be present, they had a few days to report to the office in person before their names were removed. By and large the system seemed to work very well.

One of the first things that I noticed was that many of the houses had a small area fenced off inside like a self-contained corner, which seemed to be out of place in the general concept of the house. When I asked Bill about it he told me that many of the Indians considered that when a woman had her monthly period she was reckoned to be unclean and as such could not live in contact with the other members of the household, so she was banished to the small isolation area until her period was over, after which she could be purified and rejoin the family again. This solved another mystery for me, for sometimes in the garden when I had noticed that one of the good workers was missing and I had asked her friends why she was not at work, they answered that she was having her period. At the time I thought that it must have been one hell of a period to make her as ill as that, but then of course the mystery was solved, because if she had come to work then everyone that she had contact with would have been contaminated. This was the way we learned many of the facts of life about work on the tea estates, and it meant we always had to be very careful, for quite often simple things were not as straightforward as they appeared at first sight.

Another surprising thing that we noticed was that very often some men had anything up to four wives all living together in the one house as a happy family. When I asked one of them about it he said, 'I am allowed up to four wives if I can support them and keep them happy, so myself and two of my wives work in the garden and bring in the money, while the oldest one looks after the house and the children, and the youngest one cooks the meals and is for my pleasure'. They all seemed quite happy with the arrangement, and I can imagine that when the workers came home cold and hungry in the afternoon after a wet day's plucking, they were very pleased that they didn't have to start a fire and cook a meal before they could get dry and eat.

Although the new houses we were building were made of hollow concrete block walls, with a steel roof structure and asbestos cement roof sheets, all the older houses consisted of a metal frame and roof structure, with wooden walls and a corrugated iron sheet roof. A standard house had a living area, a small kitchen, a sleeping area and a veranda, and usually housed a family of up to six people. Larger or extended families were allocated two or three houses which were usually joined together, in which they all lived as one big happy family. As we went round the lines we inspected the houses and each householder told us what repairs or improvements he would like, then we told him what we considered he should have and wrote our recommendations in the register. From these notes lists of materials were drawn up and allocated to the carpenters who repaired the houses, and by doing this the householder could check that he was getting the correct repairs done and also the quality of the work. If he was dissatisfied he would make a complaint at the office, and this ensured that the carpenters maintained a good standard of work and also showed the labourers that we had their welfare at heart.

In addition to the ration details, the registers also held the records of the amount of land that was allocated to each family for growing rice. All the areas of land in the river valleys and wild areas which were not suitable for tea but which had a good supply of water during the monsoon were covered in *dhan khets*. This enabled the workers to grow at least some of their own food and the amount of land allocated to them depended on the number of workers they had in the family. The khets were planted with young rice plants as soon as the monsoon broke and grew at a tremendous rate until October when the rice started to ripen, then this was the moment that the wild pigs from the forest had been waiting for. Large groups would come across the river under cover of darkness and lie up in the tea during the day, then at evening time and in the early morning they would leave their cover and wreak havoc in the khets, feasting on the ripening rice grains and crushing down the plants that they didn't eat. Of course the labourers did everything they could to keep them out and very often tracked them to their lairs so that we could have a hunt and shoot them, so once I had my rifle it was a favourite pastime of mine to visit the khets for an hour or so just as it was getting dark to see if I could bag one. In early September I had one superb evening in which I killed three pigs with four shots. I had several labourers with me, and after I had taken a couple of legs for Bill and ourselves, they had a whale of a time cutting the rest up into pieces so that they could share them out to all the lads who normally went on shikar with us, so they must have thought that all their Christmases had come at once.

It was in September that I met 'Old Donald' Mackenzie for the first time. We had three Mackenzies working in the company, Old Donald who was commonly known as Old Mac, his son Donald who was nicknamed Big Mac, and Ronald Ross Mackenzie, who was not related but who was known as Wee Mac. Old Mac had come into tea in the 1920s, and after he had done his time he and his wife had returned to Scotland to retire and settle down. I think he had been the manager of Nagaisuree Tea Estate for about fifteen years. After so many years in India they hated life in the UK and couldn't settle down, as to them the weather was awful, the food not to their liking and they just could not adjust to the pace of life, so they decided to go back to India and he approached Duncan Brothers to see whether he could be re-employed. Evidently he was an excellent planter with loads of experience and although they were unable to help him, our company, Goodrickes, was short of junior staff and offered him work as a Senior Assistant on our estates for a few years, so that his pay would augment his existing pension and thus enable him to stay on in the work he loved and also give him a comfortable retirement. Of course he jumped at the offer and in September he was in charge of Saugaon, the separate, smaller division of Bagracote Tea Estate, until February 1952, after which he was due to transfer to Zurrantee to stand in for Bill Milne while Bill was on home leave.

Old Mac was a very colourful character and normally dressed in a pair of very baggy military-style shorts and an old khaki singlet, with long socks and a soft hat with a feather stuck in it. If it was exceptionally cold he would wear a faded bush shirt, and he always carried a lady's handbag in which he kept his spectacles, pen, handkerchiefs, pen knife, magnifying glass and other small items, and usually had a thumb stick with him. At some time he and Mrs Mackenzie had taken in a small orphan from some estate who idolised him and prided himself on being Mac's personal servant, and as they were all the family he had he would fetch and carry and also looked after Copper, Mac's dog, a lovely big, coppery coloured pie dog with a tight curly tail that Mac had also adopted. Each afternoon in the cold weather Mac, the boy and the dog would go for a walk along the roads through the tea in the cool of the evening. This was usually a very leisurely and incident-free affair, but unfortunately on this September evening things were very different, because they were attacked by a wild boar that had been injured.

Unknown to Mac some of the Saugaon labourers had been out hunting in the tea that afternoon and after they had wounded a boar quite severely without actually killing it, it had run away into the tea and they hadn't followed it up to finish it off. It had three arrows in it and was wounded so severely that it would have died later, but when the three strolled along the road near to where it was holed up, it was very much alive and in a terrible temper and out it charged, determined to get its revenge. Other than the Himalayan Bear, a wounded boar is probably the most dangerous of all the animals in Northern India, inasmuch as once it attacks it doesn't leave until its enemy is dead. It has large, curved, razor sharp tusks, called tushes, protruding from its upper jaw, and once it has knocked its assailant down its one aim is to rip his stomach open and disembowel him and then finish him off.

Mac was quite a big, thick set, well-built man and luckily when the boar charged out it went for him instead of the boy and knocked him off his feet. As he went down he realised that his only hope was to try to keep it away from him, so he managed to scramble onto his knees facing the boar, then grabbed one of its tushes in each hand and held on for all he was worth. Although he had quite big forearms and was very strong, had he been by himself and it had been able to move about, he would have tired very quickly, but fortunately Copper grabbed hold of a back leg and between them they managed to stretch it out so that holding it was not quite so difficult and it became a contest of durability. However Mac realised that they would not be able to hang on indefinitely, so he told the boy to run back to the bungalow as speedily as possible and tell Mrs. Mackenzie to bring the shotgun to shoot it. Off the boy ran while the fight turned into a wrestling cum tug-of-war match between the three. In its fury the boar kept gnashing its teeth which lacerated Mac's hands and forearms, but he realised that if he let go he would be finished, so he managed to hold on and it was a welcome sight when he saw his wife hurrying along the road towards him with the shotgun. Just before she reached them the boar's injuries and exertions proved to be too much for it, and suddenly it gave a great shudder and dropped dead, to Mac's great relief.

Although he was sore and bruised where it had felled him and his lacerated hands and arms were bleeding quite profusely, he walked back to the bungalow, where the estate doctor treated him, gave him some antibiotic injections and then sent him to bed, which was where I met him the next day. News travelled very quickly in the tea districts and Bill Milne heard about it that night, so the next afternoon after work we went down to Saugaon to see him. There we found him lying in bed with his hands bandaged up like a boxer's, but still able to grasp his glass of whisky, and absolutely determined to be up and out to work the next day. We heard later that he had already torn a strip off the men who had wounded the boar, not because they had wounded it, but because they had not warned anyone about it and if it had attacked anyone less able than Mac it could have resulted in a fatality.

After a lifetime in tea Mac could converse quite fluently with many of the labourers in their own tribal languages, and most of them had a great regard and respect for him, so many stories made the rounds about things that he had said and done. On most estates there was a minority of troublemakers whose main aim in life seemed to be to stir up as much agitation as possible, and a typical story concerned some of these on Bagracote when Mac was acting for the Manager while he was on home leave. At that time he had to carry out some company orders which were unpopular with some of the labourers. One afternoon he was working in the office when he was surrounded by a crowd of about 200 of them, led by troublemakers who hoped to frighten him into rescinding his orders. For a while he worked quietly inside while the ringleaders shouted insults and threats. Finally he laid down his pen, took off his glasses and walked out onto the office veranda, where he looked them over and identified the ringleaders. Then he told them in fluent Nepalese that they were like a pack of jackals, very brave when they were in a mob but cowards when they were on their own, and he thought that they were a disgrace to the Gurkha race. He said that he was only carrying out company policy and that if all they wanted to do was beat him up then they had better go on and do it, because he was only an old man on his own and there was nothing he could do about it. However if they wanted some fun, then if they weren't afraid of him he was very willing to fight them all one at a time until somebody beat him. Then, taking off his hat and bush shirt, he fixed his eye on the man he thought was the main troublemaker and told him that as he was the one who had had been making the most noise, perhaps he would like to be the first to step up and have a go with bare fists.

Of course the thought of this man fighting Mac amused a lot of his friends, and once they were laughing and he was on his own all the bravado left him and he backed down, protesting his innocence. Then after asking several more whether they would like to come up and fight him and getting no response, he told them that there was no way that he was able to change his orders, so the best thing for them to do was to stop wasting everybody's time and go home and do something useful. Then he turned and walked back into the office while the now leaderless crowd gradually melted away. He was quite a colourful character.

I think Mac had three children, one daughter whom I never met and two sons, one of whom went to work in one of the

Arabian Gulf states while the other, young Donald, later to be known as Big Mac, was born and brought up on the tea estates and could speak several languages like a native. As a result he joined our company as an assistant before he was twenty, and in 1951 was working on Dangua Jhar, our estate near Jalpaiguri. He was tall and well built just like his father and almost as strong, and one of the tales told about them recounted how they were out in the car one day and had a puncture. Unfortunately their car jack was missing, so in order to change the wheel they both lifted the back of the car off the ground, then Big Mac held it up by himself while Donald removed the punctured wheel and fitted the spare. He was also a born shikari, and it was said that he had shot two man-eating tigers by the time he was 18 years old and the local people adored him. Because he was brought up with the labourers and one of his childhood friends became his driver and hunting companion when he joined tea, he had the knack of being able to think and reason like a native, which was a big advantage that us home boys did not have. Because Dangua Jhar was the most distant of our gardens and about 100 miles away, I had never met him before, but as fate would have it I was to meet him again a few months later under rather tragic circumstances and we were to remain good friends for the rest of our time in tea.

CHAPTER SEVENTEEN

Puja time

As we worked a six-day week every week and very often part of the seventh day as well during the monsoon, we treasured our days off very much indeed and as Ian Munro had bought himself an ex-army Jeep soon after I had arrived on Zurrantee he was looking forward to a few days in Darjeeling at the end of the month. The whole garden got four days' paid leave at the end of September to celebrate the Durga puja, and while the company policy was for some of the managerial staff to stay on the estate at that time to deal with any incidents that might occur, Bill granted him leave to go up to Darjeeling for the whole four days, provided he was back ready for work on the next working day. However as Robert Burns once wrote, 'The best laid schemes o' mice and men gang aft agley' and at that time little did he think that although he would get his stay in Darjeeling it didn't happen quite as he had planned it.

All the roads on the garden were topped with clay and shale from the river beds and got very rough and washed out during the rains, but his Jeep had enabled Ian to drive into some of the more inaccessible areas of the garden to check the work, which saved him a lot of time. However it was notoriously unstable on slippery shale corners, and one morning just before the puja he was returning from a visit to the top garden when he tried to bring it down a rocky short cut with two hairpin bends and a steep slope in it. Although he was usually a competent driver, for some reason he drove over the side of one hairpin and went straight down the side of the steep slope until the Jeep burrowed its bonnet into a big rock at the bottom, then fell over on its side. Shocked and stunned, Ian managed to scramble out with a cut head and badly gashed legs and ran to the nearest houses for help, where a labourer saw him coming covered in blood. Thinking he had been mauled by a tiger which was chasing him he immediately cried out, 'Tiger! Tiger!' and ran away as fast as his legs could carry him. Luckily the accident had occurred quite near to the Doctor Babu's house, so he was treated and stitched up there and then, but because the gash in his one leg was quite severe and could cause complications, it was decided that he should be taken up to the Dooars and Darjeeling Medical Association Hospital in Darjeeling for specialist treatment, where he stayed for ten days over the puja instead of four. Fate plays strange tricks on us sometimes.

As regards Bill and myself, we had arranged to go shooting in the Naura forest just before the puja to try to get some meat for the labourers, but despite our best efforts we saw absolutely nothing to shoot at despite the fact that the shikaris had seen the fresh tracks of several animals the day before. Then towards the end of the day when we were all very tired and fed up all was made clear. When we were shooting we were always accompanied by our own experienced hunter/tracker whose senses of hearing, sight and smell were vastly superior to ours, and very often they could hear or smell an animal in the forest and give warning when it was completely out of sight. So it happened that during the last beat of the day I was standing on the edge of the river bank about ten yards from the edge of the jungle with the shikari who always accompanied me, an Uraon named Dushroo. For a while everything was quiet except for the noises and calls of the distant beaters, when suddenly Dushroo gave me the sign that he could see something and quietly pointed at a spot in the undergrowth with his finger. I could see nothing, but he stared at the spot and sniffed the air for several seconds, then as I slipped the safety catch off my rifle he put his hand on my arm and said quietly, '*Mut maro Sahib. Burra bagh hai*' (Don't shoot Sahib, it is a tiger'. Then he gave a quiet cough and after another few seconds he relaxed and said quietly, 'It's all right now. It has gone', so we went over to the edge of the cover and there in the sand behind a large clump of grassy jungle we found the brand new pug marks of a very large tiger. Evidently it had stood there and stared at us while we waited about 25 feet away and Dushroo had realised that as I was quite inexperienced, if it had charged us I would have stood very little chance of killing it outright at that range, so very sensibly he had coughed to let it know that we were there and that we meant it no harm. On hearing that it had avoided us and slipped away as quickly and quietly as it had arrived, and I hadn't heard a thing.

When the beat had finished, Bill walked over from where he had been stationed about 200 yards away and said that he too had caught a momentary glimpse of it as it had passed by in front of him and hoped that I wouldn't lose my cool and take a pot shot at it, thinking that it was a deer, so Dushroo had done the right thing. Actually he was an excellent shikari and even after I had been transferred from Zurrantee, whenever I went shooting with Bill he always came with me. After the shoot the beaters said that there had been two tigers in that area of forest that we had been beating, and obviously they had scared off all the game that had been there the day before. It was a pity, but we were not after tiger and shooting was like that.

According to the Hindu religion the world developed from a great 'world egg' which was deposited by the first supreme God. From this egg proceeded the triad of the great Hindu gods, Brahma The Creator; Vishnu the Preserver; and Shiva The Destroyer. All these three Gods could appear on earth and be worshipped in a variety of different forms and guises. Shiva's consort was named Parvati, and she could be worshipped in several different ways. As Durga she was represented as the 'Earth Mother' who was the epitome of female power, and in her puja she was portrayed as the victory of good over evil, while in the Kali puja, which was celebrated a little later, she was shown as the goddess of death and destruction. The Durga puja was celebrated in late September or early October each year, depending on the phases of the moon, and for the festival a life sized, brilliantly painted effigy of the goddess was brought to the garden and installed in a special shelter on the football field where she could oversee all the festivities. These effigies were made in the bazaar by traditional craftsmen whose families had made them for generations, and were constructed of sculptured clay on a rice straw and bamboo frame, and then brightly painted to a traditional design. In most of them she was depicted standing on a demon that she was killing, and was equipped with ten arms, all of which were holding weapons that had been given to her by the other Hindu Gods.

During the four days of the puja the drums thumped and

thudded night and day with hardly a let up and I think some rather serious drinking was done at this time. Then on the main festival day when the mela was held on the football field, Bill and I went down at 9 am and found just about the whole of the labour force all dressed up in new clothes especially bought for the occasion, singing and dancing and really enjoying themselves. After distributing puja *baksheesh* of cigarettes, sweets and cash to them all, we went out onto the field to see what was going on and I was absolutely fascinated by a 'men only' dance that was held inside a bamboo fence circle, which they rotated round and round for hundreds of times rather like whirling Dervishes, until their eyes became glazed and they almost went into a hypnotic trance and fell down. As they were unable to walk they were dragged out of the circle and then left to recover, which was something that often took quite a long time and when they did they looked completely shattered, so I was unable to imagine what the object of the dance was.

Most of the women danced circular dances with very repetitive steps and with their arms round their neighbours, rather like the Palais Glide, and it delighted them to get us to join in and see us make a mess of the footwork. Actually having danced at home I picked it up quite easily and managed to enter into the spirit of the thing, but poor old Bill caused a lot of hilarity as he hopped and jumped and did his own steps in time to the music. Still he was always willing to have a go which was what the labourers liked about him, and when he finally retired from Zurrantee in 1961 they gave him a tremendous send off.

While we were at the mela we had to do the rounds and were offered drinks. We also had to dance with all the labourers from the different labour lines, as none of them wanted to be left out, so after a couple of hours, as we were both very tired, we finally excused ourselves and went down to the club for a couple of hours. When we got back all the festivities were still in full swing, and because each group of dancers had three or four drummers, even in the bungalow the noise of the drums was tremendous and disturbed my sleep. These only ceased on the last night when the image of Durga was loaded onto the back of a lorry and taken down to the Teesta River to be immersed in the water, which allowed her spirit to leave the celebrations and return to her home in the Himalayas. As can be imagined, as each place held its own celebration there were hundreds of lorries and processions carrying images of Durga down to the different rivers that night, so the roads got a bit choked at times.

As we visited each group of dancers we were offered both *haria* and the vile smelling *darhu* to drink, but a couple of weeks previously I had had a rather unnecessary and painful experience regarding the latter and there was no way I was going to have any of it because just the thought of it affected me. On the Sunday morning I was alone in the bungalow and decided to take my rifle down to the khets to see if I could bag a pig. The road down to the Naura forest passed through the Naura labour lines, and as luck would have it the head man's son was being married on that day so as I walked by I was invited in. As I didn't want to offend him I said I would go in for a few minutes to wish the couple good luck and then would have to be off, but all his family were adamant that I should stay for drinks. These drinks seemed to get stronger and stronger as I stayed on for the dinner, the dancing and the ceremony, until at last by the middle of the afternoon I was so far gone that they had to escort me back to the bungalow. My companions weren't very much better than me, but with one man on each side and a third one carrying my rifle we all staggered up to the bungalow and they went back to the festivities. And this was where my troubles began, because I soon developed a terribly upset stomach and also vomited at the same time, and bringing up this vile liquor with all its fumes affected me so much that finally I went into the bathroom and sat on the toilet while being sick into the wash basin at the same time. I didn't dare move, and at one time I went to sleep for a while still leaning on the basin with my head in my hands and feeling absolutely awful.

It must have been at this time that Bill came into the bungalow in the Jaguar to enquire whether I would like to go over to Nagrakata club with him to see the Sunday film, and as the servants hadn't seen me come back they told him that they didn't know where I was. Of course I didn't hear anything of this so off he went and I didn't wake up until about 5.30, just as a red sun was sinking behind the Naura forest. By this time I had brought up or pushed out all the food and poisonous hooch from my stomach and although I had a splitting headache I did feel a little better, so I had a bath to cleanse myself and crawled into bed, but it took several days for my digestion to recover completely. Of course when I told Bill he was very amused and told me that if it had taught me a lesson then it was not a bad thing. He was quite right, for I never touched darhu again; just the smell of it was enough to nauseate me. And as for the labourers I had been drinking with, they said they were amazed that I had been able to walk home after the amount that they had given me. Bill told me later that they thought that I had 'put up a good show and would make a good Sahib' so perhaps it was worth it, but I have my doubts. Of course they never knew what had happened once I got back to the bungalow. Even now just the memory of the smell of darhu is still enough to make me feel uneasy.

After the Durga puja came Diwali, supposedly on the darkest night of the year when all the spirits were supposed to be around, rather like our Halloween. In order to keep them away everyone lit every lamp they possessed and decorated the outsides of their houses with hundreds of tiny clay dishes filled with oil and a wick that burned for several hours. It was really moving and mystical to see all the houses softly illuminated by these tiny lights instead of our modern version, where we have gangs of children dressed in ghostly costumes 'tricking and treating' everywhere.

This was followed by the *Kali puja,* in which Parvati was worshipped in the form of Kali, 'The Black One', the Goddess of Death and Destruction. Her effigies were painted black with white teeth and a very red mouth dripping blood and looked very spectacular with a necklace of severed human heads. Looking at her I suppose that she was designed to scare the living daylight out of anybody who got on the wrong side of her; some of her greatest devotees were the Thuggees, or Deceivers, from whom we get our word 'Thug', the killers and thieves who preyed on travellers crossing India for over 300 years from the early 1500s until the 1840s. They got their name from the Hindustani verb *thugna,* to deceive, and belonged to a federation of professional murderers who killed not principally for gain, but because it was part of their religion and their worship of Kali. It is hard to understand that the Thugs killed and plundered because they believed they had been instructed to do so by the Goddess, who told them it was the right, moral and godly thing to do. Seldom did a gang kill or plunder within a hundred miles of their home villages, so the disappearance of victims could never be connected to them. Operations were organised with a meticulous care born of centuries of experience and practice, which meant that no Europeans were ever molested because they were few in number and in positions of responsibility and were easily traceable.

The Thugs did not deal in the easily traceable. Instead they took advantage of the fact that in those days travel across India was very slow and fraught with all sorts of dangers from men and beasts, so as single travellers and small groups of people were especially at risk, many of them joined together into larger groups in the belief that there was safety in numbers. Unfortunately for them this was not always the case, for the method of killing and robbery was for specially trained Deceivers to pretend to be making a journey as well. On the road they would join a larger group of travellers in order to travel in safety, and by their pleasant manner and ability to sing and play music they would entertain the group over the tedious journey until their victims had no suspicions and they had gained their confidence. Other members of the gang would join the group as the journey progressed, and as they had immense patience they would accompany their intended prey for days on end until the perfect opportunity for a successful and secret killing arrived. On that day some gang members would leave the party on some pretext and travel on ahead to decide on the killing place and dig the graves for their victims, usually in a sacred grove of trees dedicated to Kali. Then in the evening, when they had stopped for the night and had gathered round the fire for a meal and a sing song, the Thugs placed themselves in suitable places for the killing. There were usually two or three of them to every victim. When the leader could see that everything was ready, he would give the arranged death call and the stranglers would throw a yellow silk scarf weighted with a silver rupee round the neck of the victims and strangle them.

If for any reason it was not convenient to kill them round the fire, then plan B was adopted and they were killed that night. At a pre-arranged time they would ready themselves beside their sleeping victims and then as the death call came and the victims sat up wondering what on earth was happening, the yellow scarves would be thrown round their necks from the back and the results were the same. After the killing the dead bodies were pillaged and then doubled up and buried in the prepared graves, which were then filled in and the surfaces walked on and tramped down by the Thugs until it was so flat that no one would think it had ever been disturbed. After this it was covered with dead leaves etc. The victims had disappeared as though they had vanished into thin air.

All the travellers were murdered simultaneously so they were unable to help each other, and as women and children were not spared there were no survivors to bear witness. As these activities were confined entirely to the men of the tribe, the women were never told where their men went or what they did, so that if they were ever questioned they could give nothing away. The boys of the families were gradually inducted into the profession over a period of many years, details of the final killings being kept from them until it was certain that they would keep everything secret.

Although written records are very few, from the reliable ones that were available it has been estimated that over a period of three hundred years up to the 1830s, that anything up to forty thousand victims fell annually to the killers of the yellow scarf. It is possible that when the methods of communication improved and the steam trains reached India, the profession of thuggee might have died a natural death, but in the Indian political service at that time was an officer who devoted himself to ridding India of these human beasts of prey. This was a man named William Henry Sleeman, later to become Sir Henry. He joined the IPS in 1821 and as he gained seniority he heard more and more tales of travellers being lost without trace and rumours of the Thugs. He decided that something must be done, and almost single handed set up a secret network of spies and informers who fed him any scraps of information they came across. From these he was able to make some arrests, and by questioning his prisoners in a subtle and humane manner he was able to obtain a tremendous amount of information as well as learn their language. Once he could do this progress was swift. In 1830 he not only caught the main Thug leader, a man named Feringheea, with most of his gang, but persuaded him to turn approver and give evidence and betray his accomplices in order to save his own life. Once he had done this their secrets were revealed and thousands of Thugs were arrested. An assessment in 1840 showed that up until then 3689 men had been committed for trial, of whom 466 were hanged, 1564 transported for life, 933 imprisoned for life, 81 imprisoned for lesser periods, 86 set free under security for good behaviour, 97 acquitted, and 56 reprieved as approvers.

By 1848 the organisation had virtually collapsed, but Sir Henry realised that the remaining members needed some help to live, and before he died in 1856 he founded schools of industry to teach them trades and crafts of all types. Because they had never done any work these were not very popular with the Thugs at first, but later their carpet weaving became so famous that Queen Victoria ordered that they should make a carpet for her for Windsor Castle, and as a result Sleeman's Thugs wove a great, 80 foot by 40 foot seamless carpet which weighed about two tons for the Waterloo Chamber, and it can still be seen in there to this day.

Although the garden was closed for both pujas, the Kali puja was rather a quiet affair and was not celebrated as riotously as the Durga puja was, and I am pleased to say that to the best of my knowledge we never lost any of our labour force, although the Nepalese workers did have evening celebrations at which large bonfires were lit and quite large hot air balloons were filled and released, some of which travelled for long distances. These were made of very fine bamboo frames tied together with silk threads and covered with glued tissue paper, often four or five feet in diameter. They were completely airtight except for a hole in the bottom across which was a frame to hold a small lamp. When they were to be released they were held above the fire so that they were filled with hot air, then the lamp was lit and fixed to the platform. This served the dual purpose of keeping the air inside the balloon hot and illuminating it. The weight of it also kept it upright, so once it was released it rose swiftly up to several hundred feet and sailed along on the evening breeze. The first one I came across completely mystified me, as I saw it as a large, illuminated globe against a background of stars. As we didn't have satellites or space stations in those days, I thought I was seeing some slow-moving shooting star until someone explained, and then it seemed so simple.

One unique thing I was involved at that time was the first

proper General Election since Independence in 1947, held in India during the winter of 1951-52. Because India was such a vast country and resources and experienced officials scarce, an election on this scale had never been attempted before and it took almost four months from October 1951 to February 1952 to be completed. Election day on Zurrantee was held in the middle of December and we had been asked to make all our garden registers of workers and dependents available to the scrutineers, and also make the garden school together with a number of voting booths ready for use as well. Of course none of the labourers had ever participated in anything like this before, but they were all very keen and on that day the football field was a mass of hundreds of people who had all turned out to cast their votes. The main drawback that really confused them was that over the whole of India there were over 50 different parties involved and as they didn't really know the differences between many of them they had no idea who they should vote for. As a result many of them came to us and asked for our advice. As the most experienced and stable party we advised them to back the Congress Party, and this appeared to be the case all over India because as it turned out Congress won 364 out of 489 seats contested.

There were many tales of how some of the smaller local parties fared, and one that appeared in the press concerned a villager who did not know who to vote for. Every party had its own sign or logo, which was printed alongside its candidate's name for the benefit of people who were unable to read. When he asked his friend what he thought he told him to cast his vote at the side of the burning lantern, and in he went to vote. When he came out his friend asked him how he had got on and he said 'Oh, I was fine. The only trouble was that they gave me a piece of paper and I looked around, but I couldn't see a burning lantern around anywhere so I threw it on the fire'!

Roll on Christmas!

After the heat and humidity of the monsoon the cold weather was absolute bliss, and as we knew that we shouldn't get any more rain until February at the earliest this was the time when all the cricket matches and tennis and golf championships were held. Until the atmosphere got really dusty, once the sun rose the days were like those in an English summer, with a blue sky, bright sun and temperatures in the lower seventies. Early morning was quite cold and chilly with a very heavy dew, and often when it was misty and very cold the labourers would arrive on the mela muffled up in coats and blankets and would build a fire of pruning twigs to warm themselves before starting work. Then after a lovely day, once the sun went down at about 5.30pm and it got dark and quite cold very quickly, we were very happy to don our sweaters when we went back to our bungalow.

Here we had our tea in front of a blazing fire while we listened to Radio Ceylon, which broadcast an English speaking service from 4 pm to 10 pm each day with a news bulletin at 6 pm. Unlike All India Radio, whose broadcasting quality varied from day to day, Radio Ceylon always came through loud and clear and I think that at this time it was the most powerful commercial radio station in the world, probably due to the fact that it had taken over the transmitters of the Allied Forces South East Asia Command at their headquarters in Ceylon after the war.

Usually we had hot, buttered toast with either jam or cheese for our tea, but one evening Ian said, 'Roll on Christmas, and we'll have some cake', and John laughed. At the time I didn't realise the significance of the remark and thought, 'Of course we will have a bit of cake at Christmas,' little realising just how much cake we would get, but more about this later.

It wasn't very long after this that I saw my first dead man and it was then that I began to appreciate what it must have been like for Dad during the first World War when he was in France on his 18th birthday and lost many of his friends, and it made me realise just how fragile life is. To have a friend here one moment and gone the next must have had a very traumatic effect on him, so much so that he never spoke about it at home. Engo Tea Estate was a small garden situated north west of Zurrantee, sandwiched between our tea and the Naura River and their transport had to use our roads to travel to Matelli bazaar. Usually they passed through without incident, but one morning when one of their lorries was taking a load of tea chests to the railhead it swerved to avoid a dog and ran off the road near our factory. This was raised about five feet above the surrounding land, with a deep storm drain on both sides and as it slid sideways into the drain it shed its load and toppled over on its side.

On most estates a lorry crew consisted of a driver together with three loaders who usually travelled in the back on top of the load, and unfortunately as the truck went over one of these had tried to jump clear and it had toppled on top of him. News of the crash reached me in the factory and when I reached the site I could just see the top of his head and one arm sticking out from beneath the side of the truck, but as this was weighted down with spilled tea chests they had to be moved before we could try to lift it off him. Then we got some long bamboos and using these as levers we managed to lift the vehicle enough to drag him out. Despite our best efforts we could see that his chest had been badly crushed and he died soon afterwards.

There was one small coincidence that occurred at that time that also gave me an insight into the labourer's sense of humour, because there was a horrible smell in the vicinity of the wrecked lorry the whole of the time we were working on it, and later I was told that the same lorry had run over and killed a dog two days before in exactly the same place where it had run off the road. Then as luck would have it, when we finally moved it the decomposing body of the dog was discovered actually lying beneath the cab and causing this horrendous stench. This very unusual coincidence caused some of the labourers to say that the God of the Dogs had been responsible for the accident, and it was his way of getting revenge for the killing! Such is the power of the imagination.

It was also at this time that I saw another sight, the memory of which has stayed with me ever since. Our company accountant Martin Hawes had his own bungalow on Sam Sing, with an absolutely superb garden that he had designed and built himself, but although he had joined tea in the late 1920s he had never married and was a confirmed bachelor. He had travelled extensively all over the world during which he made friends with many people both male and female, and was one of the very few people that I ever met that was able to hold a conversation with anyone on just about any subject in which they were interested and also had the knack of being able to talk to everyone without being intrusive. In addition he was always ready to advise and help new assistants when they arrived and as he had a large Studebaker car he was also willing to give anyone without transport a lift to see the film at Nagrakata club on a Sunday night if he was asked. As a result it was no surprise to us when we received a note in our post one evening, saying that he was going to a very special religious festival that was being held the next night at a temple near Mynaguri about 30 miles away and would we like to go with him? Well of course we jumped at the chance and it was three very excited young men that arrived at the temple the next night not knowing what to expect. The whole place was ablaze with lights and the din was absolutely terrible, with horns, bells, drums and chanting making a cacophony of noise, and there seemed to be hundreds of Fakirs or Devotees who had deliberately mutilated or harmed themselves for some reason. Some had dozens of hooks with weights hanging from them embedded in their flesh, others had metal skewers pushed through their cheeks, in one side and out the other, and there were many others who had invented dozens of different ways of hurting themselves wandering around as though in a trance.

However the one thing that attracted us was the fire walking, and even though I have seen recent programmes on television that were supposed to explain how this is done, they do not go anywhere near to explaining what we saw that night. The fire pit was about 18 feet long by four feet wide and was absolutely filled from end to end with a glowing bed of coals that gave out a tremendous heat. Anyone who has ever been near a blazing bonfire knows that it is impossible to stand any closer that four or five feet as the heat is too intense and the heat in Mynaguri was much worse than this as the nearest that we could get to it without feeling discomfort was about 12 feet away. Strangely the devotees who were going to walk the coals seemed to feel no discomfort at all and stood in a group about 10 feet from the end of the pit with bare feet and dressed only in a plain cotton, skirt-like garment that reached to their knees. Then after being blessed by a priest, one by one they walked to the end of the pit and without a moment's fear or hesitation walked unhurriedly down the length of the pit and out the other end without seeming to experience any discomfort whatsoever. It was almost as though they were out for an afternoon stroll and though they must have spent at least 20 to 30 seconds traversing the pit their feet and skins were unmarked and even their clothing didn't seem to become charred at all. It was almost beyond belief. On the television the theory was that there was a certain amount of moisture on the soles of the feet and if they were not in contact with the embers for any length of time they did not burn. I suppose this is possible, although on the programme one lady got her feet quite badly burned and they certainly didn't explain how the almost nude walkers would have been able to get anywhere near any fire with the radiant heat that we experienced in the first place. Even Martin was unable to explain how they were able to do it, although he had seen it several times before. All he could tell us was that once when he enquired how it was done, he was informed that in order to do it you had to be a 'believer' and the method was a secret that had been passed down through the priests over the centuries, so even he did not know. It was a very thought-provoking evening.

Two of Martin's many interests were plays and films, about which he had written articles for many newspapers, and he also had a circle of friends in show business through whom he had attended West End Premiers when he was home on leave, although he never boasted about the many stars that he had met at the subsequent 'First Night' parties. One day we were chatting about films when I mentioned that I loved the film *Ben Hur* and said I thought that Charlton Heston must have been scared stiff when he drove his team in the chariot race. Typically Martin let me finish, then told me that he had had almost the same conversation with him when they were chatting one day and CH had said that the chariot race was all organised as the other drivers had stayed out of his way. Evidently they were all professional cowboy drivers from the rodeos in the USA and Canada and it was all organised and planned so that they made it easy for him. However there was one exception when his chariot accidentally ran over some wreckage that was left on the track so that he was thrown into the air and when he came down he fell half in and half out of the chariot and had to claw his way back in again. Evidently this was unintentional and completely unrehearsed, but it looked so effective that it was kept in the film and was one of the highlights of the race.

He also said that the one time he was actually scared was in the film *The Wreck of the Mary Deare,* when he had to climb up a swinging rope to board her in a storm. He did most of his own stunts, and although this sequence was not actually filmed in a storm the ship was moving quite a lot and the rope was wet and oily, which caused his hands to slip. This caused him to bang against the side. When he was about half way up his hands got so cramped that he almost panicked and fell, so it was only with the greatest difficulty that he was able to pull himself together and struggle up to the rail. For the film the storm was dubbed in afterwards and it was very realistic and made compulsive viewing, but that incident had such an effect on him that he was determined not to do anything like it again.

Because of this interest and also because some of the planters in the Nagrakata Club had started an amateur dramatic society, in 1950 Martin decided that if there was enough support in the Chulsa district he too would try to form one. As a result a meeting was held at the club, and the Chulsa Amateur Dramatic Society, or the CADS, as it was nicknamed, was launched. It was an immediate success. There were several planters and wives in the area who had had some experience of acting and there was an excellent stage in the club, and as all the managers were willing to supply some craftsmen, labourers or equipment in order to make all the scenery and goods etc that were needed to put on a successful play, they were all of a very high standard indeed. Evidently the first one was a sell-out, with people coming from all over the Dooars to see it.

In November 1951 they performed *Blithe Spirit*. Martin had had the scripts sent out from some theatrical agency in London and although I had done a bit of acting in Coaley it was nothing like that standard, so I kept my head well down when he was having a reading and enjoyed myself helping to paint the backdrop and scenery and also working a spotlight on the night. After helping serve on the bar afterwards it was about 3.30 am when I finally got home the next morning. After having had so little decent entertainment during the year, I found that I had had a really enjoyable evening and decided that I would do everything I could to make sure that Martin would produce another one in 1952.

One of the first things I had been instructed to do when I joined Zurrantee was to go up to the office at Sam Sing to meet the Superintendent, Mr Laurence Tocher. Although this informal first visit was just a courtesy call that enabled us to sum each other up and an opportunity for him to give me an introductory talk regarding what I should and should not do, it was also an opportunity for me to ask any questions I had. In addition he also made it clear what the company expected of me. He told me that until I could speak Hindi I was virtually useless on the garden, so this was to be my number one priority. Although my visits to the labour lines in the afternoons had helped me a great deal and I had learned a whole list of Hindi verbs and nouns during my seven months on the garden, I still could not hold a conversation, and I had to think of what I wanted to say in English and then translate it into Hindi. As a result I was best employed in doing practical jobs wherever possible. Once the house repair register and census had been completed and the urgent work in the factory had been done, Bill put me onto preparing the uprooted area for replanting.

The old Zurrantee Estate had been bought by the Goodricke's Tea Company just before WW I, but I believe the garden had been planted out in the late 1800s, so most of the tea bushes were more than 60 years old. It was generally accepted that tea bushes were at their best between the ages of 20 to 40 years of age, after which their yield dropped off rapidly, but the Zurrantee bushes were still giving an excellent yield of good quality tea even at that age. The Company policy regarding replanting was that providing funds permitted, every year a maximum of 2.5% of the total mature tea area would be uprooted and replanted, which meant that theoretically if there were no delays it would be replaced every 40 years.

However young tea bushes produced very little tea during the first five years of their lives, and as the replanted areas got larger each year the amount of tea being plucked got smaller and reduced the crop, which caused financial complications. In addition the young tea areas needed very much more weeding, feeding and general looking after than the mature tea did, which caused the cultivation costs to rise, so in reality if you managed to replant 1.5% of your tea each year you were doing really well.

During WWII no improvement work of any kind was done, but in the late 1940s Zurrantee had made some small profits and in 1952 we had the finance to replant an area of the oldest tea up near the Manager's bungalow. In the previous cold weather the men were put onto clearing this land, a job they loved, so shade trees were felled and the roots dug out, while the bushes were uprooted. The big wood was taken away to be allocated as fuel for the labourers, but there was always enough small wood and branches for them to take large bundles home with them to augment their fuel supply. Once this was done the whole area was cleared of jungle and levelled out, after which it was planted up with a nitrogen fixing, ground cover crop and left fallow for the whole of the monsoon until we were ready to work on it. Once the cold weather arrived, the first job was to hoe all this off and leave it to dry, as it was to be used as a mulch later on, after which the whole area had to be staked out to provide a pattern for the planting, and this is where I came in.

On flat land tea bushes were planted out in 10-acre blocks bounded by vehicle roads, with lines of bushes and access paths running from side to side. Usually they were planted in a rectangular or triangular pattern with about four or five feet between them and with the shade trees planted in a 40-foot-square pattern. However, on the hillsides where the slope and the undulations of the ground made it impossible for square planting to be used, contour planting was done so that the lines of tea followed the contours of the land. That first morning Bill took me up to the work site and gave me a quick lesson on how to use a Dumpy Level and graduated pole and then left me to it, and once I got the hang of it I really enjoyed it. Part of the area was on a steep slope which levelled out to a flat area at the bottom, so I had to use my common sense as to whether I should use the contour or the square method. Thousands of bamboo stakes about two feet long had been prepared previously, and with me on the Dumpy and a good lad on the pole we laid out the framework of the planting pattern, after which a squad of men with Gunter surveying chains came along behind and filled it in with the bamboo stakes at the correct number of plants per acre. It was a very rewarding job as each day the staked area got larger and larger so that we could see our progress. Finally at the end of October the twenty acres were completed. This enabled the next part of the operation to begin when three-foot-deep drains were dug between the rows of stakes at regular intervals and the shade trees were planted in a 20-foot square pattern all over the area. These supplied shade for the pluckers as well as the tea during the hot weather, but after a few years as they grew larger the intermediate ones were cut out for firewood, leaving the permanent trees in at the correct spacing.

One flat space in the corner of the area to be planted had been used as the tea nursery in 1950, when tea seeds from some mature seed trees in Aibheel had been placed in pits in the ground filled with damp sand until the plumules had emerged.

They were sorted each day by the old women, and the ones that had developed shoots about 1 cm long were planted out in the nursery beds at eight inches triangular spacing. These beds were five feet wide so that they could be weeded from the sides without anyone standing on them and were kept perfectly weed free during the monsoon, usually by the nursing mothers, as it was no use spending large sums of money on planting out sub-standard plants which were stunted or deformed through being smothered by weeds. By December, when the time came for planting, the seedlings had developed into healthy single-stemmed plants over two feet high with a good root system about 12 inches deep and were ready for planting out.

At this time, although the nights were cold and damp there was a hot sun by day and because we had had no rain for two months the soil was very dry. As a result the replanting was done in the early morning as soon as it was light and went on without a stop until the day's task was complete. On Zurrantee this was based on 50 plants per person per day and was strictly regulated. A squad of men arrived at the nursery at first light and were allocated a seed bed each. After digging a two-foot-deep 'squatting' hole at the end of them, they cut away the soil around the plants with a large, machete shaped knife with a square end until the roots, encased in their own ball of soil and completely undisturbed, were only attached to the bed by a thin column of earth. Then after placing a 'U' shaped piece of bent metal plate against the outer edge as a support, the digging knife was inserted down to cut the remaining column, and the *dhela* of earth containing the roots was prised away and laid upon the ground on its support. Each man had selected a woman to work with him and it was her job to carry the plants safely from the nursery to where the planting was being done, so normally he would cut 50 plants and she would carry them away on her head over to where the planters were working. However if there was an accident and she damaged some, as all damaged plants with broken dhelas were useless and were thrown away, he had to cut additional ones to make up the deficit, which didn't make her very popular.

While they were doing this the same number of hole diggers came early and were busy, as each one was allocated a line of stakes and used a hoe to dig 50 holes, one at each stake. A little later the same number of planting men arrived and started planting, taking great care to ensure that the plants were in line in every direction, and that the undamaged dhelas were firmly planted in the hole with long bamboo tampers and then the stake was replaced. Again women were employed to carry an earthenware pot of water for each plant from a nearby source. After watering it she covered the wet earth around the stem with the old ground cover so that the hot sun would not dry it out. Here again their goal was 50 plants. After a few teething troubles each worker knew exactly what he or she was supposed to do. By starting really early and sometimes helping each other, most of them had finished and were home by midday. Sometimes this varied depending on how far the nursery was from the actual planting area, but by maintaining a standard 50 plants as a task and taking the rough with the smooth, the labourers were quite happy with this arrangement. I think that on some estates the task varied from day to day and also that in many cases it was considerably higher than our 50, but it was Bill's opinion that he would rather keep the task at a reasonable level and have good planting that would live, rather than get it over quickly with a poor standard of work and then have a large number of deaths which would have to be infilled later on, and I think his way was the best.

Both Bill and I were out in the nursery at 4.30 am when the work started. It was quite eerie to see some of the diggers already there and working by the light of kerosene lamps that they had brought with them. It was also quite strange to see the long lines of men walking through the half-light, muffled up in blankets and with woollen hats on their heads against the morning chill, until finally the sun rose over the mountains and warmed us up. Bill usually stayed until about nine o'clock, when he went to have his breakfast and then worked the rest of the day as normal, while I stayed on for the whole time until the last of the work was done. This meant that I usually got back to the bungalow just after mid day. Then, after having my combined breakfast and lunch and a lie back, I had the rest of the day off. This suited me fine for about two weeks until one day I sat down to eat my lunch and had a violent, burning pain in my stomach which was only relieved by me vomiting. Once I had done this and brought up some filthy tasting acid bile I was fine for the rest of the day, but the next day when I came in from the planting I had the same excruciating pain and had to vomit again before it went. As it got steadily worse I decided to see our district medical man, Dr Maguire, so I biked over to his bungalow at Chulsa and explained what was wrong. He asked me if I had changed my eating habits at all recently and of course I had to tell him that I was rising at 4 am with no breakfast and then not eating until midday. He immediately said this was the cause. What I had described to him were the classic symptoms of the start of a stomach ulcer. My stomach lining was being irritated by gastric juices which were being produced to deal with a normal breakfast that never came, so they stayed there with the acids gradually eating away at the lining until I vomited them away. He said I should take a bottle of milk to work with me and have a regular drink, and also take something with fat in it to eat at the normal breakfast time to give my stomach a fatty lining, and said that if I did this I should be all right.

I considered this as I rode back. Although the drink of milk presented no difficulty whatsoever, getting something fatty to eat which I could carry with me at that time of the morning was more of a problem, until I had a brainwave. All I had to do was to get the cook to prepare some pieces of fried bread in the evening, then I could nibble them in the morning whenever I wanted to.

This worked a treat. I drank my milk and ate my pieces of cold fried bread whenever I felt hunger pains coming on, and after a few days my digestion was back to normal, my burning and vomiting a thing of the past. I still love to eat cold fried bread with lemon curd on it, which is an absolutely superb bonus for me.

Christmas and New Year, 1951/52

Another thing the Superintendent went to great lengths to impress upon me when I met him was that with one exception, at no time under any circumstances was I to accept cash backhanders or 'sweeteners' from any of the local tradesmen or businessmen I would be having dealings with. He explained to me that commerce in India was based on a system in which bribes or *baksheesh* were commonplace and expected from top to bottom to obtain a service or contract. However it was accepted that Europeans did not do this, and as I was a member of the managerial staff and I would be dealing with ever growing amounts of cash and contracts, now was the time to show everyone concerned that I did not accept bribes. This would make things easier for me later on. Once the locals knew this, it would be accepted that I was not to be bought and they wouldn't bother me again. The planters who could be bought did make some money on the side initially, but sometimes reaped untold trouble in their dealings with the local businessmen later on in life. It was almost as though it was expected that to a British gentleman his word was his bond, and those who were tempted lost a certain amount of respect and trust.

Luckily the one exception that he mentioned was at Christmas, when just about every businessman who had any dealings with the estate took the opportunity to bring gifts for everyone concerned, not with any intention of getting preferential attention regarding a specific business deal, but rather as a means of saying 'thank you' for the business done with them through the past year, and even more important in the hope of more in the year ahead. All the Europeans on the estate were visited during the few days leading up to Christmas and even the shopkeepers from Siliguri 50 miles away would come in hired Jeeps to bring trays of sweets, nuts, fruits of various kinds, bottles of whisky and brandy and always the obligatory Christmas cake complete with icing, snowmen, robins and Santa Claus etc.

When I had arrived in February, Ian and John were still having big slices of cake every evening at tea time, and this lasted well into March, but it was only when they began their visits in December 1951 that I realised the reason why. Because there were three of us in the bungalow, it was very rare for us to have less than two cakes left by each tradesman and usually we got one each, so as the big day approached and very often several of them queued up at the end of our drive to wait their turn to bring us their 'Christmas Baksheesh,' we had a collection of cakes that looked like a cake shop. The gifts that were left were commensurate with your importance on the estate and remembering the amount that we had, goodness knows what Bill did with his. Probably he had enough booze given to him to last him for several months, but the three of us talked it over and after keeping our liquor, some of the better cakes that would last us a couple of months and also enough of the sweets and nuts etc to ensure that we had a merry Christmas, we gave the rest to our bungalow servants to share out and take home. I think they enjoyed the festival almost as much as we did.

Although there were a few Christians on the garden who were allowed leave to celebrate the festival, for the rest of the labourers it was work as usual and so for us it should have been a normal working day. However Bill said that if we supervised the first few hours of work as normal, provided everything was going as planned we could finish work in the morning and have the rest of the day off, so we had a lovely Christmas. On the afternoon of Christmas Eve we began to decorate the front veranda and living room with bamboos, ferns, plantains, and bougainvillaea flowers. In addition the Christmas flower Poinsettia which is so expensive over here is used as a hedgerow plant by the labourers and grows into quite large bushes, so we also cut a large quantity of these and tied them to all the front veranda posts for a bit of colour, and they looked wonderful. Also during the Durga and Kali pujas the Indians used vast amounts of coloured paper trimmings, rather like the ones we used to have at home before the advent of plastic, so we were able to buy a cheap boxful from the bazaar and hang them up. The bungalow looked really festive, like a forest grotto.

In the morning we all worked until midday then went back to the bungalow, where we found that all the Christian labourers had come up with garlands and small presents to wish us a Happy Christmas (and to get a drink of course), and then we had to have dancing to the drums. By this time all the other

labourers were leaving work and had diverted their way home
to come by the bungalow and see what was going on, so for a
while our compound was absolutely crowded and it was
complete bedlam, but finally they all departed and we settled
down to enjoying the rest of the day. We had invited Bill to
lunch, for which we had a cold store turkey nicely stuffed by
the cook, mixed vegetables and gravy, Christmas pudding with
flaming brandy sauce, mince pies, brandy butter and coffee.
We ate so much that all we could do in the afternoon was sit
around drinking our brandies and whiskies and chatting and
it was really lovely. Then as the icing on the cake the *dakwalla* came up to the bungalow with the post and as he had
brought a load of Christmas cards from home, these together
with the local ones brightened up the living room no end.
Having sampled all the goodies and drinks the shopkeepers
had brought, by the time evening came we were really ready
for Bill to take us over to Sam Sing to a party in Martin Hawes'
bungalow, which was a lovely end to the day. Besides all his
other accomplishments Martin was quite a talented amateur
magician, and that evening he entertained and mystified us all
by acting the part of a snake charmer and making a snake
appear and disappear inside a basket simply by moving his
hands. It was only many years later that he explained that he
was able to do it by using extremely fine black threads attached
to the snake which were invisible to us in the darkened room.

Like Christmas our New Year's Day was another normal
working day for the labourers, but for us it was a very different
affair because the English planters were outnumbered by the
Scots by about two to one and as a result, while Christmas was
celebrated quite quietly and was usually an individual
bungalow affair, Hogmanay was celebrated by a dance at one

of the clubs, attended by just about all the planters in the area and a very hard drinking event this was too. The 'band' was usually flown up from Calcutta especially for the event and because most of the best bands preferred to stay down there where the money was, we usually got one of the second class outfits. They usually began to play at 8 pm, and by the time most of us had had a few 'wee drams' and begun dancing some of the more obscure Scottish dances, nobody seemed to worry what the band was playing and a good time was had by all, including the musicians. There was no time limit and some of the really hardened drinkers didn't go home until morning, but it was an unwritten rule that no matter what time you got home, you were out for your work on the garden at 7 am the next morning, the same as on any other working day. I think this was a case of 'National Pride' as everyone seemed to think that they should be able to do this, and I have heard of lads who arrived back on the estate at 7 am and then not having time to change their clothes went straight out to see the garden work still wearing their dress trousers and bow ties. Of course what they were like for the rest of the day I do not know and probably they were absolutely shattered, but at least they knew how to celebrate Hogmanay.

Actually I only experienced these goings on much later because that first New Year's Eve we had all been invited to a Hogmanay party at the Superintendent's bungalow, where we had an absolutely fabulous evening, with singing, dancing, games, and Martin performing some more magic and conjuring tricks which were really first class. I was quite glad that I didn't have to go to the club, not because I was unsociable but partly because I had to be up at 4.30 am to visit the replanting work as usual and also because I was still paying back the loan I had borrowed from the company to buy my motor bike. In addition Mum and Dad had been given the opportunity to buy our old home at Watkins Terrace as the owner wished to sell it, and they had asked me for my advice and some help if possible. The price was £375, quite a big sum in those days, but as I thought it was a good idea and they were having difficulty in raising the money and were short of the required amount by £90, I said I would try to help them. I talked to Bill about it and he arranged for me to borrow the amount they required to be repaid on a monthly basis, so as I was still paying that back as well I was quite happy to not go to the club.

Although we didn't get back to the bungalow until 1 am and I only had about four hours' sleep, when I faced the dawn the next morning, eating my cold, fried bread with a clear head and thinking of all the things I had done and seen in the past eleven months, I realised how fortunate I was to have been able to take this momentous step in my life and wondered what the coming year would bring.

Actually 1951 went out very successfully with a completely unexpected stroke of good fortune for me. When the Dooars Golf Meet was held in November they sold tickets for a charity draw, and although I wasn't there Mr Tocher had bought a ticket for every assistant in our group. When it was drawn just before Christmas my ticket came out and I had a prize of Rs. 450, about £32 in sterling, which was a lovely Christmas surprise and about four week's pay a year before when I was still working at Lister's, so this came in very handy to help pay back what I owed.

Early in January John Mitchell completed his year's experience on Zurrantee and transferred to Fagu, another of our estates in Mal district, before returning to the UK to take up his job with the company. Looking forward to my own prospects in 1952, Bill had told me that it was normal practice for a new assistant to stay on his first garden for the first two years, then be transferred to another to get some different experience at the beginning of his third. As far as he knew I would stay on Zurrantee until 1953, which suited me fine because I got on very well with both Bill and the labourers. I was enjoying the shooting and my football and the only doubt I had in my mind was that Bill was going to the UK on seven months' home leave in February and Old Donald Mac was due to act for him while he was away. I had seen him just the once and had been told he could be rather abrupt and didn't take kindly to Englishmen, but although I had some reservations I thought I should be able to get on with him all right, even though he was a totally different kind of person to Bill. Still, this was all in the future and I had a lot to do.

The replanting ended early in January and as machinery parts were beginning to come back from the workshops and spare parts arrived, I began to spend more time in the factory, supervising the reassembly of all the machinery, pumps, driers, cutters, rollers and the large steam engine, and also building the mist chamber. My other responsibility was the repair and refurbishment of the engineer's bungalow which was built on the hillside above the factory. This had a wooden structure on a steel frame, and as it had not been used since the war it had fallen into a sad state of repair. It was planned that I should move into it as soon as it was ready, so as labour had become available in the cold weather, the corrugated roofing sheets had been replaced and our Chinese carpenters were repairing the floors and walls and fitting new doors and windows. The one big drawback was that it did not have its own piped water supply and although the piping from the factory supply had been laid, the pump which was due to be used was unable to pump the water 250 feet up the hillside to the bungalow tank. This rotary pump, which had already been in stock in the garden stores, had a limited lift on it, which was insufficient for the job, so we had to wait for a piston type pump to arrive from the suppliers in Calcutta before the water system could be completed and I could move in.

With Bill due to leave the garden to go on home leave on February 24th the new year seemed to fly by, especially as Old Donald decided he would not stay in Bill's bungalow as this was built on a hill top. He was still having his afternoon walk with his boy and Copper, and as our bungalow stood in a level area of the garden he decided he would live there while Ian could live in Bill's while he was away and I could move to the factory bungalow. Of course this meant that all three of us had to pack up all our stuff ready for the changeover as soon as Bill left, but the extra work did not stop our Wednesday afternoon shoots in the forest. The last two we had were very memorable as everything seemed to go exactly as planned. In the first one we had had an invitation from Soongachi tea estate, who had asked Bill if he could shoot a leopard which was causing absolute havoc amongst the labourer's goats and cattle. Soongachi was on the other side of the River Naura two miles south west of Zurrantee and as several of our workers had relatives living on the garden, obviously the knowledge of his prowess as a shikari had travelled there. Evidently the leopard was very brazen and had very little fear of humans, for although it had not injured anyone so far it had chased several people out of the area of jungle on the edge of the tea where it was believed to rest up during the day. Then after dark it roamed round the labour lines looking for prey. As it had killed several goats and calves they were afraid it could take a child, so they implored him to go and shoot it for them. Well Bill was never one to refuse a request like this, so we took a lorry load of our best labourers down to the Soongachi jungle. The animal had so little fear of the beaters that during the first drive it didn't even run from the noise, but just walked casually out of the jungle in front of Bill, then stopped and looked at him. As he was only about 20 yards away he killed it with one shot behind the shoulder. Of course the Soongachi people were absolutely delighted that it was dead. Much to everyone's amusement one old girl who had lost her goat, took a stick and vented her fury on it by trying to beat the corpse to death, so I think she would have killed it even if Bill hadn't.

In the last shoot before he went we had an afternoon in the Naura forest, and because it was special and nobody wanted to miss it we had about 100 beaters. As the jungle had not been fired there was plenty of cover for all the game and consequently we had the most successful shoot we ever had in one afternoon, during which I shot a very large wild boar, a barking deer and a large civet cat, while Bill got four jungle fowl and another barking deer. After we had selected our joints of meat from one of them, the beaters cut up all the rest and divided it out so that they all went home with about 4 lbs of meat each. It was a wonderful farewell to Bill that was not to be repeated.

He left the garden on Sunday morning on the early morning Jamair flight from Grassmore airstrip. He went out with a bang, as the pilot was a friend who agreed to fly over the garden on their way out, so we were woken up at about 7.30 am to the tremendous din of a DC3 roaring over our bungalow at roof top height, after which he circled round for another pass and we waved him on his way. He flew from Calcutta on February 27th and although Heathrow Airport was opened in 1946, I see from my records that he actually flew by BOAC direct to Northolt, so they couldn't have been doing very much business in 1952.

The next day we moved up to the Manager's bungalow and Mac arrived from Saugaon complete with Copper the dog and his little boy, although he came alone as his wife had travelled to Calcutta to stay for a while, but because he had moved so many times during his 30 years in tea he must have had it off to a fine art as he had everything unpacked and tidy by the end of the day. As for myself, because the factory bungalow was still not ready for occupation I arranged to share with Ian until it was and actually I didn't move into it until the beginning of April.

Mac was a totally different type of planter from Bill. During his first two months on Zurrantee he made several subtle improvements to the way work was done which showed that he had a lifetime of experience behind him, and I felt I could learn a lot from him. However he was rather abrupt and surly in the way he spoke to some people and didn't suffer fools gladly, and I'm sorry to say that he came down on me several times for what I thought were quite small mistakes, rather like Dad used to. Maybe it was his way of correcting assistants who made mistakes or maybe he thought I had more experience than I actually had.

In the event I never had the opportunity to find out, as he died unexpectedly soon after. In the last week of April he went down with a stomach upset and although he had intermittent discomfort, because he was a very strong and robust person he tended to laugh it off and said that it was nothing that a dose of Andrew's liver salts wouldn't cure. Unfortunately the pains got worse and after he began to run a very high temperature he died of a burst appendix on May 6th. Young Donald had come up from Dangua Jhar during the night and was with him when he died. The next afternoon we used the Commer diesel truck as a hearse and after a very simple service he was buried in the small cemetery at Nagrakata. With no undertakers or facilities for keeping bodies in India it made me realise just how quickly things like this happened, but what really amazed me was that although the telephone service at that time was almost non- existent and we often had to book a call and wait for it for several hours, in some way the news of his death and funeral spread over the whole of the Dooars some 100 miles in 24 hours, and there were old friends from the Eastern Dooars there that afternoon. It must have been by some form of inexplicable jungle telegraph, but it was something I was to wonder at several times afterwards.

Mac's passing left Zurrantee without a manager until Bill returned, so Sandy Frain, the most senior assistant in the company, was instructed to transfer immediately and take over as Acting Manager. At that time he was working on Sathkyah estate as a garden assistant, so his transfer left the manager John de la Mare a man short and to replace him I was ordered to transfer there on May 18th. John de la Mare, or De La as we knew him socially, was a very refined Englishman who had been imprisoned in a Japanese prisoner of war camp during the war, and as a result suffered from chronic ill health for the rest of his life. Nevertheless he was a very conscientious and efficient planter and I got on with him very well indeed. It was said that he was related to the poet Walter de la Mare, but he never mentioned it and I never did find out whether this was fact or fiction.

On the Saturday evening all the lorry crews, my engineering staff and some of the shikaris combined to give me a farewell party in the factory labour lines in front of Lopo's house. They had borrowed some tables and chairs from the school nearby, and as he had asked me to take some of my 78 rpm jazz records down for entertainment we had a very interesting and enjoyable evening. I didn't have very much to drink, but the food was good and we listened to records of Hindi film songs and Dixieland jazz records on an old wind-up gramophone, which they really enjoyed. About 25 children came and sat around outside the circle of chairs to listen to the music, and it was quite a revelation to see them muffled up in their blankets up to their noses and their bright eyes just showing over the top, jigging about in time to the music.

Sadly it was soon over and the next morning I loaded all my belongings, plus Kancha and the paniwalla, Rufus, Titch the kitten, Bubble and Squeak, my two Guinea Pigs, and a pigeon one of the workers gave me as a going away present into the garden lorry and transferred to Sathkyah. Sunday was always the best day for transfers as this was also bazaar day and the lorry was not required for other garden work. Because the Sathkyah engineer's bungalow was due to be redecorated before I moved into it, I was told to move in with the other assistant for a few days until it was ready. He was living in the Dangee bungalow in the lower division of the garden and on the 18th he had been away shooting all day, so I did not meet him until I returned from the factory at 9.30 am on Monday for breakfast. He was already eating his and at the same time reading a book supported on a book stand in the middle of the table. Wishing to be sociable I said 'good morning', which was returned with a grunt. A few moments later I asked him whether he had had any luck with his shooting the day before, and with a great sigh he laid down his knife and fork and said, 'Can you read? If so, get yourself a b***** book and read it, because we don't talk at mealtimes in this bungalow'. Then he went on with his breakfast. Obviously he had not had a good day's shooting the previous day.

As it so happened I loved reading, so it was no hardship for me to spend our meal times reading in a semi companionable silence, but it was something that got me into trouble later on. After I went home and married Jan, on our first morning together after our honeymoon I took the daily paper and started reading it while eating my breakfast. 'What do you think you are doing?' demanded an irate Jan, snatching the newspaper away from in front of my nose. 'Oh, I'm just reading at the table', I replied, 'we always do this out in India'. 'Well, you're not in India now and you can stop that this minute', she retorted, 'If you can't be decent and talk to me while we're eating, you're certainly not going to read a blasted newspaper!' I learned very quickly that she had a very persuasive manner, because I have never done it since.

Until the early 1950s all the tea bushes were grown from good-quality seeds obtained from specially-selected mature trees which received special treatment in seed tree areas. Unfortunately, because of the need for pollination, the quality and size of crop that was obtained from individual bushes varied a great deal, so the Indian Tea Association (ITA) decided to conduct experiments at their research facility at Tocklai in Assam to investigate the use of leaf cuttings from proven quality, exceptional bushes. All tea bushes have a certain amount of hair on their leaf buds, and in their tests they discovered that in a lot of cases more hairs meant better quality. Nowadays, some 50 years afterwards, just about all the replanting is done with clonal material developed over the years as a matter of course, but in those days many of the older traditional planters thought it was just a nine-day wonder and didn't take very much interest in it.

Fortunately De La was not one of these. He had always had a scientific mind and could see the benefits in this type of bush selection, so by the time I arrived he had already started selecting very hairy mother bushes which provided leaf cuttings that were planted out in special nursery beds. Rather like developing fuchsias, all the plants in any one bed had been developed from one mother bush, and although it was a slow process, ultimately enough plants were obtained to be able to manufacture small samples of tea that had originated from the one plant in order to evaluate the quality of the tea it would produce. However in 1952 this work was in its infancy, so as De La was already looking after the top garden and the other assistant was supervising Dangee, he told me I was to look after the factory and in my spare time to wander through as much tea as I was able, examining each healthy bush in an effort to discover the 'super hairy' one. As a result I began to spend my mornings in the factory and my afternoons in the garden, examining each bush closely with a magnifying glass to see just how hairy its buds were. I found it fascinating to see just how much this varied from bush to bush. When I found an exceptional one I stuck a flag marked with a code number in it so that it would not be plucked and it was left to develop suitable shoots to make cuttings. If any cuttings became unidentifiable or the records became mixed up then the whole of the work was useless, so I devised a system of coloured letters, numbers and symbols which showed the block number, row number, and the number of the bush within that row, so that at any time we knew exactly where on the estate any individual clones had originated, and the clonal beds were all marked in the same way. This was fascinating work as I took great satisfaction in keeping the records , and my system appeared to stand the test of time because it was still in use many years afterwards.

I loved doing this sort of work, roaming through the tea by myself looking for THE top quality bush, and felt what the old-time gold prospectors must have experienced when they were looking for the elusive lost gold seam. Over the next few weeks I must have examined many tens of thousands of bushes. I had a certain amount of success, and evidently this must have been noticed, because the next thing I knew I had been selected to attend a clonal course at Tocklai on the 10th and 11th of June. During the last week of May and the beginning of June we had a heatwave during which we had temperatures as high as 109 degrees F. in the shade on several days, and with a very high humidity as well even the labourers were affected. Several of the women collapsed while plucking and one afternoon after I had been out in the sun all the morning, I had an attack of heatstroke while I was sitting in the office checking some papers. At about 4 pm I started getting large red and green blotches before my eyes. Within a few minutes I had lost my sight completely, but fortunately the Doctor Babu was nearby and he made me lie out on my back on the concrete slab in front of the office safes which was nice and cold, then kept covering my forehead with cold water compresses until my sight came back. In all I suppose I must have been blind for about an hour. All I was left with was a vicious headache, but it did teach me a lesson and for the first and only time in my life I wore a hat for a few days until I was back to normal.

On June 8th I flew down to Calcutta from Bagdogra in an Indian Airlines DC3 on the first stage of my visit to Assam. I was soon jolted back to reality, for when we alighted from the aircraft the heat and humidity was even worse, rather like stepping into a Turkish bath, and even the air conditioning in the Grand Hotel did little to dissipate the heat. Early the next morning, after a very hot and sticky night with very little sleep, I went out to Dum Dum to catch the Bharat Airways flight to Jorehaut airstrip, the nearest airfield to Tocklai, via Agartala, Gauhati and Tezpur. As we waited for the DC3 to take off there was a very dull, oppressive feel about the weather which gave us a foreboding that something big was going to happen, almost as though a boiler was building up pressure ready to explode. We did not realise just how big it was going to be.

We took off on time and reached Agartala without incident, but then our troubles began. Between Agartala and Gauhati lie the Khasi-Jaintia hills, and these were covered by an absolutely ferocious electrical storm which also seemed to be covering the whole of Assam. Within a few minutes of leaving Agartala the old Dakota was being thrown about like a leaf in a gale, until this finally became so violent that the pilot decided to turn back as he deemed it too dangerous to proceed. After waiting for two hours at the airfield he decided to try again. Thinking he might be able to pass over the top of the storm he started climbing as soon as he was airborne, but soon we were being thrown about all over the sky again and as I watched the wing tip vibrating and moving up and down while the aircraft rose and fell suddenly as though it was a lift. I felt so frightened that I was relieved when he decided that enough was enough and he returned to Calcutta, where we spent another sweltering night in the Grand.

The next morning we tried again. Although the plane was riding up and down like a switchback and lightning was playing about on the wings, we finally reached Jorehaut and I attended the course over the next two days, intending to fly back to Calcutta on Saturday afternoon, but this was not to be. When the plane arrived the pilot told us that for the last two days there had been tremendous storms over the whole of East Pakistan (now Bangladesh), which had also battered the Dooars and Assam with high winds and absolutely torrential rain, and he had been instructed not to return to Calcutta until the following day, so we were able to have another very pleasant evening in the club before we returned on Sunday. However, although he had told us as much as he knew we were not prepared for the sights we saw as we flew over the Brahmaputra and the low lying plains of East Pakistan at about 5000 feet. From the air it all looked like one vast lake, with here and there small hillocks rising out of the water on which a few houses were perched. In some places only the tops of the trees showed above the flood water, while thatched roofs floated on the surface and marooned cattle stood on isolated bits of higher ground, but where the proper rivers flowed their positions showed up as chocolate-coloured swirls in the grey floodwaters, and thousands of square miles must have been inundated. Although parts of Calcutta had been flooded it was not quite so bad flying up to Bagdogra airport on Monday afternoon, and it was not until I reached Bagrakote on the western edge of the storm area that I began to realise what absolute havoc and devastation had been wreaked over the whole of the Dooars.

The airfield staff told me that road and rail bridges had been swept away throughout the whole of the Dooars and that no transport was getting through to the affected area any further than Bagracote as the bridge there had been swept away, so I had no means of getting back to Sathkyah. Fortunately I was able to hire a taxi for the journey to Bagrakote, which took about an hour, and then it took me the rest of the day to cover the 15 miles back to Sathkyah, as most of the way I walked along the railway lines. Where the bridges or the embankments had been washed away the rails hung suspended over the gaps, but as they still had their sleepers attached to them I was able to use them as bridges, though I had my heart in my mouth at times. All the way back I saw scenes of devastation, but these didn't prepare me for the sights that met my eyes when I reached Sathkyah, where our rain gauge recorded that 36 inches of rain had fallen in nine hours. The factory was actually built on the bank of the Kurti river, which normally ran at the bottom of its own valley about 50 feet below the floor level and into which all the factory drains emptied. However at the height of the storm the valley was so full of flood water that it surged up through the drain pipes and flooded the factory, as well as washing away 20 labourer's houses and drowning six buffaloes.

Below the factory the Kurti was crossed by both a road and a rail bridge, and although the road bridge stood fast, one of the few to do so, the railway bridge was completely demolished, with just the dangling rails remaining over a 60-foot gap. Columns, piers, buttresses, everything was swept away and two-ton steel 'I' beams with two-foot-deep webs were twisted like strands of spaghetti and left lying in the river bed a hundred yards downstream. The force of the water surging down the valley must have been tremendous.

Life on Sathkyah

Possibly there were two reasons why the road bridge survived the torrent while the rail bridge didn't. The first was that it was built some 150 yards downstream from the railway at a point where the river had entered the plain and widened out, so by the time it reached there its velocity and power could have been reduced. Secondly the road bridge was considerably longer and much less sturdily made, with slender steel support columns, open angle iron sides, and a road surface made of thick, wooden planks covered with a thin, asphalt layer. This method of construction did not block or dam the water but allowed it to flow unhindered between the supports, even when it was almost submerged. At the height of the storm the flood was flowing over the decking, but although some of the decking lifted and the planks floated away, it stayed intact and was repaired quite easily afterwards. However its structure must have been weakened, because it was completely washed away two years later in 1954 by another tremendous monsoon deluge. Later it was replaced by a modern, stressed concrete bridge which was still standing when we revisited Sathkyah in 2007.

During the storm several areas of tea had been eroded and had fallen into the river and many of the garden roads were blocked with landslides and fallen trees, so it took us a week to bring it back to normality. Then it was back to the vegetative propagation. Armed with all the knowledge I had gained at Tocklai I had to write a report for the Superintendent which was then sent to all our gardens. To my surprise this made me the so-called clonal 'expert'. New style cutting beds with variable shade were prepared in the clonal nursery and then most afternoons in the cool of the evening, a group of specially selected reliable men gathered the long shoots from the mother bushes and in the nursery area these were cut into hundreds of single leaf cuttings with a length of stem attached which were then dusted with rooting powder and planted. Although I did a lot of demonstration at first, as the men became more proficient I was able to adopt a more supervisory role and concentrate on ensuring that all the records were maintained and absolutely correct.

The engineer's bungalow was built in a lovely situation on top of the hill above the factory, and as the redecoration was completed while I was in Assam I moved up from Dangee the following week. As I had shared bungalows with other assistants ever since I had arrived in tea, I was very happy to move out and live on my own at last, and as it was built to the same design as our one on Zurrantee I felt at home as soon as I moved in. Sathkyah was about three miles south of Zurrantee, with Aibheel, another of our gardens, sandwiched in between, so from the bungalow I could look across the other estates to the tree-clad Himalayan foothills beyond. During the cold weather the 22,000-foot mountains between India and Tibet were clearly visible some 25 miles away. To the south the hillside dropped steeply down to the plain where the factory, office and the Dangee out-division were situated and beyond this there was a vast expanse of tea and forest to the distant horizon.

The only drawback to where it was situated was that it was divided neatly in two by the only road and rail links between West Bengal and Assam, and these ran a few yards from the factory. On the Eastern bank of the Kurti was Chulsa Station, with several acres of shunting and goods yards, and this was a tremendous advantage when it came to despatching invoices of tea to Calcutta, for we never had any trouble in being allocated an empty wagon and we only had a few yards to carry the chests. Unfortunately one of the consequences of being right on the main roadside was that it was a prime area for thieves from Siliguri and the local Mal bazaar to operate in, and we had several incidents of break-ins and thefts of both tea and vehicle parts during my time there. Even the managerial bungalows were not immune to attention from thieves, and there had been an incident on one of the estates near Mal Bazaar only a few months before, when one of the assistants who had been to the club one Wednesday evening returned to find that his bungalow had been completely ransacked and numerous items stolen. Obviously it was clear that some of his staff had not been doing their jobs properly, because according to what we heard the thieves had taken just about everything of any value, including his clothes, his wife's clothes and jewellery and all their wedding presents. I believe they had only recently returned from his first home leave and they were so disillusioned that they decided that it would be a mistake to stay in India, so he resigned and left tea soon afterwards.

This story had made quite an impression on me and put me on my guard, so one night a few weeks after I had moved into the top bungalow, it came as no surprise to me when I too received a visit from an unwelcome friend. Although I did employ a night watchman to stay awake and guard the bungalow while I was away at night, he was allowed to sleep on the back veranda during the night while I was in the bungalow. Most nights once the manufacture was complete and the factory machinery stopped the electric lighting was switched off, so this night the bungalow was in complete darkness when an unusual noise woke me up in the early hours of the morning. In those days I came to fully awake as soon as my eyes opened and I realised that what had wakened me was the sound of someone who had scrambled up onto my bedroom window sill and was trying to break into the room. From the noise he was making I can only assume he was under the impression that the bungalow was still unoccupied, for even when I got out of bed he didn't stop. All the windows were covered with brass wire mesh mosquito netting screens. As I always slept with the small top windows wide open to allow some fresh air in, by the time I had woken up he had managed to reach inside and open the main window, but had been unable to break in through the wire netting, which he was trying to cut with a knife. Living on my own I always slept with my loaded rifle and a Gurkha kukri by the side of my bed. There was a moon that night and I could see his shape silhouetted against the night sky, so I quickly lifted the rifle and squeezed off a shot through the open window just above his head. In the silence of the night the unexpected report must have been terrifying and ear-shattering, for with an agonising cry he fell backwards off the window sill and crashed down onto the stones and bricks that edged the flower border beneath the window. The fall must have knocked the stuffing out of him and possibly injured him, because when I opened the front door and ran out onto the veranda, he was stumbling across the lawn trying to escape through the compound gate. It wasn't in my interests to shoot and injure him because all I wanted to do was frighten him silly, so in the half-light I aimed at the gate and fired another couple of shots that ricocheted off the cast iron gatepost and whined away into the tea. These caused him to speed up spectacularly, and he disappeared into the night.

I was left with a small hole in my mosquito wire netting which was easily repaired, and a sense of satisfaction in the way I had got rid of him, but for him it must have been a very traumatic experience as it probably scared him witless. No doubt he passed the word around, because I never had any further visits of this nature during the remainder of my time on Sathkyah.

However the event did have a sequel, because a few weeks later I was woken up again in the early hours of the morning by something strange. Although I got out of bed and had a wander around I couldn't find anything amiss, so I went back to bed. I had no idea what it was that had woken me, so I lay awake for a while in the hope that it would be repeated. When I was almost asleep I heard a very faint sound which seemed to be coming from the direction of the window. It sounded like a rustling, chewing noise, so I took my torch and shone it on the flower bed beneath the window and there, having a picnic and sitting quietly nibbling my flowers, were two large hares. Obviously I had very sharp hearing in those days.

With very minor variations the garden work was basically the same on all our gardens, and we issued the subsidised rations to the garden labourers in the office compound every two weeks exactly as we had done on Zurrantee. However, the difference here was that many of the labourers who lived south of the main road also lived east of the Kurti river, and during the rains the only way that they could cross over to the office was by way of the road bridge. Normally this presented no difficulty, but one day in October the number of labourers taking rations seemed to dry up for no reason at all, and when we made enquiries somebody reported that a drunken man with a naked kukri had taken over the bridge and was preventing everyone, including lorries, from crossing over. As the man was one of our labourers this seemed to be a serious business, so Dela instructed me to take Soona, one of the lower garden sirdars, with me and go and see whether we could remove him.

When we reached the bridge we saw a scene of utter confusion. He had stopped five lorries, three on the one side and two on the other, and a crowd of about 250 labourers had gathered around the bridge but were unable to cross. Evidently one of the lorry drivers had attempted to pass over, but the man had jumped on his running board and threatened that he would carve him up with the kukri if he didn't go back, so he did. In reality it was rather like a comic film, for the man was only wearing a very skimpy loin cloth and each time anybody tried to run the gauntlet and get across he would chase him off and then sing a little song and do a 'victory dance' in the middle of the bridge.

After watching him for a couple of minutes I told Soona that we would go onto the bridge together and while he went to the left and attempted to talk to him, I would go quietly up the right hand side and try to get behind him, and this we did. In actual fact he took absolutely no notice of me whatsoever.

Once I had sidled up behind him I was able to pinion his arms to his sides while Soona took the kukri out of his hand, and after that he was as quiet as a lamb.

Holding him between us, we started to march him off the bridge and the change that came over the crowd was absolutely amazing, because while he was free and in charge of the bridge nobody would go near him, but as soon as we had him immobilised and they could get close all they wanted to do was beat him to a pulp. It was with the greatest difficulty that we finally managed to get him to the office. He was obviously as high as a kite on liquor and stank like a skunk. When we asked him what he thought he had been doing, he said that he had forgotten to worship his God, who had told him to go and patrol the bridge and keep the people off it. When we asked him why he had stopped the lorries, he said that the drivers were driving very fast and dangerously and as they didn't know how to cross the bridge properly he was giving them directions with his kukri, but he wasn't going to hit them. However they seemed to see it differently, and certainly only the one of them tried to get across, but to be fair to him he didn't try to hit us. Once we had questioned him and realised that really he was quite out of his mind and didn't know what he was doing, we tied him up and the Doctor Babu gave him an injection to knock him out. Then once he had slept it off his relatives took him back to his house as quiet as a lamb and that was the last of the incident, just one of the many facets of life in India.

That bridge did make a lasting impression on me during my eight months on Sathkyah, for it also featured in another very memorable incident which could have had much more serious consequences. The new clonal tea nurseries down in the Dangee out garden meant I had to cross the bridge several times a day. One afternoon in October I finished work there and went back to the office at about 5 pm. As I came out onto the main road the Sathkyah shopkeeper's lorry passed in front of me, so I fell in behind it and followed it down to the bridge, travelling about 20 yards behind him at about 30 mph. The bridge with its approaches was about 60 yards in length and just wide enough for one vehicle to cross at a time, and as we drove onto it everything was fine. It was a lovely evening and the road was dry, so I wasn't really concentrating as I idly wondered whether the dak walla might have brought any letters from home for me, when I realised to my horror that the truck had stopped dead. It had no brake lights, so I had no warning until I realised that it was no longer moving.

A a sickening feeling came up in my stomach. For a split second I wondered whether I could squeeze the bike through the small gap between the lorry and the side pieces of the bridge, but a few days before I had seen the mangled side of a Jeep that had scraped along a similar structure, and realising the mess that angle iron and nuts and bolts can make of flesh when you hit them, I decided that the best thing I could do was to hit the back of the lorry as gently as possible.

As the bike wheels locked and I slid along the road, I heeled her over onto her right hand side until she was sliding sideways towards the back of the lorry, rather like a cinder track rider, and as we reached the tailboard I stepped off and took the collision with my outstretched arms while the bike slid beneath it with a tremendous crash and wedged itself beneath the back axle. Luckily I wasn't travelling very fast when I struck, and other than a cut leg and bruised and strained arms and shoulders I was otherwise uninjured. However I was quite shaken and dazed. I was just checking myself to see if there was any more damage when the driver and his mate ran round to the back to see what the crash was. They were absolutely dumbfounded to see me standing there, and with me shaken up and livid about what had happened the conversation was like something out of a classic Laurel and Hardy film and went something like this:

'Why are you standing there like that, Sahib?'

'I hit your lorry.'

'What did you hit the lorry with?'

'I was on my motor bike'

'Where's the motor bike now?'

'That's it underneath your back axle'.

'Oh father. What is it doing there?'

'Because it hit the back of your lorry'

'Why did you hit the back of my lorry?'

At this I gave up and lost my temper, and answered, 'Because you stopped without any warning, you fool, and I couldn't stop. Why did you do it?'

'Oh Sahib, there are a lot of goats asleep on the bridge, and I thought that when they saw me they would get up and run away but they didn't, so I had to stop or I would have run over them.'

Well there was no answer to that, because I had been daydreaming and not paying attention to my riding and it really was my fault. Fortunately I wasn't really injured, so all we had to do was drag the bike out from underneath the differential and assess the damage, and here again it was not too bad. One of the footrests was bent, there were numerous small dents and scratches and the silencer box had come adrift again, but the main damage was that the handlebar damping mechanism had been bent backwards through 90 degrees from the normal position, which meant it was jammed solid. Of course I was unable to ride it, so we loaded it onto the truck and they gave me a lift back to the factory.

To add insult to injury there was no home mail in the post that night, but when Satya the shopkeeper was told he was very sorry that it had happened, and although it had not been his driver's fault he offered to take the bike into Siliguri for me where it could be repaired at a garage owned by a friend of his. At the time I had my doubts about what kind of a job they would do, but beggars can't be choosers so I agreed and I was very pleasantly surprised when he brought it back three weeks later looking like new. Without examining it very closely it was very difficult to see where it had been damaged. Even better he must have had a word with his friend, because the bill was nothing like as much as I thought it would be, so I was well pleased with the outcome.

While the bike was away I was allowed to borrow a cycle which was kept at the factory office for people doing odd jobs and delivering messages, so I was able to cycle down to the clonal nurseries in the afternoons. I now realised just how much I had come to rely on the bike. I had forgotten that without it I was virtually a prisoner in the bungalow and could only visit the club if someone collected me, so in one way I longed for the day when I would get it back and be properly mobile once again. On the other hand the crash had made a big impression on me and the more I considered it the more I thought just how fortunate I had been. Not having been wearing proper boots, a crash helmet or protective clothing, I had been extremely lucky that I had not been seriously injured, and I realised that I might not get away with it so lightly the next time. Serious injury could possibly result in the ending of

My mother in a
pensive mood on
her 18th birthday,
May 1st 1917

An official company postcard of the P&O ship *Strathaird*, 1951

Jan on holiday in August 1952

'Bum boats' trading with the passengers in Port Said harbour, January 1951

Me posing by the first-class companionway on the Strathaird, while moored in Port Said harbour

The Zurrantee assistants at Chulsa Club on our first Sunday morning.

L-R John Mitchell, Ian Munro and "Shortie" Rod Brown.

The new Howrah Bridge across the River Hoogly, which looked as though it had been made from a giant Meccano set.

The Superintendent, Mr Lawrence Tocher, in front of his pride and joy, a Canadian Ford V8 saloon.

The Zurrantee manager's bungalow

The nine-foot-four-inch tigress shot in the Nagaisuree jungle.
The group squatting behind her (L-R) are Noel Barker, Johnny Adams,
Rod Brown, Sandie Frain's wife Nora with her baby and Bill Milne,
with the beaters grouped behind.

The tigress loaded into the back of the Zurrantee lorry. Bill's first bullet hole can be seen in its nose, and its size is evident in comparison with the lorry driver.

March 12th 1951. This was the leopard we shot behind our bungalow at lunchtime. John Mitchell is introducing our kitten to its big cousin.

The leopard with onlookers

Ian Munro with
myself and Rufus
on the lawn in front
of the bungalow,
March 1951.

Geared up with my rifle and kukri before taking a visit to the dhan khets to look for pig in the evening.

Ian Munro and me in the back of Martin Hawes' sports car after a trip up the Teesta Valley road.

Workers on Zurrantee. Somra, the tractor driver who taught me to drive, together with his wife and young son. His bandage marks the place where I cracked his bone with a shot at football.

Lopo Munda, my Chief Engineer in the Zurrantee factory, who made me my first bow and arrows.

One of the girls from the labour line going down to the river to wash her cooking pots.

Two of the nursing mothers who carried water to the tea seed beds after planting out. They would carry about five gallons of water on their heads in these "ghilas".

Leaf weighments in the garden, using a bamboo tripod and a calibrated brass scale which was checked by the authorities each year. The leaf is being carried away in the tractor trailer.

At the Killcott swimming pool, where I inadvertently swam alongside a large snake. Note the tea growing at the top of the bank.

With friends at the swimming pool

The two snakes the labourers killed while going to work one morning. The smaller one was a delicate pink and speckled grey in colour and I was unable to identify it. The other was a very large banded krait, probably more than six feet long.

Posing with my great shikari friend Dushroo behind the Soongachie leopard which Bill shot just before he went home on leave. Skinning the animal was a very specialised job which only the most capable shikaris were entrusted with.

On the Triumph 500 Speed Twin (the Red Peril), which I later rode underneath a lorry.

Our best-ever shoot, February 1952. Dushroo is pointing at the boar while Bill`s shikari is on the other side. I shot the boar, the civet cat and one of the barking deer, while Bill bagged the other deer and the four jungle fowl.

The Coronation Bridge which crosses the River Teesta at Sevoke.

Albert Ager's farewell. Seated in the front row, L-R: the Head Clerk, the Doctor Babu, Lionel Hoadley, Albert Ager, Molly Hoadley, Rod Brown, Brian Seymour the Crossley Engineer and the Head Factory Clerk. The head of the local Communist party is peeking round the corner on the left hand side.

Wee Mac posing with his bearer's wife and son. It looks as though he was tickling her.

Bagracote manager's bungalow. Cool downstairs, but hot and very smelly upstairs.

The Bagracote Assistant's bungalow by the roadside. This is where my friend the snake charmer visited me.

Albert Ager's farewell. He is standing in the doorway of the plane saying goodbye to his staff grouped round below. The freight has just been unloaded off the aircraft.

Donald Mackenzie's boyhood friend Ram with his wife and two children.

Maila Rai, a very jolly and efficient Nepalese gentleman who was my Chief Factory Engineer on Bagracote, with his four children at puja time..

My Morris Minor parked outside the wire room at the Saugaon bungalow.

The mess it made when I hit the tree going backward. She was never the same again. April 1954.

My second car, the Standard Vanguard Phase 1 Saloon
which once belonged to Lionel Hoadley.

Our lorry driver Bandhna in a jovial mood soon after he returned
from Calcutta.

The Mark 1 Ford Consul I bought in August 1954

One of the very large boars I shot during our shoots in the summer of 1954

Our record-breaking shoot at Makligunj when we shot 16 pigs.
This was my "chariot", with Ash Wason having a lift.

The three pigs I shot laid out to be recorded for posterity before they joined the rest.

First he was up... Bob Grey posed leaning back on his wagon
after he had shot one pig.

Then he was down. Bob after he had cartwheeled backwards when
his pole broke with his weight.

The wreckage of Jamair DC3 VT-DGO after the accidental landing
on May 15th 1954. She looked like a wounded bird nestling on the edge
of the 30-foot drop into the dhan khets.

My leopard, shot at Saugaon on
October 23rd 1954.

Donald Mackenzie, with myself seated
and Bob Grey, awaiting the start of the
shoot for the man-eating tiger in Cooch
Behar.

The Maharaja of Cooch Behar's shikar elephants waiting for us to be allocated our mounts. Donald Mackenzie third left, Bob Grey fifth left, T K Roy sixth left, Rod Brown fifth from the right.

The Bagracote leaf unloader in action. The "ladder" on the Ford Thames lorry
is being attached to the tree trunk.

Driving away with the leaf unrolling onto the unloading floor.

The leaf unloaded in one operation, with the ladder lying on the top of the heap ready to be reinstalled in the lorry for the next weighment.

Replanting. The men making up the tea seed beds ready for planting.

A staking man tapping a marker into the ground with a wooden mallet.

One of the women takes a drink from the pani wallah.

Women who have been carrying plants to the planting area take a rest.

Rod Brown with the small Ford 10 hp pickup at the replanting area, December 1954.

The old Bhutia woman who helped us carry the luggage down across the land slides on the Darjeeling road. The trunk was heavily loaded, but she carried it unaided by the woven strap round her forehead. She is resting the trunk on the edge of the railway line alongside the road.

Her daughter, who carried the lighter items in a similar way.

Farewell Victoria. A goodbye photo taken in front of the stern while she was berthed in Genoa harbour.

The Victoria. This large colour photograph was taken and given to me by another passenger as we returned from our visit to the Crater Market in Aden. She was moored in the Crater Harbour and it was the first time I was able to see her in all her beauty.

Santi Stores in Matelli. This was the only local store, from which the dakwalla bought all our essentials. The next nearest one was 12 miles away in Mal Bazaar.

Our local bus, the "Siliguri Flyer", ready to leave on its 50-mile long journey to the town of Siliguri.

The road from Zurrantee to Matelli Bazaar through Nagaisuree.

The valley between the two bungalows on Zurrantee, showing the tea on the top of the cliff where we shot the leopard. The "clack pump" lived in the metal housing on the valley bottom at the right hand corner of the photo.

Main Street, Matelli Bazaar.

my career in tea. Even after the bike was returned to me I continued to think about it, until finally I decided that although I would keep it for the time being, I would look around for a suitable car and sell the bike as soon as possible.

Then, as luck would have it, no sooner had I made my mind up than I heard that one of the local assistants who had decided to resign from tea and go home early in 1953 intended to sell his car, and as it seemed to be a good buy I decided to go for it. It was an original 1950/51 model Morris Minor MM with a split front windscreen, black with red upholstery in excellent condition, and it appeared to be just what I needed. Satya had already told me that if I ever wanted to sell the Triumph he had a friend in Siliguri who would like to buy it, so I had no difficulty there, and without more ado I agreed a purchase price for the Minor, arranged for my loan, and then all I had to do was wait for the vendor to go on leave. She looked a lovely car and although she was not really suitable for the road conditions in India and had some basic design faults which didn't come to light until later, with her flowing lines and gleaming paintwork I fell in love with her the moment I saw her.

Once Bill Milne had arrived back from his eight months' home leave at the end of October, Sandy Frain handed the garden back to him and returned to Sathkyah, where he took over as Engineer Assistant once more, before acting as manager for John De La Mare when John went home on leave in 1953. Had things gone as planned I knew that I should have stayed on Zurrantee for my first two years and Bill had warned me that I would probably be moving to another garden in 1953, so I moved out of the Engineer's bungalow and went back down to share the Dangee bungalow with my friendly assistant once more until it was time to transfer, but this time I knew what to expect, so things weren't quite as traumatic as they had been the first time and we got on well.

The clonal cutting nurseries were only a short distance away from the bungalow, and as my work was to get them planted up and growing as soon as possible most of my normal working time was spent there, supervising the bed-making and shade erection and keeping detailed records of all the mother bushes and cuttings as they were planted. Because the midday sun was still very hot I found that cuttings gathered and planted in the heat of the day did very badly compared with others that had been planted in the evening, so I introduced a system of working by which all the shade construction and bed-making work was done in the early morning, while the cuttings were taken and planted during the late afternoon and well into the evening using a small portable generating set for light. Once they had got used to it the labourers seemed to enjoy this work pattern as it gave them extra time off during the day, and as we got to know exactly how many cuttings we could deal with in any one evening, the work continued apace right up until the time I left. In addition the two men I had trained and put in charge of the squad became so proficient and reliable that on the nights when I had to knock off early to attend play rehearsals at the club the planting was completed satisfactorily, so that when I had to transfer to another estate in the new year I knew that they would be able to continue the good work.

I had enjoyed being involved with *Blithe Spirit* in 1951 and was quite happy to give some help in the same way again. Martin Hawes decided that in order to include more people and spread the enjoyment, the 1952 production would be

Agatha Christie's murder mystery, *Ten Little Nigger Boys* for which he needed a larger cast to be killed off one by one, so when he suggested that I took the part of Rogers, the manservant who disappears quite early in the play, I jumped at the chance. Actually as far as I was concerned, preparing and rehearsing for the play was even better than the actual performance, because after rehearsals the wives of the planters involved took it in turn to bring the supper, which usually consisted of spicy soup, sandwiches and rolls with cheese and butter, and sitting round chatting and having a social get together seemed like heaven to me. Of course the title is not accepted nowadays and has been changed to *And Then There Were None* to reflect current attitudes, but it didn't seem to matter then and when we performed it at Chulsa Club on November 26th it was a tremendous success. I was on stage when the curtain went up, with grey hair and smartly dressed in a bow tie and a tail coat, and although my part was not a large one I enjoyed every minute of it. A bonus for me was that I got to know several of the planters in Chulsa much better through being involved. After the play the evening was completed by supper, and then dancing to music on some new records brought out by one of the planters who had been on leave, so a really good time was had by all.

It was at this time that Bill Milne invited me up one evening to hear about his home leave and tell me all about the slump that had occurred in tea sales in the UK. I hadn't realised that all through the war years and until 1951, all the tea produced was sold directly through a Ministry of Food contract. As the crops were down owing to the fact that many of the male labourers were away in Assam and Burma working on military projects, the priority was on quantity not quality and the Government took as much tea as could be produced. Now the wheel had turned full circle. As the gardens returned to normality after the war and partition and the crops increased, this coincided with the export to the UK of large quantities of tea from estates in Africa which had been planted out after the war and soon there was a glut of poor quality tea on the market. Tea was still rationed in the UK at 2 oz per head per week, so when the Government decided to end the Ministry of Food contract and re-open the tea auctions in Mincing Lane in 1951, with the large amount of tea to choose from the buyers became very selective and only the best quality teas were sold. Even when tea was taken off the ration in late 1951 the situation improved very little, and things got so bad that by the beginning of 1952 up to 50% of the teas offered for sale in the London auctions failed to attract any bids whatsoever. This meant that many of the estates didn't cover the cost of manufacture and made large losses. In most cases estates that were part of a large Agency House such as our Company were able to weather the storm, but many of the smaller estates that were privately owned were forced to close, although some of them re-opened when the market improved.

During the 1951/52 cold weather, some of them went on to a three or four-day working week in order to save cash and stay afloat until plucking started once more. Fortunately our estates were never forced to resort to methods such as this, although we did do our best to ensure that unnecessary expenditure was kept to a minimum, so I suppose we were very lucky that we had our Superintendent living locally on Sam Sing and he was able to keep his eye on matters. Actually for the 1951 season, of the ten gardens that made up our group only two, Dangua Jhar and Zurrantee had made profits, so that night after a few drinks Bill was very pleased to tell me that we were 'flavour of the month back home' and that we had been 'mentioned in despatches' whatever that signified, so we must have done something right.

Because most of the preparations for the play, such as backdrop painting, scenery erection and electrical wiring were done on the Wednesday afternoon 'club days', this meant that I was unable to get up to Zurrantee to join Bill for any of the afternoon shoots over in the Naura forest, but one Sunday at the beginning of December I went up to Sam Sing and joined a shoot in the forest organised by John Adams. For most of the morning we drew a blank. Bill had brought some of the beaters from Zurrantee, including Dushroo, my shikari from Zurrantee days, and it was a real pleasure to be able to shoot with him again. Because we had had some late rain at the end of the monsoon the jungle was still very thick and visibility was limited, but this didn't account for the fact that there seemed to be no game around. However late in the morning when we were thinking of giving up and going off for tiffin, the beaters started whistling and knocking the trunks of trees to show that they had disturbed something big that had run away in front of them, although they hadn't actually seen what it was.

We were positioned on a small path right in the middle of the tract of jungle with limited visibility through the undergrowth, and as we knew that the beaters were driving whatever it was towards us, we waited very expectantly without speaking hoping that it would come our way. It always amazed me how quietly large animals could move through the jungle when they were being cautious and this day was no exception, because everything was quiet until suddenly without any warning, there was a tremendous crashing noise and I saw the head, neck and antlers of a big sambhar stag charging through the undergrowth about 20 yards away. From a standing start it was going like a racehorse and it really made me jump. As Dushroo said 'maro, Sahib, maro!' (shoot, Sahib, shoot), because I was unable to see its body clearly I instinctively swung the rifle and aimed a little below and behind where I thought the base of the neck would be. Then I followed it round and squeezed the trigger. Unfortunately I only had time for the one shot. As we looked at each other it stormed off through the jungle like an express train until there was silence.

Of course I thought I had missed and was very disappointed, especially as we finished the day's shooting soon afterwards without seeing anything else. Then as we all gathered round to discuss the day's events and tried to work out why the animals were not there, Dushroo and Bill's shikari, a man named Nando who had been having an animated conversation, suddenly announced that they thought I had hit the stag and were going to go back in to have another look. What it was Dushroo had seen that I hadn't I never did find out and I can only think that maybe he had some special sixth sense when it came to hunting. To be honest, although I knew it had been a good shot under the circumstances, I didn't think that I had hit it because it hadn't faltered or missed a step in its flight.

There was nobody more surprised than me when they came back twenty minutes later with the news that they had found it. Evidently they had found a spatter of blood on the foliage of the bushes where Dushroo had thought it had been at the moment I fired, and excited by this find they had followed the track it had made as it smashed through the jungle for about 200 yards, until finally they had found it lying stone dead with my bullet hole through the base of its neck. It was a big stag, about as big as a medium-sized horse, and it took eight men to carry it out of the forest slung on bamboo poles. Even after all the guns had had a lump of venison rump for the pot all the beaters had several pounds of meat each, so everyone went home happy.

Even the antlers were not wasted, for when the animal was cut up they were removed and presented to me as a trophy, so when I went home on leave in 1955 I took them with me and gave them to Dad. Mum didn't think very much of them but he thought they were wonderful and after he had made a wooden shield to attach them to, he fixed them to the living room wall, where they hung for over 30 years. Finally when he was no longer able to live at Watkins Terrace we cleared the house out and I took them home, and I have had them packed away ever since, so I suppose it can be said that they are 'out of sight and out of mind,' but every so often when I see them my mind goes back to that day when a small, Indian hunter had a niggle in his mind and the courage of his convictions and surprised us all.

It was at about this time that I lost Rufus after his long illness, and I buried him in the shade of a jacaranda tree in the bungalow compound. It hurt so much to lose him that I decided I would not replace him at that time, especially as we had a very troublesome leopard that was roaming round the estate at night which had snatched several dogs. For some reason leopards love to eat dog flesh and as it had been known for a more brazen one to snatch a sleeping dog from a bungalow veranda in broad daylight, I always had to keep a very special watch over Rufus whenever he went out for a run in the bungalow compound in the evening, so I decided that I would not have another dog for the time being. However plans are made to be broken and we never can be sure what lies ahead, because I had made friends with a Scottish lad named Bill Phillips who had joined tea just after me. I suppose that both being new lads we had a common bond and got on well together. He had a car and also a small Bhutia terrier dog, and one night not long after Rufus died he came down to visit me for a drink and a chat and left his dog in the car. Then while we were talking he said laughingly, 'She's nearly ready for her pups, I hope she doesn't have them in the car!' but that's just what she did. When he opened the door to go home there was a big squeaking and she'd had four. Of course Bill said that as she had had them in my bungalow, destiny intended for me to have one, so which one did I want? After a moment's hesitation I chose the only brown one in the litter. He was russet brown with a black muzzle, ears, back and tail, with four white feet, and as he had a lot of black tiger stripes down his flanks, I named him Tiger and he came to me in the middle of December.

Another bit of rather sad news I heard at this time was that the Engineer's bungalow on Zurrantee had been completely destroyed in an accidental fire not long after I had been up to visit Bill. Because of the change of plans he only had Ian Munro as his assistant, so luckily it was not occupied at the time and nobody knew what had caused it. Maybe if I had been there it would never have started, but once it did it must have spread like wildfire and become an inferno, because although they tried to put it out, when I went over and saw it a few days later all that was left were twisted steel support posts mixed up with distorted corrugated iron sheets and charred wooden planks. Indeed the damage was so bad that it was never repaired and a new replacement bungalow was built down in the lower division a few years later.

After this we started looking forward to Christmas with its avalanche of 'sweeteners', and it began in earnest on the 18th when we had our first visit from one of the tradesmen from Siliguri with his tray of goodies. Cake, fruit, nuts, sweets, a calendar, even the bottle of whisky were all there. We looked forward to many more, but on the 22nd I had a unexpected Christmas present in the form of a letter from the Superintendent instructing me to transfer to Bagracote on Friday January 2nd 1953. When I read it my heart sank, because I knew Bagracote had a reputation for being a rather troublesome garden with a lot of the agitation caused by outside interference from the local bazaar and it was not the place that I would have chosen to go to, but I knew it was no use complaining and I would have to make the best of it. The one good thing about it was that although Mr Tocher gave the impression of being a rather grumpy, dour Scotsman when I met him for the first time, after a while I had realised that he was an excellent planter and very fair, and when I read it again it struck me that at least he had a bit of a heart, inasmuch as he hadn't told me to transfer on New Year's Day after a hectic Hogmanay night at the club.

After that the time went by very quickly and Christmas Day was a rather low key affair as it so happened that I was in the bungalow on my own, though to keep up the festive spirit I did have a small turkey which I had arranged to be included in the cold stores that had come up from Calcutta. However, things didn't go exactly as planned. Kancha, who was acting as cook as well as bearer, said he knew how to roast it properly, but when it was brought in at lunchtime, although roasted to a turn, there was nothing else with it, no stuffing, no gravy and no vegetables, so I had turkey and bread and butter for my lunch. Still it taught me a lesson. Afterwards I knew that when I wanted something done by the servants or labourers that was strange to their way of life, I had to make sure that they knew exactly what they had to do down to the last detail.

This even applied to the office staff. When I began writing letters and reports and sent them to the office for typing, I found that although some of the clerks were excellent English speakers, when it came to reading handwriting, if they were unable to read the scribble they usually made a guess at what the words were and this often made no sense at all. So to avoid mistakes and having to get it all retyped, I made sure that my handwriting became absolutely clear, and this paid dividends. Unfortunately even after I came home this trait never completely left me, so Jan often tells me that I go into too much unnecessary detail when I am describing something and that I would have made a good teacher.

But to complete Christmas Day, the one good thing was that I had been invited out to a party that evening at Martin Hawes' bungalow, where we played games and I made up for my lack of lunch with a lovely dinner. I finally got home at 4.30 am after having had a really lovely time.

Once Christmas was over I packed up all my bits and pieces and prepared to move on the 2nd , but I was a little apprehensive about going to the Hogmanay dance and when the 31st arrived I decided that as I didn't have a car I would stay at home and see 1953 in by myself. However as so often happens, plans are made to be broken. At about 7.30 pm I heard a car coming up the drive and in walked Bill Phillips. As we were both new boys we got on well together, and as he was going to Mal Club to the dance, he decided to call in to see if I would like to go as well, so once I had someone to go with I didn't take much persuading and had a great time.

A six-piece band which played a variety of dance music had come up from Calcutta, and as there were only the planters' wives as partners not much dancing was done, but they were great to listen to while taking a drink or three and the time passed all too quickly.

I think the highlight of the evening for the younger men was when we played the game of stopping the electric fan with your head, which took some doing. Above the bar was an old, worn-out three-bladed fan suspended from the ceiling by a rod, and as we only had 110 volt DC current it was not very powerful and could be easily stopped by the hand when it was on its lowest speed. However the game was to climb up on the bar and get beneath the fan, where its blades were just below head height, then gently straighten the legs until the top of the head was just brushing the inclined lower faces of the blades as they rotated. Then by gradually rising up the friction of the blade on the head slowed it down until it stopped completely. It usually took about 20 knocks and the winner was the one who could do it in the least number. It wasn't actually as dangerous as it sounds, but it certainly gave you a queer sensation in the back of the neck as the blades swished by over your head before they started touching, and then the 'tonk - tonk - tonk' as the fan stopped. It was quite an experience and one not to be repeated

Unfortunately that night was the last I saw of Bill. I stayed on at Bagracote until 1955 and as he was transferred to some other area early in 1953 our paths didn't cross again, so I was never able to discover if he stayed on in tea or whether he decided it was not for him and only worked his first three year contract, but I liked him very much and often wondered what finally happened to him.

I didn't have very much to drink at the Hogmanay dance so the next morning I felt fine, and as the VP work was almost complete for the year, De La told me I could have the day off to make the final preparations for my move. Unlike Zurrantee, where there was a distinct bond between the labourers and the European staff, for some reason this was not the case on Sathkyah and as I had only been there for about nine months I didn't have any farewell celebrations to go to, so I said goodbye to Rufus under his jacaranda tree and faded quietly away to Bagracote to begin my third year in tea.

CHAPTER TWENTY ONE

Hello Bagracote

JANUARY 1953

All my worldly goods took up very little room in the back of the three-ton truck, and as I rode my motor bike down Kancha was able to sit in the front with the driver and hold Tiger on his lap for safety, while Birsa the pani walla, a lad who helped Kancha in the kitchen, sat in the back with the rest of my livestock and all their goods and chattels as well and the transfer went without a hitch.

Bagracote was a medium-sized estate at the western edge of the Dooars on the road to Siliguri, about 25 miles west of Sathkyah, and totalled about 1500 acres under tea. It consisted of two divisions that occupied a roughly rectangular area of land between two rivers, the Leesh and the Geesh, which emerged from the forests and hills to the north and then joined the River Teesta about a mile apart at the bottom. One thousand acres of the Bagracote home division, with two managerial staff bungalows, factory, the offices and labour lines, together with a small village named Pillans Hat, occupied the top of the box, while the smaller Saugaon Division with another bungalow was two miles to the south on the bank of the Geesh river, and was supervised by an Assistant Manager. They were separated in the middle by Leesh River Tea Estate, so this meant a 4.5 mile trip over the garden roads to get from the one to the other.

In the north the Bagracote tea was separated from the forest by a barbed wire fence which also demarcated the official boundary between Jalpaiguri and Darjeeling Districts, but it didn't do much to deter the herds of wild elephants that roamed the hill forests, especially in the cold weather when the vegetation and the surface water had dried up, and sometimes they broke down the fence and caused tremendous damage to our labourer's houses and tea areas. This was to be a new experience for me as we had never had this sort of trouble in Chulsa area.

The Manager of Bagracote was Albert Agar, but as he was due to retire in February and his successor Lionel Hoadley was living in the assistant's bungalow until he took over, the Superintendent had instructed me to move into the Saugaon bungalow and share with 'Wee' Mac until the changeover was complete. This was the bungalow Old Donald had been in when he wrestled with the boar, and Wee Mac had moved to Saugaon when the old man had made his ill fated move to Zurrantee in early 1952. Unlike the bungalows I had been in before, the one on Saugaon was an old-fashioned wooden structure with a corrugated iron roof built right on the bank of the River Geesh, which at this point was about a half a mile wide with the Apalchand forest on the other side. The river bed was covered with a mass of pebbles, fallen trees, silvery sand and large boulders which had been carried down by the water. When I first saw it on that day shining silvery-white in the morning sun with a shallow stream a few yards wide trickling down the main stream bed, it was very hard to visualise that once the monsoon rain began it would soon become full and un-crossable, with a foaming torrent of water half a mile wide and several feet deep raging down it.

Although the bungalow was old fashioned it was quite similar to our other ones, with a large living room, dining room, two bedrooms each with its own bathroom, and a shady veranda with a wire mesh mosquito room on the north side. It was probably built in the 1930s and looked as though it needed a bit of TLC, but it had its own Lister diesel generating set supplying 110v dc electricity, so we were quite comfortable. Probably it had had a very chequered history, because later one of the Saugaon labourers told me it was haunted by the spirit of a young girl who had been killed in it long ago by a planter, and one of his friends had actually seen her ghost, but after the incident of the trombone and the 'Tiger' on Zurrantee I always took such stories with a pinch of salt and I never came across her. The only thing I did experience was when I was disturbed one night by some unusual noises that seemed to be coming from the roof space above my bed, so much so that the next morning I went up to investigate and found it so thick with dust that nothing could have moved in there without leaving a track. They must have been made by some night bird or animal on the roof, because I never heard them again.

I think Wee Mac had joined the company in 1950 just before Ian Munro, but he was a very 'Happy go lucky' Scot who didn't stand on ceremony and as he made me very welcome it was a pleasure to share the bungalow with him. Two of his great interests were hunting and shooting, and that suited us both fine as he had a very powerful .22 centrefire rifle which he used for shooting jungle fowl and geese when they came into the *dhan khets* (paddy fields) in the evenings to feed on any rice that was left after harvesting. Because the khets were so open and there was very little cover it was impossible to get close enough to them to use a shotgun, but with great patience we were able to stalk them very gradually until they were in rifle range, and when he knew that I was a reasonable shot we spent many evenings trying to outwit these crafty birds and shoot one for the pot.

Because each khet was surrounded by an earthen wall about ten inches high to keep the water in, when they had their heads down and were actually feeding they were unable to see around them, so every so often they would straighten up and look for danger, then resume feeding. The only trouble was that they fed in groups and didn't always feed and look simultaneously. They tended to ignore any people moving around in the distance provided they didn't come too close and just kept a watchful eye on them, so we took it in turn to be the decoy and wander around while the other took the rifle and crept up on them from the other direction. It was rather like the old party game of 'statues' when the person being stalked turned round and everybody had to 'freeze', and this was quite difficult when we were creeping along over rough ground trying to keep a low profile so we did not have too much success, but we both enjoyed the challenge and did manage to get the occasional bird, which we enjoyed eating very much.

I used the rest of that first day unpacking my goods and getting things straight, then in the evening after having had a couple of drinks and a chat with Mac I went to bed and had a good night's sleep before starting work the next day. Lionel

Hoadley was also an engineer and he had spent the cold weather on Bagracote beginning the installation of a 250 BHP Crossley QVD 4 diesel engine as the prime mover in the factory. As the work was about half finished I had been instructed to take over and complete it under his guidance, which would enable him to concentrate more on garden affairs so that he would be ready to take over from Albert when he left at the end of February. It had also been arranged that because of the distance between Bagracote and Saugaon, instead of me being at the factory at 7 am and then going back to the bungalow for breakfast later, I was to have my breakfast before arriving at the factory at 8.30 am and then work through the morning. In view of this I had told Kancha to wake me at 7.00 with breakfast at 7.30, so at 6.30 I was still sleeping peacefully.

It was not to last. A few minutes later I thought all hell had broken loose. I had forgotten that the local airstrip had been built on the Saugaon grazing land, and either by accident or design Mac had omitted to tell me that the bungalow lay right beneath the flight path of the Jamair Dakotas as they came in to land. Normally later flights didn't concern us, but each morning the first flight left Dum Dum at about 4.30 am and arrived at Saugaon just after first light so that it could carry out at least two and possibly three flights in each day, and that morning was no exception. In my sleep I became aware of an absolutely terrifying noise, and as I came to I was frightened out of my wits. I thought we were being hit by an earthquake, but it had a much simpler explanation. The twin radial engines thundered throatily as the DC3 hurtled over the bungalow at an altitude of about 200 feet before landing on the airstrip some 400 yards away, but in my sleep fuddled state I shot out of bed in panic before I realised what it was. Of course Mac thought it was a great hoot when I told him and he said that I would soon get used to it, as indeed I did, so after a while I didn't even wake up as they came over. However the roar of those Pratt and Witney Twin Wasp engines is a sound I have never forgotten and I wish that I still had a morning alarm like that to wake me up nowadays. To go outside and watch the great, silver bird fly over was a lovely way to begin the day.

Our local post office was in the little village of Pillans Hat. It must have been given this name during the 1939-45 war, because on the 1932 Ordnance Survey map it was shown as Bagrakot village and railway station, so although the Hindustani word '*hat*' indicated a bazaar or market I was unable to find out who or what Pillans was. Before the war the River Leesh was impassable during the monsoon as it was completely unbridged and the Bengal-Duars Railway came up from Calcutta through what is now Bangladesh as far as Mal Bazaar. From there the main line turned east and ran through the Dooars up to the Brahmaputra, but there was a small spur line that ran westwards from Mal to Bagracote station where it ended. In those days all the tea was carried to the local station on buffalo carts and then transported to Calcutta by train, a journey of several days, and it was like this right up until the end of the war. During the monsoon all the areas were virtually cut off from their neighbours by swollen rivers, with the railway lines and bridges as the only means of direct communication, and in the Christian graveyards at Rungamutti and Nagrakata there were many gravestones which recorded the deaths of young planters who had been drowned while trying to cross the rivers on horseback and were swept away.

Lionel Hoadley had seen big changes in the area, because

one day when I was chatting to him about the old days he told me that before the war he had been an assistant on Bagracote and that during the rains the only way he had of getting to the Planter's Club at Mal was by riding his pony a journey of some 15 miles along the railway line. Then after several hours at the club he would hoist himself onto his pony and promptly fall asleep. It would walk back home until it reached the bungalow with Lionel still asleep in the saddle. Evidently it knew the road and track so well that he never fell off or had any trouble, and it never let him down.

Of course in those days there was never any regular railway traffic at night along this branch line. The only time there was an exception to this was when there was a special dance or celebration at the club. Then a 'Special' passenger train was organised which began at Bagracote and then chugged along to Mal, stopping at each local railway station to pick up all the locals in their best 'bib and tucker' along the way and then deliver them to Mal station. Then after the event at a pre-arranged time in the early morning, it was waiting in Mal station for the revellers to either climb or be carried aboard and it took them home. However it never waited for anyone after its scheduled departure time and if anyone was not there for any reason he was left behind and had to make his own way home the next morning.

In the first half of January we had some very unusual weather, which could have been caused by our close proximity to the Teesta, because we had very cold nights and a thick fog by day which made travelling up to Bagracote on my motorbike quite an unusual experience. Then on the 16th we had a very heavy rainstorm that washed all the dirt and smoke out of the atmosphere and left the view crystal clear, and from

Saugaon we got a panoramic view of the whole of the mountain range, with forest clad 'foothills' rising up to 6000 feet within a few miles of the garden and the snow clad peaks of the Kanchenjunga range hanging in the western sky. It was so lovely that I experienced the same thrill as when I first saw a similar sight on Zurrantee in 1951.

By this time Brian Seymour, the travelling Crossley engineer, had arrived to complete the commissioning of the QVD4, so as Wee Mac went to Calcutta on his two weeks' local leave early in January I was put in temporary charge of the Saugaon division. By this time my Hindi was quite fluent and as I had no difficulty in allocating and checking the work and conversing with the labourers, I got on fine. In actual fact it did me a power of good, inasmuch as it was the very first time that I was completely on my own in charge of some 400 labourers, having to use my common sense to deal with their problems and wellbeing as well as dealing with their work. I really thought for the first time about just how much power and trust had been invested in me and how much responsibility I would bear as I progressed in tea. It was a feeling I had never experienced before and as I thought about this I realised how much more self-assured and mature I had become in the two years since I left home. Gone was the boy who had cried on the *Strathaird* on the first night out from Tilbury. From that time on I was certain I had made the right decision in going to India and was eternally grateful to Mum for making it all possible.

It was also at that time that I began to formulate the rules by which I was to work with the labourers in later years. Because I came from a working class background I found I could empathise with them. I also realised that in many respects most of them were very much like myself, having the same strong family ties and problems and the same desire to do a fair day's work for a fair day's wage if they were not exploited. Very often it was like dealing with children; I found that if you treated them with friendliness and respect and also gained their confidence, they would trust you, and if you were fair but firm with them there was rarely any trouble. If I was ever in doubt I would put myself in their place and ask myself, 'If someone had to do this to me, what would be the best way for them to do it to me without annoying me?' and usually I came up with the answer. In most cases if I was able to help them or give them something, I would do so immediately without any messing around, but if I was not able to I would consider what they had to say and then tell them no and sometimes explain why not, and then never change my mind. They soon found out that with me 'No' really meant no, and once they realised this and knew it was no use cajoling me they accepted my decisions without any further hassle.

When Wee Mac came back from Calcutta my carefully ordered life in the bungalow came to an end very quickly. Ever since I had arrived in India I had managed to write very regular letters home to Jan and my Mum as well as to other friends and workmates who also sent the occasional letter. However from here on for the next few months I had the utmost difficulty, because he was a real live wire and was rarely still. He loved his shooting, so we went after wild pigs and jungle fowl most evenings, and when he knew I could play cribbage we had to have regular sessions. He had friends everywhere both in and out of tea and most evenings he would say, 'Come on, let's go and see old So-and-So', and with me being easily led we would go, but this style of life was not very conducive to letter writing. I believe he was an only child and wrote to his folks about once a month so it didn't affect him at all, but I think the fact that my letters to Mum got later and later tended to worry her, and I wish now to my shame that I had managed to write more often, even if it was only a single page with a few lines. She never complained and it was only later that I found out how she had felt, but I still get a guilty feeling when I think of what harm a bit of thoughtlessness can do.

I still had my motor cycle and I wasn't due to get the Minor until the beginning of February, but Mac had an Austin A40, so we had transport to go out in the evenings. Once we had had our evening meal the servants were free to go and then the night watchman or 'chowkidhar' took over. Ours was a Santal named Mangra, who was tall and thin and wore a perpetual grin whenever we spoke to him. To keep himself warm during the night chill he always wore a thick, multi-coloured woollen scarf that Mac's mother had sent out to him that he didn't want and a battered old trilby hat that someone had left at the club and Mac had brought home for him. It was unique, for nobody else had one at all like it and he was thrilled to bits, so he wore it all the time rather like his badge of office. Mac also had a cocker spaniel dog named Sheila, but unfortunately she had had an accident when she was quite small which had stunted her growth. As a result, although she was fully grown, she was only about half the normal size and Mac had been told that she would never grow any larger. Because she would have great difficulty in giving birth because of her small frame he had to ensure that he kept her from other dogs when she was on heat.

Well girls being what they are, toward the end of 1952 Sheila got herself a boyfriend, and by January she had puffed up until she was absolutely enormous and looked as though she was going to explode at any moment. However she was in good health and didn't look as if she was in any difficulty. One evening we had arranged to visit a friend in Siliguri and Mac warned Mangra about Sheila before we left. He explained to him that she might begin to give birth to her pups while we were away so he was to keep his eye on her, help her if she was in distress and look after the pups once they were born. Well Mangra grinned from ear to ear while this was going on, saying he knew all about dogs giving birth to pups and he would be like a father to them, so feeling that she was in good hands off we went.

When we got back at about 11 pm Mangra was waiting for us by the garage as the car stopped, obviously very excited with the news that Sheila had had her pups and was all right, and as the Sahib had told him to take care of the pups he had them on the back veranda. This was reached by a flight of stone steps, so we quickly climbed up and found a row of ten little bodies laid out very carefully on the top step. It was a sad sight to see, because they were much smaller than baby kittens and although they were absolutely perfect they had all been stillborn. However Sheila met us with a wagging tail, so everything seemed fine - until we got inside the bungalow, and what a mess greeted us. Obviously she had wandered from room to room while she was having them and instead of shutting her up in one of the rooms Mangra had let her roam. She had had two on the mat in front of the living room fire, one on the settee, two on my bed covers, one on the mat by my bedside and the rest in Mac's bedroom, and there was blood and mess everywhere. It appeared that Mangra had followed her around and as she gave birth to each one he would pick it up and tenderly carry it out to join all the others in a tidy row on the top step, not worrying about the mess she was making. It took us quite a while to clear everything up. Later when we asked him why he hadn't shut her up in one of the bathrooms to have them, he said that the Sahib had told him to watch her, which he had, and help her if she got into difficulties, which she hadn't, and as the Sahib hadn't said anything about shutting her in the bathroom and she seemed to be doing quite well by herself he didn't interfere with her, so that was that. Luckily Sheila didn't seem to be any the worse for her ordeal, but I think that afterwards Mac learned his lesson and took her into the vets in Jalpaiguri and got her sterilised so that it wouldn't happen again. She was a lovely little dog.

Dangua Jhar Tea Estate, our garden near Jalpaiguri, was only about 20 miles away from Bagracote as the crow flies, but because it was on the other side of the Teesta river it was about 75 miles away by road via the Teesta bridge and Siliguri and took about one and a half hours to get there. However on January 26th, which was celebrated as Indian Republic Day and so a public holiday, Big Mac and Ian Leith invited us together with some of their other friends from the Chulsa area down to Jalpaiguri Club for a celebratory curry and a 'round of drinks'. Really this was not quite what it appears at first sight, because the Government of India had decided that in view of the fact that they were short of sterling it would ban the import of unnecessary luxury goods with immediate effect, which meant that there would be no more foreign liquor coming into our clubs. In view of this Donald and Ian decided that as a farewell celebration we would have this special dinner in Jalpaiguri club, during which we would have a single drink of every kind of alcoholic drink it still had in stock until we couldn't drink any more, and then during this 'booze up' we would have peacock curry for supper. Evidently they had been shooting out in Jalpaiguri Forest the previous weekend and had shot a peacock, and as it was a really big bird and much too large for two to eat they decided to have this party, so down we went.

What a wonderful meal it was. The starter was tomato soup followed by fish mayonnaise, then roast breast of peafowl with vegetables and gravy and finally the main course was curried peafowl with a rice pilau. It was absolutely superb and well worth the 150-mile round trip, even though we all felt really awful the next day. It really was a lovely way to spend a holiday and I saved a couple of tail feathers from the bird to send to Mum, but she refused them saying that they brought bad luck. I thought this was a bit over the top, but strange as it may seem within a few days Ian turned his Jeep over and finished up in Jalpaiguri hospital with bad gashes on his head and legs, while the barrels of Donald's shotgun, the gun that had killed it, were so badly twisted in the accident that it could never be fired again. However all that happened to me was that I had a very painful boil come up on my arm which was probably a punishment for me eating it, but there again probably it was just a coincidence.

At the beginning of February I was able to collect the Minor from her owner in Mal, who had decided that life in India was not for him and was departing for pastures new, so Mac took me over in his car and I drove her back. I am unable to say exactly how much I paid for her because I didn't write and tell Mum anything about her in case she worried, but they were selling for about £250 in the UK at that time, and the sum of Rs. 2000 (£175) comes to mind. The revolutionary Morris Minor which was launched at the Earls Court Motor Show in September 1948 was the brainchild of a team led by

Alec Issigonis, who later designed the Mini, and was the star of the show. He considered that it was a vehicle which combined the style and conveniences of a good motor car with a price suitable for the working classes, and it was a roomy vehicle with excellent handling and cornering characteristics. The early cars had a split windscreen and the headlights mounted inside the front radiator grill, but in 1949 this was changed to comply with new US regulations, so from late 1950 the headlights were mounted on the front of the wings of all the Minor models. My car had been bought new in 1951 and still retained the split windscreen but had the new headlight arrangement, so she was only just at the beginning of her third year when I bought her. She was in lovely condition but in reality she was rather under powered and not really a suitable first car for me to use on the rough, bumpy, often washed-out estate roads. As she had a cast aluminium oil sump I managed to crack it twice by running over unseen boulders in the road during the first few months. With no spare parts available I was able to get this welded at our Sam Sing Workshops without too much inconvenience, but after the second incident I designed a stainless steel skid plate which was fitted beneath the sump and protected it while the car slid over unseen boulders in the road. Many times afterwards when I heard the grating sound of the stones rubbing along underneath after a bit of careless driving I praised the day when they fitted that for me.

There were two other drawbacks which weren't apparent at that time, but which were recognised and rectified on the later models. The first was that there was only one windscreen wiper on the driver's side of the split windscreen, which made observation during the rains very difficult indeed - this contributed to an accident I had later on. The second was that there was no retaining safety catch on the bonnet after it had been opened. This was hinged at two points beneath the windscreen, and as it fitted very snugly over the radiator grill and didn't rattle when it was down, it was quite difficult to see whether it was securely fastened or not. This didn't make any difference while I was travelling at a few miles an hour in the garden, but once I got on the main road and built up speed, suddenly the wind would get beneath the bonnet and drive it up and over against the windscreen with a frightening crash, and as I couldn't see ahead all I could do was stop as quickly as possible and bang it down again. Unfortunately this tended to distort the hinges, so I had to make a rule with myself that if I ever had to open the bonnet, before I left I ALWAYS shut it with a bang, which didn't do the hinges much good but at least it stopped it attacking me like a striking cobra when I least expected it.

With the benefit of hindsight, I feel now that she was much too refined and modern a car for me to begin with and it would have been better for me if I had been able to keep my motor cycle as well and use this for the rough work on the garden while using the car for pleasure, but I could not afford this, so the bike had to go. Still, Satya on Sathkyah was true to his word and got me a good price for it from his friend. Learning to drive and maintain the Minor was a significant point on my learning curve at that time and gave me experience for when I bought and drove other cars in the years ahead.

CHAPTER TWENTY TWO

All change

Albert Ager handed the garden over to Lionel on February 25th
and flew down to Calcutta on the following Tuesday, so as a
farewell gift the clerks made him a small presentation of models
of a traditional Indian house and a woman tea picker and
arranged for a group photograph to be taken of all the garden
staff. On that morning a large group of staff and friends
gathered round the Jamair plane to wish him farewell. As he
said his goodbyes he seemed to be a rather timeworn old man
who had done his 30 years in India and had become very
disillusioned with what had happened there after partition,
which was all rather sad.

In comparison with most of our Managers' bungalows, the
one at Bagracote was in very poor condition and looked as
though it needed a lot of TLC. Albert's great interest had been
silviculture and tree surgery, and as he had devoted a lot of his
time to the Flame of the Forest trees surrounding his bungalow
they looked an absolute picture when they were in bloom.
However as far as I know he had never married and as a result
it seemed to me that the care of the bungalow had held very
little interest for him. I think Lionel felt the same way, because

he decided that it had to be cleaned, repaired and redecorated thoroughly before he moved into it. Consequently I was ordered to move up from Saugaon and live in it while this was being done, because I would be very near the factory and able to supervise the bungalow work as well, so I moved up a few days later.

The bungalow was built in a very unusual style and must have been unique, because I didn't come across another one like it during my time in tea. It had two storeys and was shaped like a giant, classical looking shoebox, with very large, airy living rooms on the ground floor, rather dark and dismal bedrooms upstairs and a corrugated iron roof. There was a large, pillared veranda with seven arches all the way down the front of the building, which made the ground floor delightfully cool during the hot weather, but although the bedrooms also had a veranda, the sheet roof turned them into hot boxes and made them unbearable to sleep in.

It wasn't this that kept me awake during my first night though but the fact that a large colony of bats had managed to infiltrate the roof space and had made their home there. During the night they bumped and scratched above my head, but the worst thing was the smell. The bedroom ceilings were quite low. As I hadn't taken particular notice of this during the day when the windows were fully open, I thought the room smelt just a little musty, but it was quite a different matter at night when the mosquito screens were closed on the inside, because very little fresh air penetrated and an evil-smelling stench permeated the room from several patches of sticky, yellow excrement which had leaked through the ceiling and trickled down the walls. This colony of several hundred large bats had managed to enter through holes in the wire netting covering the eaves where it had rusted away, and although this could be replaced by new netting quite easily, getting them to move out while this was done was more difficult. We didn't want to kill them. Finally, after several unsuccessful attempts to make them fly out in daylight, we cut a hole in the upper veranda ceiling, made a smouldering, smoky fire from damp straw and cow dung on the floor and then ducted the smoke up into the roof space through a length of old chimney pipe. At first they refused to move, but eventually when the cloud of smoke grew so thick that it became too much for them, out they all came and we were able to make the wire netting bat proof and clean up the mess. This proved to be a very time-consuming and unpleasant job, but once it was done we were able to repair and redecorate the bungalow and several weeks later than he had intended Lionel was able to move in.

Although the monsoon wasn't due to break until the middle of May, because we had had some unusually heavy storms earlier in the year and an extremely heavy downpour on March 5th during which 1.5 inches of rain fell in a few hours, by the middle of March we were able to pluck the skiffed tea and were making some 1600 lbs of excellent quality tea each day. Because this first flush tea grew very slowly at the end of the cold weather it had a distinctive flavour all of its own and was always in great demand by the buyers in the UK, so we had orders from the London office to make sure that only the best leaf was plucked and manufactured to the highest standards. This was something that hadn't been done on Bagracote since the war, but we did our best and when Mr Tocher got back from his three months home leave and visited us a few weeks later, he told us that our early samples had received very favourable reports from the brokers.

In the lead up to the rains we had several weeks of quite severe electrical storms, during which we had violent hailstorms which damaged the tea quite badly. Several lightning strikes damaged the shade trees and tea, without us getting very much rain, and it was fascinating to see these storms brewing up. Great banks of brilliant white cumulo-nimbus clouds would build up in the clear, blue sky and although they never seemed to be moving when looked at casually with the naked eye, when studied carefully over a period of several minutes with binoculars, the edges of the clouds could be seen roiling and boiling right up to an altitude of 20,000 feet. The flashes of lightning inside the cloud banks belied their peaceful appearance. When these storms actually hit an area they could cause a lot of damage, and when one descended on Jalpaiguri town on April 7th it was accompanied by very strong winds during which hailstones as large as golf balls fell for several minutes. It so happened that a circus was performing to a full house there at that time, and as the winds got stronger the management warned the crowd that the big top was unsafe and in danger of collapsing and advised them to leave, but most of them were loathe to do so. They were afraid to go out in the hailstorm so decided to stay put, but unfortunately they made the wrong decision, because just at the height of the storm the big top collapsed and fell on top of them, killing four people and injuring over a hundred. This must have been an unlucky period for the circus manager, because the previous week a tiger and a lion from their menagerie had managed to get together and fight, and the lion had been killed before they could separate them.

Although that hailstorm missed us we did get the wind, and the next morning we found that our main water supply that came from the hills about three miles away had failed. Here a stream had been dammed in a valley at about 2000 feet above sea level, and from there a three-inch diameter pipe ran down the river valley and through the top garden before it discharged into the factory water tanks. This supplied the factory, bungalows, clerks' houses and the labour lines and for this to fail for a long period was a serious business as the factory was unable to operate without water.

A couple of men were sent up to check the pipe and see what had had happened. When they returned they reported that a large tree had fallen and destroyed a section of the pipeline, so I organised a couple of my factory engineers together with some men to carry some spare lengths of piping and we went up to see what we could do. This was the first time I had ever been up into these high hill forests, and it was a wonderful experience, because at first the path alongside the pipeline was quite wide as it was used by the forestry workers to carry out bamboos and timber, but as we started climbing it gradually became narrower and rougher until finally we were virtually scrambling up the stream bed, and the higher we climbed the more it became choked with fallen trees and large boulders. The valley was quite narrow with high, jungle clad, cliff-like sides that rose up to the clear blue sky and it was almost like walking into a green wonderland from a science fiction novel. Wild life abounded and at one place we surprised a large band of monkeys that took off through the trees in fright, chattering angrily and with the babies clinging on beneath their mothers' front legs for dear life. The pipeline was fractured in an open glade about halfway up to the dam, so I made two journeys up and back that day.

On the way back in the afternoon I made a rather stupid

mistake that could have had very serious consequences. About halfway down I reached a place where the stream had cut its way through a rock shelf and was flowing through a small canyon with very steep sides. Earlier in the day I had noticed that although they were almost sheer, they were only about 40 feet high and as there seemed to be plenty of ledges and handholds all the way up the face, I thought I should be able to climb up to the top, from where I could get a rather unique view of Bagracote and the surrounding countryside. The only drawback was that although I had climbed trees and farm buildings when I was a boy I was really afraid of heights, but as the climb didn't seem too bad I thrust caution and common sense to one side and decided to have a go.

At the bottom of the cliff was a steeply-sloping bank of scree which had weathered off the rock face and I quickly scrambled up this and climbed up the first 20 feet, but after this I had to start looking for hand and foot holds and the ascent became more difficult. Finally I reached a spot about ten feet from the top where there was an overhang with no hand holds or ledges to assist me any further. Had I been an experienced climber it would have been chicken feed, but as I clung to the wall and looked above and to each side to see whether there was any way in which I could climb on up, I realised that I was beaten and knew I would have to make my way back down again.

This was where I made my big mistake - I looked down. 30 feet up from the ground doesn't sound very high, but when I looked vertically down it seemed one hell of a way and I panicked with an attack of vertigo. My teeth started chattering, my hands shook and my knees turned to jelly and started trembling. For a couple of minutes I was so badly affected that I thought I would faint and fall off, but I shut my eyes and managed to hang on and by talking to myself I managed to calm myself sufficiently to look for the hand and footholds I had used to ascend, and I began a very slow descent. Gradually I came down. I would like to say I managed to make it without incident, but unfortunately just when I was thinking that I was almost safe, I lost my grip and fell for the last 12 feet until I hit the scree slope at the bottom with such force that it knocked all the wind out of me. Luckily this dissipated some of the force of the landing, and I rolled for the remaining 12 feet down the slope until I clattered up against some boulders in the stream, where I lay in the cold water for several seconds until some semblance of reality came back to me.

As I was only wearing a T shirt, shorts and plimsolls I could have been quite badly injured, but much to my relief I found that no bones had been broken and I got away with nothing worse than a very stiff back and several severe bruises and abrasions, so I was very fortunate. However thinking about it later I realised that it was an extremely stupid thing to do, as the labourers would probably have gone home a different way, and as there was nobody else in the vicinity I could have been there with a broken back or leg all night, so it was something I never did again.

One of the things Albert Ager had left behind when he retired was a very antiquated wireless in a wooden case which I discovered in the back of a wardrobe. Its reception was very poor and listening to the Overseas Service of the BBC was almost unbearable because of the static electricity, but as I didn't have a radio of my own it was better than nothing. One of the things I was determined not to miss if I could help it was the FA Cup Final, which was due to be played on May 2nd between Blackpool and Bolton Wanderers. This held a special attraction for me because my boyhood hero had been Stanley Matthews, and despite his obvious skills he had never been able to win a cup winner's medal. Due to the time difference the kick off was at 8.30 pm Indian time, so I decided not to go to Mal Club for the film but had an early tea and then settled down to enjoy listening to how Matthews had won his first Cup Final winner's medal instead. When I heard the crowd singing 'Abide with me' I felt the tears welling up in my eyes and I felt quite homesick, but once the match began I felt quite confident that this was to be Stan's big day, only to have my hopes dashed almost immediately when Nat Lofthouse scored a goal in the second minute and then dominated the play in the rest of the first half so that Bolton were leading 2-1 at half time.

In the second half Blackpool realised they had to score as quickly as possible to get back into the match, but despite all their efforts it was Bolton that scored again and when they were still leading 3-1 with only 22 minutes left to play I thought all hope of a Blackpool victory had gone. Although Stan had played well it sounded as though he had just had an ordinary game, but it was at that time that he must have realised that unless they threw caution to the winds the match would slip away and he came more into it. In the 68th minute Stan Mortensen scored his second goal from a goal mouth scramble to give them a chance, and then for some reason Stanley proceeded to turn the Bolton defence inside out and run them ragged, until in the 88th minute Blackpool were awarded a free kick just outside the penalty area. Mortensen normally took the free kicks near goal and the captain instructed him to lob the ball to the players at the far post in the hope that somebody could score with a header, but he had other ideas and completely unpredictably he took a long run and hammered it straight into the top, right hand corner of the Bolton net to give him his hat trick and bring Blackpool back from the brink of defeat.

By this time the Bolton players were bags of nerves, and when the referee indicated that there would be four minutes of injury time to be played, Stan decided that now was his last chance and he became absolutely inspired and completely unstoppable, as though he had been given some divine strength. It was in the second added minute that he was given the ball once more, and he made a mazy run down the right hand touchline, beating three Bolton defenders on the way. When he reached the goal line he pulled the ball back into the path of Bill Perry, who calmly drilled it into the back of the net.

Wembley Stadium erupted. The noise was terrific and for a moment I sat listening to the uproar in stunned silence. Then, realising what had happened, I went wild too, and leaping into the air I ran round and round the living room waving my arms in triumph and yelling and cheering at the top of my voice. At this point the night watchman came crashing in through the back veranda door brandishing a kukri and a six foot long pig spear ready to do battle with whatever or whoever I was fighting inside. I had given all the servants leave to go once I had settled down, but I had completely forgotten that the watchman had come on duty and it turned out that he had been sitting by the fire in the cookhouse half asleep when this terrible racket broke out inside the bungalow. As he was quite drowsy he thought I was being attacked either by some wild animal or thieves and he sailed in to the rescue, only to be confronted by me leaping and cavorting around the room and yelling at the top of my voice. He recoiled in horror, as he thought I had gone *pugla* (off my rocker). It took me quite a while to convince him that all I had got so excited over was a game of football, but finally I calmed him down and praised him for risking his life and limb in coming to my defence and he went back out to the cookhouse and left me to celebrate the victory with an extra peg of Indian whisky.

I was jubilant that Stanley had got his winner's medal at last because I realised that at 38 years of age this was probably his last chance as he only had a few more years of first class football left in him. At that time I thought it was this that had spurred him on to play in such a magnificent and unforgettable manner, but it appears I was very wrong.

It was only much later, when I read his autobiography *The Way it Was* in 2001, that I realised something much more important than that had driven him on to play as though he had been inspired. He wrote that his father, Jack Matthews, had always been a boxer and had wanted him to follow in his footsteps, but after he had realised that all Stan was ever interested in was football he relented and gave him as much encouragement as he could to fulfil his dream of being a pro. Then when he died in 1945 Stan visited him on his death bed. As his last request his father had asked him to promise that he would look after his mother after he had gone, and also that he would try to win a Cup Final medal for him. Evidently it was the memory of this that had driven Stan to such heights on that day, because afterwards when he came down from the royal box after being presented with his medal by the new Queen Elizabeth II, he raised it above his head and looked at the heavens and said, 'There it is, Dad'.

There is an interesting footnote to the match itself, because

I think all the Bolton players were English with the exception of one Scot, Willie Moir, while Blackpool had eight Englishmen and three Scots in their team and both the managers were English as well, which is a vast difference compared with the makeup of English Premier League teams nowadays.

One good thing about Bagracote was that it had a very good football team, and once the rain came and the grass started growing there was a practice game on the football field most evenings. The three small towns of Mal, Dam Dim and Odlabari all had excellent teams and the Dam Dim club hosted regular tournaments in which all the local garden and bazaar teams entered. These cup matches usually took place on Sunday afternoons after the market had finished, and were graced by a local band consisting of two drummers and two Indian pipers who made a horrible lot of squealing noises and a trumpeter who played the tune. For most of the time when the football was a bit boring they played Indian music, but every time a goal was scored they launched into an up tempo version of 'The Isle of Capri'. To see them marching along the touchline belting out "Twas on the Isle of Capri that I found her, beneath the shade of an old apple tree' was a sight and sound never to be forgotten, and it made the scoring of a goal a very memorable business indeed. Nobody seemed to know why they played it or how they came to know the tune, so I can only think it had been carried over from the days of the Raj.

Because Odlabari Bazaar was only two miles away we played friendly games against them several times a year. One evening when we arrived to play them after a day of torrential rain we found that the pitch was half flooded to a depth of a couple of inches, and were told that during the night somebody had stolen the goalposts and crossbars. As the theft had only been noticed that afternoon they hadn't had time to replace them, but after waiting for a while four bamboos were brought to be used as posts. As they couldn't get any long enough to use as crossbars, we had to stretch pieces of soggy rope across. This was fine, so the game went ahead as planned and we sloshed our way over the flooded pitch, slipping and sliding everywhere, until near the end of the game our right winger put in a shot that hit the 'cross rope' up and it went in beneath it. I thought it had gone in, but the referee was an Odlabari man and he ruled that it had gone over and disallowed the goal, much to the fury of our supporters. As I think some of the spectators had gambled on the result, it looked for a while as though a fight might break out. Fortunately after a while things calmed down, and as we finally won the game 2–1 our folks went home happy and it was all forgotten by the time the next bazaar day came round.

Unfortunately the pre-monsoon storms didn't last very long, and it was not long before drought conditions began again and the leaf growth slowed down, which was a bit annoying because some of our early invoices had got excellent valuations in London. However by the first week of May things had got back to normal and we experienced some more extremely violent storms, which culminated in one on the night of May 11th when we had seven inches of rain and a bolt of lightning hit the office building and blew part of the roof off. There was a tremendous, sizzling crash and the office watchman who was asleep inside thought that the end of the world had come, while I was asleep in the Manager's bungalow about 50 yards away and thought that we had been bombed. It was quite a memorable experience, although we were all very thankful that it wasn't repeated. In the absence of the monsoon the day temperatures continued to rise, until by May 20th we were getting bright, sunny days with temperatures in the upper eighties.

Under our terms of employment we were allowed to take two weeks' local leave each year, but as I had only taken a few days off to play sporting fixtures at various times and had not been on any local leave, I decided to fly down to Calcutta for a few days to do some shopping and also try to buy a suitable gift to send home to Jan for her 21st birthday on July 23rd. However there was one big drawback to this plan - lack of money. I was still paying back my various loans for my car etc, while both the return air fare to Calcutta and a stay in the better hotels were quite expensive, so if I needed spending money as well then I had to do something about it, and I decided to have a word with the Jamair pilots. Saugaon airfield was built on a flat area of cattle grazing land alongside the Leesh river about 400 yards from the bungalow, and so we often met the planes and became great friends with many of the crew members. The mixed passenger/freight flight that arrived at about 6.30 am never stayed for very long, only allowing enough time for the passengers to disembark and unload the cargo before reloading again for Calcutta, but the second flight that only carried freight and arrived at about midday was a very much more leisurely affair. The actual airstrip had been bulldozed and scraped flat during WWII and surfaced with gravel and shale from the river bed, then gradually over the years it had been consolidated by a mat of thick grass that was kept cropped short by herds of cattle and goats that roamed over it all day long. The *chokras* (boys) who acted as goat and cowherds were not allowed to bring them out until after the morning plane had departed for Calcutta, but any subsequent flights were a different matter and the moment the distant drone of the approaching DC3 could be heard, the Jamair Office Clerk would shout to warn them and there would be a general stampede in the direction of the river so that the strip was cleared before the 'big bird' arrived. Of course the herd boys loved this and seeing the way in which some of the cows and goats kicked up their heels and ran I suspect that they enjoyed the exercise as well.

I seem to remember that on the mixed flights, the cargo load weight had to be reduced by 700 lbs for every passenger carried, so this meant that on a cargo flight where much more freight was carried, the unloading and reloading took much longer, very often as long as a couple of hours. There were no motorised facilities available, so every item had to be manhandled out of the aircraft, then carried by labourers to the store shed some 30 yards away, and the plane was loaded in the same way. In addition when the weather was very hot and sticky in Calcutta the crew members enjoyed our weather upcountry, so very often when it was their last flight of the day and they were in no hurry to get back, we used to take them back to the bungalow for a comfortable rest and some food and drink. Two of them, Johnny Leyland and 'Shaky' Blake, were both ex-RAF pilots and we got to know them well. Captain Blake was a family man and had his young son at school in Darjeeling, but Johnny was the exact opposite because his face had obviously been damaged and quite disfigured at some time, probably in a crash, and rumours claimed that he had served in 617 Squadron at some time after the Dambuster raid and had been injured when he crash-landed a badly damaged Lancaster back at base. He seemed to be quite a loner. How and why he came out to India after the war to fly old DC3s for a company like Jamair we never did find out, but he loved the independence of this kind of flying, and it could have been that he preferred the 'happy go lucky' type of life those pilots led when compared with working for more regimented airlines. Anyway flying was in his blood, so he was a wonderful pilot and tremendous company.

One day when we were in the bungalow he said to us that if we ever wanted a trip down to Calcutta to let him know. Recalling this, the next time I saw him I explained my circumstances and asked him whether there was any way he could help me travel down without paying the full passenger fare. He came up trumps straight away. Evidently the DC3s normally carried a crew of two, a pilot and co-pilot for short flights, although in the cabin there was a spare seat that was used by an extra crew member such as a Flight Engineer on longer ones and also a small curtained bunk behind the pilot's seat where a man could rest. He said that although these could not be used on a passenger flight, if I was willing to fly down and back on freight flights it would be permissible for me to use the extra seat and fly with the crew free of charge. In addition he added that as he had his own flat in Calcutta, although he only had the one bedroom, if I was willing to sleep on the couch in his living room I was very welcome to stay with him so I jumped at the chance. This seemed to be the answer to my prayers and my trip turned out to be much better than I ever thought possible.

The following Saturday afternoon I turned up at the airstrip as arranged. The flight down was an absolute delight, because from my seat in the cabin I watched all the preparations for the flight, and when the engines started and were run up it was quite easy for me to imagine that I was going to fly the plane, as I always did have a fertile imagination when it came to aircraft! As we took off I had a panoramic view of the Himalayas stretching right back into Nepal and Tibet and the gleaming white peaks of the Kanchenjunga range shining in the bright sunshine.

We overflew tea estates and forests until we reached the Ganges. From there until we reached the outskirts of Calcutta the land below was rather monotonous, although it was of some interest because the last time that I had seen it was when I had flown up after my trip to Assam the previous year when it had been under several feet of water, so it was hard to imagine that it was the same countryside. However once we approached Dum Dum it was fascinating to see the small clusters of houses and arable land all spread out beneath us, with very little wasted.

It was extremely hot in Calcutta at 107 degrees F in the shade, so I tried to do my shopping either in the early morning or evening, with a nice long 'lie-back' in the afternoons that prepared me for a trip out with Johnny in the evenings. How he managed to get enough sleep I never found out, because the early morning flights left Dum Dum at about 4.45 am and he had to be away from the flat at four, then he returned at about 4.30 pm to have a bath and a meal before we went out to one of the clubs with his friends until about 11. By this time we were all merry.

During his walk back to his flat one of his favourite games was what he called 'Cow Jumping'. The pavements were absolutely littered with dozens of unwanted cows and bullocks that had been abandoned as a token of faith to roam the streets and find food wherever they could, and at night they lay and slept in any comfortable spot until morning. They were the most docile creatures I ever came across. Johnny's fun was to start with the first of a group of bullocks and jump up on his back, then leap from back to back to see how many he could cross before he had to touch the pavement again. One would have thought they would have been distressed, but he was on and off so fast that he could cover as many as 12 or 14 animals before he was forced to 'land' and not one of them took a blind bit of notice. They just lazily chewed the cud as if he didn't exist.

With antics like this my four days in Calcutta passed only too swiftly, and on the following Wednesday I took the freight flight back to Saugaon after having had a wonderful break. After the heat of Calcutta the icing on the cake was the delightful cooling breeze which met me when I left the plane, which brought home to me just how much the aircrews must have enjoyed their short stays up country. The only drawback to my trip was the fact that I had been unable to get anything suitable for Jan's birthday, but as it happened it wasn't too much of a disaster because the following week I was able to buy a gold Swiss Movado wristlet watch from a dealer in Mal Club, which was just what I had in mind. In addition I was also able to make arrangements with a friend who was going on UK leave to take it home for me and let her have it in time for her birthday, so I thought everything had turned out really well.

Unfortunately things didn't go just as I had planned, because although Jan was really delighted with it as a watch to wear, it was a terrible time keeper, usually losing up to five minutes in a day and sometimes stopping completely. After I had bought it I had kept it in my bedroom for several days, during which it kept excellent time, but nothing she did had any lasting effect until finally it stopped completely and refused to restart, so she took it up to a watchmaker's shop in Gloucester for them to look at it, and there the mystery was solved. Once they knew that it had originated in India they opened it up and found that before leaving the factory it had been oiled with a specially thick lubricant in order to counteract the high temperatures and humidity in which it would have to operate. As the colder autumn weather had set in at home it had got so thick that it had clogged the works. Once this was completely cleaned out and the works re-lubricated with normal European oil it kept perfect time, and has run well ever since.

A few days after this I had an absolutely enchanting experience which is still as clear now as it was then. Lionel had told me that as very little maintenance and repair work had been done on the water supply line since the war and the walls of the dam were leaking like a sieve, the company had given permission for the dam to have a thorough overhaul and repair, with some of the more doubtful sections of the pipeline being rerouted if necessary. In order to do this he asked me to take a trip up to the dam and see what was required in the hope that it could be done in the next cold weather. Well this was just up my street, so I made arrangements for all the garden work to be supervised and the next morning I had my breakfast early and away I went. On my previous excursion I had only been about half way up and as the dam was about three miles up into the hills, the further I climbed the more spectacular the scenery became. The sides of the valley were almost sheer, with rocky outcrops and tree-clad slopes, and the stream bed became choked with fallen trees and immense boulders several feet high over which I had to scramble. The higher I climbed the more restricted it became, but finally I emerged onto a small plateau where the dam was built and found that this was quite a small affair, some 12 feet wide and two feet deep in the middle with a small pool behind it. Although it was leaking steadily in several places, because there was always a steady stream of water running into it 24 hours a day it was sufficient for our needs.

It must have been extremely old and exhibited the signs of having been repaired many times. I realised that very few people in the company had any idea what the whole setup looked like, so I measured it up and made a rough plan of the dam and basin from which I could make a finished drawing when I got back and decided to follow the actual pipeline down the hillside and check it on my return journey. Then, as I had several hours to spare before I had to be back, I thought I might as well have a look around further up the hillside while I had the chance and decided to scramble up the stream bed as far as I could to find out where our water came from. I don't remember what I actually expected to see, but after two hundred yards of slipping and scrambling up over the rocks and fallen trees, I emerged into a fantastically lovely place. During the monsoon the stream must have developed into a torrent raging down the hillside, for it had carved a six-foot-wide cleft through a gap in the rock wall through which it emerged, although at that time the water was only a few inches deep. Inside the cleft in the rock the stream had cut and ground away an overhang which was virtually a tunnel about 20 feet long, the upper end emerging into a large flat area on the hillside. Here the main stream bed was quite dry, but our water was flowing out of a quite a large, deep pool of clear water fed by a cascade that tumbled down over the rocks on the top side. To my surprise the water was a lovely shade of green and several quite large fish were swimming in it. How these had come to live in a place several hundred feet up the side of a hill I had no idea, although later it was suggested to me that possibly the pool had been made by some of the local hill villagers who had 'planted' the young fish in there with the idea of harvesting them before the monsoon overwhelmed the pool and flooded them away. However I was very surprised at the size of some of them. Thinking about it later I came to the conclusion that the main stream could have been dammed with boulders further up the hillside at the beginning of the cold weather, so that the reduced flow of water was diverted into the pool, and then once the monsoon came they could have been removed to allow it to surge down its original channel once more until they were replaced at the end of the rains.

Unfortunately, although I had intended going further on up the hill side, this pool was so delightful, the sort of place folks at home paid good money to see, that I spent the rest of the afternoon there, deciding that I would come back up again in my own time so that I could find out whether my ideas were correct and discover what other delights might be hidden further up.

Unfortunately the road to Hell is paved with good intentions, and although I did go up as far as the dam several times afterwards, much to my regret I never did go up to my pool again. I wonder what I missed.

CHAPTER TWENTY THREE

God Save The Queen!
Down with hookworms!

Despite the fact that the *barsaat* or monsoon had officially broken (I seem to remember that the day was cold and wet at home), the morning of The Queen's Coronation Day, June 2nd 1953 broke fine and clear without a hint of rain, and as the event was so special we were all given the whole day off to celebrate, the first and only time I ever knew it to happen. Because the Europeans were so few in number, it was decided that a combined celebration for all the members of the United Kingdom's Citizens Association in Mal, Chulsa and Nagrakata Districts would be held at Nagrakata Club and the idea was that we would all get there in the morning to attend a church service for all denominations, followed by the drinking of the Loyal Toast to the new Queen. After this a cricket match had been organised and we could have drinks before eating an absolutely superb lunch that the Nagrakata ladies had prepared, and then have some more drinks before we were all supposed to gather round a wireless and listen to the actual Coronation.

That morning Wee Mac and I decided to go to Nagrakata together in the Minor. As we reached the Nagrakata forest we saw an old car lying on its side at the bottom of the embankment, but were unable to see the driver. Later we were told that it belonged to a young planter who had bought two old Austin Sevens and made one good car out of them, but although it was fine as a museum piece its reliability was very suspect and evidently it had had a front wheel blow out that caused it to wander off the road before it rolled down the embankment and trapped him beneath it. Luckily Bill Milne had come along a few minutes later and managed to pull him out from beneath the car, and after binding up a cut on his head took him on to the club where he had some stitches inserted by the doctor. Really it was a quite minor incident and he didn't suffer any lasting injuries, but I don't think he ever anticipated celebrating the coronation like that.

Because of the time difference between India and the UK the ceremony was scheduled to begin at about 3.30 pm our time, but unfortunately the wireless reception was absolutely abysmal due to static interference caused by electric storms in the Himalayas, so after having had several drinks to celebrate the event most people gave it up as a bad job. As there was to be a dance at Mal Club in the evening very few bothered to listen to it and most of us went home. However one thing that was announced as I was eating my lunch was the news that Everest had been conquered by Hilary and Tenzing, and the thought came to me that just at the time that they had been preparing to mount their assault on the summit, I must have been climbing up to my secret pool above the dam, so we all had something to celebrate. Still I shall always regret the fact that I never made the extra effort to climb up to see what lay beyond it, but it was a case of 'Always tomorrow, never today' and I only have myself to blame.

Despite tumbling down the bank the old car was not badly damaged and was soon repaired and on the road again, but I saw it later on and thought it was a death trap. The two cars from which he had constructed it were already absolutely worn out as they had been used as taxis to carry passengers across the two miles of sandy track that separated Jalpaiguri town from the Teesta ferry during the cold weather. As long as the ferry was running during the hours of daylight, they carried passengers, goods and livestock over the sandy, dusty track without resting and must have covered hundreds of thousands of miles in this way, but once the rains began and the ferry was unable to operate they were left on the bank above high water level, covered with a tarpaulin and then buried under a big mound of sand and abandoned until the next cold weather, when they were cleaned and started again. They were absolutely basic and in the car he had 'made' the small fuel tank was mounted above the engine on the bulkhead below the windscreen so that it had a gravity feed. As there were several small leaks in the piping there was quite a strong smell of petrol in the engine compartment. Normally this would not have been too serious, but someone had told the lad that his engine would run much better if his sparks were 'hotter' and advised him to insert a shirt button with the centre removed in each of his sparking plug leads. These were cut and the buttons inserted so that the spark jumped across the gap and increased in strength before it reached the spark plug, theoretically increasing the efficiency of the engine. Never having had very much to do with cars, when he showed me I couldn't see quite how this would happen, but I did appreciate that there was a very strong smell of petrol fumes around an engine that flashed and sparked like a manic Christmas tree every time the engine ran, and I thought it could only be a matter of time before the whole lot would explode with a hell of a bang, so I left with the minimum of delay. To be fair, to the best of my knowledge this never occurred, and I believe he ran it without any incident for the rest of his short time in tea.

Someone else who gave Wee Mac a lot of inconvenience was another lad who was mad keen on shooting. Because the Saugaon bungalow was right on the edge of the Geesh river, he would leave his car there while he walked across the river to the Apalchand forest on the other side and then come back in the early hours of the morning after roaming around the jungle paths for several hours. This would not have been too bad except that he was usually cold, wet and thirsty and liked to wake Mac up to get warm and talk about what he had seen, which didn't go down very well.

Finally after several warnings things got so bad that one night Mac decided to teach him a lesson. Whenever he crossed the river he used to leave a lighted lantern hanging in the branches of a tree in the bungalow compound to guide him back across the river, and one night after he had gone Mac told his driver to take it down and then tie it in another tree on the riverbank about a half a mile downstream below the bungalow and leave it there. As a result, when he re-crossed the river bed late that night using the lantern as a guiding light, once he reached the bank he had absolutely no idea where he was and had a long walk back up the river bed before he got his bearings and found his way back to his car. According to Mac nothing was ever said about the light being moved, but it had the desired effect and afterwards he found somewhere else to leave his car for his treks across the river.

After the coronation the monsoon set in with a vengeance. Although the annual rainfall at Bagracote was only about 200 inches, which was considerably less than the amount that fell on the gardens in the Chulsa area, we still had plenty of days when we got 10 or 12 inches of rain over 24 hours. Probably this was due to the fact that Bagracote lay on the plain at the base of the foothills at an altitude of about 200 feet, whereas the Chulsa gardens were on a rising bank of red soil at 600 or 800 feet and received up to an additional 150 inches of rain. Because the Bagracote soil was very sandy the football field drained quickly, so we were always able to play a match even during the heaviest rain. As a result I played very much more than I had done previously, but inexplicably my standard of play deteriorated. It seemed to me that I was always tired and got fatigued very easily, which was something I had never experienced before.

Then towards the end of the rains I began to have unusual bouts of sickness and diarrhoea. In themselves these were not uncommon, because like most Europeans I had had periodic attacks of amoebic dysentery, enteritis and other stomach upsets ever since I had arrived in India, but with the correct medication these were soon cleared up. What I had now was something much more serious, for I suddenly realised that I had lost 14 lbs in weight over the course of three months and that meant that there was something very wrong. When I left home I was really fit and weighed 11.5 stones. Although I had lost 8lbs during my first few weeks in India, my weight soon settled down and had remained at a constant 11 stones ever since. Now I had lost 14 lbs, and although I was always hungry and ate like a horse I didn't put on any weight. In addition I was always tired and could drop off to sleep in a chair at a moment's notice. At first I thought this was due to excessive exercise and playing too much football in the enervating heat, but finally when I realised just how much it was affecting me, I spoke to our District Medical Officer about it and the answer was simple. I had a severe attack of hookworm.

The hookworm is a parasitic roundworm with hooks around its mouth which enable it to cling to the wall of the small intestine of its human host. It lives mainly in tropical and sub-tropical regions where it is humid, and is very common in India during the monsoon. The worm's eggs are hatched in damp soil and then the minute larvae bore their way through the host's skin into the flesh, usually through the lower leg or the soles of their feet. Once through the skin they enter the bloodstream and make their way to the small intestine, where they attach themselves to the wall by their mouth hooks and live by sucking the host's blood and extracting the goodness. When they are mature the worms lay eggs, some of which hatch inside the host and others that are expelled with faeces onto the soil, and the cycle starts all over again. The human hookworm causes anaemia, tiredness, weakness and abdominal upsets and pain and is quite common in areas where the people go to the lavatory outdoors, thus passing on the infection.

Once this was explained to me I understood why I was always feeling so under par and also eating so much and not getting fat. It was simply because I was playing 'Happy Families' with a giant colony of hookworms. And where had I got them from? I had absolutely no idea, because from the day I had arrived on Zurrantee I had been told repeatedly, 'Because of snakes and hookworm, NEVER walk around anywhere without wearing something on your feet' and to the best of my knowledge I had never consciously done so. However, somewhere along the line I had slipped up for a few minutes, so I had to pay the penalty.

The cure for hookworm was very straightforward but absolutely awful. The senna bush is a shrub of the genus Cassia which bears yellow flowers and flat, greenish seed pods, and senna leaf tea is made from its leaflets, rather like normal tea. For a great many years this infusion has been drunk as a mild homeopathic purgative and before the development of modern drugs was used extensively to cure cases of constipation. Indeed Grandfather Brown always declared that a good dose of senna tea would always put him right whenever he felt 'costive'. The senna oil that was used to kill hookworms was however obtained from the crushed pods and seeds of the bush and as it was many more times concentrated than the 'tea' it really did the job.

After my diagnosis I didn't really understand what was involved when the doctor told me to arrange a suitable day for me to have off work so that I could take the medicine, then make sure that I ate or drank nothing after my evening meal the night before and present myself at the hospital the next morning with a completely empty stomach to take the treatment, but obediently I did this. On the appointed day I turned up at the garden hospital, where I was greeted by our Doctor Babu, who presented me with a glass of evil-tasting, oily, yellow-brownish liquid which smelt horribly. He said that the best way to take it was to hold the nose and then swallow it down in a couple of gulps before the taste buds realised just how bad it tasted, and was I glad I did. I don't think I have ever tasted anything so bitter and nasty. Even as I write this after 55 years, the memory of it still makes me shudder.

Once it was down the doctor told me to hurry back to the bungalow and stay near the toilet, then let nature take its course! By this time I was feeling quite nauseated, so I hurried off. The poor old hookworms didn't stand a chance, because for the whole of the day I kept belching up horrible tasting wind and felt sick, while I kept going to the toilet and ran like a tap. It was an absolutely horrible experience, but it must have completely cleaned out my digestive system and poisoned the worms so that they couldn't hold on, because my condition gradually improved in the evening and after drinking a bottle of water which tasted like nectar I felt fine. That was that, except that there was one small disappointment; the oil had no effect on the eggs that were already in my body, so I had to have another smaller dose of the medicine two weeks later in order to destroy any baby roundworms that had hatched from eggs that had been left. Luckily this was nothing like as bad as the first one, and once it was over I began to gain weight and my general health began to improve.

For some reason or other hookworm was very prevalent on Bagracote that year. As it caused a very high rate of absenteeism and was responsible for other associated illnesses that affected the standards of work on the garden, Lionel decided to purge the labour force over a two-week period. It was arranged that 10% of the labourers would turn up at the hospital each day together with their dependents, and provided they took the medicine they were all granted a day's paid leave to recover while their families got a small cash payment. Because many of them suffered so badly from various types of stomach worms, most of them were only too glad to have a day off and take the medicine, and although it was the first time the scheme had been tried on Bagracote it paid dividends.

The other thing that made a lasting impression on me at this time was the death of a young Nepalese girl who had contracted rabies from her pet dog. She had not actually been bitten, but she had petted and played with it before it ran away from home, and although she searched for it unsuccessfully she didn't think anything about it until about two weeks later when she began to feel nauseated and went to the estate hospital. Here she was admitted to the care unit, but despite the best of treatment her condition gradually deteriorated until after five days she was paralysed, with her body bent like a bow and only able to make animal noises. It was a merciful release when she finally died, because there was nothing anybody could do for her once the final stage had begun. It so happened that I was in our hospital when she passed away and this made a big impact on me, because she was an excellent worker who I knew well, and it brought home to me just how fragile life is and demonstrated to me just what a terrible disease rabies is. Dog lovers travelling abroad and petting the local pooches should really be careful.

To my great relief my hookworm treatment proved to be a resounding success. Once I was no longer playing host to masses of worms all my normal energy returned and I felt like my old self again. In fact my health improved so much that although we had a very wet July, during which we hardly saw the sun and had almost non-stop torrential rain day and night for four weeks, I played football for the Odlabari team in the Jalpaiguri tournament and we beat Siliguri Town 6-1. It was quite a memorable match, because the river which flows through the town was so flooded that it inundated most of the town under two feet of very dirty water and the first game was cancelled. However by the next day the water level had fallen and we were able to play the match, even though the pitch was terribly soft and muddy and had been covered with clumps of water hyacinth that had been left stranded.

The mauve water hyacinth had been introduced into India at some time as a decorative water plant and a mass of them with their light mauve flowers was a sight to see, but once it had escaped into the wild it became an absolute menace. Conditions suited it so well that it grew like a weed until its thick, fleshy stems and leaves choked the waterways, and even when it was taken out by hand and thrown onto the bank it took ages to die. Then when the rivers were swollen in the monsoon, large rafts of the plants were torn up and drifted against the bridges, so that in next to no time they were absolutely choked with a solid mass of vegetation and sometimes gave way under the pressure. Unfortunately it was a plant that neither man, the goats or the cows could eat, so it had no agricultural use and as far as I know it is still there making a nuisance of itself. There was one time just before I left India that someone discovered that if it was shredded and dried, then boiled and mixed with various chemicals and glue, a type of fibre board could be made that was excellent for building. It could be cut and painted and seemed to be an excellent solution to the problem, until it was discovered that if it ever got wet in the rains new shoots began to appear all over it and before long you had a wall that had started growing, so that idea came to a dismal end.

It took us about four month's work to repair and redecorate the manager's bungalow and it wasn't until the middle of July that Lionel was able to move in and I moved over to the assistant's bungalow, but I didn't mind because as far as I was concerned it was the most modern and the best of the three. This was where the day watchman had beaten the snake charmer with his bamboo lathi because I didn't want to see his snakes dance. The only thing I didn't like about it was that it seemed to have a plague of ants. These were only tiny, red things that lived outside in the compound, but they invaded the kitchen and dining room at every opportunity. The only way that we could stop them getting onto the tables and into the food cabinets was by placing their legs in large tins filled with water. It seemed that the ants were only interested in food, the sweeter the better, because they completely ignored the rest of the bungalow.

One humorous thing that happened with me at this time concerned the Hoadleys' dog, a very nice, friendly little dachshund named Fritz which unfortunately had a very nasty habit of letting people walk past him and then quickly running in behind them and nipping their ankles. He did this to me on several occasions until I got tired of it and finally decided to teach him a lesson. That evening I had played football and after the match Lionel invited me back to the bungalow for a cup of tea and a drink, so I still had my kit on. I knew that Fritz liked to hide behind a chair on the veranda until his victims came by, but I had also noticed that as he ran across the floor his claws made a clicking noise on the polished surface and realised this would give me warning of his attack. As I followed Lionel along the veranda into the living room I heard the claws running up behind me and waited for the optimum moment before I gave a quick back heel and hit him smack in the face with my football boot. He was coming in so fast that it almost bowled him over and he gave a strangled yelp and disappeared back under his chair. When Lionel asked what had happened to him I said that something must have frightened him, because he had run along the veranda and under his chair, which was quite true and that was that, but the good thing was that although I didn't really hurt him at all he never attacked my ankles again although he still did it to other people, so he had really learned his lesson so far as I was concerned and knew that I was not to be trifled with.

Unfortunately a very sad thing also happened at the same time and that was that I lost Tiger. He was a very loving and friendly little dog, and ever since he had been a puppy, if he met me or someone that he knew as a friend he would roll over on his back, all four legs kicking in the air to have his tummy tickled. Unfortunately he had something wrong with his 'waterworks', and if he was really excited and his bladder was full he would lie on his back and spray wee everywhere, rather like a small stirrup pump. He would also do this if I scolded him or if he was frightened at all, so I tried to keep him as calm as possible, but he was less than a year old when he began to produce blood in his urine. Not being able to help him myself I took him into Jalpaiguri and left him with the nearest reputable veterinary surgeon for treatment, but he was unable to save him and he died there. Later when I went in to collect him he told me that his kidneys had not developed properly and he had suffered from an acute attack of nephritis which had proved to be too much for his constitution, but whether this was fact or just something he told me to justify the very large bill he presented me with I never did find out.

Once Tiger was gone I missed him terribly, for he was one of the most affectionate little creatures it has ever been my good fortune to meet. My favourite memory of him relates to a day soon after I had moved back to Bagracote. In his short life he had only known life in the Saugaon bungalow and seen the garden women outside in their rather dull working clothes.

However one afternoon soon after we had moved up to the wide open spaces of the Manager's bungalow, Mollie Hoadley walked over to the factory for some books I had promised her and we went to collect them. She usually wore lovely flowing sun dresses with big brimmed hats, and this day her dress was a flaming red with a very full skirt. As we walked onto the veranda Tiger heard our footsteps and came running out from the living room to greet me, only to be scared stiff when he saw her. He'd never seen anything so big and colourful in the bungalow in his life and was so completely petrified that he started to wee and was unable to stop himself as a he skidded along in it in a shower of spray. As he tried to find the door and escape his hackles were raised and his coat was bristling, and it was ages before he plucked up enough courage to come back in and have another go, but luckily she was very quiet with him and once he had come up and smelt her he settled down and accepted her as a friend. It was a great pity that I didn't have him for longer, because I think that of the three dogs I had he was my favourite. Still, such is life.

After the downpour we had had in July the monsoon finished quite early in September, but we continued to get useful quantities of rain for the autumnal flushes and we finished the plucking year in November on a high note. Because the drop in temperatures caused the bushes to grow much more slowly, these autumnal teas were noted for their quality and flavour and were always in great demand, so we continued to concentrate on maintaining the quality of the leaf plucked and it paid dividends. Indeed, despite the disruptions that had been made to the garden work by the rain, the standard of leaf plucked and that of the tea manufactured had improved so much that we all got a pat on the back from both the Superintendent and the London office. It had been a long time since autumnal tea of this quality had been made on Bagracote, so this was a feather in Lionel's cap.

CHAPTER TWENTY FOUR

Two weddings and a tiger

Soon after Tiger's death I received two items of very unexpected news. The first was that my sister Marion was going to be married in December to a man I had never met, while the second was that I was going to have to move back down to Saugaon to share with Wee Mac again. Life in those days was full of surprises.

Regarding Marion's wedding, evidently she and Jan had gone on a cycling holiday together to the Isle of Wight in 1952, and during a visit to Portsmouth she had met Peter Fox, a Royal Naval officer who was training to be a pilot in the Fleet Air Arm and who attracted her very much. In fact, when she returned from her holiday she told Mum that she had met the man she was going to marry, and true to her words the romance blossomed. After he had visited our home several times, they decided to get married, on December 19th 1953. Of course I had never met him, but the fact that he was in the FAA and learning to fly a plane was good enough for me. Although I would be unable to be at the wedding, Jan was going to be her bridesmaid and I was sure that we would get on well together when I met him. The one thing that did interest me but about which I could find out very little at that time was that Peter's father had spent several years in Tibet. Mum had heard a very simplified version of the story and told me that she thought he was living in either Darjeeling or Kalimpong, but wasn't able to give me any details. As I had heard nothing about a Reggie Fox, I missed a golden opportunity to meet him before he died in Kalimpong soon afterwards.

Peter was born in 1932, followed by his sister Meryl approximately two years later. For some reason their parents parted and later divorced, and subsequently his father Reginald married a Tibetan woman and they had several children. It appears that by trade he was a radio engineer and worked in India in the early 1930s, but it is probable that he first visited Tibet with a British Indian mission that visited Lhasa in 1936. It was at this time that China was beginning to make claims of sovereignty over Tibet, and in 1937 he was employed by the Tibetan government to set up a radio station in Lhasa to facilitate speedy communications with the outside world. I have a print of a photograph that was taken of him in Tibetan dress at a New Year's reception in Lhasa in 1940/41. Then in 1942 matters came to a head when it was realised that Chinese troops had penetrated deep into Tibetan territory without anyone in Lhasa knowing, and it was decided to establish wireless communications throughout Tibet using transmitters and receivers supplied by the British and American governments. The training of Tibetan operators was first undertaken in Lhasa, and then the programme was later enlarged and improved by radio operator Reggie Fox and a RAF radio instructor Robert Ford, both of whom who were granted the status of fully-fledged Tibetan government officials, and their trainees served as operators on the transmitters in various areas of Tibet as well as the Tibetan army in Kham.

In 1948 Radio Lhasa started the first of its daily broadcasts to the outside world and each day at 5 pm when the station went on the air, the news was read in English by Reggie Fox. He must have become quite a celebrity, because when the Chinese People's Liberation Army invaded Tibet in 1949 he was accused of being a spy. According to Chinese sources he organised resistance to their forces and the Tibetan army operated basically in accordance with his instructions from then until he was forced to flee to India with the Dalai Lama in 1951. Although the Dalai Lama returned to Lhasa from 1951 to 1959, Reggie Fox never went back. He spent the rest of his days with his Tibetan wife and children in a small house on the outskirts of Kalimpong, a small, hill town near the Tibetan frontier about 50 miles from Darjeeling, where I think he died in either 1954 or 1955. Had I known this earlier I would have been able to visit him but fate decreed otherwise, and this was a pity because he would have been a very interesting person to know.

As for my very unexpected return to Saugaon, when Lionel and I had exchanged bungalows in July I had been told that the plan was that I would stay in the roadside bungalow as Engineer until after he came back from his UK leave in a year's time, after which I would probably be moved to another garden for my last year, so I thought I knew what my future was. However Big Donald Mackenzie had gone on his eight months long UK leave from Dangua Jhar TE at the beginning of March, and we were told that although he was not due back officially until November he had unexpectedly got married while in London, and having spent all his money had decided to come back a month early. As a result of this he had been posted to Bagracote early, ready to act as Acting Manager for

Lionel while he was on home leave in 1954, and he would arrive at the beginning of October.

Realising that he would know very few people in the UK and as far as we knew he had no family members there either, I had arranged for him to go and stay with my folks at Coaley for a while if he got stuck during his furlough with nowhere to go. As Mum had not mentioned him during the period I had wondered how he had managed, and now I knew. He had surprised everyone by getting married, and it was only right that as a young married couple, he and Betty should have the best bungalow to themselves, so I packed up my gear once more and moved back to Saugaon with Wee Mac. In actual fact, as I loved the wild, open spaces in Saugaon so close to the airfield this was not a hardship for me, so I moved as soon as possible and it was a real pleasure to be woken up by the roar of the Jamair DC3s once more.

When Donald and Betty arrived we were all very surprised, because she was nothing like what we thought a wife of Donald's would be. Both Betty and her sister Meryl were London models, and as I boasted to Mum in a letter, they had appeared in a photograph for a very popular newspaper advertisement that asked, 'Which twin has the Toni?' (a brand of home hair perm). She was tall and slim with what we lads thought were the latest lines in makeup and fashion. We wondered how he could have persuaded her to come out to plantation life in India after being used to the celebrities, the bright lights and the night clubs of London, and even more how she would settle down. Well we needn't have worried, because she made herself completely at home and soon settled down quite happily as though she had been there for years.

Because Donald had spent most of his childhood in India,

either away at school or at home on whichever estate his father was managing at the time, he gave the impression that he was rather naive about life and affairs outside India and the way that it was lived in the UK. However, when it came to living in India he was worldly wise and full of confidence and he had joined the Goodricke's Group as an Assistant as soon as he was old enough and had played and associated with the workers' children ever since he was a baby. As a result he could speak Hindustani like a native, as well as Bengali, Nepalese and several of the tribal languages that were spoken by the labourers.

His great friend and playmate from his early years was a lad of about his own age named Ram who stayed with him during the whole of his time in tea. They were almost inseparable. Ram worked in the bungalow as Donald's personal servant, acting as his driver, and whenever Donald was out shooting he was there in charge of the firearms. They were almost like two brothers, and I often wonder what happened to him when Donald finally left India in the early 1970s.

From the tales I heard about him it seems that Old Mac had taught Donald to shoot while he was still a young boy, and it was said that he shot his first man-eating tiger near Jalpaiguri when he was 18, so after that shooting and shikar became one of his great interests in life and was the subject of a story he told me. This visit on home leave had been the first time Donald had been back to England since he was a boy and he loved to visit fairgrounds where there were .22 rifle ranges which gave prizes of cash and cigarettes for winning scores. As he told it to me, he went to a fair with Betty, and when they were by a shooting range she asked him to have a go, to which Donald replied quite loudly that it was a waste of time as the sights on the rifles had been doctored. Of course the showman heard this and told him indignantly that the sights had not been doctored, and if he wasn't man enough or good enough to use a rifle properly, then he should clear off as he would give the shooting range a bad name. They argued for a while and ultimately a small crowd gathered. This was like a red rag to a bull for Donald, so he handed over £2 for 20 sets of five shots and selected a rifle. He used his first shots to sight it in and found that if he aimed at the bulls eye it fired 3 inches high and to the right, so with his next attempt he corrected his aim to low down on the left-hand side and had three bulls and two in the next ring, which was not quite good enough for a prize, but after that it was just like taking sweets off a baby. There was very little he didn't know about guns and shooting. From then on he put five shots into each bull's-eye with monotonous regularity and won a packet of 20 cigarettes each time, while the showman had to change the target. As time went on Donald never seemed to miss, while the pile of cigarette cartons mounted up on the counter. The showman began to get worried as he realised that Donald was not quite so big and simple as he had appeared at first sight and he could see his profits melting away, so he told Donald that he thought there *was* something wrong with the sights and felt that he should change the rifle for him. Well this didn't go down well with the people in the crowd, who were absolutely delighted that somebody was teaching the showman a lesson, and when they heard this they began to boo, so Donald demurred and said 'No, I'm sorry but you were quite right about the sights. There is nothing wrong with them, so I'll keep this rifle. Actually I was thinking of having another five pounds worth of goes with it.' The crowd loved it. As Donald was about twice the showman's size and the mob were on his side as well, the man knew he could not use strong-arm tactics with him. He also realised that if he didn't want his business ruined for the remainder of his stay he would have to back down, so he took Donald to one side and whispered to him, 'How much do you want to clear off quietly and not bother me again?' Well Donald had proved his point and didn't want to cause a rumpus, so he thought for a few seconds and then settled for £10 and took Betty and his cigarettes off elsewhere, much to Donald's amusement and the showman's relief.

He hadn't been back many days before it was evident that his prowess must have become well known throughout the Dooars, because soon after the newlyweds had arrived back on Bagracote he received a message from one of his 'friends', the Maharaja of Cooch Bihar, asking for help with another man-eater. This tiger was causing a great deal of trouble in the Cooch Bihar district in the Eastern Dooars, and although the Maharaja had a herd of shikar elephants which had been specially trained for hunting game, he did not have enough hunters experienced enough to deal with this type of animal to use them, so knowing that many of the planters were sportsmen he called on Donald to help.

Of course this was just up Donald's street and he soon arranged for several of us to travel over to Cooch Bihar as soon as it was known for certain that the tiger was in the area once more, and this occurred towards the end of October. On Saturday afternoon Donald received the news that the tiger had killed a woman in a village about ten miles from Cooch Bihar town, but after being driven off the body it was thought that it had gone into hiding in an area covered with thick grass and scrub jungle nearby to rest up.

Despite the short notice it was decided to try for it. It had already been arranged that when the news came Wee Mac and I would travel over together in his Austin A40, so we were away early the next morning. It was a journey of some 120 miles from Bagracote by the only road and as this passed through numerous villages it was crowded with buffalo carts, buses, lorries, cycle rickshaws, animals, children playing and masses of people walking to the bazaars , and although we set off at 5 am it was nearly 10 am by the time we reached the village where the victim had lived and the elephants had been assembled.

There were 12 of them, mostly big bulls well able to look after themselves and in addition several of them carried wooden clubs in their trunks which they swung from side to side as they walked. They were quite adept at using them as weapons if attacked. Since early morning local hunters had been sent out to various vantage points in the area so that we could be warned if the tiger showed itself and moved during the day, and as soon as we arrived the head shikari explained how he planned to conduct the beats over the area where the tiger was thought to be in hiding. Each elephant would have one gun on it and they would advance across it side by side about 30 yards apart, then they would be followed by a loose line of beaters whose job it was to make a noise to distract the tiger if it tried to break back through the elephant line. In addition another line of beaters would walk ahead of the elephant line on each side of the tract of jungle in case the tiger tried to escape out through the sides. However most tigers hated moving about during the heat of the day, and if it was there it was likely that it would hide up in a thick patch of jungle in the hope that the elephants would pass it by. He said that if an elephant got too near and it got worried it would usually growl a warning, and if this occurred the nearest elephants were trained to stop and wait while those on either side would gradually curve round it with the minimum of noise, thus tightening the cordon until the circle was complete. Then, no matter which way the tiger tried to escape, it would present a target for at least two or three guns.

The final instruction was to keep our safety catches on for the whole of the time until we got a clear view of it, because the last thing we needed was for a shot to be fired accidentally by somebody with an itchy finger if the tiger attacked and the elephants were milling round trying to get into a shooting position. As he said, that was the way in which people got killed.

Once we had had this pep talk we were allocated an elephant each, and as each one had a number chalked on its forehead we knew which was to be our mount for the rest of the shoot. Elephants always rest up during the heat of the day, so we were only going to be able to beat for a couple of hours in the morning, then for three hours late in the afternoon, and were to take our lunch while the elephants rested. Although old pictures of hunters shooting tigers in India show them standing safely in large howdas on the elephants' backs, all we had was a flat, straw-filled tarpaulin pad lashed on top on which to sit or kneel and the motion of riding on the elephant was something like being in a small boat on a choppy sea.

At first all I was able to do was hang on to the lashings as tight as possible and not worry about shooting a tiger. Then as we moved into the first beat I gradually adjusted my balance so that I moved with the motion, but how I would have coped with shooting had we seen the tiger I never did find out, because despite beating over several large tracts of jungle, the head shikari finally came to the conclusion that because the tiger had been driven off its kill, instead of lying up nearby as it had done previously, it had decided that discretion was the better part of valour and had left the area immediately. They are great travellers and can wander anything up to 20 miles in a night looking for prey, so in all probability our tiger was many miles away before we arrived and it was nobody's fault that the shoot was not a success.

It was a big disappointment for everybody, because the locals still had to live with the knowledge that it would probably return, and also for us because we saw all sorts of other game that we were not allowed to shoot. The only bit of excitement came when we thought we had found the tiger in a thick patch of thorn jungle. The elephants sensed that there was a large animal in it and the mahouts were just beginning to tighten the circle when there was a crashing and squealing from the undergrowth and out shot an enormous wild sow accompanied by a sounder of eight or nine piglets, which dashed away through the elephants to freedom, running like the wind. After this the remainder of the beats seemed to be a bit of an anti-climax as the pads became more and more uncomfortable as the day wore on, and when it was decided to call it a day at about 5.30 pm we were all very pleased to slide down off our elephants and try to shake the kinks out of our spines.

However we all cheered up when we realised that a superb Indian meal had been prepared for us by the Maharaja's staff in a large field tent that had been pitched at the side of the clearing. We sat on camp stools and really filled ourselves after virtually starving all day. Considering where we were it was a really excellent spread, especially as it was accompanied by a well-stocked bar, and as we sat and relaxed and talked over the events of the day we realised that this was a type of 'shooting in style' which was unlikely to be repeated and for me we were right. Later we heard that although the tiger did not return for some reason, the elephants were used for the filming of the part of the film *Around the World in 80 Days*, which was shot in India, and that actress Shirley MacLaine had stayed at the Palace of Cooch Bihar while they were filming it, so she might have ridden on my elephant! What a thought.

Finally at about 9 pm we decided it was time to head for home. As luck would have it Donald and his party were first away while we followed a few minutes later, and with hindsight it was rather unfortunate that we did so. The first part of our journey was quite uneventful as there was rarely very much traffic on the roads at that time of night, so as Mac was a very good driver and I had nothing to do I settled down and drifted in and out of sleep. However about half way home as we neared the town of Maynaguri, Mac saw the reflection of four eyes in the distant darkness and realised it was a buffalo cart coming towards us. Normally this didn't present any difficulties as they were very docile animals, but I think this pair must have taken exception to a pair of blazing headlights bearing down on them and when we were some 100 yards away they began to veer to the right and come over onto our side of the road.

Unfortunately at this point the road was quite narrow and bounded on each side by a four-foot-high bank topped with shade trees. As the driver frantically tried to pull his animals back to his side of the road and Mac steered for the gradually-closing gap on our side, he realised that he was going to hit something and shouted to warn me. As I came out of my doze I realised that we were in trouble, but I could only sit horror struck as I watched the gap slowly opening once more as the driver pulled his animals over. For a moment I thought we were going to get through, then with a sickening crash the car hit one of the buffaloes and its horn smashed the windscreen, then it bounced off the back of the cart and buried its front end into the bank.

After the rending noise of the smash the subsequent darkness and silence were uncanny. The silence was only broken by the slurping noise I was making as I tried to spit out several fragments of glass which had entered my mouth when the windscreen shattered. In those early Austin cars the windscreens disintegrated into thousands of small glass chunks similar in size and shape to the cells in a honey bee comb, and several entered my mouth when I opened it to shout a warning at Mac and the screen came in. As I sat in the darkness with my fingers in my mouth trying to fish out the glass, I was making queer, gurgling noises and trying to speak to him at the same time while he kept saying 'Don't die, Rod, don't die'. I don't know which one of us was the most relieved when I finally managed to coax the last of the bits out and I was able to speak to him properly.

As there was no such thing as seat belts in those days we were both severely shaken up, but luckily I was completely unharmed. Mac had just one gash on his left forearm caused by a piece of flying glass. What we didn't realise at the time was that it had actually entered his arm and had lodged beneath the skin, and it was only several days later when the gash refused to heal up that he noticed a lump further up his arm and when he pressed it the piece of glass popped out.

When we got out of the car we found the cart had stopped a few yards back up the road, and one of the buffaloes had a broken back leg. Despite the fact that the loss of his buffalo would cause him great hardship, the driver was worried more about hitting us than he was about his injured animal, but when he knew that we were both all right he said that as he lived nearby he would tie it up by the side of the road and then go and get some help to carry it home. Of course with a lot of damage to its steering and front end, the car could not be driven, but luckily Mac knew the Manager of a nearby estate quite well, so I stayed with the car to look after our gear and firearms while he walked to his bungalow to see if he could arrange for some transport to take us home and he came up trumps. Luckily he was still up when Mac arrived at his bungalow and he quickly sent for his driver and lent us the garden pickup to take us home to Bagracote, where we finally arrived at about midnight, extremely tired after a long, exhausting day. Still, we knew we were both very lucky to have come out of it as lightly as we had.

The next afternoon after work Mac was allowed to take our Ford truck over to Maynaguri to collect his car, and after delivering a couple of bottles of whisky to his friend and leaving some baksheesh for the driver, he manhandled it onto the back of the lorry and then visited the village where the cart driver lived to give him some compensation. Here he found that the villagers had made a sling from hessian cloth that passed beneath the belly of the buffalo and had suspended it from a branch of a jackfruit tree by some ropes. Lying in the sling, its legs passed through three holes in the belly band so that its feet just touched the floor, except for its broken leg which was bandaged and splinted and hung over a depression which had been dug beneath it, thus keeping it straight. The sling enabled it to be fed and watered without difficulty and supported it when it slept, and it also allowed it to relieve itself when necessary. It seemed to be quite happy and contented dangling there and evidently it stayed there for several days until it was able to move about on its splint, and we heard later that it made a full recovery.

Regarding Mac's car, it was taken to Siliguri for repair, where the 'iron fighters' were able to bash out the dents and repair the front panels and steering quite successfully within a few days. Unfortunately the new windscreen and headlights were not available locally, so they had to be obtained from Calcutta and this took a couple of weeks, but once they were fitted the repairs and paint work had been done so professionally that it was not apparent that the car had ever been damaged.

CHAPTER TWENTY FIVE

1953/1954 - a cold weather to remember

Once Donald had settled in he took over the assistant's work on Bagracote in conjunction with Lionel while I replaced him in the factory once more, so once again I ate my breakfast before I left Saugaon then returned to the bungalow for my lunch, and as I had the only transport Wee Mac came back up with me in the afternoon. Once plucking stopped and the final manufacture and sorting was finished it was a race to dismantle and check all the machines in order to get faulty parts away for repair or replacement as quickly as possible, for with all the estates finishing at the same time it was a case of 'first in, first out' and days counted when the factories had to be ready for manufacture in March.

Our final crop was a total of 18,000 maunds of good quality tea, a maund weighing 80 lbs, so this equated to 1,440,000 lbs or 640 tons, which was all exported to London to be sold at the tea auctions in Mincing Lane. At a ratio of 5lbs of green leaf to 1lb of made tea, this took 3200 tons of green leaf ,and when you consider that this was all plucked by some 1800 labourers over the eight months of the plucking season, it can be imagined how much pressure everyone worked under at that time.

It was at this time of year that the season's work and tea sales were analysed in the London office and the estimates of expenditures and the programmes of work for the coming year were worked out, and when we received them we were very pleasantly surprised. Because the quality of the tea produced and the sale prices had improved while the production costs had been reduced, it was forecast that the estate would make a profit for the first time in several years, and we all got a pat on the back. We were also given permission to make the necessary preparations for some replanting to be done in the 1954/55 cold weather and also begin our plans for the rebuilding of our dam in the hills.

Once the monsoon finished and we started to get clear days and cool nights again it was almost as though an oppressive weight had been lifted from us all, and it can be imagined how much everybody enjoyed the Durga Puja in October and the Kali Puja at the beginning of November. The Kali Puja was especially enjoyed by the Nepalese labourers, for it was at this time that they made full sized swinging boats and ferris wheels out of bamboos and ropes, and as even the adults could play on these they were rarely still. They also made their large hot air balloons, often as large as six feet in diameter, out of very thin slivers of bamboo and tissue paper. By holding them over a large fire they would fill them with hot air and then light a large lamp fixed in the aperture beneath. Once they were released they would float off, often up to an altitude of several hundred feet, where they would sail along in the dark night sky like artificial full moons.

At this time the Hoadleys went up to Darjeeling to take their two weeks' annual local leave, leaving Donald in charge, while Wee Mac went down to the Teesta forest for some shikar. I stayed in the Saugaon bungalow, but even there I had some excitement because a leopard which had crossed the river from the Apalchand forest had killed a small cow near the labour lines and eaten most of it in the night. The owner said it had escaped from its pen and he couldn't get it back before nightfall, but I think he had turned it out in the tea to graze. I didn't really want to shoot the leopard, but it was a bit too close to the houses for comfort, so when the labourers asked me to sit up over what remained of the carcass so that I could shoot it if it came back to finish it up, reluctantly I agreed.

As there were no trees in the vicinity I had to wait for it on the ground, but there was a ditch about ten yards away beneath a nearby hedge and once this was dug out I had quite a comfortable hole in which I was able to sit or kneel with only my shoulders and rifle showing above ground. Because I was so close to the kill I was not too happy about taking a shot at a big leopard at that range, but I never needed to because it didn't return. Probably it had eaten so much the night before that it didn't need to eat for a couple of days. I had a lovely night sitting in a hole being eaten alive by mosquitoes, but I was rewarded by the amount of wildlife that I did see, ranging from jackals to a monitor lizard and two porcupines.

Finally at about 5 am I decided to call it a night and walked back to the bungalow, very stiff and sore, where I found several of the labourers waiting for me. They were overjoyed that I had stayed there for so long in an effort 'to help them'. They said that they were all rather worried about me being on the ground with the leopard and if they had heard a shot they would all have come running in case I needed any help! It was a lovely thought, although what they could have done with kerosene lanterns, bows and arrows and spears against a wounded leopard hardly bears thinking about, but I was very touched by their concern. I think that because I had tried I went up in their estimation as well.

Two nights later I had some more excitement when two houses in the labour lines burned down and we had great difficulty in stopping the flames from spreading to several others. Fireworks were always very popular with the labourers at puja time, especially the jumping explosive kind, and as they had been letting them off all day I wasn't surprised when I heard a loud bang. However I was startled when I heard a loud uproar start in the lines. When I hurried outside I found somebody had lit a cracker which had finished up on the thatched roof of one of the houses and set it alight. Because there were large areas of thatch grass on Saugaon, very few of the labour houses had corrugated iron roofs, so for an hour we worked like demons damping down the neighbouring houses and trying to stop the flames from spreading. Luckily there was a very light wind that night and as the labour line was quite near the river bank there was plenty of water to throw around, but unfortunately we were unable to save the first two and many of the occupants' belongings were destroyed.

Wee Mac got his car back in the middle of November and then on the 22nd received an instruction from the Superintendent telling him to transfer to Sam Sing Tea Estate on December 1st. He was not too happy about this because he loved being his own boss tucked away in the 'backwoods' in Saugaon, and did not relish the thought of being right under the Superintendent's nose on Sam Sing. Also because they were both very keen on shooting he had looked forward to a spell on Bagracote with Donald, but orders were orders and he transferred on the 1st. Lionel resumed control of the factory work while I took sole charge of the Saugaon division. This arrangement suited me fine, partly because it meant I only had to make one trip up to Bagracote on most days, and also because it gave me an excellent opportunity to gain an intimate knowledge of the cold weather work on the garden and also of the labourers and their lives. I was solely responsible for paying them all out on pay days and ration days. I issued the rations every second week, checked the houses to record what repairs were required and gave the orders for the different works that were to be done each day, then checked them to ensure that they were being done properly.

Ever since I was a small boy I have always been a 'loner' and quite happy with my own company, so being on my own for 20 hours a day only speaking Hindi didn't seem to worry me at all. Although I was on the go from early morning until the late afternoon when I went up to Bagracote to get my post and receive any orders for the next day, I felt I was really enjoying life and fulfilling my potential. Unfortunately this didn't leave much time for writing letters home, much to Mum's distress. Now with hindsight I wish that I had written more frequently, even if it had only been just a few lines to tell her I was still thinking about her and that I was still well. I learned later that each morning when she was on her way to work in Dursley she always met the postman wherever he was on his round, and if there was a letter he always had it out ready to give to her. Still, we can all be wise after the event.

With so much work and activity, December passed by in a whirl, Although I had intended to send a congratulatory telegram to Marion and Peter for their wedding, it was on me before I realised it, and actually I forgot it completely. Fortunately I did send a cheque to them earlier in the month, but sadly their wedding day, December 19th, also happened to be the day when we had to renew our firearms licences at Mal Police Station. This was a very serious annual event supervised by the local Chief of Police, when every firearm had to be presented by the owner and inspected and the licence checked. If it was not being maintained properly it could be confiscated, and if for some reason it was not renewed on this day then there was only a short period of grace during which it could be taken to Jalpaiguri to be seen, which necessitated a round trip of some 150 miles. For many people this was a major operation. If it was not done the licence could be revoked and the weapon seized, so on inspection morning the whole of the parade area in front of the police station was a mass of owners all waiting patiently for their names to be called, and there was no favouritism.

In India it was a very high status symbol if a person owned a firearm, and even a small village headman usually had a couple of battered old shotguns, so this crowd of several hundred people usually consisted of many different ages and nationalities and people from different parts of India. Records of licences for rifles, shotguns and handguns were all detailed in different registers in a strictly numerical order instead of all being under one name, so the clerks ploughed through the lists of numbers while everybody waited for theirs to come up and their name to be called. The more firearms you had the longer the wait, and as each one had to be done separately sometimes the waiting seemed endless. However I got there early in the morning and as I only had my rifle and a .410 shotgun to renew I managed to return to Saugaon in time to check the work that had been done that day. However I forgot about the wedding, and it was not until I was getting ready to go to Mal Club that evening to see the weekly film that it came to me. Of course with the Post Office closed for the weekend and no telephone system, sadly it was much too late to do anything about it. In these days of mobile phones, video links and emails, people cannot imagine that once the Post and Telegraph Office had closed on a Saturday night we had no way of contacting anyone outside the district before Monday morning, and even an air letter took from four to eight days to get home. Of course I was very sorry that this had happened, especially as it might have seemed to some people that I had done it on purpose, but in due course I think I managed to convince Marion that it had been a genuine mistake and she forgave me.

After this the next thing was Christmas. Although I was on my own I was determined to celebrate as much as possible, and decorated the bungalow up with large clumps of poinsettia bushes, banana plants and other jungle, and with paper trimmings that I had got from the bazaar I made it look really festive. The only thing lacking was someone to share it with. On Christmas morning I worked as normal until 10 am making sure that all the work was proceeding as normal, then I went up to Mal Club for a game of cricket and a lunch which some of the ladies had organised consisting of turkey, ham, salads and Christmas pudding with brandy sauce and mince pies. As I had to go back in the afternoon to check some work in the factory I had very little to drink, but I made up for it later as Lionel and Molly had invited us to a small party in the evening and opened several bottles of champagne. This was the first time I had ever tasted this, and although it was rather too dry for my taste I had several glasses, plus other things, and I felt fine when I drove back down to Saugaon that night. However the next morning was rather different as I woke up with a splitting headache, and when I went out in the hot sun I gradually felt it affecting my eyesight until I was completely blind and seeing bright flashes if I closed my eyes. The only thing I could do was stumble back to the bungalow and crawl into bed until the afternoon, when my eyesight gradually recovered and everything came back to normal. Since then champagne has never been my favourite drink, although I can take a sip if necessary.

Normally during the cold weather from October to February we got hardly any rain and everywhere became arid and dry, with visibility reduced to two or three miles, but at the beginning of January we had several very unexpected and unseasonal storms of rain which damped down all the dust and washed all the smoke and impurities out of the air. This meant that the mornings became crystal clear, and to my joy I was able to see the Kanchenjunga range once more, silhouetted against the Western sky and glistening in the morning sun. Because Bagracote was situated so close under the foothills this view was not possible from there, but from Saugaon two miles to the south I got an absolutely superb view of the whole range. Unfortunately this was not to last, because that was all the rain that we were to get for three and a half months. Even at the beginning of March when we usually got the early rain or hail storms, all we received were several really severe wind storms that sucked up sand and dust from the parched earth and threw them around like miniature sand storms. The riverside areas down in Saugaon were particularly hard hit, and at times they looked like the Sahara desert, especially when one of the Jamair planes took off.

In the middle of March Lionel and Molly Hoadley flew down to Calcutta at the start of their six months' UK leave and Donald moved over to the manager's bungalow, which left the other bungalow free for a new Assistant who arrived a few days later. Ashwani Wason, a young Indian army officer who had decided to join tea, was one of the first Indian lads to join our company, and we liked each other from our first meeting and got on so well together that we became firm friends. His arrival also resulted in something which I think was unique for our company and possibly for all the other firms as well, and something I never heard of happening anywhere else. The Manager (Acting) was Donald aged 23, then myself, the Senior Assistant at 25, and then Ash the junior assistant was aged about 27, which was a complete reversal of seniority and must have been something of a record.

Indeed Ash and I gelled so well together that when I was given leave to visit Darjeeling during the Holi Puja on the 20th, he came up with me and we stayed at the Swiss Hotel. On the Monday morning I was asleep in bed when I was woken up by a terrific rumbling, rushing noise which was exactly like the sound a tube train makes when it emerges from the tunnel into the station. For a few seconds I wondered what on earth was happening, until I realised that the bed was bumping and shaking beneath me and everything in the room was rattling merrily. The doors and windows also rattled for about three minutes while I wondered whether to stay put or rush outside, but gradually the tremors subsided until everything was quiet once more. Later we found out that the epicentre of the earthquake was in Manipur, in Assam about 400 miles away. Although there was some damage done, luckily there were no casualties.

The other exciting thing that happened to me on that weekend was that I was introduced to 'Tiger' Tenzing for the first time. After the conquest of Everest in 1953, the Indian Government had set up a mountaineering training centre and Everest Museum in Darjeeling named the Himalayan Mountaineering Institute and as a reward for his success had appointed him as its Head and Chief Instructor. Consequently he had made his home just along the road from the hotel. On the Sunday morning he was walking along towards the town with his two daughters, Pem Pem and Nima, when he stopped to chat to a mutual friend who introduced me to him. My friend Erach Avari was a well-known businessman in Darjeeling who had been an officer in the British army during the war, and besides being a great friend of many of the planters he had been of great help to Tenzing when he was making a name for himself as a Sherpa mountaineer. Indeed he had such a high regard for him that when he returned from the conquest of Everest he brought back two stones he had picked up from Everest, one of which he gave to the President of India and the other to Erach as a token of his gratitude. He treasured this so much that he had it mounted in a silver picture frame together with a photograph and a note from Tenzing, and I was to see this many times when we visited the family at home in later years.

As a result of this meeting, on the Monday afternoon we went up to the HMI where we visited the museum, which contained many items of equipment that had been used on this and previous climbs, together with hundreds of photographs, boots, ropes, ice axes, clothes and flags and many gifts, messages and medals he had been given, and we spent a very interesting afternoon there. During our visit he came and introduced himself to us again and shook hands, and then after chatting for a while he gave us each an autographed photograph of himself which I still have. He was a lovely man, very unassuming and unspoilt, for his fame seemed to lie very lightly on his shoulders. Several years later I was very pleased when Erach was able to introduce Jan to him as well. It was almost as though the wheel of fate had turned full circle.

CHAPTER TWENTY SIX

One bent car, two parakeets and a hokoos in a shade tree

Unfortunately that visit to Darjeeling was the last long trip I was destined to make in the Minor, because at the beginning of April she was badly damaged in an unusual accident. After a period of very dry, dusty weather in March a storm had brewed up, and on April 7th we had the first of the pre-monsoon downpours, during which several inches of rain fell within a few hours. After the final leaf weighment in the afternoon I had driven into Siliguri to the nearest hardware store to get some items we needed for use in the factory and was returning at about 7 pm when I ran into this absolutely blinding downpour, which was very unlucky because it was the only one we had and within a few days it had all dried up and the rest of the month was hot and dry.

However on that night I was driving back from the Teesta Bridge on a road which consisted of a single ribbon of tarmac with ragged edges which played havoc with car tyres, and these were flanked by a grass-covered verge on each side about ten feet wide. It was the accepted custom when two vehicles met for them to pass each other 'two up and two down', with two wheels on the road and two on the verge. This was fine as long as everyone played the game fairly and the verges were not slippery, but not everyone played it the same way. That night was pitch black and I had my windscreen wiper full on when through the teeming rain I saw the headlights of a vehicle approaching in the middle of the road. On seeing him I drove my two nearside wheels onto the verge as usual. Then to my horror I realised that it was a Jeep with very poor lights and no windscreen wipers and obviously the driver had not seen me, because unless I left the road completely there would be a head on collision.

Hauling the wheel over I went up onto the grass and missed him by a coat of paint, but the Minor started sliding and turning on the wet turf and before I could correct it I found I was travelling backwards. Then I hit something with a most horrendous crash. Luckily I was not travelling fast so I only experienced a severe jolt and some whiplash, but as I sat in my seat quite stunned by the shock I was aware of the engine still running and of something banging and clanging on the roof of the car as though someone was hitting it with a hammer. By this time the Jeep had vanished into the darkness without stopping. I sat there for a while before I switched off the engine and got out to see the damage.

Normally the grass verges were kept clear of any trees or bushes, but for some reason a large tree had been left growing at this point, the only one in about two miles of road, and it was this I had hit going backwards. The trunk was embedded in the boot of the car and the hammering I had heard was the sound of branches and dry wood raining down from the top of the tree onto the roof. The Minor was not built with a chassis, and the force of the smash shortened the floor pan by a couple of inches and caused the roof to bend in from back to front, thus giving the car a humpy backed appearance. Nevertheless after checking that the petrol tank was not leaking, I managed to drive her back to the bungalow and later sent her off to Siliguri for repairs.

I was now down in Saugaon with no transport, and because I was now the engineer again I was having to come up to the factory first thing each morning as well as supervising the lower garden. Still, difficulties are meant to be overcome and quite often when one door closes another one opens, so very luckily there was a solution. Lionel Hoadley had had a Standard Vanguard Phase 1 car which I believe he had brought back with him after his UK leave in 1949/50, and after using it for four years he had sold it to the Bagracote kyah (garden shopkeeper) before he went home in March. It was one of the models with the beetle-shaped back which to me looked like a fancy loaf of bread. Because its suspension and steering were of more robust construction than that the Minor and its ground clearance was also greater, it was a much more suitable car for use on the garden roads than the little Minor was, even though it only did about 25 miles to the gallon. Talking to him I don't think that the kyah was terribly interested in using it on rough roads and for him I think it was more of a status symbol for his wife and family. However with her pretty lines and 40+ miles to the gallon, I think he had always coveted the Minor, and once he had said to me that if I ever wanted to sell it he would like first refusal Nevertheless I was very surprised when he came up to me a few days later to see if I would consider a deal. He knew that I was badly in need of a set of wheels and although my car was newer than his it had cost less when new, so the resale values of the two were just about the same, and what he proposed was a straight swop between us, my Minor for his Vanguard. Because the Vanguard needed some minor work done on it, he proposed that if I would accept it as seen, he would accept my damaged Minor as it was and also pay for the repairs being done in Siliguri.

Well I knew that Lionel had taken good care of his car, so this seemed to be too good a chance to miss. When I spoke to Donald about it he too thought that under the circumstances it was an excellent deal, so I decided to take the plunge, and the next day I was the proud owner of a metallic silver Vanguard. After driving the Minor she felt like a tank, really beefy and solid, and rode the bumps and ruts really well, but although she served her purpose at that time, I never felt really comfortable in her because it transpired that on occasions the 'dog' on the starter motor would jam in the starter ring and refused to disengage, which meant that sometimes I would have to leave her engaged in top gear and then bump her violently up and down until it slipped free. This didn't happen all that often, but as spares were not available it meant I had to put up with this until I could get some, which really was a nuisance. In the back of my mind I had the idea that I would probably only keep her until after I had been on my UK furlough in 1955 and then replace her, but how wrong I was to be again.

Regarding the repairs to the Minor, the workshops in Siliguri cut her in half, straightened out the floor pan, the roof and the rear end then welded her back together again, and after they had finished and she had been repainted it was not possible to see that she had been in a smash, so it was a really good job done on a car that would have been a write off in the UK and one of which the kyah was justly proud.

After I had settled down to life by myself in Saugaon, I was able to indulge myself by doing something I had waited to do for several months, and that was to have a pet bird. In my youth I had always loved the British songbirds, especially the blackbirds and the robins, and although India had nothing to compare with these songsters they did have some really unusual native birds, like the hill mynahs and the parakeets, which were not difficult to tame and made wonderful pets. The mynahs were excellent talkers and a friend of mine had one that was able to say quite clearly, 'Give the man a drink. Get him a cold beer, Bearer' as soon as anyone walked into the room and it was almost as though it had spoken fluent English all its life.

The hill mynahs were not common down on the plains, but Saugaon was the home of several large flocks of colourful Alexandrine or large Indian parakeets. These were also known as ring-necked parakeets and they squawked and chattered in the treetops all day long, using holes and cracks in the garden trees in which to nest rather like woodpeckers. Their heads and backs were green, with yellow breasts and maroon patches on their wings and they had large orange/red bills and a distinct dark collar round their necks from which they got their name. I had wanted a parakeet ever since I first saw them on Saugaon, but although they could be bought in the bazaar, these were just captive wild adults which had been trapped, and these were not what I wanted. My idea was to get a couple of youngsters which I could rear by hand, and then once they could fly I would release them by the bungalow in the hope that they would stay in the vicinity and come back to me when called. So once I had really settled in I told a couple of garden chowkidhars (watchmen) that if they ever came across a nest with young in and could get me a couple I would be very grateful.

A few days later I returned to the bungalow after work to find them waiting for me with two of the ugliest little things imaginable. They said that there were several young in the nest so they would not be missed by the parents. The chicks were completely bald, with protruding eyes, queerly-shaped heads and beaks almost as big as their bodies. At first I kept them in a wickerwork basket in the living room and to simulate the warmth and security of the nest hole I covered it over with a small square of blanket, but as they were taken out and fed by hand at regular intervals during the day they soon became used to being out in the open. In the wild they were fed with partially-digested food regurgitated by the parents, so to simulate this we fed them with a mixture of mashed-up boiled rice, papayas, bananas and any other soft fruits available, and it worked a treat. We pushed this disgusting mess into their ever-open beaks, from where they filled their crops and then digested it later. Probably they got more food from us than they would ever have done in the wild, because they developed so quickly that it was almost possible to see them growing.

After several weeks they had fledged and become more adventurous. When Titch the kitten became interested in them I transferred them to the wire room at the front of the bungalow. This was an area of the front veranda about 10 feet square, which had a wooden framework covered with fine mosquito-proof wire-netting. Once I had given them a couple of large tree branches to fly around and clamber about in they settled in quite happily. From then on, once they could feed themselves on more varied food, they grew rapidly, and within a matter of weeks they had developed into a pair of beautiful birds which became part of our household. They were very friendly and loved being handled, so whenever anybody entered the room they got excited and hopped up and down on their perches until they received some attention. If I gave a certain whistle they fluttered over to me and sat on my hand or shoulder, at the same time talking to me and watching my every movement with their small, black, beady eyes. If I was in a different part of the bungalow and whistled to them they would answer. I suppose they must have thought of me as their father. Finally they became so tame that I was able to open the door of the wire room and let them fly freely around the trees in the bungalow compound until it was time for them to come back in, and there was never any trouble when I whistled for them to come back to my hand so that I could carry them back into what they regarded as their home.

Bringing up these two young birds was a very pleasurable and unforgettable experience for me. It lasted until the middle of 1954, when I lost one of them in a rather freakish accident. Periodically when the branches were well worn and dirty they were replaced with new ones, and when it was done this time, on one of them two of the smaller side branches had been distorted and rubbed against each other. Normally the birds were very agile and careful when they climbed about, but on this occasion one of them slipped and trapped its head and neck between the two branches, and as it struggled to get free it strangled itself. Evidently Kancha had heard a rumpus coming from the wire room, but as they were always squawking and play fighting he thought nothing of it until he went to feed them and found it hanging dead. He was terribly cut up about it because he had done a lot of the feeding when they were very young and had become attached to them and looked on them almost as his pets, but there was nothing we could do about it.

Afterwards I kept the other one for a while, but they had been constant companions and all the life and playfulness seemed to go out of the remaining one when he was on his own, so finally I decided to let him fly free if he wished to do so. Consequently I increased the length of time he was allowed to fly around outside the bungalow, until one day when we had a large flock of parakeets fluttering around in the trees surrounding the bungalow I let him out. After a few minutes' hesitation in which he worked out that they were his own kind, he flew up and joined them as though he had been a wild parakeet all his life. They stayed in the vicinity of the bungalow for another couple of hours and to my joy, when they flew away he went with them. Although we all kept a good lookout for several days just in case he had been rejected by the flock, we never saw any solitary birds at all, so presumably he never stuck out in the crowd. He was a lovely bird and I like to think that he was accepted by the rest of the group and possibly was reunited with his parents. I hope so anyway.

Since then there have been many reports of flocks of Alexandrine parakeets being found living wild in western Europe, especially in the London parks, Surrey, East Anglia and Kent. It has been suggested that these were originally pet birds that escaped from captivity, or that they were released deliberately for some reason. Still, whatever their origins, a combination of mild winters, a lack of natural predators, food being readily available from bird tables and an increase in breeding partners have caused a population boom, and recently it has been estimated that there is a total of more than 20,000 birds now living wild in the eastern counties of England, so it appears that they have come to stay.

It was also at this time that I came across another different but equally interesting bird, when one Sunday morning I woke up to a sound I had never heard before, which sounded like a rather musical fog horn or the bellowing of a bull with a sore throat. It was repeated every 30 seconds or so and grated on my ear so much that when Kancha brought in the morning tea I asked him what was making the noise. He said he had no idea either, but he would go and find out. A few minutes later he returned and told me that it was the call of a *hokoos* sitting in a tree about 300 yards from the bungalow. I had never heard of a hokoos. When I asked him what it was he replied that it was a black and white bird as big as a man, with a big nose and a long tail. The idea of a man-sized bird with a big nose intrigued me, so I dressed quickly and hurried to the tree to view this wonder. I was rewarded by my first and only close up view of a Great Hornbill (*Buceros bicornis*) in the wild. These birds live in the forests and jungles of the Himalayas and South East Asia and can grow up to four feet in length. They have an extremely powerful down curved bill with a very large, bony growth or 'casque' at the top which at first sight does give the impression of a nose, so Kancha was quite right. Their beaks, casques and necks are coloured a bright yellow, while they have black and white plumage and their black and white barred tail feathers are greatly prized by the Naga tribesmen of the North East Frontier area, as they make their headdresses from them.

Although I had seen them in the distance while out shooting with Bill Milne in the Naura forest, this was the first one I had ever seen at close quarters. As it perched fifteen feet up in the tree and 'sang' its horrible song I stood below and watched, absolutely enthralled as I marvelled at its size and wondered why it had bothered to cross the river from the Apalchand forest and was making such a noise. They have a very unusual lifestyle because in all the forest-dwelling species, the female becomes a 'prisoner' for many weeks as she sits in her nest. These are built in holes in trees, rock faces and earth banks and at first the entrance holes are partially blocked with mud from the outside. Once it is small enough to keep out predators the female squeezes through and then continues to block up the entrance from the inside, using her own droppings and food remains, while the male helps her by bringing her more mud and food. Finally, when the entrance is complete, there is only a tiny slit left, through which she looks out as he feeds her while she incubates the eggs. She also keeps the nest clean by passing out her droppings and food scraps to him through the slit. When the eggs hatch he has to bring back large quantities of food to feed the chicks as well until they are ready to leave the nest, so they are entirely dependent on him.

As I stood there the crowd of onlookers who were gathered around the base of the tree gradually increased as more and more people came to see the free show. The hokoos stayed for about 20 minutes until it was disturbed, then clumsily launched itself into the air like an underpowered flying boat, after which it laboriously flapped its way back across the river. Afterwards I read about its habits in a book of Indian birds, and this made me wonder if it had been looking after a family and then, having lost them in some natural catastrophe, it had been mourning them. From the noise it had been making it certainly sounded that way.

The hot dry weather at the end of April meant that the leaf

growth slowed again and was ideal for shooting, and Donald was not the kind of man to miss an opportunity like that. One of his favourite places was on the bank of the Teesta river near the town of Dhupguri, where the villagers had huge areas of rice khets and bhabni thatch grass which the local wild pigs visited in large numbers at this time of year, so much so that they became a big pest and caused considerable loss, because they came out during the evenings and early morning and ate the ripened grain and then rested up in the thatch during the day. Donald knew these villagers very well as he had visited them many times when he was on Dangua Jhar, so on Sunday April 11th we set off in the garden Ford V8 pickup truck at 6 am accompanied by a lorryload of labourers all armed with spears and bows and arrows and full of confidence.

Unfortunately when we reached the bhabni jungle we were in for a rude awakening, because although the pigs were there in plenty the grass was so tall that when we walked through it looking for them we were unable to see a thing. It was no use sending our men through as beaters as they just got disoriented. The pigs made lovely little shelters in the middle of patches of extra thick jungle by smashing the thatch down into a heap and then making two holes in it, an entry at the front and a bolt hole at the back, then crawling in and stretching out on the cool ground. The thatch grew to about six feet tall and was exceptionally thick that year. As we wandered about inside searching for the elusive shelters, whenever we got near one the crafty pig would quietly sidle out of his back door and all we would find was an empty nest. Finally after two hours of fruitless wandering about we accepted that we were wasting our time and called it a day.

After eating a very nice chicken curry lunch that the

villagers had prepared for us, Donald had a meeting with the village headmen. He explained our difficulties and said we would be prepared to come down the following Sunday provided they would arrange for each of us to have the use of a country cart pulled by two young bullocks. Although the pigs evaded us quite easily, it appeared that they didn't take any notice of bullocks or other animals wandering through the thatch and just crouched down in their nests until they moved on, so if everybody remained absolutely silent they wouldn't realise that we were standing on the back until it was too late. The villagers accepted that we couldn't shoot something we couldn't see and thought this was a good idea. As the carts were not like the ungainly, heavy bullock carts but were very light and manoeuvrable with just a flat, bamboo bed lashed to an axle and pulled by two bullocks, in order to give us some support when we were trying to balance as we jolted over the uneven ground, it was arranged that a bamboo post would be lashed to the axle and project for five feet through above the bed so that we could brace our backs against them and have both hands free for firing our rifles. Once all the arrangements were agreed we prepared to make the 70-mile journey back to Bagracote and return the following Sunday, but before we left they asked Donald if he would shoot some giant Indian fruit bats (flying foxes) for them as a substitute for the pigs we didn't shoot. Evidently they had made arrangements for a big village feast and they had relied on us for the meat. They took him to a stand of tall trees just on the edge of the village which was festooned with thousands of bats hanging from the upper branches. They were completely out of reach of the villagers, but all Donald had to do was give them both barrels of his 12 bore shot gun and about 30 dead and injured bats came raining down like ripe fruit. They were pounced on by the villagers, who began to skin them straight away while we went home.

On the 18th we retraced our steps and found that they had not let us down, because all the carts were there with the posts firmly lashed to the framework and axles. When we climbed up on them we found that our heads were about 10 feet above ground level, which gave us an excellent view over the thatch, and as the posts sloped slightly backwards we were able to brace our legs and lean back enough to keep us absolutely steady.

Knowing that an experienced shikari would be invaluable when we actually began spotting the pigs, I had arranged for Dushroo, my trusty companion from Zurrantee days, to come with us, so I picked him up on the way and he was absolutely delighted to be shooting with me once more and greeted me like a long lost friend.

During the week the villagers had erected rows of flags tied to tall bamboos on all sides of the bhabni jungle so that when the beat started the cart drivers had marks to head for and maintain a straight line, and the idea worked like a dream. The labourers we had taken with us and all the able-bodied villagers, armed with spears and bows and arrows, were deployed round the sides of the area being beaten and their job was to deal with any pigs that had run away or had been wounded and tried to escape the guns. Once they were in place we mounted up on our individual carts and started off in line abreast about 50 feet apart in absolute silence, letting the bullocks quietly wander along until one came up to a 'nest'. No talking was allowed, but the driver would whistle to the others for the line to stop and then he would manoeuvre the cart until the shikari could see if there was a pig inside it, with a good enough view of it to get a killing shot. There were so many of them that the line was continually stopping and starting and many of them were empty, but by 1 pm, after three hours of rambling about in the hot sun, we had shot 12 pigs, while the labourers had killed another four as they tried to break through the cordon.

I had a very successful day, as I managed to shoot three of them and each was different. The first was dead easy. We positioned our cart immediately in front of the entrance to the 'nest' and instead of bolting out of the back door, the silly thing ambled out of the entrance right in front of me as though it was half asleep and paid the price. However when we found the second, I was very glad that I had Dushroo with me for without him I would never have been able to shoot. Our cart broke out into a small clearing in the thatch with a hide in the centre and the moment we stopped in front of it he whispered to me, 'There's a pig in there Sahib'. Despite the fact that we were moving about on top of the cart trying to peer inside to see exactly how it was lying, it lay absolutely motionless, presumably hoping that if we couldn't see it we would go away. In the gloom inside the hide all I could see was a patchwork of black shadows, grey patches and small white smudges which made absolutely no sense to me whatsoever, but to Dushroo's experienced shikari's eye it was as plain as daylight. Whispering very softly to me he told me exactly how the pig was facing and where to shoot to kill it, but try as I might I was unable to translate what he was saying into what I was seeing inside the hide, and I thought that there was no way that I could imagine enough to shoot at it. Finally, getting a bit exasperated, he whispered to me, 'Look Sahib, it's lying on its belly facing the left side of the hole and with its face on the ground. If you can see a white smudge about two inches long that is its tush and then the small white spot a little bit above and behind that is its eye watching us. If you aim just behind and below the eye you will hit it just at the base of its ear and kill it. Now shoot it Sahib.' Well with instructions like that there was no way I could miss, so I located the things he had described, then I aimed carefully and squeezed the trigger. To my surprise the pig hardly moved as it twitched its legs a couple of times and then lay still. When we dragged it out of its shelter we were both delighted, Dushroo because it was a monster and one of the largest pigs we got that day and me because his instructions had been so exact that my shot had struck it exactly at the base of its ear and shattered its brain, killing it instantly. We were like a couple of brothers as we loaded it on our cart.

The third one was much more of a problem as it broke out of the back of the hide and I had to have a moving shot at it as it bolted for the long grass. This hit one of its back legs and broke it, but despite this it kept running and managed to escape through the outside cordon. Dushroo, plus myself and a couple of Bagracote men followed its blood trail through the thatch and scrub jungle for about two miles on foot. It had been hit very hard and was losing a lot of blood, for every few hundred yards it had to stop and rest. No doubt the poor beast was almost beside itself with pain, but finally we got close and heard it moving through the scrub jungle in front of us, so I ran round to head it off and shot it through the head as it approached me. This too was a very large pig and it was all the two Bagracote men could do to sling it on a bamboo pole and carry it back to where our cart was waiting for us.

By this time the shoot was over and everyone returned to the village, where we rested in the shade and drank some beers we had brought with us before we tucked into a superb curried meal which the villagers had prepared, and after a hot, dusty and very exciting day it was absolutely wonderful. While we did so we discussed the events of the day. The highlight was a fall Bob Grey had had from his cart when the line had stopped and while he waited he leaned back against his post with all his weight. He was a big lad and evidently the post was not up to it, for one moment he was resting peacefully on top of the cart and the next it had broken and he did a cartwheel over the back of it and finished up sprawling on the ground. Luckily the ground was soft and he wasn't injured, nor was his rifle damaged, so the only thing dented was his pride, because it so happened that I was on the next cart and managed to take some photographs of him. Unfortunately the lads with cameras took so many pictures of the actual shoot that when it came to the big share out of the meat nobody had any film left, so the sight of our 16 pigs laid out in a row, the most we ever had in one shoot, could not be recorded for posterity.

While we were eating we told our shikaris exactly what cuts of meat we wanted to take for our own use, and then the villagers and our men decided how the rest of the kill should be distributed amongst all the men who had taken part in the shoot. This seemed to take a lot of very earnest discussion, but finally it was agreed that our men would take five of them and divide them up when we got home, while the cart drivers and the other villagers would take the other eleven and share them out between themselves on a household basis. This meant that everybody received about 15 pounds of meat each, undoubtedly the best result we ever had.

CHAPTER TWENTY SEVEN

A tea thief and a tiger

The weather that April was very unusual, because after the absolute downpour we got on the 7th during which I pranged the Minor we didn't get any more rain until well into May, and this together with a hot sun and day temperatures in the mid-eighties quickly resulted in drought conditions. The bushes needed regular rainfall to produce the very tender, young green leaves from which the top quality, first flush teas were produced, so they really suffered from the lack of moisture.

Day after day great banks of cloud would gather over the hills and really violent electrical storms would develop, but in the evening they would gradually die away and we would have another dry night until the sun began to burn things up again the next day. What added to my trials and tribulations was that my diesel engine broke down at the beginning of April, and as I was dependent on this for my electricity and my water supply my life became very basic for a while until the necessary replacement parts arrived and I fitted them. A minimum quantity of water was delivered to the bungalow by the tractor each day, but I was unable to use my electric light, my wireless or my fans, so the bungalow became like a dark oven. The only relief I got was in the evening when a cooling breeze sprang up in the river valley and blew the stale air out of the bungalow. The monsoon wasn't due to arrive until the middle of May and each day we longed for some rain to arrive, little realising what tricks nature was preparing to play on us. Because there was not enough leaf to make plucking viable, other jobs had to be created for the workers to do, and while this was not difficult for the men, who could always be diverted to draining, road repairs, riverbank maintenance and making seed beds for the replanting to be done in 1955, for the women who were usually used for this very fine type of plucking this was much more difficult, so the garden got a very much more thorough hand weeding that year.

Despite the fact that leaf was at a premium we did get it stolen by people who lived in Pillans Hat village. Despite receiving several warnings they continued to trespass in the tea at night and tear off whatever leaf they could steal. They then manufactured it at home by hand, dried it in the sun and later sold it in the local bazaar at a very good profit. Our chowkidhars (watchmen) told us this was going on, and really the thing that worried us was not the value of the tea that we were losing, which was minimal, but rather the amount of damage that they were doing to the bushes in ripping the young leaf off, so as the days went on and it seemed to be on the increase Donald decided to nip it in the bud.

The next night we gathered several chowkidhars and took a roundabout route over to the area where the theft was taking place. As we neared it we could see several small lights bobbing about in the tea, so Donald's plan was to walk quietly round the perimeter road until we were between them and the bazaar and then try to catch one of them. This showed the way

Donald's mind worked, because he said if we caught several of them it just complicated things, but if we got just one we could make an example of him and that would scare the rest off, so he told us which one to target and it worked like a dream. We had approached so quietly that we were amongst them before they realised quite what was happening, so we had no difficulty in concentrating on a middle-aged Nepali man. Despite the fact that he dived beneath the bushes to avoid detection, when Donald shouted that we would send the dogs in after him he emerged very quickly and we had him tied up in next to no time while the rest all scampered back to the bazaar.

As we marched him back Donald chatted to our men in Nepalese so that the thief could understand, deliberately appearing undecided whether to take him off to the police station that night or whether it was too late and we should wait until morning. By the time we reached the factory he was absolutely begging for mercy, swearing that he would never steal any more tea again. Of course Donald ignored him completely, but told our men to lock him up in a spare, empty store room that we had at the back of the office and said he would decide what he would do to him in the morning. If we had decided to hand him over to the police it would have meant a court case for him in Jalpaiguri, with all the attendant expenditure. When Donald saw him at 7 am he told him that he had a choice; either to accept a punishment that he would decide or be handed over to the police to face prosecution. Of course during the night he had had plenty of time to think things over and knowing what it would be like if the police were involved he opted for the punishment. He must have wondered whether he had made the right decision, because he was painted all over with red and aluminium paint from the factory, marched all around the lines and bazaar for everyone to see what happened to tea thieves and then driven about eleven miles to the Teesta bridge where he was tipped out to walk home, a ramble that took him the rest of the day. Some people say deterrents do not work but this one certainly did, because theft from our green tea stopped immediately and to the best of my knowledge never restarted in my time there.

By the end of April we had made so little first flush tea that our crop was down by 1000 maunds of made tea (35 tons) compared with the same time in 1953, but to compensate for this we did get the best prices for our tea (five shillings per pound) in the first tea auctions and got a pat on the back from the Superintendent for our manufacture.

After our success the previous week, on April 25th we had an invitation to go on another shooting trip to a different village out in the bush about 15 miles south of the small town of Dhupguri. This turned out to be very memorable indeed. The report said that the villagers were experiencing a lot of trouble from pigs which were hiding up in a patch of scrub jungle near the village and causing havoc in their ripening grain. As they could do very little to stop them they begged Donald for help.

The village was about 20 miles from Dhupguri down a very dry and dusty, winding track, but when we got there we found it was an excellent area for a beat as it was roughly rectangular in shape and instead of the very long thatch grass it was covered with bushes and light scrub jungle through which the beaters could walk without much difficulty, so they began the beat spread out along the top edge while the guns were staked out at roughly 100 yard intervals around the bottom. One of our party was a young Assistant from Ranicherra Tea Estate whose name as far as I can remember was something like Heddite Hussain, known as Heddi, and for the purpose of this story I will refer to him as that. If it was something different I can only apologise. As luck would have it he and Bob Grey were allocated the bottom right hand corner, the two Mackenzies were spaced out facing the bottom edge, while Ian Leith and I were on the left. This ensured that any animals breaking out of the patch would have to pass within about 50 yards of at least one of our guns.

For a while we waited quietly as we listened to the beaters noisily crashing through the scrub towards us, but to our disappointment none of them gave us the coded whistles that told us that there were animals moving through ahead of them. Then suddenly it all changed. Over on the right the shouts changed to yells of fear and consternation, and through the noise we heard the sound of a shot followed by two more a short while later. As these were accompanied by the roaring of an enraged animal, we realised with a sinking feeling in our stomachs that somebody had wounded a tiger or leopard.

We were a couple of hundred yards away but ran around the perimeter as quickly as we could to find Heddi lying on the ground badly injured, Bob Grey sitting up near him with his face much whiter than his name and a village buffalo standing alongside with blood streaming from claw marks down its neck. There was no sign of a tiger. Donald and Wee Mac were already there, but even they had not been quick enough to see what had happened, so as we gave Heddi basic medical aid to try to staunch the bleeding, we tried to piece together what had happened.

As I recorded it in a letter home a couple of days later, the tiger must have been in a vile temper at being disturbed, as it had scattered the beaters and rushed back through them, then emerged immediately in front of Heddi and charged him on sight. It took just a few seconds to cover the few yards and he was only able to take one shot at it before it knocked him down and lay on top of him, biting and clawing at his shoulder, thigh and lower legs. He was unable to push it off. Bob Grey, who had a shot gun loaded with LG, not really suitable for shooting tiger, saw what was happening but was too far away to fire for fear of hitting Heddi, so he ran up as quickly as possible and shot it in the body from about four feet away which caused it to roll off him. This was the second shot we heard. However it was not good enough to kill it, and quick as a flash it got up and pounced on him again. Bob was still trying to place himself so that he could have a killing shot at it without endangering Heddi, but before he could do so a village buffalo which had been watching rushed up and knocked the tiger off with its horns and tossed it about ten feet away. This enabled Bob to get between it and Heddi and fire his second barrel as it leapt at him again.

Unfortunately this too was not enough to kill it. As he held his shotgun up in both hands to protect his face the tiger sprang at him, knocked the gun down and gave him such a clout in the face with its paw that it stretched him out alongside Heddi. The next thing he knew he was lying on his back with the tiger lying across his chest while it still bit and clawed at Heddi. Afterwards he told us that as he tried to push it off with his hands it turned its head and snarled in his face; he said "its breath was awful!" Actually he was very lucky, for if it had hit him in the face with its claws extended he would have had half his face torn away, but as it happened all it did was clout him with its massive paw. Although he was very badly shocked and trembling like a leaf, all he had to show for it was a bruise and a red welt along his cheek just beneath his eye.

Of course when things like this happen it is almost as if they are taking place in slow motion, and although the whole incident could only have taken a couple of minutes, Bob said that with the tiger lying on his chest they seemed to have been there for ages and thought that they were 'goners'. But then the miracle happened. The old buffalo saw what was happening and rushed in to the attack again, putting its head down and deftly lifting the tiger off without touching them. It then knocked it down twice more, preventing it from getting at the two planters. At this treatment the tiger got even more peeved and grabbed the buffalo's neck with its claws, so without more ado it got its horns beneath it and tossed it several feet in the air, after which the tiger rushed away and took cover in a small, wooded valley about two hundred yards away.

Once we knew what had happened we realised that there was no way that the wounded tiger could be left, so Donald took charge immediately. He decided that our first priority was for Ian and Bob to stay with Heddi and try to stop his bleeding, while Donald, Wee Mac and I, who all had rifles with lead-nosed bullets, went to put the tiger out of its misery. It had taken refuge in a patch of thick jungle in the bottom of the valley, and as we stood at the top of the slope about 10 yards away we could hear it growling and snarling to itself as it moved about trying to come to grips with its injuries. I felt really sorry that this had occurred. It had not been our intention to go for tiger, but these unforeseen incidents did occur on occasions and once it had been wounded, under the hunter's code of ethics it had to be followed up and finished off, and Donald was prepared to do this.

He told Wee Mac and me to go round to the other side of the valley and position ourselves at each end of the wooded area so that we could cut off its escape route if it decided to bolt that way. Then once we were in place he began to descend the sloping side of the valley towards the tiger. Really after what had gone before the end turned out to be a bit of an anticlimax thank goodness, for after each slow step he waited, rifle ready as he awaited the charge until he deemed that it was safe to take another step, until finally he was able to see it and one shot from his double barrelled .470 ended its misery. Seeing it stretched out there it seemed such a pity that it had to die like this, but unfortunately such accidents like this did occur sometimes and could not be avoided.

Leaving it there to be collected by the villagers later, we hurried back to the other three and found that Ian had managed to bind up the worst of Heddi's injuries and made him as comfortable as he could. We realised that we had to get him back to Dhupguri hospital for proper treatment as quickly as possible. In its attack the tiger had bitten quite a large lump out of the top of his shoulder, made another large wound in his buttock and then lacerated the whole of one leg from his thigh to his ankle by raking its rear claws up and down his leg, exactly like a tame puss would do at home when it was playing, leaving his trouser leg just a mass of blood-stained rags and tatters.

He was unable to stand, and we realised that in order to get him to hospital we would have to take him lying in the back of the lorry over 20 miles of rutted and bumpy roads. As we had no mattress or anything of that nature it was decided that Donald would drive, with Wee Mac and Bob Grey in the cab, while Ian and myself sat on the pickup seat cushions in the back, with our backs resting against the cab and between us supporting Heddi on our legs and arms so that he had the least amount of contact with the floor. We did this all the way back to Dhupguri. Although Donald was a good driver he realised that speed was essential, and no matter how carefully he drove and how much we tried to keep Heddi from bouncing on the floor it must have been purgatory for him and he passed out several times during the journey.

Finally, after what seemed an eternity, we reached the hospital and he received temporary medical care to prepare him for the journey of 150 miles up to Darjeeling hospital, where he stayed for the next month until he had recovered. Despite his terrible mauling he didn't suffer any permanent disability and he was soon back on Soongachi, but he was badly marked with scars that he carried for the rest of his life. Regarding Bob Grey, he received a thorough examination. Fortunately, although he was badly shocked, he had no physical injuries and was back shooting again within a few days.

Once we had delivered Heddi and Bob to hospital we took the lorry back to the village to collect the pickup, the tiger and all the labourers, and we finally got back to Bagrakote at 8 pm after a very eventful Sunday which could have ended in a fatality. Later as we had our first drinks and meal since our early breakfasts, we all agreed how very fortunate we were that things had turned out the way they did. Regarding the heroic buffalo, Donald went back to the village the next evening and paid for it to have injections to counteract the poison from the tiger's claws and bite, and when we saw it again three weeks later its injuries had healed and it was no worse for its encounter with the tiger. Without its intervention there is a distinct possibility that both Heddi and Bob could have been killed or maimed in the short time before the others arrived, because there was no way either of them could have pushed it off themselves as they lay on the ground.

However, it took more than this to deter us from our Sunday shoots, and on May 16th I shot an absolutely monstrous pig which had very large tushes and must have weighed about 240 lbs. It seemed that the older and more experienced the pigs got the more crafty they became, and this one must have been a very experienced old rascal because he was another one that waited until the beaters were right on top of him, and then instead of running away in front of them would break back through the line and escape to the rear. Knowing he was there we beat the same patch of jungle three times and each time he acted in the same way, always breaking back and never leaving the patch of jungle. As we talked about it after the third beat I remembered the one I had shot when I was out with Bill Milne on Zurrantee and I walked in behind the beaters, so we decided that provided I was extremely careful as to where I shot it was worth one more try.

As the beaters went in I told them to shout and warn me the moment that they saw anything of it and then followed about fifteen yards behind. True to pattern they had not been beating very long before I heard them shouting '*Aghi hai, Sahib, ata hai*' (It's in front, Sahib, and coming) so I ran towards the sound. I had only gone a few yards when I heard it coming directly towards me like an express train crashing through the jungle. As it rushed by me about six feet away I had no time to sight the rifle but just pointed it at him, then followed through and pulled the trigger. For a moment I thought I had missed it because it didn't even falter, but as I turned to go after it I realised that there was blood all over the jungle it had passed through and we found it lying dead a few yards further on at the end of a great 'skid mark' which it had churned up in the jungle floor as it slid to a halt. I had hit it just behind the shoulder right through the heart, and it couldn't have been a better shot even if I had sighted carefully on it, so I was very pleased.

It had a really big set of tushes which I sent home to Mum, My only regret was that because it was an old pig, so far as I was concerned I found the meat rather tough, but the others didn't seem to think this mattered very much and as it was so large that there was plenty of meat for all the beaters to share and they went home very happy. It was a very memorable porker.

This was not the only excitement we had that weekend, because on the previous day Saturday, May 15th, one of the Jamair aircraft made a crash landing at Saugaon. After the very slow start the leaf had begun to grow in record quantities and on that morning I was taking the second garden weighment on Saugaon when I heard the midday Jamair freight plane come in and land. We were working in one of the more remote areas of Saugaon and as I was concentrating on recording the quantities of leaf properly I didn't notice anything amiss as she passed over in the distance, so as a result I was very surprised when a man rushed up to me on the Jamair Office Babu's bike to tell me that the plane had crash landed and would I get over to the airfield as quickly as possible, while he pedalled the four miles up to Bagracote to ask Donald to come down as the Babu had requested assistance. Poor fellow!

He seemed to know very little about the crash, so I told him to go back and tell the Babu that I would go as soon as I had finished the weighment, and away he went on his important mission, dhoti flying in the wind of his passage and his naked legs whirling round like a demented windmill. Within a few minutes I too was on my way in a much more sedate fashion, but as I neared the airfield I was astonished to see that everything looked absolutely normal. There was no plane, no wreckage and no fire or smoke to be seen, only a crowd of people standing by the Jamair office door, so I was very pleased when the Clerk told me that the aircraft was down in one piece at the very end of the runway where it neared the Teesta river and that as far as he knew none of the crew was injured.

Immediately I drove across to where the DC3 had finished up and there I found VT-DGO neatly balanced on her side on the top of a 30-foot high bank on the edge of the dhan khets which ran away to the Teesta river. She was a Douglas C-47B-30-DK model, and after making her first flight in 1945, had served in the RAF as a DC3 Dakota IV (Serial KN461). I knew that all the Jamair aircraft were serviced regularly in Calcutta and for their routine main overhauls they were sent to Hindustan Aircraft in Bangalore for specialist attention, so I was quite surprised that DGO had come to grief on our airfield.

From a distance it appeared as though she had been flying along the edge of the airfield at ground level completely undamaged, but once I got close I realised that although there seemed to be very little structural damage, the landing gear was retracted and because she had made a 'wheels up' landing, the propellers and engines were damaged. The only crew member I knew was the flight engineer, who had come up as 'third man', while both the Captain and his Second Officer were strangers to me. As they stood discussing what they should do, it appeared that one of the engines had failed on the approach and for some reason this had caused them to make a crash landing.

They had managed to call Calcutta on DGO's radio and

another Jamair plane that had flown to Central Dooars was being diverted to pick them up, but instructions had been issued that once Donald arrived they should ask him for the hire of a truck in order to unload the aircraft and ferry all the cargo over to the storage facility alongside the office. The crew were of the opinion that once this was done, although there was no hope of DGO being repaired in situ, if she was not too badly damaged it might be possible to dismantle her and repair her on the airfield near the office. Now in retrospect I think they were grabbing at straws.

The story of the landing that we heard as we waited for the relief plane to arrive seemed to be that the Second Officer had been in charge of the aircraft and was making the landing and everything was going fine until the Captain realised that he was too high passing over the threshold and was going to make his initial grounding too far up the runway to be able to stop her before reaching the end. He had told the Second Officer to power her up and take her round again for a second attempt. He did this, but an engine failed, and with insufficient power she was forced to land. With power on one side only she veered off track. She was still running along quite fast on her wheels, and one of the crew then realised they would run out of flat land before she could be stopped and she would then career over the bank into the khets and probably break up, so he decided to retract the undercarriage and she flopped onto her belly. By this time she was crabbing sideways and still had enough speed on her to reach the khets. Luckily at the point where she reached the bank a tree had been felled and the stump still stuck two feet up into the air, and as the port wing slid sideways over this it gouged a deep furrow in it until finally it penetrated deeply into the bottom of the fuselage and acted as a brake. This left her neatly balanced on the top of the bank with her starboard wing pointing to the sky and the other down in the khets. Even in this state, though she was lying like a wounded bird, she still looked lovely.

Soon after that Donald arrived, the relief plane flew in to take the crew back to Calcutta and arrangements were made to transport the cargo over to the storage shed with one of our lorries and normal work resumed, so we thought that that was the end of the matter as far as we were concerned. However, to our surprise a few days later we received a letter from the Jamair Chief Engineer telling us that there had to be an inquiry into the crash, for which they needed the suspect engine down in Calcutta for examination, so would it be possible for Donald to assist them? Of course Jamair was our lifeline in the Dooars, so we were always willing to help if possible. Arrangements were made for two Jamair engineers to come up and remove the engine, while we supplied the labourers, lifting tackle and transport to cart it over to the office ready for it to be sent down to Calcutta.

They came up on the following Monday accompanied by a 'professional' photographer from Calcutta whose brief was to record the site of the crash and photograph the position of the aircraft for the inquiry before it was interfered with. Because he was only there for the time it took to unload and load the aircraft for the return flight time was of the essence, so I took them all down to the crash site. At the same time I thought I might just as well use the time while I was waiting with him by taking some photos as well, so I got my camera and snapped away until he had finished his work, then drove him back over to the plane and away he went. In the meantime the two engineers took the suspect engine off the plane and removed several of the instruments from the flight deck. By dint of hard labour, by Tuesday evening it was all packed up and over in the store ready for return to Calcutta.

Although our estate charged Jamair for the labour etc that had been supplied, because of our personal help we were told that there were about 160 gallons of high octane aviation fuel still in DGO's tanks that would never be used again, so if we liked to drain them we were very welcome to it to use in our cars. We were warned that it was VERY fiery stuff and if we used it neat we would probably burn our engine valves out, but by mixing it 50/50% with standard cheap petrol and adding some lubricating oil we would be able to have many months of very cheap motoring. Afterwards our cars ran like totally different vehicles.

Regarding the inquiry there was one humorous development, because a few days later I had a letter from the Chief Engineer telling me that the photographer had got back to Calcutta safely and thanking me for the help that I had given him, but it transpired that when he came to develop his pictures, to his astonishment he discovered that he hadn't put a film in the camera, so there were no pictures for the inquiry to view. However the man had told him that I had also taken some at the same time, so they asked if I was willing to send my film down for it to be developed and printed for the inquiry, after which the negatives and prints would be returned to me. I had no idea how they would turn out, but I would only have had to do the same thing later on, so I sent it down by return and ultimately got them back. To my relief, although I had taken them with quite a cheap camera, they turned out very well indeed and I got my prints free of charge.

As for the result of the inquiry, although we never heard

anything official we did hear unofficially by the 'grapevine' that parts of the official findings were very different from the first account we heard. Evidently the suspect engine was still working perfectly, and other than superficial damage to the shroud and cowling etc that had been caused by the impact there was nothing wrong with it, but the propeller had been 'feathered' deliberately. Normally when an engine failed, the propeller blades were turned end on to the airflow so that it could not 'windmill' and thus reduced drag, and it appeared that this had been done manually by using the cockpit controls prior to the crash. After this came to light some of the statements seem to have changed. The final story we heard was that the Second Officer was making the landing on only one engine in order to get some experience. This could be done quite safely, but when he shut the engine down, instead of allowing it to 'windmill' and thus keep it going so that it could be restarted immediately if needed, he feathered the propeller and stopped it completely. Either the Captain did not know about this or he had been told and forgotten, because when it was evident that the Second Officer was going to land the plane too far up the strip for her to stop safely, he told him to put the power on and take her round again for another attempt, expecting it to power up immediately, but nothing happened and poor old DGO didn't have enough airspeed to keep herself up and just flew onto the ground.

Once her wheels hit she ran fast, and because she had power on only one wing the aircraft slewed round and crabbed sideways. By the time this one was powered down as well it was evident that she would over shoot the boundary of the airfield onto the stones and boulders that edged the khets below. Fortunately, for the landing the Engineer had taken up his place standing in the middle of the cockpit behind the two pilots' seats so that he could watch what was going on, and when he realised what would happen he reached over and retracted the undercarriage so that she did a belly slide until she stopped just in time. It was probably his quick thinking that prevented an unfortunate accident from developing into a tragedy. There is no doubt that if she had gone down into the khets travelling at speed she would have broken up on the rough stone walls that bordered them and the cockpit would have borne the brunt of it.

Although I know the Engineer did keep working for Jamair, I never saw the Captain or Second Officer at Saugaon again, so what happened to them I can only surmise. Poor old DGO was a complete write off and never flew again, although on occasions men came up from Calcutta and took various parts away, presumably for use as spare parts on other aircraft. When I left Bagracote in 1955 to go on home leave, her remains were still there with her one wing still pointing forlornly at the sky, and for all I know parts of her could be there still.

As for the Jamair Company, this had been formed in 1948 by two men named Jimmie Muff and Eddie Quinn with financial assistance from the Maharajah of Nawanagar, who was also titled the Jam Sahib, which was why the company was named after him. Both Muff and Quinn had worked for the China National Aviation Corporation (CNAC) until they left the company just before its demise in 1949 and as a result they probably knew quite a lot about operating C47s. The CNAC had been formed in 1937 from a merger between the Chinese Air Company and China Airways, with Pan American owning 45% of the assets and the Nationalist Government the remainder, and during WWII its aircraft flew many thousands of tons of supplies from India 'over the Hump' into China after the Japanese cut the Burma Road. Despite the many casualties inflicted by the Japanese fighters and even more significantly the ever-changing weather over the Himalayas, these logistics flights ran round the clock from April 1942 until the end of the war, using Douglas DC2 and C47 (DC3) aircraft mainly operated with American pilots and Chinese co-pilots and radio operators. However CNAC ceased operations in November 1949 following the Chinese Communist revolution, when the Civil Aviation Administration of China took over and seized many of the CNAC aircraft.

Presumably Muff and Quinn had seen the split coming and decided to form their own company, and even after the death of the Jam Sahib in 1948 it continued to operate from Calcutta's Dum Dum airport. In 1953 it was nationalised by the Indian Government with Muff staying on as director and it finally ceased business after his death in 1977. The crash at Saugaon was the first of four the airline was to experience as three more C47s were lost later. VT-AZV crashed at Amritsar Airport on December 7th 1961, luckily without loss of life, but VT-CZC crashed on take-off at Delhi on 5th December 1970 with the loss of three crew and two passengers, and this was followed by the total loss of VT-ATT on 26th March 1971 when she strayed off course on a flight from Gauhati to Calcutta via Bagdogra and crashed in the Himalayan foothills near Hasimara in the Eastern Dooars. It took rescuers six days to locate the wreckage and finally when they did so they found that all of the 15 people on board had perished, an extremely sad ending to an airline with which I had had a very close and pleasant affinity during the whole of my life in India.

Because Bagracote had made a profit in 1953, the

expenditure for 1954 included a sum of money to benefit and entertain the labour force and as this was usually spent on sports equipment, circuses and magic shows etc, after purchasing a set of cricket gear, some footballs and a new set of shirts for the garden team, there was still enough left for some entertainments. One afternoon in May a young magician visited the garden to ask if he could give the labourers a show and as he seemed to be a bright boy and his charges were not high, Donald decided to give him an opportunity. He was driving a battered old three-ton Ford truck which carried all his props and equipment and was accompanied by a young girl and a dog as his assistants. The next day they erected a very impressive looking stage in a corner of the factory compound and by 7.30 that evening an expectant crowd of several hundred labourers had gathered to see the show. But he flattered to deceive. His act was extremely amateurish, his tricks kept going wrong, his assistant danced like a zombie to music from an old gramophone and about the only thing that was any good was the dog, as he did quite good balancing tricks. However this was not what the labourers had come to see, and as the promised magic tricks failed to materialise and they realised that they had been lured to see the show under false pretences, they became more and more angry and it seemed as though there would be a riot. Luckily the magician must have been through all this before. Knowing that he was likely to get a thumping, suddenly all three of them disappeared behind the back curtain, and the next thing we knew the Ford had gunned its motor and rattled off into the night. Evidently they spent the night in Odlabari Bazaar, because the next morning he came back to collect all the equipment he had abandoned as well as his fee, and immediately he ran into trouble. Many of the labourers had considered that the show was so bad that he should not be paid, but Donald was a fair person and after consideration decided to give him a reduced amount to cover his expenses, for which he was very grateful and finally they departed.

After that fiasco we thought we would not be seeing any more magicians for a while, but as luck would have it another one rolled up a couple of weeks later in a rather travel-worn Canadian Ford V8 saloon which looked as though it had once been an army staff car. This one was an older man with a male assistant who drove the car. When he spoke to Donald in the office he said he had studied magic and trickery under one of India's greatest magicians, so please would he allow him to perform. Thinking that it would put him off and he would go away, Donald told him the story of what had happened to the previous one, and said he had been so bad that he had only just escaped a beating, so if this one had any sense he would get back in his car and clear off while the going was good.

This man was not to be put off. To our surprise he said that it was that type of person that gave magicians a bad name and made many people very sceptical. However he suggested that if we allowed him to perform a trick before us in the office, if we were suitably impressed he would then like us to let him give a show to the labourers, for which he would not accept any payment unless Donald thought it was worth the money.

On saying this he seemed to be so genuine that Donald decided to give him a chance, and with no idea of what he was about to do he was allowed to come into the office. We thought he would perform a few card tricks or something like that, but he really surprised us, because without more ado he borrowed a three-inch long bodkin needle from the Head

Clerk which was used to sew packets of tea up with twine when they were sent to the UK by post. Then he called the office boy over to him, Jetha, a young Nepali boy in his early twenties. He said to him in Nepalese, 'When I snap my fingers you will go to sleep' and immediately Jetha shut his eyes and stood motionless. 'Now put out your tongue' he instructed. When he did this the magician immediately rammed the needle through his protruding tongue from bottom to top, until it was pressing onto his upper lip and his chin. Then he took his arm and led him to everyone in the office in turn, so that we could all see that there had been no fakery and that it was the original needle that had pierced completely through his tongue. When we were all satisfied he gripped the needle and withdrew it, then told Jetha to put his tongue in and wake up, which he did in a bleary kind of way, looking round as though he was waiting for something to happen. When we questioned him he had absolutely no recollection of anything that had happened. He had no pain anywhere, and when he showed us his tongue there wasn't a single trace of blood and only the smallest of red marks to indicate where the needle had penetrated. A bitten tongue bleeds quite profusely and is extremely sore, so it was quite uncanny that he should feel no after affects whatsoever. We were all very impressed and as it was a no-lose situation for us the deal was struck.

He didn't have a stage on which to perform, so he asked us to make him one out of planks laid on the tops of empty 40-gallon oil drums, with a bamboo pole at each corner from which he could hang his curtains and that was that. But despite this and our reservations, he gave us a show to remember. Obviously the details of the trick he had done in the office had quickly passed around the garden, because that evening another much larger, very expectant crowd gathered in front of the stage, which was illuminated by a string of electric lights strung up by one of the factory electricians. Immediately in front of the stage two rows of chairs had been placed for us and the clerical staff, and as we were only about eight feet away we had a very clear and uninterrupted view of the stage and everything he did. Not that that helped us much.

There was no doubt that he was a top notch performer, as his delivery was so slick that it was impossible to see how he did his illusions. It was an almost non-stop show for two hours, in which he did tricks with cards, coins, flags, bunches of flowers, buckets of water that contained showers of paper when he threw them at the audience and even white doves which he made disappear and reappear from the most unexpected places. The number of props he must have carried in that old car was absolutely amazing. He even hypnotised members of the audience and made them do silly things, much to the amusement of their friends in the audience, but he kept his best illusion until last and this was so baffling that I am still unable to explain how he did it, because theoretically it was impossible to do under those conditions.

He called a young lad named Saila up from the audience who actually worked in the manager's bungalow and promptly hypnotised him, then left him standing absolutely motionless at the corner of the stage. Then he and his assistant erected three wooden posts, each of which was about an inch in diameter and four feet high and supported by a cross piece at the bottom. Then they placed them in a straight line across the stage about two feet apart. Once this was done he walked over to Saila and gave him a slight push in the chest so that he fell over backwards into the arms of his assistant, who laid him out gently on his back. He was as stiff as a board, but they rearranged him by crossing his arms on his chest and crossing his legs at his ankles, then they picked him up and carefully placed him on the three posts, one beneath his neck, one in the small of his back, the last beneath his crossed ankles, and then they moved away from him to leave him lying motionless on the posts in the middle of the stage, just as though he was in his bed at home. It was absolutely uncanny to see him. He was completely rigid and by the laws of balance he should have toppled straight off, but he was breathing quite quietly, absolutely balanced, and in the crowd you could have heard a pin drop.

Then, thinking that this was the end of the trick, everyone began to applaud, but the best was still to come. Ever the consummate showman, the magician held up his hands for attention then moved over to Saila's feet, lifted his legs slightly and quietly removed the support from beneath his ankles. Then he did the same to the one beneath his back, leaving Saila floating motionless in the thin air, with only the post beneath his neck to keep him up. To demonstrate that there was no outside means of support, he took a large hoop and passed it along his body from his feet up to his head, then down the support to the floor and back again. From ten feet away it was apparent that there was nothing there, so what kept him up nobody could guess. By the normal laws of gravity what he had done was absolutely impossible, and as he could not have had any sophisticated mechanical help to do the trick and it was performed on a rickety stage erected that afternoon, what he did was unexplainable and to me has been so ever since.

They left him floating there for about a minute, then carefully replaced the supports. Finally they lifted him down and stood him upright, then woke him from his trance. On opening his eyes Saila stood and grinned self-consciously at the crowd as though he was waiting for something to happen, and when the magician thanked him and told him he could go, he just jumped down and went back to his friends. When I questioned him the next morning, he could remember absolutely nothing and he couldn't even recall being put to sleep, so it was just as though a chunk of his life was missing. Even though I have no logical explanation for what happened that night, I know what we all thought we saw.

Some people have suggested that we were all hypnotised into imagining it. However many of the labourers who also saw what we saw and who were standing in the darkness at the edge of the crowd could not have been seen from the stage, so I doubt whether he would have been able to perform a mass hypnotism on a crowd that size and at that distance away. Anyway, I know what I think I saw. I have no explanation, but I hope that maybe one day someone will tell me how he was able to do it.

Since retiring from India in 1967 I have seen a similar illusion performed on the television. Later it was revealed that the subject was supported on a strengthened glass shelf, which because of the lighting became invisible against the background, and thus was not filmed by the cameras. However he had nothing like this in his car and we were so near that we would have seen if it had been done like this. While in India I also read accounts of how some Tibetan Buddhist monks were able to levitate themselves and other objects by the power of thought alone, a type of telekinesis, but like the Indian rope trick I never actually saw it performed for myself unless this was it.

The magician was a very unassuming person. The next morning he turned up at the office and asked Donald whether his show had been worth the fee or not. Of course we all thought it was the best we had ever seen, so he was paid the agreed sum plus a bonus and off they went to their next engagement. In later years what mystified me was that although he was so good we never saw or heard anything about him again, but maybe his trip through the tea areas that year was just a working holiday or a stepping stone up to bigger things. I hope so.

CHAPTER TWENTY EIGHT

Mother Nature's little joke

Most years at the beginning of the monsoon the rainstorms came intermittently with a good downpour arriving every two or three days, but 1954 didn't abide by the rules and by the third week in May, a little later than usual, the monsoon broke and the weather changed completely, with regular daily storms bringing appreciable amounts of rain, often several inches in a few hours. This abundant rain, together with temperatures in the upper eighties, caused the bushes to flush with a vengeance, and by the end of May we were plucking 2.5 tons of excellent green leaf a day. As this was a reasonable amount of leaf to manufacture it suited us fine and we thought we would have a nice even start to the season. Silly us! Little did we know the tricks Mother Nature had in store for us.

Because 1953 had been a very good year and a profit had been made, permission had been given for extra quantities of fertilisers to be applied to the tea areas. As June also turned out to be hot and humid, with heavy rain falling most nights, once the effect of these fertilisers kicked in we were soon having great difficulty in plucking the leaf on time. To make quality tea we needed very fine shoots consisting of two leaves and a bud with no hard stalks, and as these developed from the smallest bud to a two leaved shoot in seven days, we had to work on what was known as a 'seven day round'. To do this we had to pluck the same areas of tea on the same day each week. Normally, by adjusting the numbers of labourers plucking from day to day, we were able to stay on the round without too much trouble, but as the bushes flushed more and more vigorously we found it increasingly difficult to cope with the leaf.

Normally the workers arrived at the 'mela', the area to be plucked, by 7.30 am, and then two leaf weighments were carried out in the garden in the morning, one at about 10 am and the other at midday. Between these times they were able to fill their *jhulies* (plucking cloths) and these were then hung on weighment scales. The amount of leaf was recorded and then it was tipped into the lorry for transport back to the factory. However once there was an abundance of leaf simply begging to be plucked, very soon many of the better pluckers began arriving on the mela soon after first light at 6 am so that by the first weighment they had two jhulies full of leaf which more than filled the lorry, so it had to make two trips, and we lost valuable working time while some of the pluckers had to wait by the roadside waiting for it to return. With the amount of leaf growing it was soon evident that our normal transport arrangements were going to be completely inadequate, so all the garden transport including the two pickups and the tractors were detailed onto weighment duties when necessary, and within a few days we introduced an extra one at 9 am followed by the others at 11 am and 1 pm with the final one in the factory at 3 pm.

One very big time waster was having to unload the leaf from the lorries so that it could be carried up to the storage areas above the factory until it could be manufactured. With our type of fresh leaf manufacture it had to be spread in an even carpet all over the floor no deeper than three inches thick so that it remained cool. With the ambient temperatures in the high eighties it was very easy for it to overheat, and if it did so it went limp and red and as such it was completely useless and had to be destroyed.

As tipper trucks were unknown in India, unloading had to be done by hand, and the lorry crew used three-foot-long bamboo staves with pointed ends to pull the leaf off as these did the minimum amount of damage to the leaf. However with leaf from other lorries spread all over the concrete unloading floor, this was often a time-consuming business, and sometimes the Saugaon lorry crew managed to clear their load only just in time for it to do the return journey and the next weighment. With the amount of leaf being gathered increasing daily, we realised that if nothing was done we would have to ease up on the plucking rather than pay the labourers for leaf that we couldn't manufacture, so we decided to try our own idea of a contraption which we heard was being used by some other gardens. This 'slider' consisted of a loop of half-inch diameter steel cable fitted with 3' x 2' wooden battens every two feet along its length, rather like a seven-foot-wide ladder with wooden rungs, and this was placed on the bed of the lorry with the loop hanging out of the back. Then the lorry was loaded as normal. At the factory the loop was attached to a large hook on another cable which was fixed to a steel veranda support and the lorry driven away. Theoretically, as the lorry moved forward the fixed cable prevented the slider going as well and slider and leaf slipped along to the back and off onto the floor in one operation, but we soon found that theory and practice very often do not go well together. The idea was good but we found that it only worked with lightly-loaded lorries where the friction was minimal. With a full load of several tons of green leaf the weight caused so much friction with the bed of the lorry that it refused to budge, and from a standing start the driver had to slip his clutch to get any movement at all. If he tried a moving start before taking up the strain, the jolt was so great that we were afraid we would pull the veranda down, so although the idea had possibilities, we realised that we would have to go back to the drawing board before we wrecked the clutches on all our lorries and demolished the veranda.

As we talked about it we formulated the idea of rolling the leaf out instead of sliding it, rather like making a Swiss roll, and we made the necessary alterations. The loop was lengthened so that the looped end went right up over the cab, then the 'ladder' ran vertically down the back of the cab and along the floor to the tailboard. At the factory we dug a six-foot-deep hole and 'planted' a 12 foot high by 18 inch diameter 'tree trunk' from a dead tree we had cut out of the forest. Then we concreted it in, and it worked like a dream. When the loaded lorry came in it backed up to the post and a cable fixed about eight feet up was attached to the loop on the lorry. Then when it was driven away the cable tightened horizontally, the ladder began to pull the load upward and backward, and as there was no friction it rolled backwards off the lorry and finished up on top of the heap of leaf, ready to be loaded back on the lorry for the next trip.

The only doubtful aspect was that as the main weight of the load neared the back of the bed, the front wheels of the truck came up a few inches off the ground, but as they were rear wheel drive they kept moving and soon banged down again and that was that. Once the prototype worked we equipped all the other vehicles with suitable 'ladders' and then we only had to increase the number of carrying men to keep the unloading area clear so that they could get in and out. By bringing in additional temporary labourers from the surrounding areas to help pluck the additional leaf we were able to keep on top of the extraordinary crop that was being produced.

The subsequent drawback of this was that other than a 30-minute break at 7 am each day when all the machinery was cleaned, checked and lubricated, the factory had to work virtually non-stop from Monday morning until Sunday morning to deal with it, and unfortunately at the beginning of July the Crossley QVD 4 diesel engine began to give trouble. At first it was just a small loss of power and some smoke coming out in the exhaust gases, but as this got worse and we began to hear a noise from the engine block, we realised that something serious was wrong and needed looking at before it packed in altogether. When I came to strip and examine it the next Sunday I discovered that two valve springs had broken and several of the piston rings on three of the cylinders had broken up and were just sliding up and down in their grooves without doing any work at all, and this was causing the increasing loss of power.

During the cold weather overhaul new sets of springs and piston rings had been fitted. In India you could never be sure whether spare parts that were supplied were genuine or not, so whenever possible we ensured that genuine spares were obtained from the Crossley agents in Calcutta. Under normal circumstances the engine could have kept going for several weeks, but with it having to work non-stop for long periods it was essential that we got it repaired with the minimum of delay, so a message was sent down to Crossley's on the next

Jamair flight. On Tuesday we received a telegram informing us that the parts were not in stock but they were arranging to obtain genuine parts as soon as possible and these should be ready for despatch on Thursday, so how did we want them sent? We had had a general directive from the Superintendent's office that no unscheduled flights to Calcutta on Estate business could be made until they had been cleared by him, but Donald, who was an extremely unorthodox young man and used to taking qualified risks just turned to me and said, 'We've got to have those ****** things as soon as possible and can't risk losing them, so get aboard the flight down tomorrow morning, collect them personally from Crossleys and check that they are the right ones, bring them back on the next flight and leave the Sup to me', so that's what I did.

They arrived from the suppliers in the UK on the Thursday afternoon as scheduled, so I collected them from Crossley's office and checked the paperwork to make absolutely sure that they were the correct and genuine articles, then returned on the early morning flight on Friday morning, after which we made the necessary arrangements to send some of our Saturday leaf to other gardens so that the engine could be shut down on Friday afternoon to cool down while the standby steam engine coped with the remainder. Then I gathered a team of our most reliable factory men together and we worked non-stop without any proper sleep other than a quick nap at meal breaks, from 6 pm on Friday night until 3 am on Monday morning in servicing the engine, extracting the pistons and replacing all the rings and valve springs and then rebuilding her, and it was real purgatory. The steam engine house and boiler next door was a hot place at the best of times, but at dead of night when there was very little breeze it was like an oven and the artificial lights didn't help as they seemed to attract all the insects from miles around, but we soldiered on. Finally in the wee small hours of Monday morning we were able to start her up, and she ran like a dream. I had given Donald a rough idea of what time we hoped to finish and to give him his due he got up and came over to congratulate us all for the work we had done, because we had managed to complete it in time to be used for Monday's manufacture. Even better, we had caught the trouble before the broken rings had started scoring the insides of the piston barrels. Had they done so it would have been a much more difficult operation.

So we all went home to bed. After a cooling shower to wash all the grime off, I crept into my bed and slept like a log from about 5 am until 8 pm that evening, absolutely exhausted. After having my evening meal I went back to bed and had another dreamless night's sleep until Tuesday morning. It was absolutely wonderful.

When we examined the broken bits later it was apparent that they were made from much inferior metal to the genuine ones and in all probability had been knocked out in some back street workshop in Calcutta or Bombay. Even when they were checked carefully it was impossible to say that they were defective goods because they looked identical to genuine ones, even to having the correct paint, part numbers and other identifying marks stamped on them. Several of the valve springs were pretty dubious too, although they looked identical to those I had brought up from Calcutta. How they managed to be passed off as the real thing and infiltrate the system we never did find out. There must have been somebody taking 'backhanders' somewhere in the supply system.

Regarding the Superintendent and his directive, Donald

was called up to his office to explain why he had taken it upon himself to send me down to Calcutta to collect goods that could quite easily have been sent up by airfreight without all the expense. As he was expecting to get a dressing down he decided that attack was the best form of defence, so when he was asked to explain his actions he asked Mr Tocher what he would have thought if some incorrect spares had been sent up and fitted and while the mistakes were being rectified the engine had broken down completely and put out of action for several weeks. He said that without the engine and with the amount of leaf coming in, this would have cost the company many thousands of rupees, far outweighing the cost of a return flight to Calcutta and a hotel room for a couple of nights, and by his actions he had ensured that the correct parts were brought and fitted and the engine was repaired in time for manufacture three days later. So in his capacity as Acting Manager he had decided to take this action and he was prepared to stand by it and then waited for the dressing down that never came.

The Superintendent was a stern but very fair man, and although he didn't suffer fools gladly he did recognise and acknowledge honest endeavour when he saw it, so he told him that he did agree that what Donald had done was right, but then qualified it by saying that there was always a right and a wrong way of doing things, as Donald would find out with more experience. Just because he was young he could not be allowed to ride roughshod over the system. He didn't send directives out for the fun of doing so, and what Donald should have done was explain what he had in mind and get permission first, even if this meant a trip up to Sam Sing. As this was his first acting and he had acted with the best of intentions, he was prepared to overlook his actions on this occasion but they were not to be repeated, or else! And that was that. After the 'carpeting' that he had been expecting Donald sighed with relief, but he was even more astounded when Mr Tocher then smiled at him and said, 'And now laddie, now that I have sorted you out would you like to come across to the bungalow and have a wee dram before you go back to Bagracote'? He was a lovely man, Mr Tocher.

In retrospect, it was a good job we did overhaul the engine when we did, because the monsoon rain continued to fall during June and July and with the temperatures in the low 90s F, they were ideal growing conditions for the tea. Gradually we realised that if things continued this way we were looking at making a record crop. All we had to do was ensure that good quality leaf was gathered and manufactured.

Each morning I met Donald at the factory to taste the result of the night's manufacture, and this was repeated on several occasions during the day to ensure that quality was maintained. When it seemed that the round was likely to slip out to eight or nine days, extra pluckers were lorried in from the surrounding villages to take the extra leaf off. The only drawback with this was that it was almost impossible to maintain the quality of the plucking carried out by this casual labour, because if they were given too much hassle they just refused to come anyway. Still it was better for us to take it off the bushes on time than leave it to wave in the wind as this caused the bushes to stop producing buds, so whenever possible they were used to pluck the poorer areas of tea and their leaf was manufactured and packed separately. By doing this and carefully manipulating the labour force, we were able to keep on top of things. As July wore on our crop figures were well ahead of the 1953 figures, and in our innocence we thought that all we had to do was soldier on to the end of September and then we would be able to look back on a successful season.

Little did we know that Mother Nature was laughing up her sleeve at us and preparing to play another of her little tricks to mess up our plans. During the second half of July, the states of Bihar, Bengal and Assam experienced even more severe monsoon storms and were deluged with some 30 inches of rain, so everywhere became completely waterlogged. Then on the night of July 27th there was a tremendous wind storm during which another 12 inches of rain fell over the whole area and the land and rivers just couldn't cope any more. According to the newspapers, thousands of square miles of country were flooded with water up to 12 feet deep, over 300,000 people lost their homes and nobody was able to say exactly how many lives were lost. The devastation over the whole of the Dooars was absolutely tremendous and much worse than that inflicted in 1952, and even my old friend the Sathkyah bridge, which had withstood such a pounding at that time, was swept away. Bagracote was completely cut off for a week, as there were 39 landslides blocking the road from Siliguri and all the temporary rail and road bridges over the Leesh, Geesh and Odlabari rivers were swept away as they had been before. Again the only way to go and get essential supplies from Odlabari bazaar was by walking over the sagging railway lines which were still left hanging after the bridges and embankments had been demolished, so it was something we did only when it was absolutely necessary. Some 40 yards of bridge and embankment had been carried away, and it was a rather foolhardy and very hair-raising experience edging carefully from sleeper to sleeper, with the rails vibrating and the dirty brown flood water surging along a couple of feet below. Goodness knows what was holding the sleepers in place beneath the lines, because they had no other supports. Thinking back now I wonder whether I was rather foolish to do it, because if I had slipped in I would have been carried away in the raging torrent immediately and I am unable to swim. Still, I suppose I had the confidence (or foolhardiness) of the young in those days.

Regarding our food, we were very lucky that the estate always kept a reserve of several week's supply of rice, flour meal, cooking oil and kerosene oil in hand for the labourers' rations, and as the Kyah's garden shop also carried stocks of sugar, salt, soap and other essential items such as this, we were able to get along until the roads were reopened. The one thing we did miss very much was the lack of post, so it was a great relief when a large bundle finally came through about ten days later. This was our only link with home. In normal circumstances we always hoped the afternoon's *dak* (post) would contain at least one letter from somebody, but during the floods we knew there would not be any and that really made the waiting very tedious indeed.

With no road or rail transport available, the only way our tea could be sent to Calcutta was by air. Although this was a very expensive way of shipping it, with this being the busiest time of the year there was no other option and the Jamair aircraft flew almost non-stop every day from dawn to dusk, freighting thousands of tons of tea down to Calcutta from all the various airstrips in the Dooars. Because flying directly to Calcutta from some of the Eastern Dooars airstrips would have meant overflying what was then East Pakistan, which because of some ongoing national arguments was not allowed, some of the planes ran a shuttle service to Saugaon, where invoices of tea were stored until other planes could take them to Calcutta. It was a good job the Jamair pilots were masters of their craft and had such a wealth of experience, because some of the weather in which they flew, without modern navigational aids and so close to the mountains, was absolutely horrendous.

On one occasion, a plane flying into Saugaon with a load from the Eastern Dooars appeared to be coming in with a peculiar 'tail down' attitude and it looked as though it was about to stall. It so happened that we were down on the airfield talking to the crew of another aircraft as he came in, so we watched with bated breath as the pilot managed to get her down safely, even though it was a bit of a clumsy and bumpy landing. Later he told us that not long after taking off he had flown through some clear air turbulence which had thrown the aircraft around so much that the cargo had moved and upset the centre of gravity and he had had to nurse her back the whole of the way. From the look on his face when he disembarked from the plane I think he was very relieved that he had managed to get her back in one piece, but all the pilots had the utmost faith in their aircraft and there is no doubt that the old DC3 was one of the most dependable and reliable aircraft ever built.

In a way it was a very good job it was, for some of the tales they told us about incidents which had occurred while flying were hard to believe. Once the cold weather set in and the railway system had been repaired, the amount of tea being transferred to Calcutta by air tailed off, but luckily for Jamair they had a lucrative contract to take planeloads of Indian and Pakistani Muslims to Mecca for the annual festival of the Hajj. Every Muslim is supposed to make the pilgrimage to Muhammad's birthplace at least once in his lifetime and for many of them the Hajj meant a journey of thousands of miles and the spending of their life savings. For Muslims in India the only way they could get there in comfort was by flying, so each year the Jamair pilots made several return journeys to Saudi Arabia with loads of pilgrims on board. Usually these flights were uneventful, even though many of the passengers had never been near an aircraft let alone fly in one, but on one memorable trip a crew member walked back down through the passenger cabin and found that some of the passengers were making tea over a fire they had lit in the middle of the floor and were sitting round smoking and chatting. Luckily they had built it on some flat pieces of stone they had brought aboard so the floor of the plane hadn't begun to burn, but they couldn't see anything wrong in what they were doing and weren't very happy when he put their fire out with the extinguisher.

According to the pilots one of the most demanding flights they had to make was to Katmandu, the capital of Nepal, because in those days there were only very basic navigational aids and the pilots had to feel their way up the various valleys until they could see the airfield. This was carved into the side of the mountain and the approach to the runway was the lip of the flat area where the mountainside plunged downwards for hundreds of feet. Consequently they had to get it exactly right as they came in just over the end of the runway, put her down and then stop her as quickly as possible before they ran out of space and ran into the mountainside at the other end. The return take-off was equally exciting because the plane was turned at the far end, and then the pilot stood on his brakes while he revved his engines to full throttle before he released them. Once started he couldn't stop and before he was properly airborne he shot over the edge of the precipice, rather like taking off on an aircraft carrier, and at once he was flying at several hundred feet above the bottom of the valley. As they told it, it sounded absolutely hair-raising, but they must have been really careful, because in all my seventeen years in India I never heard of a plane coming to grief there. Nowadays of course things have changed, and I believe Katmandu is now served by a very modern airport with all the facilities, but I sometimes wonder whether the old airfield is still there.

Fortunately for us, although the rivers washed away some of our tea and destroyed a number of our houses on the banks, none of our labourers were killed and Bagracote was not badly affected other than some more damage to our main water supply. The next morning I took four of my engineering lads, and it took us all the morning to scramble up the valley over rock falls and landslides until we reached the dam. This had been badly damaged by falling rocks and was leaking like a sieve, and as several sections of piping had also been carried away by landslides, it took us all day to plug the leaks and make temporary repairs to the piping, so I was dog tired when I got back to the bungalow that night. Still our efforts were well worth it, because the one thing there was plenty of up in the hills was clean water. Our temporary repairs kept it flowing until more permanent repairs could be made. Later we were informed that special expenditure would be made available in the cold weather for the dam to be rebuilt and the most vulnerable sections of the pipeline to be re-routed and replaced with new piping, so my efforts had not been in vain.

It took the civil authorities eight days to clear the 39 landslides which blocked the only road between Siliguri and Bagracote and make temporary repairs to the many damaged bridges, so it was ten days before it was finally opened to vehicular traffic and life began to return to normal. However the road and railway between Siliguri and Darjeeling was much more severely damaged, because several lengths of road had been swept away by landslides and had to be completely rebuilt, so it was impassable to motor vehicles for several months.

It was as a result of this that Donald received a letter from one of the Jamair pilots asking for our help in getting his son down from Darjeeling. Evidently he was a scholar at St. Pauls College and as the family were going away, arrangements had been made for him to come down by taxi to Bagdogra airport and then to Calcutta. However with the disruption caused by the floods these plans had completely fallen through, and as a last resort his father had asked Donald whether there was any way in which we could get him down to Bagracote. Well most people were always ready to help anybody else out in India, so we were especially ready to help the 'Fly boys' whenever possible and as we discussed it we realised there was a way we could get the lad down.

Because of the steepness of the slope the road meandered along the mountainside in a series of very sharp curves and corners for several miles, gradually gaining height as it went. Consequently, the traveller found that after several miles of road travel, he found that he had returned to a spot on the mountainside a few hundred feet above where he had begun, and then the whole process began again in a series of zig-zags until he reached the small town of Ghum, which at a height of 8000 feet above sea level was the highest point on the journey. If one of the hairpin shaped sections of road was rendered impassable, by employing teams of the local villagers as porters it was possible to move people and goods up and down the mountainside from one section of good road to the next by using very steep paths which were normally only used by goats and the local villagers. These paths were quite rough and slippery and no young boy with his luggage could have managed it by himself, but we thought that if both Ash and I went up as far as we could by car then scrambled up the paths we should be able to get him down, and that's what we did.

His father was able to contact St. Pauls, so we arranged for him to tell his son to use a taxi to bring him down to the topmost slip as early as possible on Sunday in two days' time and wait for us there, while we took Ash's Ford V8 car up as far as we could go and then parked it. It was a good job we were both quite fit and healthy and used to scrambling about in the tea, because from there it was an uphill struggle over rough, slippery tracks which wound back and forwards up the hillside, and as we were climbing at about 5000 feet we had to keep stopping to get our breath back. The locals had it very well organised, as they had developed two tracks and organised a one-way system, so from a distance it looked like two trails of ants moving up and down, but even then it took us a couple of hours to traverse three very rough climbs and two lengths of road before we emerged at the top and to our relief found the boy waiting for us. He had a large black steel trunk, a bedding roll and several smaller packages with him, so we recruited a Bhutia woman and her daughter who were obviously used to carrying quite heavy loads from straps that hung from their foreheads. They were both barefooted but this didn't seem to deter them, and while the old girl carried the trunk and her daughter took the bulk of the lighter items, Ash and I carried his hand luggage and helped the lad scramble down the path which we managed to do without any serious mishaps, but we were both very weary and very thankful when we finally reached the car.

The boy told us his Dad had instructed him to tell us that because he was so grateful he would like us to reward anybody who had helped us down really well, so we took him at his word and paid the two women considerably more than the going rate they had asked us for at the top. They could hardly believe their luck and were a very happy pair as they waved goodbye to us and began to plod back up the hillside once more. After that it was literally all downhill, as we descended the 25 miles back down to the plains and on to Bagracote, where the boy spent the night with Betty and Donald and then went down to Calcutta on the Jamair flight the next day.

His father was extremely fortunate that our roads were opened at the right time for us to help him and he must have been very grateful for everything we did for him because on a later flight he sent a bottle of Scotch malt whisky for each of us, which was a handsome gift. By 1954 Scotch could not be obtained in our part of India and no doubt it had come in duty free from somewhere else, but we didn't query its origin and enjoyed it all the more, especially as we had experienced one of the most challenging and enjoyable Sundays we had had in a long time.

CHAPTER TWENTY NINE

August 1954 - what a month!

Because August began like that it seemed as though it was setting the tone for the remainder of the month. It turned out to be a very eventful one all round, because when I joined the company in 1951 I was told I would serve five years in India and then receive eight months' home leave in year six. However, during 1953 our terms of service were amended, and in August I was informed that after four years' service I would be granted six months' fully-paid UK leave in year five.

I was already making arrangements to take my home leave in 1955 when I heard of a superb car which had unexpectedly become available in Siliguri. I hadn't thought of changing my car again and firmly intended keeping the old Vanguard on the road until I went home on leave in 1956 and then replace it later, but it seemed to me to be too good a buy to miss.

It was a 1951 model Mark I Ford Consul that had belonged to a Darjeeling planter who had brought it back with him when he returned from home leave in 1952. At that time he had had no intention of selling it, but since then he had developed a very severe form of an illness known as Tropical Sprue, an extremely debilitating illness which is endemic in India and South East Asia that is characterised by attacks of acute diarrhoea, indigestion, cramps, weight loss and malnutrition, anorexia and intense fatigue. Its cause is unknown. Although it can be treated and cured with vitamins and drugs, if the patient leaves the tropics but later returns to the affected regions he is always liable to re-infection. In this case the planter had been affected so much that his life was in danger, so in his own interests his company decided to repatriate him to hospital in the UK immediately and terminate his employment. This meant that his wife who had been left behind in India to settle up all their affairs had to sell their car as quickly as possible, and it was bought by Everest Motors in Siliguri.

This was a family-owned Bengali concern which was run on Western lines and as a result did a tremendous amount of business with the tea estates. Although they were not actual motor vehicle dealers, they did do overhauls and all types of repairs and also supplied spare parts, besides giving assistance to any planters who needed help while in Siliguri. Although owned by the old father, the company was run by his three sons, who were all in their twenties. As they were all friendly with many of the planters, they would even give us a cup of tea or a cold beer if we ever popped in to have a chat when we were passing.

I had become quite friendly with the youngest brother, named Filoo, who was about my age, and it so happened that I had to visit Siliguri in early July a few days after they had bought the Consul. It was while we were sitting and having a drink that he told me the story of how they had actually come to buy it to help the planter's wife and asked if I knew anyone who wanted to buy a good car. I knew they weren't car dealers and because I had no intention of changing the Vanguard I wasn't very interested, but just because it was such a good buy he persuaded me to go into the workshop to see it. She was painted light cream with a light blue interior and beige upholstery and with her sleek, modern lines, her bench front seat and her steering column gear change I fell in love with her the moment I saw her. She impressed me so much that I decided to take her out for a test drive straight away.

Being on a Darjeeling garden she had been used for pleasure motoring only, mainly for going up and down to the club, so she ran like a dream, and as I drove her back I realised that I had some serious thinking to do. I was going home in a year's time, where I would meet Jan again and hopefully marry her, but although she had written regularly to me three times a week over the years and we both longed to see each other again, I had no real idea of whether she would be willing to leave her family and friends and trust her well-being to me in India, or whether she would hope that I would resign from tea and look for another job in the UK before considering marriage.

However if as I hoped Jan did come back with me, then I knew from experience that travelling about the Indian countryside in an unreliable car was not a sensible thing to do, so I would have to change the Vanguard, and it was unlikely that another one of this quality would become available at that time. So I was in a quandary. Was it a sensible thing for me to take the plunge and buy it or not? Then as I drove back to the garage I realised that I didn't know the price, and if I couldn't afford her I didn't have a problem anyway. When I returned to the garage I talked it over with

Filoo and asked him what price they were asking for her, and he surprised me by quoting what I considered to be a very reasonable price, quite a lot cheaper than I had expected for a car of this quality. He explained this by saying that because they were not dealers and had only bought the car because the planter had been a friend of theirs and they had wanted to help his wife dispose of it quickly so that she could go back to the UK, they were not worried about making a large profit. Provided they could cover their costs and make a nominal profit by a quick sale they would be quite happy.

Of course I knew they were not interested in taking the Vanguard in part exchange and accepted that I would have to sell it privately, but I decided to take the plunge and came to an agreement with Filoo. Provided I could sell the Vanguard quickly and get a company loan for the balance of the money, then I would buy her and they would keep her for me until the end of July, and also throw in a box of spare parts which the owner had brought out with the car as well. On the other hand, if I was unable to do this, then I was to let them know and they could look for another buyer, so the deal was struck.

I drove back to the bungalow that night dreaming about owning her, but full of misgivings. Did I really need that car? I feared I was making a fool of myself in acting on the spur of the moment, but as it so happened I need not have worried because everything turned out fine, despite the fact that the Vanguard was hit by a bolt of lightning on the way home. This was the first time I had ever experienced this phenomenon and it came as a complete shock as I drove home through a torrential downpour which was merely a precursor to the floods to come. I had just left the Sevoke forest and was nearing the Teesta river valley when there was a vivid, blinding flash of white light accompanied by a smell of ozone and what seemed like burnt oil and then a most tremendous bang as though someone had hit the top of the car with a sledge hammer. The bolt had hit the top of the wet car, travelled down its sides and then earthed itself through the wet tyres, but other than leaving me with a ringing in my ears and quite shaken up, no damage was done to me or the car, so I was very thankful.

During the next two weeks I had no difficulty in getting my loan sanctioned by the Superintendent. The garden kyah had a friend who wanted a British car very badly and agreed to give me a very fair price for the Vanguard, so all I had to do was travel into Siliguri and complete the deal. Unfortunately things did not go as planned because the floods came to spoil things and it was the middle of August before I could collect her. However Filoo was very fair, and true to his word she was kept for me although several European planters showed an interest in her after I saw her, and they would have had no difficulty in selling her. She was in excellent condition and the only bad thing about her that I could see was that her tyres had worn out. They had been on her from new and now after three years of hammering on the stony, rutted Darjeeling roads, two of them were down to the canvas while the other two weren't very much better. Filoo had warned me that they were not available in India, so I knew I would have to 'make do and mend' for a year until I could bring a set back with me when I returned from my UK leave, which was the normal procedure for everyone who owned a British-made car in India. At that time the only car manufactured in India was the old Morris Isis with the dished bonnet. When this model was superseded in the UK by the Morris Oxford, all the jig and tool equipment and the manufacturing machinery were exported to India lock, stock and barrel and it was then made under licence and marketed as the Hindustan Standard or the Hindustan Ambassador. Today there are still tens of thousands of them still going strong, either as taxis or private cars. However at that time, India's sole tyre manufacturing firm only had enough manufacturing capacity to satisfy the market for these Hindustan cars, so if you needed different tyres you imported them as 'personal goods' for which you didn't need an import licence.

To illustrate just how popular these cars were, in 1967 when I retired from tea, three different models of car were being made under licence in India, The Triumph Herald and the Fiat 1100, both of which had a waiting time of six years from placing the order until delivery, and the Hindustan Ambassador for which you placed the order accompanied by one third of the price as a down payment and also a banker's guarantee that you personally were reliable for the rest of the money - and then waited ten years for delivery. It was quite standard procedure for fathers who wanted to give their sons a car as a wedding present to place the orders when the boys were about 10 years old so that they would get one on time. At one time a good quality, second hand Ambassador cost almost as much as a new one.

Another thing that happened towards the end of the month illustrated what made it such a joy to work with the ordinary people in India, who in a way were rather like old children. I had had enough experience to know that when orders were given, in most cases they needed to be absolutely explicit otherwise something might not get done, or they might be carried out absolutely to the letter, and that was what happened that afternoon. We were in the middle of a tropical storm and I was sitting at my desk in the office when I looked out of the window and saw an old man in the small flower garden that surrounded the office, with his umbrella up but absolutely wet through, watering the plants with a watering can. In India there never has been and still isn't a pension scheme for the majority of the ordinary people, if you don't work you don't get paid it's as simple as that, but on most of the estates we had a scheme to help our old labourers, many of whom had lived on the estate and grown old in the service of the company. We did this by giving them very simple, easy tasks for which they received the equivalent of a living allowance and also made them feel wanted, and on Bagracote this was recorded as Labour Welfare. Monbahadur was a wizened, old Nepalese man who had spent most of his life working on Bagracote, and his little job was to weed, tend, and water the plants in the office garden, so seeing him I felt I had to know what he thought he was doing, and taking shelter beneath my umbrella I went out to see him.

'Monbahadur, what are you doing?' I asked him.

Pityingly he looked at me as if to say that I must be mad if I couldn't see what he was doing, and said, 'I'm watering the flowers, Sahib'.

Wondering what his next answer would be, I indicated the sky with the rain lashing down and said, 'But don't you think that God is doing a much better job at watering the flowers than you can do'?

For a moment he thought then said, 'If the *Burra Sahib* (Manager) says 'Your job is to water the flowers, then I water the flowers' at which he finished his can and stalked off to refill it.

Afterwards I thought about this, and it was obvious that he had great pride in his job, which was about the only thing he was able to do and for which he was being paid, and in a childish sort of way he was going to do it to the best of his ability, literally come hell or high water.

I was still using Albert Ager's old radio, and although reception was pretty poor during the monsoon season, I was able to receive Radio Ceylon and also the Overseas Service of the Australian Broadcasting Corporation most of the time, so it had turned out to be a very valuable acquisition. Radio Ceylon broadcast regular English language programmes from 6 am to 9 am each morning and for another four hours each evening which gave us the world news and some music, but for some reason there was a heavy American bias. I remember that we seemed to get religious music and 'hot gospel' choir music a lot of the time and in one of the letters I wrote home to Mum I told her that I was listening to a gospel choir telling me that if I'd like to 'run behind the chariot of the Lord, I'd come from the darkness into light' and that cheered me up no end.

The drawback with the ABC was that because they were five hours ahead of Indian time they didn't operate in the evenings, but as their programmes were very varied and full of interest I tried to listen to them on Sunday afternoons. One I liked very much was specially directed at overseas listeners. Music requests were played and letters from listeners were read out, many of them asking for people in other countries with similar interests such as philately or letter writing to contact them. One afternoon there was a letter from a Mr Andy Fortuna, whose address was given as c/o The Hangchow Automobile Repair Factory, Hangchow, China, in which he wrote that he would welcome letters from anyone who cared to write to him at that address. Now this seemed very strange and made me very curious. Why should a man with a Western-sounding name be living in a city in Communist China when we were in the midst of the 'Cold War' with the Communist countries? The more I thought about it the more curious I became. Finally during the floods when I had a few minutes to spare, I decided to write to him to satisfy my curiosity, and when I received his reply a few weeks later his story was almost stranger than fiction.

Towards the end of the Korean War in 1953, the repatriation of prisoners was one of the main stumbling blocks in the long ceasefire negotiations between the forces of the United Nations and those of China and North Korea. They finally agreed that sick and wounded prisoners would be exchanged in April and May, and in June they agreed that no prisoners who did not wish to be repatriated would have to be. Under this agreement these men would be allowed to live in a neutral country to reconsider before being allowed to live in enemy territory, and as a result of this, the armistice ending the Korean War was signed on June 27th, 1953 and the main prisoner exchange was able to proceed. Subsequently, 15,823 Communist fighters and 12,773 UN soldiers were repatriated, but over 22,000 Communist prisoners, many of whom had fought for General Chiang Kai-Shek against the Communists during the Chinese civil war refused repatriation, and were helped to make their homes in the west. This was to be expected, but much to the shock, surprise and consternation of the Western nations, one British marine and 21 American soldiers refused to be repatriated and decided to stay in China. Andy Fortuna was one of those.

Later these 21 Americans were given dishonourable discharges from the US Army, but subsequently this proved to be a double-edged sword because it had the unexpected consequence of rendering them immune to court martial when they finally returned to the USA because they were deemed to be no longer on active military duty. At the time some people said they had been brainwashed by the Chinese during their captivity, while others thought they were actually deserters who were afraid to return to the USA, but from his letters Andy seemed to have a genuine liking for the Chinese people and their attitude to life. He admired their skill and ability to make the most of what assets they had with the minimum of equipment, and I could agree with that because the Cantonese carpenters on the tea estates were first-class craftsmen who could make quite complicated items with just the use of their razor sharp hatchets and a few basic tools. In his letters Andy told me he had been captured in 1950 so he had had a lot to do with the Chinese. After refusing repatriation he had been given a job in an automobile repair factory where old military vehicles, both Chinese and American, were completely stripped down and rebuilt. In most cases new spare parts were not available, so usually some of the vehicles were cannibalised or the necessary parts were hand made by the craftsmen in the workshops, and he was amazed at what they turned out. He lived in his own small house with the services of a translator, and although he did not do much sightseeing, he did have access to a car and driver if he wished to go out. He never did tell me what specific work he did, although I think he was used more as a living advertisement for the benefits of communism than as a worker.

It appeared that his food was adequate, although rather monotonous, and in many of his letters he wrote of the things he would do 'when he got back to the States'. I thought this was a rather naive attitude from someone who had deliberately turned his back on his homeland. At that time I thought that he didn't have a snowball's chance in hell of being welcomed back to the USA but I was completely wrong, because nine of these people returned from China in the late 1950s, while a further seven went back in the early 1960s. Subsequently one died in captivity, this left only another four who either stayed in China or went to live in other countries when released. It was only recently that I discovered on the internet that Andy had returned to America in 1957 and had a Japanese wife. He was a sergeant who had served in the US Army in WWII and had earned two bronze stars for gallantry in Korea before he was captured, and when he died in 1984 his last known residence was given as Inkster, Michigan.

Although his letters were interesting he never went into very much detail, and from the stilted way they were worded I always felt he suspected that they might be checked by the authorities before being sent. I also had the thought in the back of my mind that there was the possibility that the Chinese had an ulterior motive in allowing him to contact people abroad, so I was always careful what I wrote and was not surprised in 1955 when he asked me if I could send him any technical papers or instruction books that were available in India, as these were in very short supply in China. Immediately I read this I got a bit apprehensive about the way things were developing and decided to tread warily. Since the Chinese People's Liberation Army had invaded Tibet and resumed control again in 1951 and the Dalai Lama had fled to India, relations between the two countries had reached a very low ebb, and since China was also making unfriendly noises and claiming sovereignty over the two small Himalayan States of Bhutan and Sikkim which were 'protected' by India, the Indian authorities did not look very kindly on anyone who professed

Chinese sympathies and in the bazaars anti-Chinese feelings were running very high. In view of this I 'chickened out' and lost no time in writing back to him, explaining that because India was also lacking technical material of all kinds, the Indian government had placed an embargo on the export of technical information from the country and I was unable to send him any.

Afterwards we continued to correspond, but gradually the tone of his letters changed. It seemed that he had become disenchanted with life in China and was quite confident that he would be able to go back home, possibly because he had heard that four of his compatriots were to be allowed to return in 1955. Of course, I didn't know anything of this and kept writing, but finally things came to a head in late 1956 when I received another letter in which he told me how wonderful the communist way of life was and how much it benefited the ordinary people. I received this soon after the Hungarian revolt in October 1956, during which 2500 Soviet tanks were sent into Budapest to quell the uprising. Many executions followed and I was so incensed that I sent him some newspaper cuttings and wrote 'If this barbarity is what you think is so wonderful then you can keep it and you are welcome to my share as well'. That was the end. Whether he ever got the letter or whether it was stopped and censored by the Chinese authorities before he got it I don't know, but Andy never replied and I can't say I was really sorry.

Unfortunately I destroyed all his letters during the big clearout of old papers I had before leaving India. With hindsight this was rather unfortunate in view of what happened later, because I am sure they would have made very interesting reading today. However the anti-Chinese feelings continued for many years, and during 1954 and 1955 when the local people were feeling really worked up, several of the Chinese carpenters who worked on the estates were beaten up in the local bazaar simply because they happened to be Chinese. One day our Chinaman came to me and said that he was due his annual leave and had arranged to go down to Calcutta, but because of this trouble he was afraid to go, and under the circumstances would we allow him to stay in the estate for safety and also to give him some extra work to do to keep him occupied? Well we jumped at the chance as it was always a challenge to keep the more difficult jobs under control when the Chinamen were away because they were extremely skilled craftsmen and could turn their hands to anything, so we gave him extra work and he passed his leave peacefully on the garden, for which he was extremely grateful. However both Ash and I were extremely surprised and honoured when he approached us a few days later and asked us if we would be his guests at a dinner which his wife would cook especially for us as a gesture of their thanks. We both loved Chinese food, so we were very pleased to accept, and that night they treated the two of us to a most sumptuous meal which his little wife cooked in her kitchen at the back of their house. It was the best Chinese food that I have ever tasted and no food in restaurants has ever compared to it. When we thanked her later and congratulated her on her cooking, she was almost overcome at the thought that we should rate it so highly and was most embarrassed. Little did we think when we helped the old man that it would result in such a treat, because it was absolutely superb.

CHAPTER THIRTY

A time of celebration

Despite the amounts of rain that had fallen in the previous months, we continued to get deluges of heavy rain during the whole of September, and this, combined with abnormally high temperatures, resulted in tremendous quantities of leaf being plucked, so it was soon evident that if this continued until the cold weather we would make another record crop. As it was his first Acting post, Donald was overjoyed. As he was always ready for a celebration no matter what the reason, the day we passed the 1953 final crop with several weeks to spare we were invited over to his bungalow for a drink, and we made a proper evening of it.

According to the company's contract terms, my first contract with the company ran for three years from January 1st 1951 to December 31st 1953, and this was followed by a second one which finished at the end of 1956. Although they were very similar in content, the second one was very much more important, inasmuch as the Company reckoned that if you had made a success of your first three years' service and were good enough to be offered a second contract, then you were entitled to share in any profits that were made. If the estate made a loss nobody got anything, but if there was a profit everyone from the managerial staff to the clerks and labourers received bonus payments as an incentive, and in the covenanted staff, the manager received a commission of a certain percentage of the profit which varied with seniority, while as a second term assistant for this record crop that we made in 1954 I was paid 0.1% of the profit on it in 1955. This doesn't sound like very much but later it amounted to the very handy sum of £1108 12s 6d, and even though I still had to pay one quarter of this to the Indian Revenue Office as income tax and super tax, it was still enough to clear all my debts in the safe at Bagracote and also leave me with a healthy balance, which was considerably more than I could have saved had I worked for the same time at home, so all my work with Donald paid off.

Because of our ages he referred to us as the 'Three *Bachhas*' or youngsters, and because the three bachhas had done it again, that evening turned into quite a memorable 'beat up' as we used to call our drinking sessions, but that one was nothing like the party that he threw when his son Donald Mackenzie III, who was known as 'Junior' was born a few weeks later. Betty had gone up to Darjeeling to await his birth and the morning he got the news that she had had Junior he was beside himself with joy. Without any more ado I was detailed to go into Mal Bazaar to bring back whatever booze the liquor shop had, while Ash got the word out to all his friends to come to the party and Donald arranged with his cook to prepare the dinner - and what an evening that was. How the word was passed I am unable to remember, but that evening some 30 of us gathered out on his veranda and a very merry time was had by all, especially by a young assistant who had just come out to tea and was attending his first party. He was another Scot from

Aberdeen and after he had had a couple of drinks he boasted to Donald that there were very few people who could match him drink for drink. It was probably just that he wanted to make an impression on us and it was the alcohol talking, but it was like a red rag to a bull to some of the lads and within a few minutes there was a drinking competition going on which only finished when he was completely sloshed and went to sleep in his chair. Donald was also merry by this time and pronounced that if he couldn't drink then he shouldn't boast, and that as he had let the Scottish nation down he should only be drinking orange squash and had to be punished. With this solemn pronouncement he poured half a bottle of squash over the assistant's head so that it dripped down over his face and body and made a hell of a mess, but it didn't disturb him and he just went on sleeping the sleep of the just, completely oblivious to everything while the orange gunge slid down his face.

Later in the evening when he came to he staggered out into the compound to be sick. After a while he tottered back in saying that he felt much better, but unfortunately after a short while he discovered that while he was being sick he had taken out some false teeth that he was wearing and put them on the ground, but then in his subsequent discomfort had omitted to pick them up, so he asked us if we would help him find them. Unfortunately he had never been to the bungalow before and in the complete darkness out in the compound he had no idea where he had been sick, so we were very happy as we charged round like bulls in a china shop for a while until they were found. Unfortunately somebody had trodden on them during the search and they were useless. Our nearest dental surgery was up in Darjeeling a hundred miles away. Although I believe he got another plate made later, I think this turned out to be a very valuable lesson to him and taught him to be a bit careful when it came to drinking with planters, and not try to run before he could walk.

As for me, before I went to India I kept myself very fit and never felt the need to drink alcohol, and although later I was always ready to have a social drink, the occasions when I drank to excess were very rare. Having said that I have always had a sweet tooth and it was at that time that I had discovered the joys of drinking a rather potent 'short' drink of my own concoction. I discovered that if blended whisky and condensed milk were mixed in equal proportions, the result was a rather thick, creamy liquid which tasted like fiery caramel. I enjoyed this so much that I still drink it to this day if ever we have any spare condensed milk hanging around. Unfortunately to abuse Scottish whisky like this was an anathema to a true Scot like Donald, and because I knew how he felt I used to take my own tin of milk with me so that I could take my liquor neat and then mix up my own drink on the quiet. Unfortunately, although this plan worked well for the first part of the evening, later on after I had had a few I got a bit careless, and he discovered my tin of milk hidden on the corner of the window sill. Well he was not having that, and with one movement he grabbed it and hurled it out over the veranda rail into the compound with the cry, 'No bloody Sassenach is going to mix condensed milk with fine Scotch whisky at my bachha's birthday party!' Then off he stomped to get me a PROPER drink and the party continued into the small hours. As far as I can remember I finished the night well the worse for wear and rather than travel back down to Saugaon I spent the rest of the night at Ash's bungalow, but true to our principles, although we were still quite woozy and suffering from monumental hangovers, we were all out and on the job at 7 am the next morning as usual.

The next milestone in that eventful year was the Durga Puja that fell at the beginning of October, closely followed by the Kali Puja a few days later, so at this time Donald and Betty went up to Darjeeling for some local leave, leaving me in overall charge of the estate with Ash looking after Bagracote division and we got on fine. This was the first time that I had ever been in charge of a complete garden and although it was only for a very limited period it was a tremendous experience for me and gave me a taste of what could be, and was a valuable insight into what was involved when you were top man on an 1800 acre tea estate on a 3000 acres grant of land and responsible for about 4000 labourers and dependants. By this time it was apparent to me that if an estate was run properly and everyone knew what their duties were and had belief in the ability and honesty of their manager, then it should be able to operate for a few days without him being around and that is what happened. All I had to do was deal with any unforeseen incidents that cropped up and that was that.

Although we were in charge of Bagracote this didn't mean that we had to stay there during every moment of the day during the holiday. As long as we returned there at night to deal with any emergencies that cropped up, as neither of us had visited any of the mountainous area north of Darjeeling and Kalimpong, we decided to visit Kalimpong and then go as far as we could into the small, independent kingdom of Sikkim, which was the buffer state between Tibet and India in that region. Only 2471 sq. miles in area, Sikkim and its neighbouring state of Bhutan were two small countries nestling in the Himalayas north of West Bengal. On its western boundary it shared a border with Nepal and to the north and east was Tibetan China. From the early 1700s onward there were always incursions and constant threats of invasion from both these countries. However after the end of the Gurkha war in 1814, all the territory annexed by Nepal was returned to Sikkim and it became an unofficial protectorate of the East India Company. It finally became allied to Britain in 1886, although the Chinese always maintained that it was still part of Tibet and thus part of the wider Chinese Republic. In 1888 the Tibetans were defeated and northern Sikkim came under the rule of British India, and in 1894 the capital was shifted to Gangtok. From then on the country was granted more and more Home Rule until finally in 1918 complete independence in all internal affairs was restored, and this continued until the guarantees on independence were transferred to the Indian Government when it gained independence in 1947.

In 1962 India and the People's Republic of China went to war. Although Sikkim was an independent country, skirmishes occurred at the Nathu La Pass between Indian border guards and the Chinese soldiers, so after the war it was shut down and did not reopen until July 2006. The Nathu La was an important pass through the Himalayas on the Old Silk Route, an offshoot of the historic Silk Road between Western Europe and China. It was the only route between the plains of Bengal to the south and Lhasa, the capital of Tibet in the north, and connected North Eastern Sikkim with the Tibetan Chumbi Valley. It lay at an altitude of over 14,000 feet, surrounded by 20,000-foot peaks.

From Chulsa it was some 130 miles away by road, but such was the circuitous nature of the roads and tracks that led to it that during the cold weather its surrounding peaks were clearly visible from some of our estates in the Chulsa district, only 35 miles away as the crow flies. The morning was the best time to see them and they looked superb silhouetted against the northern sky with the snow clad peaks glistening in the early morning sun. The road between Kalimpong, Gangtok and Lhasa had always been the most important trade route between India and Tibet, and until it was closed in 1962 many hundreds of mules and yaks, together with many rough and bandit-like Tibetan muleteers were employed in carrying goods on the 25-day journey between the two countries. Once the mule trains left the Chumbi Valley and entered Sikkim through the Nathu La pass, the main track went on to Gantok, while a smaller one branched off southward to Kalimpong. A train was a very colourful affair, always led by the most experienced mare known as the 'bell mare' because she was decorated with bells, coloured plumes and ribbons as symbols of her authority. She was always the leader, and the others trusted her to find the best way over the perilous mountain tracks. Wherever she went they went, but without her they were lost and this could result in chaos, so the drivers treated her with great care and rightly so.

I had seen coloured photographs and slides of the mule trains arriving at Kalimpong at the end of their journey, and had always hoped to visit Gangtok to see them there, but owing to the trouble with the Chinese and the fact that it was a frontier area, it was extremely difficult for foreigners to get a visitor's permit. However, as I was resident in West Bengal and Ash had been an Indian army officer, we thought that that might help and decided to see how far we could go, so that morning we called into the office to make sure that everything was all right, then away we went. Petrol was quite expensive in India and under normal circumstances we would not have considered attempting such a long-distance jaunt in one day, but having our supply of 'free' aviation spirit made a great deal of difference, so we took the Consul and set off westwards along the Siliguri road.

After 15 miles we reached the Teesta river valley, where the road followed the ins and outs of the hillside upstream for four miles until it reached the Coronation Bridge. This section of road had suffered badly in the recent floods as it was where most of the landslides had occurred, and although essential repairs had been done, the road surface was still in a terrible mess and some falls had still not been completely cleared, so progress was very slow.

The Coronation Bridge was built to commemorate the coronation of King George VI in 1937 and I believe it was opened in the early 1940s. Before it was built the only way to cross the Teesta at that point was by walking across the railway bridge about four miles downstream. Then when the war came and the bridge was opened, the war effort against the Japanese demanded that all the rivers across the Dooars and Assam were bridged, and an all-weather road was built from the Teesta right through to Burma, so thousands of tea garden labourers and European planters were recruited to build these and many air strips across the whole of north-east India.

Constructed of reinforced concrete, it was supported on slender piles embedded in the bedrock on both sides of the river. The road crossed the bridge on a graceful arch which rose up on each side between them, and when it was approached from the south and was framed by the jungle-clad river valley behind it, it was a sight to behold. When I saw it at that time it was painted a glistening white and looked superb, but when we revisited India in 2007 the white coating had worn off and it looked what it was - concrete. However, because of its situation I still think it was one of the most picturesque and beautiful bridges I have ever seen.

Once across to the western side the ways parted downstream to Siliguri, while we turned upstream on the road to the Anderson Bridge and Kalimpong. The sides of the valley are extremely steep and very heavily forested, and as the road was quite narrow and the side bordering the river very often ended abruptly and fell almost vertically into the waters some 100 feet below, drivers had to be extremely careful. Consequently, although the two bridges were only about ten miles apart, because of the serpentine nature of the road as it followed the contours of the valley it was probably twice this distance, and it was late morning by the time we reached the Anderson Bridge. At this point the road forked, the left-hand track leaving the valley and making its tortuous way up the mountainside through Takdah, Rangli Rangliot and Ghoom until it reached Darjeeling by the back route, while the other one crossed the river over the bridge and carried on up to Kalimpong and Gangtok. This was quite an old suspension bridge which hung some ninety feet high above the river, and as we crossed over it felt so solid that it seemed as though nothing could affect it. Little did we know that fifteen years later in 1969 the river upstream would be dammed by a landslide in Sikkim, and that when this broke the subsequent tidal wave that surged down the river valley almost like a tsunami would carry it away. A flood of this magnitude is hard to comprehend. The torrent was so large and unexpected that in Jalpaiguri town thirty miles downstream the district gaol was completely submerged within minutes, and I heard later that many of the prisoners drowned in their cells because the staff members were unable to reach them and release them in time as the waters rose so quickly.

From the bridge, the road twisted and turned for ten miles up a mountainside which seemed to blaze with large stands of wild poinsettia bushes, giving us absolutely breath-taking views of the mountains and the Teesta winding its way along the valley below. We made so many stops to admire the views that it was almost midday when we arrived in Kalimpong, so we decided to have our lunch in one of the Chinese restaurants before we continued on to Gangtok. It was very picturesque and unlike Darjeeling, most of which is built on a very steep hillside, Kalimpong is situated at an altitude of about 4100 feet on the end of a mountain spur which juts out into India from central Sikkim. It gradually grew up there mainly because it was the natural terminus for the mule trains from Tibet, and consequently was an absolute hodge podge of different races and cultures. As a result it was crowded with Buddhist monks from the local monasteries in their saffron and red robes, Tibetan mule drivers with their pigtails, outlandish dress and felt hats and boots who were in town determined to have a good time, as well as the local people in their colourful costumes. There was so much to see that we would have been quite happy to spend the rest of the day there, but we resisted the idea and were soon driving north along the road to the Sikkim border - where a disappointment awaited us. Here we were stopped at a check point manned by Indian police and although they were all very friendly they were absolutely adamant that because we didn't have the necessary paperwork they were unable to let us through. Evidently the passes were issued from the DCs office in Jalpaiguri and as a resident I should have been able to get one without any trouble, but I hadn't done so and as a result, no permit, no visit.

However all was not lost, because for the last part of its journey the smaller mule trail from the Nathu La also used the motor road to Kalimpong, so we decided to drive north along it and see just how far we could go. For the first thirty miles the road followed the crest of the spur just on the Indian side of the border and was in good condition, but gradually it deteriorated until finally we reached the small town of Pedong some sixty miles from Kalimpong, where the road petered out into a narrow dirt track which we were told crossed over into Sikkim a couple of miles further on. As a result, although we were a little disappointed that we had not been able to visit Gangtok we were very pleased with the outcome of our trip, because although Pedong in itself was not very spectacular and only consisted of a school, a football field and some large buildings interspersed with Buddhist temples, the hill scenery of the area through which we had travelled was extremely wild and beautiful compared with what we were used to on the plains, and well worth the effort of getting there.

Finally we left the Consul by the soccer field and walked on to have a look at the track. It was obvious that it was the path the mule trains had used, but it was very narrow and studded with stones and boulders which would have damaged the car had we gone any further, so we realised that we had made a wise decision and decided to call it a day. By the time we had walked back to the town the light was fading, so after eating a tea of singaras and samosas in a small restaurant, we set off on the return journey and finally got back to Bagracote at 10 pm, very tired but feeling like a couple of explorers who had reached their journey's end. It was a very memorable day.

A few days after this I came across my first demonstration of water divining, or 'dowsing' as it is termed. I knew it existed, but had no idea how it was done or what it involved and had never met anyone who practised it, so it was a new experience for me when I met a stranger who was waiting on the airfield one morning. When I saw him I realised he wasn't a planter, and as we waited for the midday flight to land we chatted and he told me that he worked for a Calcutta-based water supply company which specialised in sinking deep borehole wells, often several hundred feet deep. Of course rather like oil wells, it was not economic to bore a hole this deep unless you were reasonably sure that there was water down there in the first place, so the company worked on a 'no water, no fee' basis, and employed him to use his skills to survey the prospective customer's site and ascertain whether there was a viable source of water beneath the property or not. According to him only about 10% of the Earth's fresh water supply is above the surface, while the other 90% lies underground in what is technically known as the 'groundwater saturation zone'. Finding these supplies of hidden water has been a skill known to people all over the world for hundreds of years. He also said that nobody could actually describe what this sixth sense was, but the Australian aborigines and African bushmen could 'smell' water beneath the desert, and although most humans once had this sense to some degree, in the developed countries of the modern world most people have lost the knack of using it, so in many cases it is a lost art. In his case he was taught by his father at a very young age and was able to sense pools of water and watercourses beneath the surface and also estimate quantities and rates of flow as well as purity, etc. At the time I met him he was dowsing on Leesh River tea estate in an attempt to discover whether there was a suitable site to bore a well that would give them adequate supplies of water during the dry season, and during his time there I watched him walking the paths on Leesh River on several occasions. Leesh River was originally known as Phulbari Tea Estate, after Phulbari (flower garden) market that was situated on the property on the bank of the River Gish, but was changed to its new name when it became part of the Duncan Brothers' agency after the war.

Once he had completed his tests and observations he returned to Calcutta in order to write his report and notify his employers of his findings, and I believe that when I left Bagracote in 1955 to go on home leave the manager was still waiting for their recommendations. As luck would have it fate decreed that I would never work on Bagracote again, so I never did find out whether his efforts were successful and whether a well was bored or not, which was a shame. However one thing is certain. In 1951 Zurrantee had no surface water during the dry season and from October to March all our supplies had to come from shallow surface wells, but when we revisited it in January 2007 they were irrigating the tea with copious quantities of water which was being pumped out of a borehole in the bed of the Naura river, so they had found a supply somewhere and were able to utilise it. Of course the secret of doing this was having mains electricity, because all we had in our time was 110v DC which we generated ourselves. Once the 220 AC current from the Jaldakha hydro-electric scheme came on stream in the early 1970s, deep-well pumps became a possibility and after that they never looked back. Indeed an amusing thing that happened concerning that time was when I was introduced to the members of the Dooars Branch of the

Indian Tea Association at their AGM 2007 as 'Mr. R G Brown, Manager of Aibheel, BE,' and when I asked what the BE stood for they said 'Before Electricity.'

Undoubtedly the introduction of mains electricity from the Jaldakha hydro-electric Scheme had a very profound effect on both the small towns and the tea estates, and this was demonstrated to us when we visited Sathkyah during our visit and our host asked us if we had seen Sinclair's Retreat. We knew absolutely nothing about it, so he took us there and it was a real eye opener. On a tract of some 20 acres of land on the top of a nearby hill which had been nothing more than dry, dusty scrub jungle with no grass at all in our day, a Tourist Resort and Conference Centre named Sinclair's Retreat had sprung up, complete with an irrigated cricket ground and sports field, formal gardens and lawns, bungalows and rooms for the guests, a large bar and restaurant, a keep-fit complex and a conference hall. When I asked him where all the water for this had come from he said 'Come, I'll show you' and took us to a modern pump house which housed two very large deep-well pumps. He said the water was coming from several hundred feet below ground level. After we had seen all we wanted to he took us behind the pump house, where there was something I would never have thought possible, even in my wildest dreams. It was an Olympic-sized swimming pool full of sparkling blue water. After remembering what the area had been like in our days it was like a rose bush flowering in the middle of the Sahara desert, and I just couldn't get over it. We would have given our eye teeth to have had somewhere like that to splash about in when we lived there.

I must admit that I was rather sceptical about dowsing in 1954, but since I returned from India I have come across many dowsers and other gifted people who possess amazing powers, from being able to 'sense' the whereabouts of people or bodies through looking at a map or handling their personal belongings, to finding graves or the remains of old buildings and archaeological remains beneath the surface of fields etc where there is absolutely nothing to be seen on the surface. Unfortunately I do not seem to have the gift, so I just have to content myself with reading about the doings of our local dowsing society in our weekly newspaper, a poor substitute.

After Durga the next festival was the Kali Puja a couple of weeks later. Donald said that as we had looked after the garden while he was away we could go up to Darjeeling for a couple of days at that time if we wished to do so. That was an offer that we just couldn't turn down. Although the weather was very wet and cold for that time of year, it was very pleasant to get away from the garden and see some different faces and do a bit of shopping.

For several months I had been looking forward to my home leave, but it was not until that trip to Darjeeling that it really came home to me that even though Jan was happy to marry me, she might not be willing to cut herself off from her family and come to India. If this was the case then in all probability I would not be returning either. The situation was rather complicated, because Jan's Mum had died in rather tragic circumstances when she was 14 years old, leaving her father to bring up Jan and her sister. Sadie was four years older than Jan and was already in a serious relationship, so there was a distinct possibility that she would get married first and move out, leaving Jan to look after her father, and as I knew that Jan was a very devoted and home-loving daughter I never doubted that she would be willing to do this if the need arose. Very selfishly and foolishly I had never considered these things seriously as I bumbled along in a rosy haze, loving the work and the country and the free and easy style of living, and very stupidly I thought that all I had to do was ride into Dursley and gather Jan up and marry her and then carry her back to India like a fairytale prince with his bride. Oh what a silly boy I was at that time when it came to family matters!

Then it then struck me that if I didn't return to India I had very few mementos of my five years spent in tea, just some albums filled with black and white photographs and some items of Indian craftwork, so really I had nothing that I could take home and show the folks what life had really been like. However thinking about it further, one thing that had impressed me was an 8 mm cine camera owned by our accountant Martin, who had had it for several years and had built up a considerable library of small films of events and places that he had visited. We did see the occasional Technicolor film at the club in those days, but as Martin was a bachelor and had travelled all over the world during his local and annual leaves, we loved to be invited to his bungalow for one of his film shows. They were lovely films in full colour and I thought that if I could take something like that home, not only would our families and friends enjoy seeing them, but I would have a permanent record of my life in India and the work on the estate as well.

As we drove up to Darjeeling that morning Ash and I talked it over. We decided that if I could buy the equipment it would solve my problems, the only trouble being the cost. The camera by itself was well within my budget; it was the projector that cost the big money and without that the films could not be shown

Suddenly Ash came up with a brainwave. He suggested that if I bought the camera by itself so that I could shoot the films, then for the rest of my time until my leave we could view them on Martin's projector just to ensure that I was not making any serious mistakes during filming. Afterwards when I took them home they would take up very little space in my luggage and I would be able to buy a second-hand projector in the UK to show everyone. Then I could sell it again if I came back. I thought this was a brilliant idea, and although I hadn't spoken to Martin about it, I decided to buy a camera in Darjeeling if there was one available. As it turned out later on when I did speak to Martin he said that he had an old projector which he only kept as a spare and lent it to me until I went on leave. Unfortunately 8mm cine cameras and projectors were in short supply at that time, but when I approached Mr Das, who owned Das Photographic Studios in Darjeeling, he said that although he didn't have one in stock at that moment, he could order one for me for delivery in November if that was of any use to me. I decided to take the plunge and ordered it.

In retrospect it was a great pity that I wasn't able to buy it at that time because October 23rd was my birthday and this turned out to be such an unforgettable experience that it would have been well worth recording as my first film. This was a big disappointment, but it was more than made up for by the fact that I was given the opportunity of seeing a facet of life which not many Europeans would have been fortunate enough to experience. While we were there Ash met up with several members of the Indian Army who he had known while he was in the service, and as a result we were invited down to the Army camp at what was Lebong racecourse at that time, where the main Gurkhali Kali Festival of Worship was due to take place on the Sunday morning.

Lebong is in a valley about eight miles from Darjeeling, and at just over 6000 feet above sea level it once held the record of having the highest racecourse in the world, but sadly I think it no longer exists. It was laid out by the British Army in 1885, and as a complete lap of the almost circular track was only 480 yards long, most races consisted of four or six laps and then a straight run in past the main grandstand to the finishing line. Because of the rarefied atmosphere at that altitude, the 'racehorses' were local Bhutia ponies, while most of the jockeys seemed to be a motley crew of local lads who were willing to risk life and limb in the free-for-all that usually occurred on the tiny track. Nevertheless it was quite good fun, and I was there one racing weekend when I was very successful, as I met and chatted to my hero Sherpa Tenzing once more and also managed to win quite a nice little sum on the horses. In one race one of the outsiders was a pony named Jaimanjari, and with a romantic twist of mind I managed to change this into 'Jai–Jan Marry' which had romantic connotations for me, so I had five rupees on it and it won at 50 to 1, which I thought was a very good omen indeed.

As Kali is regarded as the Goddess of War, Death and Destruction, the Gurkha regiments look on her as their patron saint, so on her feast day a prime buffalo was always sacrificed to her as an offering, and if she accepted it the men knew they would have luck and good fortune with them in the year ahead. The festival was celebrated on the morning of the Goddess' feast day, and the main event took place on the race course in the space in front of the main grandstand, so there was plenty of room for everyone who wished to attend. When we arrived there all the Gurkha soldiers had already taken their seats in the front rows. We were led to some visitors' seats at the back where Ash's friends were already seated, but we were still able to get an excellent view of the proceedings from there. Ash had told me that most of the ceremony was quite low key and rather boring, but that the moment when the sacrifice was made was really spectacular, so I waited in great anticipation. I had noticed that a very sturdy post about 15 inches in diameter and six feet high had been planted in the ground in front of the crowd and when the time for the offering came and the buffalo was led out of its pen a murmur of appreciation ran through the onlookers. It was a magnificent animal which had obviously been very well cared for during the previous weeks, for it looked sleek and well fed, while its horns shone black in the morning sunlight.

It wore a large garland of flowers round its neck and waited quietly while the serious part of the worship was completed, then it was led to the post where its head was placed against it with one horn each side and then securely lashed with rope so that it was completely immobile, as though it was heading the post. It was deemed to be a great honour to be the person who was selected to actually carry out the sacrifice, because if it was done satisfactorily he became an instant celebrity with fame that lasted for the rest of his life, so there was great rivalry for the honour and only the best man was chosen. However there was a down side to this, because if he failed to carry out his task satisfactorily and the sacrifice was a failure, then the battalion was destined to have bad luck for the next year and the unfortunate man was held to be responsible, which was a hard thing to live down, rather like a footballer missing a last minute penalty in the cup final at Wembley, only worse.

When the time came the chosen man marched out with some assistants, one of whom was carrying one of the largest kukris that I had ever seen, with a blade about two feet long that looked as though it had been sharpened and honed until it was razor sharp. Then two of the assistants took hold of the animal's tail and pulled its body backwards so that its neck was stretched and its legs braced, and while they held it motionless he ran his fingers along the line of its neck vertebrae to find the points at where they joined and noted where he was going to strike. Then without more ado he took the kukri and raised it above his head, then brought it down in one tremendous slicing blow straight between two of the vertebrae. It severed the neck completely and left the head still attached to the post, while the headless body stood motionless for several seconds before the legs collapsed in a shower of blood and it fell sideways, which showed that Kali had accepted the offering.

For a few seconds there was complete silence while the buffalo's life blood drained away, then a tremendous shout of relief rang out and the Gurkhas mobbed their hero amid great rejoicing. If he had muffed his first strike and had had to have several cuts at it in order to sever the head, his name would have been mud, but everything was fine and the drinking and celebrating could start.

Although we joined them, we had to get back to Bagracote that night so we were only able to stay until early evening. We missed the big dinner that was held that night, which was a pity because the buffalo was skinned and butchered then roasted on a spit over a monstrous fire in the middle of the parade ground, and as it was large enough for all and sundry to come and eat their fill it was not wasted. It was a pity that after all we had seen we weren't able to get our little bit.

CHAPTER THIRTY ONE

My leopard

Since the end of the monsoon we had been having trouble with a large leopard which seemed to come across from the forest most nights and roam through the labour lines looking for dogs, goats or young cattle to catch. Several dogs and goats had disappeared, and one of the dogs had been snatched while its terrified young owner had looked on from about six feet away, so as the labourers were worried that it might attack a child someday, they asked me if I could help them. When leopards are on the prowl they make a loud, unmistakable noise which sounds like somebody sawing wood, just like a pet tabby purring only about a hundred times louder, so they knew in which section of the garden it had been on any particular night, but as it didn't seem to have any regular pattern to its wanderings, this was of no use to me. However, I told them if it made a kill anywhere on the garden that was suitable for me to sit over then I would be willing to do so.

As luck would have it, it killed a cow a few days later. On the night of October 21st the animal had been allowed to graze in the thatch area on the edge of the tea, and unfortunately the owner had 'forgotten' to bring it in that evening, so the leopard had made short work of it. It was a fine, young animal which he had bought to supply milk for his family and for which he had paid quite a large sum of money, so this represented a great loss to him, but I had very little sympathy for him. He knew it was forbidden to graze animals in the tea because they damaged the bushes too much, and he had made his bed and had to lie on it. However it seemed very likely that this leopard was the one that was causing the anxiety in the labour lines, and as this had to be dealt with I decided to give it a go.

That afternoon after work some labourers took me to the site on the edge of tea near the river Leesh, about a mile from the bungalow, where I found the cow lying in a small clearing on the edge of the tea. It seemed to have put up a tremendous fight for life, because the ground was cut up and the vegetation trampled over quite a large area, but finally it had lost its battle. It looked rather pathetic lying on its side in the middle of the clearing. It had sustained damage to its throat where the leopard had throttled it, but other than this the carcase was completely unmarked, with the exception of a small area beneath its belly where the leopard had eaten a few pounds of meat. It was possible that killing the animal had exhausted it and if it was given the chance it might return for another meal later, so I thought it might be a good idea to sit up. However it seemed a pity to let all this good food go to waste, so before I made my final decision I suggested to the owner that as the animal had died naturally and not been slaughtered, in order to recoup some of his money why didn't he quietly take it away and butcher it. But he would have none of it. Even though it had died a natural death, it was still a member of the cow family and thus a holy animal, and there would be a riot if any of it was eaten so it had to be left, which was a great shame because it would have fed a lot of people.

There was one reasonably large tree near the kill, so I instructed the men to cut some bamboos from the *bari*. By tying them to its branches about eight feet from the ground, they made a simple *machan* (small platform) on which I could sit and wait. It wouldn't be very comfortable to sit on but it would suffice for one night, and from it I would get a good view of the kill about 10 yards away. Then I left them and went back to the bungalow to get ready, while they stayed by the kill in case the leopard came back early.

After supper I put new batteries in my five-cell torch, which I had taped beneath the barrel of my rifle, and once night fell I adjusted it so that it gave a good beam of light at twenty yards against which my sights were silhouetted. Then I loaded the magazine with new cartridges and was ready. Although days in October were warm like a pleasant summer day in the UK the nights were distinctly cold, and I knew from experience that sitting almost motionless halfway up a tree for several hours could chill you to the bone, so I put on a thick long-sleeved shirt and jumper, together with a pair of slacks which I tucked into some long socks to foil the mosquitoes. Then to shadow the paleness of my face I completed the ensemble by wearing an old slouch hat which had belonged to Wee Mac, and I was ready for anything.

I returned to the kill at 7 pm and to keep disturbance to a minimum, after leaving the car by the roadside I walked the last quarter of a mile as quietly as possible. While I was away the labourers had completed my platform and made a rough ladder for me to climb up to my seat. Once I was comfortable they removed the ladder and walked away. While they did so they talked and made as much noise as possible to give the impression that work was over and everyone had gone home. As I listened to their voices getting fainter in the darkness all I had to do was wait, and this gave me a distinctly uneasy feeling.

I don't recall how long I thought I would have to wait before the leopard made its appearance, but I did think that if it hadn't eaten its fill the night before it would not be too long before it came back to see if a meal was still available. I managed to sit almost motionless with my rifle across my lap for several hours, hardly daring to blink or make any sudden movements in case it had crept up to the edge of the tea and was waiting to see if there was anyone there. Despite my precautions I was almost bitten alive by mosquitoes, and as the hours dragged by my seat became more and more uncomfortable. I became cold, stiff and sore and my back began to ache, until finally at 3 am I decided that the leopard wasn't going to come and I decided to call it a night. First I lowered my rifle down to the ground on a piece of twine I had put in my pocket, then, feeling very stiff and sore, I almost fell down out of the tree. Not worrying about how much noise I made I shuffled back to the car. Relaxing in the driving seat on the way back to the bungalow was absolute heaven. If anyone says they have difficulty in sleeping, all they have to do is sit halfway up a tree on two bamboos for eight hours without moving, and I guarantee that they will sleep like a new-born babe. I know I did.

Three hours later Kancha woke me as normal at 6.30 am with my morning tea. He told me some of the labourers were waiting outside to ask me why I had not been able to shoot the leopard. Wondering what on earth they wanted I got dressed and went out to see them, and what they told me was almost beyond belief. Evidently two of the men had gone out early to see whether I was still up the tree, and they found that most of the body of the cow had been eaten, and only the head, neck, ribs and legs remained. Looking at the leopard's pug marks which had been left, they were convinced that it was the animal we had been after, so they had come to the bungalow to find out why I hadn't shot it. They looked incredulous when I said it hadn't come. I explained that I had waited until 3 am without having the faintest sniff of the leopard, so obviously it had come after I had left.

We decided to go back to the kill site to try to work out from its tracks what had happened, and what we found was absolutely amazing. Whether it had come and watched when the labourers were preparing the machan we could not determine, but we did find a worn patch of jungle about fifty yards from the kill where it had obviously laid up and watched proceedings for quite a long time. This was at a point where the dirt road ran through a cutting in the tea and had a six-foot-high bank on each side. From the clearing in the tea at the top of the bank there was an excellent view of the kill and my bamboo seat silhouetted against the sky. Evidently the crafty devil had known I was sitting in the tree, and had waited patiently on the top of the bank until I got down at 3 am. Then once I had passed by on the road about twelve feet away it jumped down and followed me along the road until I reached the car, and I hadn't realised a thing about it. We traced its pug marks in the dust from where it had landed and then along the road, and in some places they were actually superimposed on my footprints, until its tracks stopped about 50 feet from the car. After that it appeared to have watched me turn the car and drive away, and then, satisfied that it was alone, it turned and walked back up the side of the road until it reached the kill and had its feed.

After seeing the amount of meat it appeared to have eaten I didn't think it would need to eat for a couple of days, so it wouldn't be any use for me to sit up over the remains that night. But Big Mac had much more experience than me. He thought from its actions and cleverness that it must have had some experience of hunters sitting over its kills before, which was why it was so careful. He also said that in his experience a leopard would never turn a free meal down if it was available, especially one it had left, and he thought that provided I played crafty and changed my place of hiding, there was every likelihood that it would come back that night to see if there was anything left.

Because that day, the 23rd, was my birthday, and it was also the weekly film at Mal Club that night, I was rather reluctant to waste another night sitting up a tree, but he recommended that I gave it one more try. After he had seen the size of the pug marks and realised the amount of meat it had eaten, he said it was a large animal. As my .303 Mauser was quite a light rifle, he offered me his large bore hunting rifle to ensure that if I was lucky enough to get a shot at it, it would kill it cleanly and not cause complications. This was a classic Holland and Holland .470 Nitro hunting rifle, hand-made in London and a beautiful weapon which was Donald's pride and joy, and the one with which he had shot the tiger at Dhupguri. It was almost the Rolls Royce of big game rifles and for him to offer it to me was a great honour. As it was my birthday and I thought I would probably never have another chance like it again, I changed my mind.

Back at the kill I instructed the labourers to collect some rubbish to cover the remains in order to stop the vultures from visiting it, then considered what actions I should take do to outwit this clever animal. I thought it would be useless to sit up in the same tree that night as it was obviously aware of that, and the only other vantage point was a group of much smaller trees on the opposite side of the clearing. None of these was large enough to support a platform, and in any case I wanted to keep noise down to a minimum while making my preparations, but the nearest one did have large enough branches to support a chair and I thought I could make that do.

I told the men to spread the word that nobody was to go near the kill that day. After I had checked the garden work and had my breakfast, I took a basket weave easy chair from the veranda and tied it up in the branches of the tree about six feet from the ground. Although I was a little uneasy about being so low, it did give me an excellent sight of the kill about twenty feet away, and as I looked at my handiwork I thought, 'Well boy, at that range you can't miss. If you don't shoot it then it will get you'.

Nobody went near the spot all day. I had an early supper and then, remembering how cold and miserable I had been the night before, I clothed myself in two plaid shirts, two jumpers, long trousers, two pairs of socks and a coat. Then walked quietly along to the kill with two labourers at five o'clock, just before dark. I decided not to take the car because I knew the leopard associated it with me. As silently as possible they helped me up into my seat and handed me up the rifle, spare torch and also a blanket which I hoped would keep me warm and break up my outline. Lastly they gave me a short piece of bamboo and some more string. Once I was sitting comfortably,

I tied the bamboo across the two chair arms in front of me so that I could support the heavy rifle on it while I was waiting. I also thought it would prevent me falling forward out of my seat if I fell asleep. Then the men removed the rubbish from the kill and went off home, leaving me to it.

Darkness fell at 6.15 pm and the hours began to drag by once more. At 7.30 pm I began to think about the other lads arriving at the club to see the Saturday film, and reflected how stupid I was to be sitting cold and weary, halfway up a tree. At one time I almost gave it up as a bad job, but finally decided that as I was going home on leave in 1955 this would probably be the last opportunity I would get to bag a big cat, so I hunched myself down in my blanket to stay to the bitter end.

There was a cold wind blowing off the river, but despite this and all the unusual noises of the night, I was so tired that there were short periods when I dropped off to snooze, only to be jolted awake by some unusual noise nearby.

At about midnight I heard a sudden crashing through the tea, and then something stopped just below my tree and started munching. I knew by the noise it had made that it wasn't the leopard. At first I thought it was a large deer, but I could make out a dark blob in the darkness so I switched on my spare torch, and there looking up at me was an old buffalo which someone had put out into the tea to graze. We looked at each other for a few seconds, and it seemed to be unable to work out what a torch was doing halfway up a tree. Then I threw a bit of dry wood at it and it thundered away.

After that bit of activity it didn't take me long to get drowsy again, and before I knew it I was fast asleep, only to be woken up at 1 am by a tearing sound and the noise of sticks breaking in the tea. At first, as my befuddled brain interpreted the noises,

I thought that someone had come into the tea to steal firewood, but then I was fully awake in an instant. I realised the sound was coming from the kill and that the light-coloured shape I could see in the darkness was the leopard. It had come at last.

Moving very, very slowly, I gradually inched myself upright in my seat and edged the rifle along the bamboo until it was pointing in the leopard's general direction. My arms and body were very cramped, but my heart was beating like a drum as I gradually raised the rifle to the aim, slowly, oh so very slowly, so that it would not be alarmed. I took a couple of deep breaths to steady my nerves before I switched on the torch and there it was, stretched out just like a cat when it is feeding. Almost as though it had no fear it looked up into the beam of the torch straight at me. For several seconds all I could do was stare at it admiring its beauty, then I thought, 'Fool, it you don't put a bullet in him he'll be away and then you'll lose him', so I slipped the safety catch. I could see the whole of its side broadside on. Compensating for the fact that I was firing down on it, I shifted my sights to just behind the top of its shoulder blade and squeezed the trigger.

I had never fired a weapon as powerful as that before, and I was absolutely deafened by the tremendous report. The leopard jumped four feet into the air and twisted as it fell. In fact I had hit it in the right place and my bullet would have finished it, but not wishing to be a stupid hero I put the second barrel through its spine to make sure, and then reloaded.

That was that - my birthday present was all stretched out before me, and I nearly shouted for joy as I climbed down the tree. It was a big female leopard in lovely condition about seven feet six inches long from the end of her nose to the tip of her tail. As I knelt by her side to take a close look she looked so beautiful that I felt regret that I had shot her, but then when I saw her teeth and claws I realised just what a superb killing machine she was and why the labourers feared her when she stalked through the lines at night, and knew that it just had to be. As this sank in I gave thanks for the fact that everything had turned out well for me, and that I had managed to kill her without her suffering. She could have known nothing about it.

I was on a great 'high' after it was all over, for I must have knelt there for several minutes as I wound down, stroking her fur and wondering whether I had done the right thing. The next thing I knew was the sound of voices calling to me from far away asking me if I was all right. Unknown to me, my men had been uneasy at leaving me sitting so close to the ground because the leopard could easily have reached me, so being loyal, instead of going home they had decided to spend the night at the airfield office about half a mile away, just in case I needed help. When they heard my two shots and then silence they knew that either it was all over, or something had happened and I needed help, so they decided to walk up and find me, and the rest was history.

When I heard their voices I shouted back that everything was all right, and there was pandemonium when they realised their old foe was dead. They gathered round discussing her in great detail. I was dog tired and was all for leaving her where she lay until she could be collected the next morning, but they would have none of it and insisted on carrying her back to the bungalow in triumph. There she was laid out in the middle of the garage floor, and as the word went round the lines at three in the morning, a succession of people rose from their beds to come and look at her. On the other hand, after two sleepless nights I was so tired that all I wanted was my bed, so I sloped off and left them to it. When I awoke the next morning there were still labourers coming to see her before they went to the bazaar. The smaller children thought it was a wonderful show. I think they were brought up on warnings about leopards and tigers, and to actually see one of them at close quarters in the flesh was a wonderful thing for them, especially one that was dead.

I didn't sleep very much that night because I think I was too wound up. As the 24th was a Sunday there was no real need for me to get up early, but I rose at the normal time as I was keen to take Donald's rifle back and tell him what had happened. Of course he was overjoyed, and told Ram, his ever-present companion, to take the pickup down to collect the body and bring it back for skinning as soon as possible. I intended to send it down to the renowned Dutch taxidermy company Van Ingen and Van Ingen in Mysore for preservation and conversion into a rug, and Donald recommended that the sooner the pelt was removed and any excess flesh cleaned off, the less likely it would be to deteriorate.

Luckily Ram had had great experience in dealing with Donald's shikar trophies, and in next to no time he and his friends were engaged in the delicate business of removing every bit of the skin, including the eyelids, lips and claws etc, from the carcase in one piece. Once this was done all the blood and dirt was washed from the pelt, and it was laid on a piece of tarpaulin fur side down so that the whole flayed area could be covered with a thick layer of coarse salt to cure it. This had to be rubbed in and the salt layer topped up again each day, in order to stop the skin rotting in the heat and the hair dropping out. This was a process that took several weeks until the temporary cure was complete and it could be sent to Van

Ingens' for the proper job to be done. I wanted the head to be mounted complete on the top of the finished rug, and in order to model it properly Van Ingens' needed the skull as a foundation on which to work, so the head was removed and par-boiled until the meat was fairly soft, and then the top was cut off a large termite mound near the bungalow and the head placed inside. Once the top was replaced the termites were quite happy, and they worked away at this plentiful supply of free food until I re-opened the mound again two weeks later and found it picked as clean as a whistle. Every bit of flesh had gone, including the brain and the tongue, and only the skull and the teeth remained, shining spotlessly white in the sunlight. Those termites did a wonderful job.

For several weeks I tended it regularly until it had cured sufficiently for me to be able to parcel up the pelt and skull and post them to Mysore, with the instructions that I wanted it to be finished as a rug with a red felt surround, and with the head modelled and mounted in the correct position. I had had no dealings with Van Ingens' before, but I knew that they served the highest of the international nobility as well as the Maharajas of India in preserving their shikar trophies, and I felt that no matter how much it cost, MY leopard just had to have the very best.

I was not disappointed. When I got the finished rug back a few months later it looked absolutely superb. The red felt surround brought out the rich colours of her pelt, and even now, 45 years later, when I look at her hanging on our wall, I still get a thrill and remember my 26th birthday.

This should have been the end of the story, but when I got back to the bungalow that evening I had a very emotional experience. In the compound I found a small group of the labourers and their children waiting for me. Their spokesman told me that they had been extremely worried about the leopard and felt so grateful to me for what I had done that in order to express their thanks they had made a collection and brought a gift for me from the bazaar. This turned out to be a chicken, a dozen eggs and a basket of mangoes. As they presented them to me I felt really humble as I realised that what had appeared to me to be just another incident on my path to being a tea planter, to them it was a life and death affair. Had the leopard lived it could well have resulted in a tragedy for some of them, so I am pleased that it had a happy ending.

CHAPTER THIRTY TWO

Repairs, replanting, rest and relaxation

Lionel and Molly Hoadley returned from their Home Furlough on October 28th and after handing over the managership of the garden to Lionel, Donald Mac transferred to Sam Sing Tea Estate on November 1st. It seemed to me that Lionel was not in a very good frame of mind and was not happy to be back, and later I wondered whether the fact that Donald had made a record crop of excellent quality tea and had had a very successful acting had something to do with it. Success is a very hard act to follow, and with me going on my home leave and an unknown assistant coming to take my place, it must have looked to him as though he had a very hard time ahead.

An added complication was the fact that the company had allocated finance in the 1953/54 budget for 17 acres of replanting to be done on Bagracote, which I would be looking after, and as I would be supervising the cold weather overhaul in the factory as well, I would have to move up to the Assistant's bungalow on Bagracote while Ash moved down to Saugaon to replace me. In addition Ash had some annual local leave due to him which he had to take by the end of the year, so for three weeks there would be just Lionel and myself holding the fort, and I don't think he was really looking forward to that.

It was at that time that I had my one and only difference of opinion with Mr Tocher. By our terms of employment we were allowed two weeks' local leave each year, for which we could draw an allowance of Rs 200 provided we left the garden and went somewhere else for a real change of scenery. However because I was quite happy in my work and as there were always so many new things and places to be seen locally, I had never bothered to take any before. I had considered taking my 1954 local leave during September, but because we were working flat out making Donald's record crop he asked me to defer it and take it later when the work eased. Of course I was quite happy to do this, but we both forgot that Ash would have to take his three weeks' leave during the period and I would be involved with the replanting, which meant I would be unable to take mine until January at the earliest.

To me this seemed quite straightforward and I didn't anticipate any trouble, so I wrote a letter to the Superintendent's office with the request that I should be allowed to take my local leave in January after the replanting was finished. His reply was a real bombshell. The answer was a resounding no. Mr Tocher explained that company rules stated that annual leave should be taken in the year it was due and could not be carried over, and even if it had been possible to do so, then it was not permissible to take both annual leave and UK furlough in the same year, so I should have taken my local leave when it was convenient. Now this annoyed me, because I had never taken any local leave before, and the more

I thought about it the more determined I was that I would not give up without a fight. I showed the letter to Lionel and asked him whether he would allow me to take my leave during December. Naturally he said no, because the planting would be in full flow at that time and would continue until mid January, and although he had no objection to me going after it was finished if regulations permitted, that was as far as he would go, so my next step was to have it out with the Superintendent. I had always found him to be a very fair and straight person to deal with. Remembering how he had dealt with Donald I thought the best thing for me to do would be to request an interview with him so that I could put my case personally. Really I didn't mind when I had my leave, December, January or February, but I was determined that I was going to have one at some time, come hell or high water.

I sent my letter off and was very surprised to get a reply the following day, because in order to do so he must have answered it as soon as he got it. I was requested to present myself at his office at 4 pm the following afternoon. During the evening I felt a bit apprehensive as I rehearsed what I intended to say, but I remembered Donald's experience and was determined to speak to him firmly but not aggressively and see what he had to say before planning my next move. However I was quite surprised when his clerk showed me into his office and without any preamble he said, 'Well, what's all this about, Brown? Didn't you understand what I wrote in my letter?' I had not expected the interview to begin like this and it rather took the wind out of my sails, but I quickly gathered my wits about me and replied, 'Oh yes sir, it was perfectly clear, but as far as I am concerned it was not a satisfactory answer. I have never taken a local leave since I joined the company, and so far this year I have been unable to take it because of the pressure of work during Donald Mackenzie's acting. I could take it next month, but here again I can't because of the planting I have been asked to do. Now I did replanting when I was on Zurrantee and would love to do it again, but if this means the temporary transfer of an assistant from another garden for two weeks while I am away, then I am quite happy. Otherwise Mr Hoadley has said that he has no objection if I go away after the work is finished if permission is granted, so under the circumstances I should be grateful if you could reassess the situation and reconsider your decision, sir'.

After I had finished he stayed quiet for a few seconds, then said, 'You seem to be very keen on taking this leave, Brown. Are you thinking of going somewhere special?' Well, at that time I wasn't, so I replied, 'No sir, it is just a matter of principle. I've not taken any leave for three years, but this doesn't appear to make any difference. In order to help Donald make his record crop we were working flat out so he asked me to take it later, which I was quite happy to do. Now I am willing to do the replanting and defer my leave until January in order to help Lionel, but it seems to me that no matter how much I try to help people this doesn't seem to count in my favour and I get left holding the dirty end of the stick, and I'm absolutely sick and fed up with it.'

At hearing this he laughed and with a twinkle in his eyes said 'Well now laddie, you listen to this carefully. It is fine to be considerate to other people, but in this life if you are allowed something by right then take it when it is due, because nobody will think any the better of you if you don't. If you don't take it because you don't want it then that is entirely up to you, but don't be a martyr and then expect to be thanked for doing so afterwards. Regarding the work done during the rains, you did an excellent job in repairing the diesel engine so very well done, but never get the idea that anybody is completely indispensable. I don't think Bagracote would have come to a grinding halt if you had taken a few days' leave at some time. I know Mackenzie can be very persuasive and I was an assistant myself once, but all I can say to you is be fair and straight in dealing with people, but if something is due to you take it, because it's yours, and in most cases once it is gone you won't get it afterwards. So, now what do you say to that?'

I thought for a few moments, then said, 'Thanks very much for pointing things out to me, sir. What you have said has made sense and made me realise that I have been rather naive in some ways, and this made me overestimate my own importance, so I will not be making the same mistake again. Regarding my leave, if company rules do not allow it to be carried over, then I still have enough time to arrange with Mr Hoadley for me to take it in December, and then if I am still needed I can work on the replanting when I return. I think that is all I have to say, sir, other than to thank you for seeing me and putting me straight. We can always live and learn'.

Mr Tocher was a very astute and crafty old character. After hearing this he smiled and said, 'Ah well, now you have learned your lesson, I've got something more to say to you. Although I said in my letter that company rules state that annual leave must be taken in the year in which it is due and cannot be carried over and that is quite true, what I didn't add was that they also say that this can be amended by the Superintendent in some special circumstances when he considers it necessary. Now in my opinion this could be one of those cases, so as Hoadley is only just back from leave and is finding his feet again, at this time and for this time only, I would like you to do the planting and then take your leave once that is completed. Does this meet with your approval?'

This was just what I had wanted, and I now realised that the suggestion had had to come from the Superintendent and not me, as I had got a bit big for my boots and he had had to teach me a lesson. As far as I was concerned I bore him no ill will and agreed straight away with a smile of relief, upon which he said, ' Well, that's decided then laddie, keep up the good work. Now let's go back to the bungalow and see what Nora's got for tea before you go back to Bagracote' and that was that.

I have carried the two lessons I learned that afternoon with me for the rest of my life, and since then I have always tried not to overvalue my own importance, but also I have always made sure that if something is due to me I take it. As he pointed out, nobody loves a martyr.

Two days later Ash and I exchanged bungalows again, and with the last of the high-quality autumnal leaf manufactured we were able to begin the factory overhaul. The 170 men who normally manned the factory were not enough to do the job in the time available, so other reliable garden men were drafted in to work with the more skilled factory staff as labourers and cleaners. They worked in teams of eight to ten men and every machine was numbered and then dismantled and its components laid out in a designated area on the floor, after which they were thoroughly cleaned. When they were ready for inspection I examined them all in company with the Head Engineer, a very jolly Nepalese man named Maila Rai and one of the factory clerks, and we decided which ones could be dealt with by our engineering staff, and then separated the items that would have to be sent away to the Sam Sing Workshops for repair or overhaul.

Once this was done the parts were stamped or painted with identifying numbers and then sent away as quickly as possible, because the workshops dealt with all the work from our gardens in the order in which it was received, so speed was of the essence to ensure that the factory would be completely ready to receive the first of the new season's crop in four months' time. The individual components of all our machines were always kept separate and never mixed up, and as I checked each item I made a list of all the parts that went away, detailing when, where and how they went away, what was being done to them and also a space for when they were returned. Later these notes were typed up into a comprehensive list by the clerk and updated when items were returned, so we always knew exactly what the situation was with any machine and when we needed to apply for a bit of priority if the lack of a certain item was holding up other important work.

Once this work was organised and the operation was running smoothly, I was able to concentrate on the preparations for the replanting. The area where this was to be done was on the edge of the forest boundary in the north-east corner of Bagracote. It had been uprooted and cleared earlier in the year by a tractor-mounted winch while I was on Saugaon, but in order to subdue the rank growth and also put some goodness back into the soil it had been planted with a ground cover crop of nitrogen fixing plants. This had done well, but unfortunately it was now a favourite feeding ground for a herd of wild elephants which roamed in the tract of forest on the hills above. They had become a real nuisance since the beginning of the cold weather as they broke down the barbed-wire fence which demarcated the forest boundary in order to gorge themselves at our expense. They were also very fond of entering a nearby labour line at night in search of any rice, maize or fruit which had been left outside the houses, much to the residents' consternation, and sometimes the men had to sally forth with flaming kerosene torches in order to drive them away. Normally a fence kept them out, but when they were determined to come in the barbed wire made not a scrap of difference, because all they did was push a succession of fencing posts down with their foreheads and in a few minutes several yards of wire fencing were lying on the ground and the elephants were strolling over. It was like trying to stop a brigade of tanks with sticks and knitting wool.

The preparation work was of the utmost importance. All the ground cover and weeds had to be uprooted using a chain flail and a harrow mounted behind the tractor. Then the men were used to carry it away to the edges of the area to be dried so that it could be used as a mulch around the collars of the young tea plants once they were planted to stop the soil around them drying out in the hot sun. Once this was complete, they hoed and cleaned the soil, then moved it to make the surface of the area as flat as possible. While this was being done I used a Dumpy Level and a team of staking men using Gunter's chains to lay out the roads, paths, drains and the boundaries of the blocks of tea over the whole area. Although the Gunter's chain was invented and introduced in 1620 by an English clergyman named Edmund Gunter, long before the development of more sophisticated methods of surveying, it is so simple yet so efficient that it has been used to survey and map plots of land for commercial and legal purposes ever since and is still in regular daily use. Today all over the world the Gunter's chain's most famous legacy is that it gives us an absolutely accurate length for a cricket pitch, and there are very few clubs that do not have at least one in their groundsman's kit.

The Romans were the first to use a unit of long distance named 'mille passum', which literally meant 'one thousand paces' in Latin, and as a Roman army pace was a complete two steps, a 'left-right-left', it denoted a distance of 1000 paces, which equated to about 5000 Roman feet, now estimated to have been about 1600 yards. The English word 'mile' was derived from this and the English Statute Mile was defined by an Act of Parliament in 1592 as being 1760 yards long, consisting of eight furlongs of 220 yards each. In traditional units, the acre measured 4840 sq yards. The Reverend Gunter knew that if 220 is divided by 10 the answer is 22, but he was also clever enough to realise that if you squared 22 yards you finished up with 484 sq yards, and then if you multiplied this by 10 you finished up with 4840 sq. yards, exactly an acre. It was then that he had his brilliant idea. He made a 66-foot-long metal chain which consisted of 100 links, each link being 7.92 inches long, while each group of 10 links was marked off with brass rings to simplify intermediate measurement. On the face of it the dimensions made no sense, but in reality he had combined what appeared to be two incompatible systems, the traditional English land measurements based on the number four and the newly-introduced system of decimals based on the number 10. Gunter's chain allowed either method to be used. An acre measured 4840 sq. yards in traditional units and 10 square chains in his system, so the entire process of land measurement could be computed in decimalised chains and links, and then converted into acres by dividing the results by 10.

In practice, the method of surveying or laying out an area of land was for a surveyor assisted by several chainmen, to place marker poles at significant locations and then measure the distances between them by chaining. A ranging rod, usually a coloured wooden pole, was placed in the ground at the destination point, and starting at the origination point the chain was laid out and stretched taut by using a sighting rod directly in line with the ranging rod. A pin was then put in the ground at the forward end of the chain, and the whole chain was then moved towards the rod and the process repeated until it was finally reached, leaving a dead straight line of pins at chain intervals. The process is surprisingly accurate and requires very little expertise if the land is level and continuous. On a slope the chain had to be levelled by raising or lowering one end of it as needed, so that undulations did not alter the apparent length of the side or the area of the tract. By the 1950s this was accomplished by using a Dumpy Level, a high-powered telescopic sight fitted with cross hairs mounted on a tripod which could be adjusted to get the instrument absolutely level and vertical. This was sighted on a graduated staff held by one of the chainmen. Once the Dumpy was sighted and locked onto the distant ranging rod it was simple to keep it dead in line with it, and by reading the graduations on the sighting rod the height of the chain could be adjusted accordingly. The only disadvantage in using it was that when viewed through the eyepiece the image was inverted. The sighting rod was engraved with inverted figures, so that when viewed through the instrument it was the right way up, even though the person holding it was standing on his head, so once you had got used to this it was quite easy to work out just how much adjustment the chain needed.

Once the main markers had been connected with a series of one-chain squares, it was easy to fill them in with planting stakes which represented the exact spot at which each new seedling would be planted, and over the years this spacing had varied from garden to garden. Before World War II and the arrival of large numbers of military surplus motor vehicles on the estates, most of the freight was carried by buffalo carts and the pluckers worked to a different work pattern. After plucking the leaf for two hours they would carry it back to the factory, where it would be weighed then carried up to the storage sheds, after which they would have some refreshment and then walk back to the plucking area to gather some more leaf before carrying it back again. This was done twice and possibly three times in a day's work, which meant they wasted a lot of good plucking time walking to and from their work areas. However, once mechanised transport became available, roads were built through the tea so that the leaf could be weighed and collected on site at regular intervals, and then it was carried back to the factory without delay so that the leaf was kept as fresh as possible, and all subsequent planting took this into consideration.

Planting out an area of tea was not a haphazard business and to do it successfully required a lot of thought and planning. Normally when the pluckers began work at 7.30 am they started from one edge of a block of tea and each individual was allocated two rows of bushes to pluck, and then he worked his way across it by walking up between them and plucking the bushes on each side. By doing this it was easy for an individual plucker's work to be checked and substandard plucking to be detected. Bearing this in mind the roads were placed so that by 10 am, the normal time for the first field weighment, the pluckers had reached the vicinity of the road and didn't have far to carry their leaf. The other service roads were spaced accordingly. However they had to be planned very carefully because unnecessary roads meant more upkeep, and also reduced the planted area by several lines of bushes, causing loss of crop.

The number of tea plants required to cover an acre of ground varied quite considerably with different types of planting, and this differed from garden to garden, but the general idea was for the bushes to spread reasonably quickly so that they touched the adjacent plants and cut off the light to the jungle beneath. If the bushes were planted close together they filled up the space quickly, but it became more difficult for the labourers to walk between them, and because many more plants were required to cover the area, planting became very much more expensive. On the other hand, planting the bushes further apart meant less plants were needed per acre, and this meant cheaper planting, but it took longer for them to spread out and subdue the jungle, so more money had to be spent on cultivation for several years until they matured.

Most of the tea in our areas had been planted out at either 4x4 feet square planting, which needed 2768 plants per acre, or 5x5 feet triangular which took only 2000 per acre but left terrible gaps if one died. We had decided on the first as it seemed to be the most suitable. However this was one of the last areas to be planted like this in our estates, because the Tea Industry Research Institute in Assam had done experiments on planting patterns and decided that by far the best one was to plant the tea in rows with 2.5 feet between plants and 5 feet between rows. This took 3380 plants per acre, but the initial extra cost of planting was more than compensated for by the speed with which the bushes could be pruned and trained to cover the ground sideways, thus reducing cultivation costs, and the ease with which the labourers could pass along the lines. Subsequently all our estates adopted this pattern of planting as standard procedure.

With my other work as well it took me about two weeks to lay out a skeleton of one-chain squares over the area to be planted, during which time Ash continued to supervise the work on Bagracote while also familiarising himself with Saugaon. Then he left for Calcutta on his three weeks' leave. He had bought himself a Canadian Ford V8 beetle-backed saloon car, and as he intended staying with a friend who lived several miles out of the city he needed it while he was there. Unfortunately the road journey down to Calcutta involved the crossing of several channels of the Ganges on small country ferries. As he didn't want to waste part of his leave by driving it down himself, he arranged with Bandhna, our senior lorry driver, to take some of his annual leave and drive it down for him. He was a member of the Uraon tribe of people whose home villages were situated in the Ranchi area of the state of Bihar, about 300 miles west of Calcutta, but his forefathers had left this homeland and settled in Bagracote when the estate was planted out in the late 1890s. Bandhna himself belonged to a second generation born on Bagracote and had never seen any town larger than Darjeeling, so to visit Calcutta was like an English country boy who had never been away from home before visiting London for the first time. It was quite an experience for him.

Calcutta was about 400 miles away by road, which with the ferry crossings would take three days' driving to complete, so he had decided to take a friend with him. On the morning of their departure the intrepid adventurers loaded their bags and bedding rolls into the back of the car and set off like Captain

Scott setting out to reach the South Pole. It was quite a send off, and I'm pleased to say they completed their journey quite successfully so that Ash found his car waiting for him when he reached Calcutta by air two days later. Of course Ash stayed on, but a few days later Bandhna returned on the train and for weeks afterwards he entertained us all with tales of his adventures in the big city. He was amazed at the size of the place and the crowds of people everywhere. He said that one day he had really blotted his copybook when he was walking along gawping at the sights and bumped straight into a young Bengali girl who was walking to school, causing her to drop all her books and papers, which blew all over the pavement. Normally someone of Bandhna's status in Calcutta would always have been very careful and would have avoided contact with her at all costs, but of course he didn't know any better. He was very surprised that although he offered to help her pick them up she shouted at him and her male school friends chased him along the street until he lost them in the crowds. He said that he had been afraid that if they had caught him they would have killed him. It made quite a lasting impression on him when he compared it with the much more free and easy atmosphere of life on the tea estates.

His most amusing story was about where he had stayed while there. Although Ash had given him money for his food and accommodation, soon after he had arrived he was in a tea shop and overheard two men of about his own age chatting to each other in their common tribal language. As a result he introduced himself and it turned out that one of the men had originated in a small village just a few miles from where Bandhna's grandfather had been born, and although his family still lived there he had moved to Calcutta to find work. He seemed delighted that he had found another local in Calcutta, and they got on so well together that he invited Bandhna to stay with him while he was there. He said the man lived and cooked in a small room in a big house, and as there wasn't enough room to sleep in there as well he slept in his 'work room', which he said he used to carry Sahibs all over the house. This sounded very odd, but some more questions revealed that his friend was talking about a lift. He was night duty lift attendant in a large block of flats. His shift began at 7 pm and lasted until 7 am and he operated the lift all the evening as the residents came and went until about 11 pm when they were all accounted for. Then as a system of night security he got out his bedding roll and slept on the floor of the lift until the morning, when the day man arrived. This seemed to be such a common arrangement in blocks of flats in India that it must have been very successful.

Of course, not knowing that things like lifts existed in the world, Bandhna was absolutely enthralled with this little magic room which seemed to have a mind of its own and wandered about the flats without any visible effort. He said it was just like a 'jadhu ghar,' a magician's house, because you got in at one place and shut the door and a few seconds later you opened it again and were somewhere else, like a Calcutta-style Tardis before its time. During the evening when passengers were few his friend took him for many trips up and down the 16 floors, opening the doors and exploring at each stop. It left such a lasting impression on him that it was the highlight of his trip.

While Ash was away, Lionel dealt with the managerial office work as well as all the cold weather work on Bagracote, while I had to supervise Saugaon as well as keeping an eye on developments in the factory and the work on the replanting area, so we didn't see very much of each other for almost three weeks. The arrangement was that once Ash had returned he would take over Saugaon again while I concentrated on the factory and the preparations for the replanting, and from the planting I had supervised on Zurrantee in 1951/52 I knew that only the best and most conscientious labourers should be used. Experience had proved that it was better to plant a small area properly so that the plants lived, rather than scamp the work and cover a large area quickly and then have to repeat the work and infill the vacancies when the plants died. On the other hand there was only a certain time window during which this work could be done, so I decided that I would try to plant about two thirds of an acre per day. The basic daily task for this was 50 plants per planter, but in order to plant the 1846 seedlings needed to accomplish this I needed 200 of our most reliable labourers and supervisors, plus two tea women and two boys each day. This force was made up of 38 teams of three men and two women, each of whom planted out 50 perfect seedlings as their daily task. One man was responsible for cutting out the plants, while the second dug the 50 holes in which they were to be planted by the third man. The seedlings were carried from the seed beds by one of the women, while the other carried large jars of water on her head to water the plants in and then applied the mulch around their collars so that the soil didn't dry out, so in order to foster a good team spirit one of the men was appointed Team Leader and then he recruited his own four co-workers from his family and friends, so that if a member was unable to work one day for any reason then he could bring his own suitable replacement.

Because the mornings were very chilly and the 'digging out' men got very cramped and cold squatting in a two-foot-deep hole, the two extra women kept them very well supplied with copious amounts of hot tea at any time they required it, and because I supplied some sugar to sweeten it instead of adding the normal salt to it, it proved to be a very popular 'perk' with all the workers. And what were the two boys needed for? Well their job was to carry baskets full of chemical fertiliser from bags in the back of the pickup truck to the planting area, and then mix 2 oz per plant with the soil excavated from the planting holes before it was used to plant the seedlings and this gave them a good start in life. Then once they had done this they gathered up all the discarded marker stakes and tied them up in bundles of a hundred so that they could be used again when required.

By the time Ash returned I had all my workers selected and everything was ready to begin the work. In order to take advantage of the cool of the early morning the 'taking out' men reached the seed beds by first light, and by the time the planters arrived with the women at about 6.30 the holing men had fifteen or twenty holes dug. One year old plants had tap roots about 18 inches long with a very compact root system, so it was imperative that the earth surrounding them was cut away on three sides as well as beneath the end of the root so that when the long extracting knife was sliced down behind it and then levered forward it came out cleanly into a long, curved tray into which it fitted snugly and was then carried to the hole by the woman. Any sub-standard plants, as well as any that were dropped or damaged while being dug out or carried to the planting area, were thrown away and had to be replaced, so great care was taken to ensure that only the very best plants were used and the team spirit ensured that they all worked together and maintained the highest standard of work.

The holing men dug their holes with long, narrow-bladed hoes, exactly on the spot where the stakes had been, and when one was deep enough, the plant was brought on its tray and placed in the hole so that the top of the earth *dela* which covered the roots was exactly level with the surface of the earth and roughly in the correct place. Then supervisors sighted along the lines of planted tea from three different directions and its position was adjusted until it was in its exact spot, after which the planting man firmed it in with large bamboo tamping poles about six inches in diameter until it was firmly planted and could be watered and mulched. This continued until about 11 am, when the planted area had been transformed from what had been an untidy patch of weed-covered soil into a beautifully clean and tidy area covered with straight lines of tea plants with not a weed in sight. There was no doubt that these plains labourers were born agriculturalists and took a real pride in their work, so with the additional bonus of being able to complete their day's work by mid morning and having the rest of the day off, there was never a shortage of volunteers if required and by carefully checking the work as it progressed we could always ensure that we had the best men that were available at the time.

As a result of this the work went according to plan. Just before Christmas we completed almost 20 acres and the whole area looked superb. Because it had gone so well I thought the labourers deserved our thanks, so on the last morning I arranged for some *haria* and *darhu* from the local liquor shop to be brought, together with some biscuits that I supplied, and after pouring a glassful onto the roots of the last plants so that they realised why we were celebrating, everybody gathered round a fire we had made from all the rubbish and had a celebration, and they thoroughly enjoyed it. I don't think that they had ever had an 'end of planting party' like that before and it was talked about for weeks afterwards.

CHAPTER THIRTY THREE

Local leave I -
the Land of the Moguls

Once the replanting was finished I was free to take my local leave, but the trouble was that despite the front I had presented in the Superintendent's office, I still had nothing planned and nowhere to go. Because the tribal people in the area around Shillong in Assam were still very pro-British, many of the Assistants went there for their leaves, and indeed some of them married the local Khasi girls. However because my home leave was imminent this didn't interest me, and as Calcutta left much to be desired I was at a complete loss as to what to do.

Historically I had always been very interested in the Mogul emperors and anything that remained of the Indian Mutiny, but I knew that the cost of spending two weeks in Delhi plus the return air fares was completely outside my budget. On the other hand I realised that after the episode in the Superintendent's office, if I didn't take my leave it would be frowned on in high places. I couldn't see any way out until a few days later when Ash invited me down for supper and drinks with some of his friends. These were Indian Assistants from neighbouring gardens whom I knew well. During the evening we chatted about my leave plans and my thoughts of visiting Delhi that weren't likely to mature.

As we talked several schemes were proposed but discarded, mainly for financial reasons, until one of them said, 'Well, I've got an idea, why don't take your car and drive up there? My parents live quite near Delhi and although they are not there at the moment, they do have a small guest bungalow in the garden that they allow friends and guests to use, and I am sure that they would allow you to use it if I arranged it with them. Other than the cost of some food stuffs and some pay and *baksheesh* for the servants it would cost you nothing to stay, so all you would have to find would be your own food and with your own car you could come and go as you please. The round journey would be about 2000 miles for which you would need some 80 gallons of petrol, but Ash says that you have a lot of aviation fuel left from the Jamair crash, so you would be able to take forty gallons with you and only have to buy enough to get back. How does that sound to you?'

Well at that point I didn't know quite what to think, as the size and complexity of the journey rather overawed me, but as we sat and talked it over the plan seemed to fall into place. I realised that if my friend could obtain permission from his parents for me to stay, I could see much more of the real India than I ever would have done if I had flown down to Calcutta. I'm sure the old Vanguard would never have made the journey, but now that I had the Consul in good condition and as I loved driving I had no fear of the distance.

The main complication was time. The Grand Trunk Road from Calcutta to Delhi ran on the south side of the Ganges, and for me to join it the car would have to be ferried across the Ganges on a country ferry boat. This entailed a 100-mile journey upriver from Manihari to Bhagalpur, and as the country boats didn't possess engines, they were either 'punted' with 18-foot-long bamboo poles or pulled by the crew with ropes at about 3 miles per hour. Unfortunately, below Bhagalpur the river widened out and became studded with quite large sandbanks on which the boat could easily go aground, so they would have their work cut out to pole and steer it up what they knew to be the safe deep channels. Luckily I would be travelling at the easiest time of the year, when the river was at its lowest and the prevailing wind was blowing upstream, but because they were unable to move during the hours of darkness and had to anchor in midstream to avoid being attacked by local dacoits, I would have to sleep the night in the car, while the crossing would take two complete days to cover with a second night at the end of it and a further 800 miles to Delhi.

Fortunately the main railway line from Assam to Delhi ran along the north bank of the river until it crossed a bridge and reached a small town named Mokama on the south side, from where it was straightforward to reach the Grand Trunk Road. I remembered how Ash had sent his car on ahead to Calcutta.

I thought that if I could persuade Bandhna to start off three days before I began my leave, he could drive the Consul down to Manihari, ferry it up to Bhagalpur and then drive up to Mokama, where he could wait for me at the station. Then three days later I would be able to take the evening train from Siliguri and arrive in Mokama in the morning, where the car should be waiting for me. Then I could begin my leave well on the way while Bandhna could go back on the train.

These suggestions seemed to be the answer to my dilemma,

so hoping that I would hear from Madhan in due course I decided to make some preparatory arrangements. Regarding Bandhna, I don't know whether his trip to Calcutta had opened his eyes to the wider world outside the tea areas, but once I mentioned it to him he was very keen to have another jaunt away from the garden, so a lengthy ferry passage up the Mother Ganges represented another challenge which he was only too willing to accept, especially as he was being paid to do it. He was by far the best driver on Bagracote. He rarely drank liquor, and as he had managed to find his way around Calcutta without any difficulty, I had no worries about his being able to drive the car to Mokama Station, so I told him to ready himself. I also arranged for Kancha and a friend of his to accompany me, partly for company and partly in case of any emergencies along the way.

It took a week for Madhan to confirm that his parents would be delighted if I would use their guest house while they were away. Once I received his message I decided to leave as soon as possible, and although my two weeks' local leave officially began on the Monday, Lionel said that I could have the previous Saturday off as casual leave, so I booked our tickets for the evening train from Mal Station on Friday evening January 21st, which would get us into Mokama at about 6 am the following morning. Then all that remained for me to do was to pack the car with everything we would need for the journey, so that it would be ready for Bandhna to begin his journey on Tuesday, January 18th. This was not quite as simple as it would appear, because in addition to the four ten-gallon petrol cans, I had to carry blankets in case we had to sleep in the car, bedding rolls, two four-gallon cans of drinking water, a first aid kit, a can of engine oil and a comprehensive tool kit, some spare parts for the engine, some emergency food items and cooking utensils, and our clothes. Luckily at this time of year rain was unlikely, so our clothes were mainly T-shirts and shorts, with some underclothes, socks and plimsolls, but we did take a spare jumper, a pair of slacks and a warm coat to wear in the cool of the evening. As for anything else we needed, we would have to buy this along the way. The one good thing was that with only three passengers in the car there was plenty of room on the spare back seat for everything we needed, so I had no difficulty in having the car ready for departure on the 18th morning.

It was only about 200 miles from Bagracote to the *Ghat* (ferry point) at Manihari in Bihar. Once I had given Bandhna his expenses money and a letter of authority which certified that I was the owner of the car and he had my permission to drive it outside the State of West Bengal, I was confident when they left at 9 am that they would arrive there well before nightfall. This would enable him to arrange for the ferry passage that night and set sail the next morning. Then, because of the twists and turns in the course of the Ganges, it was about 100 miles to Bhagalpur, so they would have two full days to complete this and still reach Mokama by Saturday morning. However if things went wrong and they didn't make it, I would just have to wait there until he arrived.

Without my car the next three days seemed to crawl by, but finally Friday evening arrived and Ash drove us up to Mal station. The Delhi Express was two hours late when it finally arrived, but it must have made up time on the journey, because we were only a few minutes late when we arrived at Mokama at 6 am after a sleepless night. We found a grinning Bandhna waiting on the platform to welcome us and the Consul safe and sound in the car park. Evidently the ferry trip had taken two and a half days owing to contrary winds and the presence of several large sandbanks which had been exposed by the low water level, so they had had to spend the two nights anchored in mid stream, but the subsequent road trip from Bhagalpur to Mokama had been without incident, and they had spent the remainder of the night sleeping in the car. Knowing I would have to do the same ferry trip on my return journey I had instructed Bandhna to ask the boatman about it, and he confirmed that as we would be travelling downstream on the current, we would only have to anchor for one night and should reach Manihari at about noon the next day. With this information I knew that if I was back at Bhagalpur by the Friday night, I could be back on Bagracote on Sunday evening ready to begin work on Monday, so all would be well. Now all I had to do was make sure that Bandhna and his friend had everything they needed to get home, and I could be away to enjoy my holiday.

While I was planning it I had studied a detailed map of India for the first time, and realised that the Grand Trunk Road crossed the Ganges at Banares (now Vanarasi) and then ran onward in a roundabout route through Allahabad, Kanpur and Agra to Delhi. However the most direct route was by another main road that branched off and then ran north-westerly straight to Delhi via Lucknow. With my interest in the Mutiny, for some reason the siege of the Residency in Lucknow in 1857 and its subsequent relief and evacuation by Sir Colin Campbell had always held a fascination for me, so there was no way that I was going to pass it by without making an effort to visit the site if I could help it. Lucknow was about 420 miles from Mokama and more than halfway to Delhi, so

I decided to try to reach it that evening and spend the night in a hotel, then use the following morning to visit the ruins of the Residency in the Old Town before attempting to reach Delhi by Sunday evening.

Once I had ensured that all was well with Bandhna I was away. The 190 miles of first-class main road from Mokama to where it joined the Grand Trunk Road was very narrow, and because of its close proximity to the river, in many places it was covered with a thick blanket of red dust and sand which made visibility quite difficult, so I was quite relieved when we finally reached the junction. From there it was only another 50 miles to Banares. Despite the fact that there was very much more traffic on it, especially lorries, we made good progress, and after we had crossed the Ganges on another steel girder bridge which looked as though some lad had made it out of his Meccano set, we reached the city at lunchtime. From the bridge I got a very clear view of the flights of steps leading down to the water's edge which were used for ceremonial bathing, but they held very little interest for me and as the city seemed very crowded and dirty I decided to press on to Lucknow without stopping. In fact it was a very good thing I did, because although I had only another 200 miles to cover, owing to the fact that there was much more traffic on the road and also because I had to drive directly into the dazzle of a very bright, low setting sun for over an hour, the journey took much longer than it should have done. Actually driving on that road was quite a hair-raising experience, but also very amusing at times, because there were far more lorries than cars and many of them had slogans such as 'GOD HELP CAR DRIVER', 'I AM KING OF THE ROAD, GIVE WAY' and the very cheery 'IF I HIT YOU, I KILL YOU' painted on fascia boards mounted above their wind screens. There was also a great number of camels wandering about, the first that I had seen in India, and what with these, herds of goats, buffalo carts, cycle rickshaws and thousands of pedestrians, progress was necessarily slow.

It was past 7 pm and I was dog tired when I reached Lucknow and found a small, inexpensive hotel which was suitable both for myself and servants. Although it wasn't the Lucknow Hilton, it was reasonably furnished and clean and the bed was comfortable, although the toilet facilities, which were housed in a separate building, left a lot to be desired. However, it was only for one night and as the food was quite simple but well cooked and I had plenty of Bagracote water to drink, I had a good curry dinner and then slept like a log. The main drawback in an establishment like that was that the locals were up and about soon after dawn, so by 7 am I was up, washed and dressed and ready to discover what Lucknow had to offer. After a so-called 'English' breakfast of papaya, two boiled eggs, toast and mango jam, I packed my bedding and toiletries in the car and set off.

The hotelier had given me instructions on how to reach the ruins of the Residency, which consisted of a group of buildings built in 1800 AD by the Nawab of Oudh to serve as the residence of the British Resident General, who represented the British authorities in his court. During the next 46 years nothing very much happened to disturb the tranquillity of the cluster of red brick buildings, but when the Indian Mutiny broke out in 1857 things changed. In 1856, after the princely state of Oudh was annexed by the East India Company, the first British Commissioner to be appointed proved to be so inefficient that he was soon replaced by Sir Henry Lawrence, a man who knew and loved India from top to bottom. He was appointed as the new Governor in March 1857, and with his knowledge of India and his experience as an administrator, when the Indian soldiers in Meerut broke out into open rebellion on May 10th he realised that the situation was critical. He began to fortify the Residency buildings and lay in supplies of food and water in case of a siege. This began in earnest on June 30th, by which time there were almost 3000 persons inside it, consisting of 855 British Army officers and men, 712 loyal Indian sepoys, 153 civilian volunteers and 1280 non combatants, mainly women and children who had sought refuge from the carnage outside. History records that some of the ladies brought large quantities of furniture and other valuables with them which they didn't want to lose if there was any trouble, and they were very irate when Sir Henry commandeered anything that would stop a bullet in order to use it to reinforce the defences.

With the mutineers bombarding the buildings with cannons and their windows and doors blocked and being used as firing points by the defenders, it was too dangerous for the rooms to be used by the refugees, so they had to make their living quarters in the cellars beneath the Residency, or what was left of the stables and outbuildings. As a result, whenever the bombardments and attacks began, all the wounded and non-combatants took refuge in the dark, damp cellars, where life went on in clouds of dust illuminated only by the flickering of a few candles. Women who had not done a thing for themselves for years now found themselves in the stifling heat occupied constantly with the chores of washing clothes, cooking, cleaning, and looking after their children and tending the sick. Many of them died of malnutrition, cholera, smallpox and dysentery and whole families were wiped out. Usually the husband died first, shot down in the defences, then the exhausted wife and finally the orphaned children. As a result of this conditions became very primitive and corpses could not be disposed of properly.

On November 27th after 150 days of siege, General Sir Colin Campbell's Relief Column managed to fight its way through to the Residency and succeeded to withdraw successfully with all the survivors, but more than 2500 soldiers and civilians had perished. These included Sir Henry Lawrence, who died from disease a few days before the relieving force arrived. After the Mutiny ended, his body, together with those of many of the others, were interred in the burial ground of a nearby Christian church, the ruins of which are still in existence, together with a memorial to the siege and Lawrence himself.

After the end of the Mutiny the ruins of the Residency and its associated buildings were maintained and preserved as they had been at the time of the final relief. The shattered walls are still scarred by cannon shot and bullets, but since Indian Independence they have been surrounded by lawns and flowerbeds and have become a tourist attraction. Standing in the early morning sunshine it was hard for me to imagine the sufferings and heartaches that had been experienced there 98 years before. However when I wandered through the gloom and damp of the old cellars a very strong feeling of deep depression came over me, as though the very bricks had been imbued with all the pain and suffering experienced there during the months of fighting.

Although I knew I had another very long drive to Delhi ahead of me that afternoon, I was very reluctant to tear myself away, so it was 2.30 pm by the time I took to the road once more. It was 350 miles to Delhi, but luckily the highway was in much better condition and considerably less crowded than those south of the Ganges and despite the fact that I was chasing a very low, dazzling setting sun again for a long period, I was able to maintain a very good average speed and reach the outskirts at about 9.30 pm.

Ancient Indian history records that it is possible that centres of civilisation existed all down the valley of the Jumna river from 300 BC Onward. The first city named Delhi was originally a large fortified area built by the Hindu Emperor Pritvi Raj on the west bank of the River Jumna in the 12th Century AD, but his army was defeated by Turkish Mohammedan invaders in 1192 AD and subsequently the city was gradually abandoned and fell into disrepair until today there is very little left. The only parts left intact of the remains of the first Delhi are the Qutab Mosque and the Qutab Minar tower.

To replace it, a second city, also named Delhi, was built nearby in 1303 AD. Since then another six cities have been destroyed and rebuilt over the extended site, so New Delhi is the eighth city to bear the name. The seventh city, now named Old Delhi, was built between 1633 and 1658 by the Mogul Emperor Shah Jahan of Taj Mahal fame. Subsequently its walls and fortifications were restored and strengthened by the East India Company and are still in good condition. New Delhi, now the capital city of India, was built to the south of the old town and designed by English architect Sir Edwin Lutyens to replace Calcutta as the seat of British Government in 1912. Officially inaugurated in 1931, it grew rapidly and is now India's largest commercial and communications centre.

As a result of the centuries of building and the demise of

the previous six cities, the remains are now a mass of ruins scattered all over the plain and nobody seemed to take any notice of them. Madhan's parental home was built on one of many large rectangular plots of land situated on the outskirts of the old city. These had many ancient tombs, memorials and other historical ruins scattered about in them, which seemed to be absorbed into the scenery. The buildings and walls were all made of red bricks, presumably manufactured from the local red clay, and the whole area was covered with a thick film of red dust. Fortunately Madhan had given me a map of the area, so I had no difficulty in locating the house. When we finally arrived there I was relieved and very happy to find that the bearer and cook were waiting for me in a small but very comfortable bungalow just inside the main gate of the compound. They gave us a tremendous welcome and had a delicious curry waiting for me.

The guest bungalow consisted of a small sitting room, two large, well-equipped bedrooms, a toilet, a shower room and a basic kitchen in which the bearer said they would prepare any meals for me when I needed them. He also said that that he had been told that I would be coming and going sightseeing, but as the main house would be empty while I was there, one of them would always be on duty in the bungalow whenever I came back, even if it was late at night. Regarding the size of the living room compared to the bedrooms, I was rather puzzled until he told me that normally when visitors came they spent the whole of the day up in the main house as guests and only used the bedrooms at night, hence there was no need for a large living room, and of course then it made sense.

Once I had eaten my supper and showered I went to bed. As I had had no proper sleep since the previous Thursday night

I slept like a log until morning, but I was still so tired that I decided not to begin my sightseeing until the next day. There was one thing I needed to do on Monday and this was to get some money from the bank, but as it happened this turned out to be much more tiring than any sightseeing would ever have been. In 1951 I had opened a bank account with Messrs. Grindlays' Bank in Calcutta and through them I was able to transfer money home to Lloyds' branch in Dursley. However internal transactions in India were not as simple then as they are nowadays. Most banks and establishments would not accept cheques from strangers or supply cash unless the necessary arrangements had been made beforehand. Accordingly I had written to the Manager and instructed him to make arrangements for me to withdraw cash from their Delhi Branch during my holiday On the Monday morning I looked up its address from the directory in the guesthouse, checked its position on the map of Delhi that I had bought - and proceeded to get hopelessly lost. Either the map was totally out of date or the mapmakers hadn't bothered to include anything they considered unimportant, because it was late morning before I arrived at the Bank and it was with a sigh of relief that I hurried inside. Here the clerks were very helpful, but were very reluctant to give me any cash until finally I tired of being played with and asked to see the Head Clerk. After a while an extremely tall and thin individual wearing gold-rimmed spectacles made his appearance. He told me that despite my assurances that arrangements had been made, he was absolutely certain that they had no record of any correspondence arriving from Calcutta, and although he did not doubt my veracity and would like to help me, the bank policy was that until they had made contact with them and received permission to pay me the cash I would have to wait, 'possibly one or two days, sir'.

Well I hadn't carried very much cash with me on the journey deliberately and knew that this delay would make things very difficult, so not willing to give up without a struggle I took out my letter from Calcutta and gave it to him. Slowly he read it through, silently mouthing the words to himself as he did so, until suddenly he gave a triumphant laugh which sounded like a horse neighing and said, 'Ah, here it is, as plain as a pikestaff and the nose on my face. You sir have made one disastrous mistake! You instructed them to send cash to Delhi Branch, but this is not it. This is NEW Delhi Branch where we look after the gentlemen. The Delhi Branch where the others keep their money is in Chandni Chowk Street in OLD Delhi, and it is there that you told them to send your money. Oh yes indeed sir, your money is here, but it is there, and it is there that you will find it.' He neighed again as though he had told me the joke of the year.

Well I wasn't very happy about this, but I knew that the worst thing I could do was show it or lose my temper, so I asked him how far it was and also if he would be good enough to draw me a map of how to get there. 'Oh yes indeed sir,'he replied. 'It is about five miles by fast car and my maps are noted for their authenticity so I will draw one for you immediately.' Hearing this I didn't bother to ask him how far it was by a slow car, but thanked him and waited patiently while he drew a very artistic map coloured in with red and green ink. With it I had no difficulty in finding Chandni Chowk Street.

Unfortunately he had made one basic mistake. Chandni Chowk actually means 'Silver Bazaar' and it is a street nearly a mile long in the Bazaar area of Old Delhi that is the centre of the Indian silver and gold trade. It is renowned for the quality of its Indian jewellery and is lined with silver and gold manufacturing workshops and shops, as well as being the home of some of the secure vaults where many of the local people keep their family valuables safe until they are needed for a marriage or other celebration. The actual street is some 20 yards wide, but because hundreds of small shopkeepers have set up their market stalls in it the actual vehicular road is only a few yards wide. When I arrived there I found that this narrow passage was a flood of vehicles, animals and people, with buffalo and camel carts, Brahma bulls, cycle rickshaws, motor cycles and thousands of pedestrians all flowing down the street like a slow-moving river of humanity. I had seen crowded streets before in Calcutta, but I had never experienced anything like this.

For a few moments I pulled up and gazed at it in wonder, but then I realised that if I didn't fight my way through it then I wouldn't get my cash, so I edged the car in and with my horn blaring gradually forced my way up the street until I found my way blocked by a very smart young police constable who flagged me down and motioned for me to get out. Judging the Delhi police force to be something like our local one in Matelli Bazaar, I knew that very few of them spoke any English, so I said to him in my best Hindi, *'Salaam Constable, Apko kya chahie?'*, (Greetings, Constable. What do you want?) to which he replied in faultless English, 'Good morning sir, what do you think you are doing? Didn't you see the notice?'

At this I was taken aback. I told him that I hadn't seen any notice at all and asked him what it had said, to which he replied, 'It said that this is a one way street and you are driving the wrong way up it. What are you going to do about it?' To say that I was surprised was an understatement, but immediately he said this to me I realised why there had been so much traffic coming towards me and why I had received so many dirty looks from the locals. To this day I am unable to understand why I didn't realise that mine was the only car fighting against the flood.

Thinking quickly, I realised that the best thing to do was to plead ignorance and apologise profusely, so speaking in English I told him that I was a complete stranger who had never visited Delhi before, but I was very sorry for breaking the law and if he would let me off this time I would turn around and drive back down to the exit. Then I would find my way up to the entrance and come back down the proper way. At this he looked at my number plate and asked, 'And what is a car registered in Darjeeling, West Bengal, doing driving the wrong way up the Chandni Chowk in Delhi?'

I told him about my holiday, of the mix-up with my money and how I was trying to reach the bank and then how the bank clerk had drawn his 'authentic' map for me and how he had omitted to tell me about the one-way street. This delighted him. 'Aha, those money chaps. They think they know everything but in fact they know nothing' he chortled. 'If you had asked him about a one-way street he would probably have said that we don't have such things in India!'

Then he told me that the white-painted building about 100 yards further on up the street was the bank and that as I was a visitor, if I drove carefully on and then entered into the official car park then he would say nothing more. However, I was to make sure that when I left to go home I was to drive carefully DOWN the street as he would not let me off the next time. I thought what a nice policeman he was, so I complimented him on his mastery of the English language and chatted with him for a while, then thanked him again and drove on.

Now I knew what I was doing it didn't take me long to reach the bank. When I did so I realised that stopping a car as he had done must have been something of a landmark for him, because although it had quite a large parking area which must have dated back to the days when the bank catered for 'gentlemen' there were only two cars in there, both of which looked as though they belonged to the senior bank staff, and most of the customers were arriving on foot or riding in cycle rickshaws. Because I was there on bank business parking was not a problem.

Once I had my money I was able to leave the car and explore the Chowk on foot, and what an experience that was. It was an absolute mass of gold, silver and jewellery shops all crammed in with very little space between them. As they all looked similar it wasn't long before I lost my bearings, so it was quite a while before I could find my way out. I suppose in a way this was a form of protection against robbers and thieves, because no stranger could have run out of there without losing his way, so the locals could have picked him up in next to no time. When I tired of fighting the crowds and decided to call it a day, I had not been able to see a half of it.

CHAPTER THIRTY FOUR

Local leave II - sight-seeing in Delhi

While I was wandering I found a shop which sold maps and guide books and was able to buy several tourist guides for the Delhi and Agra districts, so the next morning I decided to plan my tourist itinerary. In order to make sure I was back on Bagracote on the Sunday, I knew it would be essential to start the return journey on the second Thursday morning, which allowed me nine clear days to see the sights. Although there were enough in Delhi alone to occupy this time, I decided that there were three things outside the Delhi area that I must see while I had the chance. These were the Taj Mahal, the town and palace of the Jat Maharaja of Bharatpur, and the deserted city of Fatehpur Sikri, all of which were about 130 miles away near Agra. In all probability it seemed that I would be able to combine visits to the first two in a single day, but Fatehpur Sikri was so huge that it needed a full day's tour on its own, so I decided to space them out in the middle of my stay and visit the local sights in between, beginning with oldest first.

Nowadays both the Iron Pillar and the Qutab Minar stand

only a few hundred yards apart in the UNESCO Qutab World Heritage Site and are surrounded by several other ancient and medieval ruins collectively known as the Qutab Complex. This is in what had been the heart of the first Delhi, about 11 miles south west of the present city, so the next morning I decided to pay them a visit and it was not long before I could see the Minar towering high above the horizon several miles away. The Iron Pillar is an old Hindu relic dating back to the 4th Century AD which stands in the ruins of an old temple. It is a solid metal shaft which is mainly made of iron some 30 feet high, and tapers from 16 inches in diameter at the base to 12 inches in diameter at the top, and there is another three feet buried in the ground where it terminates in a large knob that is firmly fixed by eight strong iron bars attached to massive stone blocks. According to the guide books it weighs approximately six tons, but the strange thing is that although it is supposed to be made of pure iron it has not rusted and its surface is still as smooth and polished as it was when it was forged. It is said that in 1738 an invading general named Nadir Shah was so fascinated by the pillar that he tried to dig it out to take it away as a victory trophy but was unsuccessful. Not pleased with having his plans thwarted he fired a cannon ball at it in an attempt to knock it down, but it just bounced off, leaving a small depression which can still be seen. Finally he gave up in disgust.

Compared to the simplicity of the Pillar, the Qutab Minar Tower is truly magnificent as it soars to a height of 238 feet above its plinth and is built in five sections. Indian historians still differ as to whether the first storey was built to a height of 95 feet by Prithvi Raj Chauhan, the last Hindu ruler of Delhi, to enable his wife to see the sacred river Jumna as part of her worship each day without actually visiting it, or whether it was actually begun by his successor, Qutab-ud-Din Aibak, as a memorial tower to commemorate his victory over him. Then after his death the other four sections were added by two subsequent rulers between the years 1210 and 1280 AD together with a 13-foot-high cupola, which was thrown down by an earthquake in 1803. The tower itself was also damaged and was repaired, but as a result it has a lean of 25 inches to the south west which is considered to be 'satisfactory', for which I was quite glad when I was at the top.

From my guide books it seems they can't even agree whether it was actually named after Qutab –ud-Din Aibak or whether it was in honour of a much-venerated saint who came to live in Delhi later, named Qutab–ud-Din Bakhtiar Kaki, but whoever built it or where its name came from seemed immaterial to me when I saw this graceful tower soaring up into the cloudless blue sky. Built of fluted red sandstone and white marble, with its ground floor plan in the shape of a lotus flower, it is 47 feet in diameter at the base and tapers down to nine feet in diameter at the top. This is reached by a circular staircase of 379 stone steps, and from the viewing platform a breathtaking view of several miles across the city to the river and plains beyond is obtained. The five storeys are separated from each other by ornate balconies which are reached from the stairs. When I visited it there were so few visitors that I climbed to the top with no difficulty and spent almost an hour up there completely alone, taking in the marvellous view.

As tourism became more popular and the sightseeing crowds grew larger it became almost impossible for the two streams of people, one upstairs and one down to pass each other on the narrow stairs or see anything from the top, until finally jams began to occur and some people became overcome by the heat and stress or were accidentally injured. Added to this was the fact that because the top was only guarded by a simple iron rail which was easy to scale, it became a convenient way of escape for people who wished to end their lives, so later I was not surprised when I heard that casual entry had been banned and the tower could only be accessed by prior appointment. In view of this I feel that I was very fortunate and privileged to have been able to visit it at that time, and it is an experience I shall never forget. Standing on the top I was so high up, with only the sigh of the breeze through the railings as company, that it felt as if I was in another world, and as I watched the human ants scurrying about on the ground 238 feet beneath me, I thought it was almost as though I was the Greek God Zeus standing on Mount Olympus, while he watched mankind struggling on the Earth below, as portrayed in Greek mythology. It was an absolutely wonderful feeling.

A few hundred yards north of the Qutab Minar is Ala-ud-Din's Minar, a tower that was begun in 1311 AD by another ruler, Ala-ud-Din Khiliji, who must have been very vain. He considered that as he was twice as great a ruler as Qutab-ud-Din Aibak, his tower would be twice the size of the Qutab Minar. The first storey had a diameter of about 90 feet and should have reached a height of 200 feet when completed, but it had only reached a height of 87 feet when he died in 1315 AD and it was never completed. Standing alongside the gigantic stump one realises what a tremendous undertaking it would have been to build the whole thing up to a total height of nearly 500 feet with only bamboo scaffolding and human labour, and with no powered machines to raise the blocks to the top. I think he must have been 'power crazy,' so maybe it was a good thing he died when he did!

By the time I had visited the tower it was time to call it a day. Tired but happy, I returned to the Guest House, where I found the two servants waiting for me as promised. They had told me that they didn't mind cooking and looking after me, because during the periods when the family was away and the house deserted, the security duties were shared by them with an additional night watchman accompanied by a terrifying pie dog, who always stayed awake from 10 pm until 7 am the next morning. In actual fact I think he slept for a while during the night and relied on the dog to wake him up, but it seemed that although there was always at least one person on duty, with very little actual work to do the time dragged and they tended to find it very boring, so they welcomed a change of routine. The cook was also looking forward to the opportunity of using his creative talents instead of being given orders all the time. Once I knew this I arranged to give them money to buy supplies for me from the bazaar and they agreed to prepare what they called an 'English breakfast' for me each morning. This consisted of corn flakes or puffed rice, fruit such as papayas, bananas or mangos, and eggs cooked in some way with fried rice and toast. They also gave me sandwiches and fruit for my midday meal, which was sufficient to carry me through until the evening. Then, because I was a visitor, for my evening meal they said they would like to cook a variety of Punjabi and Northern Indian meals for me in order to give me a true taste of the local food. As I knew this was quite different from that which we could get in Bengal, I was very happy to agree because it solved all my food problems. Although I was prepared to give Kancha money to buy his food in the local bazaar, I told him the arrangements I had made and asked him whether he had any personal or religious objections to eating the same food as me if I could arrange it. He was delighted at this suggestion as it saved him a lot of hassle, so I proposed to the bearer that I would give him sufficient cash to buy enough groceries to feed myself, Kancha and his friend, together with himself and the cook. He leapt at the chance and the deal was struck. In fact I thought that I was getting off very lightly indeed, because although it would cost me a little more to feed the five of us, it was absolute peanuts when compared with what it would have cost me to stay in a hotel for 10 days, and with the cook eating his own cooking it ensured that he would be striving to impress. I was not mistaken.

The attraction of true Indian cuisine lies in the variety of its regional foods and menus, and what many of the 'Indian' restaurants in Britain serve up is a very pallid representation of what true Indian food is like, which is a great shame. There is no comparison between the flavours of freshly ground and prepared spices and those bought in packets in supermarkets, or between the taste of meats that have actually been cooked with the spices and sauces and those that have been cooked in our normal fashion beforehand and then served with the appropriate curry sauce, such as 'MILD', 'MEDIUM', 'HOT', and 'VERY HOT' poured over them, as they are served in many places. To cook many Indian dishes the cooking medium is either ghee (clarified butter) or oil of some kind. As this is usually the locally-produced oil it tends to vary from region to region, such as coconut oil in South India, mustard oil in Bengal and Assam and peanut or sesame oil in Northern India, all of which influence the flavour of the food.

Either through preference or necessity, many Indians are vegetarians, and as a result of this over hundreds of years they have developed a balanced and varied vegetarian cuisine based on various kinds of *dhal*, such as lentils, split peas, black eyed peas and chick peas, all cooked 'wet' or 'dry' with many different combinations of spices and a tremendous variety of vegetables. In addition to this in South and Eastern India curries are usually served with rice, whereas wheat grows abundantly in Northern India, so breads such as naans, chapattis and parathas are eaten, while others made from besan (gram flour), maize meal, sorghum and millet are predominant in the Punjab and Western India, so it is very evident that when compared with the real thing, very few of us have ever had the good fortune to taste real Indian food. After I had tasted my first curry on Bombay railway station in 1951 I developed a great liking for it, and as increasing numbers of young Indian Assistants joined tea as the years went by, I had more and more opportunities of being invited to dinner with them and was introduced to many delicious dishes to which I would not normally have had access, so when the bearer and cook told me of their plan I was absolutely delighted.

I made only two stipulations. No matter how much I had tried I was unable to stomach brain curry, which was a delicacy to some people but I hated it, so there was to be none of that. The other thing was that for my sweet each night they were to get me some rasgullas, Bengal's favourite sweet, which I absolutely adore. Although many people find them much too sweet for their taste, they are superb if you have a very sweet tooth and in my opinion we have nothing to compare with them. Basically they are made from milk that has been continually boiled until only the solid curds are left, then these are kneaded into small balls which are simmered for a period in a thick, sugar syrup which has been lightly perfumed until they have swelled a little and become solid. Then they are transferred into a less concentrated sugar syrup which is then cooled. When they are eaten they are popped into the mouth, and as they are bitten they squeak and all the syrup trapped inside them squishes out into the mouth, giving what I think is a wonderful sensation.

As I sat sipping a cold Tiger beer and waiting to see what the cook had prepared for me, I chatted to the bearer. Both of them were very intrigued with the fact that I was able to converse with them in very fluent Hindi, as I don't think either of them had met a European planter before. The bearer was very pleased to talk to me about the Qutab Minar and give me his thoughts on how they had managed to lift the very large blocks of sandstone to the top of the tower, as there was not enough room to carry them up the stairs. It seemed he had given the matter quite a lot of thought. I was really surprised when he came up with the theory that if they had made a suitable sloping ramp of timber and bamboos from ground level to the height at which they were working, they would have been able to slide the blocks up on rollers, then as the tower got higher the slideway would have had to have been made higher and longer, but the workable angle could have remained the same. As he spoke I realised that I had been thinking the same thing, as I had remembered how the Roman army was supposed to have built a sloping causeway by which they were able to climb up to the walls when they besieged the Jewish natural fortress of Masada, and also how the Egyptians were thought to have built the pyramids.

I asked him what had made him think of that and whether he had read anything about the Qutab at school. 'Oh no', he replied, 'I never went to school, but I was born and raised very near the tower, so it was just like an old uncle looking over us and we often used to sit around and look at it and try to work out how it had been made. The more I considered it, the more I thought that with unlimited labour and with elephants to pull the blocks up by ropes running over wheels whenever possible, then that could have been how it was done, but probably I was wrong.'

Well I thought that probably he was right, and if he had been born in a different country under different circumstances, with a reasoning brain like that he could have been something like myself, but fate had decreed that he had been raised in the shadow of the Qutab and become a household servant, while I was fortunate enough to have been born in 'Glorious Gloucestershire' and become a 'Rambling wreck from Gloucester Tech and a hell of an engineer!' As the old saying has it, 'There, but for the Grace of God go I'.

A few minutes later the dinner was served. When you consider that it was prepared in a small kitchen at the rear of the guest house on a coal burning stove it was absolutely superb. I can safely say that since I returned to the UK in 1967, I have never eaten any commercial Indian food to compare with that meal and the others I enjoyed over the next eight nights. To give details would be boring and take too much space, but usually they consisted of a starter of small, savoury items such as samosas and pakorhas, served with spicy dips, and then the main course was usually two dishes, one either of meat or fish, and the other vegetarian, accompanied by a variety of chutneys and different types of piping hot bread straight from the stove. My personal favourites were pooris, a deep fried, unleavened wholemeal bread which puffs up with air like a crisp brown snooker ball, luchis, which are very similar but made out of white flour and look like a crunchy , white tennis ball, and parathas, which is a kind of puffed bread that is crisp and flaky on the outside, but soft in the middle. I loved them when they were stuffed with fried egg. Once I had had my meal the other four ate outside and I suppose it is possible that they did not eat all the things that I did, but the next day I asked Kancha if he had had sufficient food and I was very pleased when he gave me one of his grins and said that he had never had any food like it, so at least he was satisfied, and I know I was.

With food like this to come back to each evening, all I had to do now was decide which other sights I wanted to see and visit them with the minimum amount of travelling. I had told Kancha that as most of them were only a few miles away, there was no need for him to come everywhere with me if he did not wish to do so. However he seemed to be genuinely interested in seeing as much as he could and he said that as his food arrangements had been made he would like to go with me wherever possible, so although we did separate once I had parked the car and he went off and did his own thing, that is what we did. Over the next two days we visited the Red Fort and many of the sites on the walls of the old city where the most fierce fighting occurred during the Mutiny.

The building of the Red Fort was begun by the Mogul Emperor Shah Jehan when he moved his capital from Agra to Delhi in 1638 AD and took ten years to complete. Its shape is an irregular octagon about 1.5 miles in circumference. Although the city was also fortified with walls and ditches, the Red Fort was to be his palace, so he decided to make it virtually impregnable, with defensive walls 60 feet in height on the river front, while those on the landward side rose to 75 feet and were bounded by an immense ditch 30 feet deep and 75 feet wide. However inside the public and private rooms no expense was spared to decorate them with ivory, gold, silver, diamonds and other precious stones, to the extent that some early visitors declared that it was 'the most magnificent palace in the East, possibly in the whole world'. His masterpiece was the erection of the 'Peacock Throne,' which consisted of a golden seat measuring six feet by four standing on six massive golden legs inlaid with diamonds and other precious stones. It was covered by a golden canopy supported by twelve pillars which were also encrusted with emeralds and decorated with the life-sized figures of two peacocks made of solid gold which were inlaid with precious stones of the appropriate colours so that they resembled living birds. Unfortunately this was looted and carried off by the Persian invader Nadir Shah in 1739, together with most of the other palace treasures, and these included a solid block of purest crystal four feet long by three feet wide by two feet deep, described as 'the most beautiful stone ever seen'. Although these marvels were never replaced, fortunately most of the rooms are still brightly decorated and in good condition, and I spent several days wandering through them and imagining what life had been like in those days. Unfortunately the fort was so large and there were so many wonderful sights that I was unable to see them all.

By doing this I was able to walk the city walls and fortified gateways which had played such a crucial part during the mutiny, and it was only when I saw their size and complexity that I realised just how difficult it must have been for the British army to break through when the final attack was made on the morning of the 14th. September 1857. The section of wall on the northern side of the city from the Kabul Gate and the Mori Bastion to the Kashmir gate had been hammered by the British siege cannons for seven days, until two breaches had been made which were deemed large enough to enable the first attackers to fight their way through. Unfortunately, although the debris from the breaches had collapsed into the ditch, it was not enough to serve as a bridge, so the men of A and B Columns were forced to cross individually by running across scaling ladders laid horizontally to bridge the ditch. It was only after intense hand-to-hand fighting that the breaches were taken and more than 1500 men entered the city and tried to fight their way to the two gates. However they were totally unprepared for the maze of twisting alleys and houses they encountered and the ferocity of the hand-to-hand fighting that ensued, so they often got lost and progress was extremely slow. So many atrocities had been committed that the mutineers knew they could expect no mercy if they were captured, so the fighting was totally savage and unforgiving and no quarter was asked or given. Although the Kashmir Gate was finally blown up by a mine so that the rest of the attacking force could enter, it was not until September 20th that they were able to force their way into the palace and the old King of Delhi surrendered. This in turn sparked off an orgy of revenge killings and looting which lasted for several days, until everybody was sick of the slaughter and their desire for revenge satiated. Similarly to the Residency in Lucknow, the ruined wall between the gate and the Mori Bastion was left as it was after the battle and remains a testament to the ferocious fighting which took place there. When I saw the scale of the ditch and the fortifications and the size of the two breaches, I wondered how on earth the British soldiers had been crazy enough or brave enough to storm them, because it must have been like hell on earth.

The area around the Kashmir Gate is now the centre of a

fashionable shopping area, but just outside it in a small, well-kept garden stands a statue in memory of the legendary General John Nicholson, known as 'Nickal Sen Sahib', who headed the successful attack on the Kashmir Gate. Tradition has it that his statue stands on the exact spot where his horse was standing that day when he was waiting for the bugle call to announce that the gate had been successfully blown up. He led his own personal regiment of local troops, who revered him so much that when he was killed a few hours later during another attack on the Lahore Gate, they refused to fight for anyone else and went back to their homes. There was only one Nickal Sen.

Just inside the gate is the Memorial Church of St. James, built by Col. James Skinner, who also formed his own regiment. Besides his grave and those of several members of his family who were buried there, it also contains many monuments and memorials to those who fell in the mutiny. It was a fascinating place. The day I spent looking round the building and wandering round the burial ground seemed to pass as though it was a couple of hours instead of a complete day, and even then I wished that I had had a bit more time.

Because New Delhi was so modern, as it had been built in 1931 specifically to replace Calcutta as the capital of present-day India, there was only one thing there of interest to me and that was the *Janter Manter*. In the colloquial Hindustani everyone spoke on the Tea Gardens, known as the '*garden bhat*', the term '*janter manter*' was given to any mixed up collection of different items, rather like we use the term 'humble, jumble' in English, and although this one was only a few hundred yards away from the very swish centre of Connaught Place in New Delhi, it was exactly that, only it was built out of stone. Viewing it for the first time it looked as though some baby giants had been playing with their toy blocks and after erecting a few buildings they had tired and gone away to play elsewhere. In fact it was a celestial observatory built in 1724 on the orders of the Emperor Mohammed Shah. He was absolutely obsessed with the mysteries of the solar system and was a competent mathematician, so he commissioned the best astronomers and mathematical wizards of his time to build the various erections and these were used to study the movements of the sun, moon and other celestial objects, very much as Stonehenge is thought to have been in prehistoric times. It was fascinating to wander round the various buildings and stairways trying to work out how they could have been used.

On the Friday of my stay I decided I would visit Agra, so I got away early in the cool of the morning and as I made very good time I decided to stop to visit the Mausoleum of Itmud-Ud-Daula on the bank of the River Jumna just outside Agra. Itmud-Ud-Daula was a Persian adventurer from Teheran who after his daughter Nurjahan married the Mogul Emperor Jahangir in 1611, became Lord High Treasurer and later Prime Minister serving him. Then after his death in 1622, Nurjahan decided to build a mausoleum for him, which was completed in 1628. Ash had told me to make a special effort to view it if I had the chance, because he thought it was something special, and he was quite right. Situated in a large walled garden, it was nothing like most of the very large, pretentious Mogul tombs I had visited, but instead was fashioned entirely of white marble and looked like a large wedding cake, with a pavilion on the top and a small tower at each corner. Light admitted to the rooms through beautifully-pierced marble screens, and these, together with the extremely beautiful inlay and mosaic work with which it was covered both inside and out, made it one of the loveliest buildings I have ever seen. I thought its elegant simplicity was absolute perfection.

The mausoleum predated the Taj Mahal by only three years. In its own way the Taj Mahal was just as beautiful, but I think part of its charm is due to the romantic story of its erection. The Taj has a mystique all of its own and when I walked through its entrance arch that morning, it looked like a fairy tale palace straight out of an illustration in my book of 'Arabian Nights' stories that I had as a child. It looked as though it was floating in the air, with a sense of mystery about it, but when I got close up it was apparent that the ravages of time had played havoc with some of the masonry and many of the panels of inlaid work had been damaged. There was an aura of neglect about it, and I was told that for many years the gardens had been overgrown and very little work had been done to preserve the building. I suppose the authorities thought that in the Indian climate, it had stood unprotected for so long that it would do so in the future.

According to the guide book, which I still have, entrance to the Taj Mahal, the Itmud-Ud-Daula and most of the other Mogul tombs was free, the Red Fort in Agra being the only one for which an entrance charge (2 annas) was made, the equivalent of about two pence in sterling. There were very few other visitors around and nobody seemed to worry who went in and out, the only proviso being that when I went inside I had to take my shoes off, so in I went and spent an hour wandering round in splendid near-isolation. There were no electric lights, but flickering lamps added a softer, more authentic aura to the interior and as I was able to visit the actual tombs in the crypt below the main building which modern visitors are unable to do, it made me feel that this was how it must have been when Shah Jahan visited the tomb to pray at the side of the love of his life, Mumtaz Mahal.

This was in marked contrast to how it was 50 years later when Jan and I made a return visit. Because of the damage done to the masonry by exhaust fumes, no motor vehicles are allowed nearer than a half a mile away, where they park and electric buggies take the visitors to the site. The entry cost now is 50 rupees for Indian nationals, which is about 75 pence in sterling and represents an agricultural labourer's daily wage, while for foreign visitors it is 1000 Rupees, or about £12.50 per person. When I asked one of the staff why this was so high he replied, 'You know, we have visited your country and have seen that you are willing to pay prices like this to view your own National Treasures, so why should you not pay the same amount when you want to come and see ours?' As the income was being used to preserve such a beautiful building I could quite see the logic in this. However despite these prices the outside gardens were crowded with visitors waiting to go inside, and although the authorities had done a wonderful job of repairing the fabric of the building, when we entered there were no artificial lights at all and we shuffled round the inside like a living stream in semi darkness through which we could see very little of its beauty, which was quite a disappointment compared to my first visit. When I enquired of one of the attendants why they didn't have any lights on inside he said, 'We did once, but so many people want to come in that if we leave the lights on they all stand around and gawk at everything so that the rest of the visitors can never come in, so we just shut the lights off and keep them flowing through'.

So as far as I was concerned, although from the outside it

still looks fantastic, once inside it is not what is expected. I suppose for most of the visitors the main thing is that they can say they have visited the Taj and they don't worry whether they have seen very much else or not, which is a pity really because the inside was absolutely unique when you could actually see it.

Shah Jehan was so affected by his wife's death that he swore he would build a tomb for her which would surpass anything the world had ever seen before or would ever see again, and the Taj Mahal, right on the bank of the Jumna, was the result. He imported the finest stone carvers, masons, craftsmen and engineers he could obtain from far and wide. Construction was begun in 1631, two years after her death, and it took about 17 years to complete. However according to legend this was only the first part of his great idea, which was to build another identical building of black marble for himself on the opposite bank and then connect the two with a golden bridge spanning the river. Had he been able to complete this grandiose scheme it would have been absolutely magnificent, but unfortunately his son Aurangzeb was more interested in wine, women, song and the good life and was not in favour of his father frittering away the family fortune on useless things like that, so in 1658 when Shah Jahan was struck down with a sudden illness, he usurped the throne in a bloodless coup and imprisoned his father in a suite of rooms in the Red Fort until he died in 1666. From a balcony in one of these rooms there is a lovely view of the Taj Mahal about a mile away, and it is said that each day Shah Jehan would sit and gaze at it all day, meditating about his beloved wife until night fell, until finally his death brought him a merciful release and he was buried by her side in the crypt.

And what happened to the naughty Aurangzeb, you may ask? Well he must have been a really nasty piece of work, because he proclaimed himself Emperor and 'Conqueror of the World' in 1658, then put all his brothers to death so that there should be no dispute for the throne. Subsequently he persecuted the Hindu population and destroyed many famous Hindu temples, schools, and libraries. He also revived an invidious ancient type of poll-tax which non-Mohammedans had to pay in order to finance his excesses. When Aurangzeb died at Ahmadnagar in 1707 at the age of 90, it seems he was mourned by very few people, either Muslim or Hindu, as he was buried in a very ordinary mausoleum there. Probably they thought it was 'good riddance to bad rubbish'.

Because my visit to the Taj Mahal was quite short, I was able to pay a quick visit to the Red Fort in the afternoon, mainly to see the areas where Shah Jahan had been imprisoned and the view of it from his personal balcony really was delightful, but it made me feel quite sad when I thought that it was his own son who had ensured that it was the only thing that he would look at for the last eight years of his life, so I decided not to view the rest of the Fort but to visit the palace of the Jat Maharajas of Bharatpur instead.

There are about 11 million Jats living in India at the present time. They are the descendants of an ethnic group of farmers and agricultural labourers who migrated from Persia to India around 100 AD and settled in an area west of Agra. For centuries they tilled the land and lived a peaceful, agricultural life, but in the early 18th Century they were persecuted by their Moslem rulers until they were united by one of their leaders named Badan Singh. Their rebellion was so successful that he was accepted by them as their King and the title of Rajah was conferred on him by the Mughals. He established the town of Bharatpur in 1743 and built a palace and a fort there so that he could use it as his capital. Over the next ten years he and his sons built the city walls, fortified many of the towns and built many almost impregnable forts in inaccessible places which defied the efforts of many invaders to take them. By 1750 they had grown so powerful that they were able to capture Delhi in 1753 and Agra in 1761, and they remained in their possession until 1774. After this their power gradually waned, but Bharatpur remained a Princely State with its Maharaja warranting a 17-gun salute under British rule until it became part of the new Indian State of Rajastan in 1947.

It was only an hour's drive from Agra to Bharatpur town, and when I arrived there I found it an absolutely enchanting sight as it looked like a long-forgotten Indian time warp. The imposing city walls had been whitewashed and shone like an iced wedding cake in the afternoon sun, while life-sized pictures of black fighting elephants had been painted on each side of the main entrance gate. It seemed to me that the hustle and bustle of a normal Indian town were missing, and the air hung heavy in the streets as I parked the car and walked to the town museum and then on to the Maharaja's palace, which was no longer in use. Both places were full of dusty exhibits and relics of bygone ages, while the palace contained a great many faded hunting trophies mounted on the walls which looked down on the visitors with dull, unseeing glass eyes. There seemed to be very little evidence of the city's royal grandeur and its warlike past. Had I had more time to spend there is no doubt that there were many fascinating things to be seen there, especially the walls and fortifications, but by this time I felt quite tired so I quickly called it a day and hurried back to Delhi for a cold shower and another delectable dinner.

CHAPTER THIRTY FIVE

Local leave III - Fatehpur Sikri

Despite having a sound night's sleep, when I awoke the next morning I still felt very tired, so I decided to have a couple of easy days relaxing over the weekend before driving down to Agra again to visit Fatehpur Sikri on Monday. While driving back from Bharatpur I thought I had detected a strange thrumming noise which seemed to be coming from the engine, but when I ran her back at the guest house I could hear nothing strange and the engine sounded normal. However when I drove out to see some of the local sights later in the day it began again. By listening carefully I realised that it was coming up through the floor above where I judged the gearbox was likely to be, and when I looked beneath the car I found it was plastered with a thick layer of filth. On closer inspection it looked as though the gearbox rear oil seal had worn so badly that it was allowing the hot oil to run outside along the drive shaft until it was thrown off by the centrifugal force and sprayed over the floor panel, where it was mixed with the clouds of red dust thrown up from the roads until it looked like a thick, greasy pan cake and it was in a hell of a mess.

The oil filler cap and the dipstick were situated on top of the gearbox. These could be accessed from inside the car by unscrewing a circular panel in the floor which revealed a circular hole with the dipstick and filler just below. When I checked the oil level I found it was non-existent, which made the trouble clear. The box was completely empty and the rumbling noise I had heard was that of the gears meshing together without lubrication. It was only a matter of time before something seized up and wrecked it completely.

Gearbox oil was something I had not considered bringing with me. I was able to buy a very expensive tin at a local garage, so I knew I would be able to keep topping her up for the foreseeable future. The trouble was that I didn't know just how badly the seal was leaking and if I needed to fill it too many times on the journey home supplies might not be available. Spares for any type of foreign car were completely unavailable in India at that time. Everest Motors had told me that they would be able to import small spares directly from the UK for me, provided they could be sent out by post and that I was willing to pay for them in advance with a sterling cheque, so I knew that once I was home they would be able to fix her. I decided to fill her up and hope for the best. I thought that I should not look for trouble until trouble found me, and just keep on with the sight-seeing.

As a result I was up early on Monday morning and away before the roads became crowded, so I had a good run down to Agra and then another 23 miles to Fatehpur Sikri along a very dusty track. I had read a lot about it but was completely taken aback by what it was really like. I found a magnificent rose-red city some six miles in circumference around its defending walls, standing in an absolutely barren desert and completely deserted, as it has been for the last 400 years. Although from a distance it looks as though it was abandoned only yesterday, the modern mind can only wonder at the despotic power of a ruler who had it built as his capital on a whim and then abandoned it after living in it for less than 30 years. History records that in the mid 16th century Sikri was only a small cluster of huts inhabited by stonecutters who worked in some nearby quarries which also boasted a cave where a celebrated religious recluse named Sheikh Salim Chishti lived, who was renowned for his piety and miraculous powers. The ruler at that time was Akbar, perhaps the greatest of all the Mughal Emperors, but he had a problem, because although he was 27 years of age and had fathered children who had died in infancy, he didn't have a son and heir, and his favourite wife Maryam seemed to be unable to conceive a child. It appears that when he was getting desperate he decided to visit the Saint and asked for his help. He told him that if he sent his wife to stay with him for a year, he felt that in due time she would give birth to a son for him. Well Akbar must have been a very trusting kind of a chap because he did send her on holiday to stay with the Saint and he must have had some miraculous powers, because within a year she gave birth to a baby boy, who he named Salim after the Saint. He was so overjoyed that he told Chishti to say what he would like in payment, to which he replied that his God had told him that he wanted Akbar to build him a city at Sikri where the miracle had happened that would last beyond time, so he did just that.

On a rocky outcrop in the middle of the otherwise flat desert he built his city, surrounded by fortified walls about six miles in circumference and pierced by seven splendid gates. Inside it there were magnificent palaces, public rooms, accommodation for 800 concubines, a treasury and a mint where he struck his own gold coins, mosques, towers, courtyards and stables for his elephants, horses and his own private menagerie, living quarters for his private servants and his army, and for an entire private population whose history has not been recorded. Beginning it in 1570 it took him four years to complete.

I spent the whole day wandering round marvelling that anything so magnificent and grandiose could have been built on a whim like that. Although there was an artificial lake on the north-west side which was partially dried up, so far as I could see the only things missing were any fountains or pools of cool water. He must have known that if he built a city in the middle of a desert on the highest ground available, there would be no water to spare as it is very difficult to make water flow uphill. There was an unlimited supply in the River Jumna, but that was 25 miles away, and as rainfall in the area was very infrequent every drop of water used had to be carried in from outside which would have been a horrendous undertaking. In 1585 Akbar must have decided that he had had enough and moved his court to Lahore and then to Agra, where he died in 1605. Subsequently other rulers made fleeting visits to the city, but none remained for very long. In fact Fatehpur Sikri was completely deserted within fifty years of its foundation, and so it has remained ever since, with only a few echoing buildings to remind us of the greatness that once was.

Sheikh Salim Chishti died in 1571 and in accordance with his wishes he was buried in the vault of a magnificent white marble tomb which was incorporated into the city as it was built. Viewed against the backdrop of the other red sandstone buildings, it still looks absolutely magnificent. It is only a small, square building measuring about 50 feet on each side, but the floors were decorated with marble mosaics while the portico and walls were made of thin white marble screens perforated with beautiful designs which could only be appreciated properly when they were viewed from the inside against the daylight.

One unusual thing about it was that from a distance it looked as though there were coloured birds of some sort moving about on the screens, but when I got close I could see that the effect was caused by hundreds of small bows of coloured ribbon tied to the fret work which were fluttering in the breeze. Later I was told that in accordance with its history it is still visited by thousands of barren women every year, in the belief that the dead Saint will grant them a son, and as a token of their faith they leave a ribbon for him, which they remove later if their prayers are answered. I have no idea if this is still the case, but judging from the number of ribbons that were fluttering there on that day it appeared that there were still a lot of women who hadn't given up hope entirely.

When I left my car in the car park I was approached by a very smart bearded gentleman who had been watching me. He was dressed in a long robe and wearing a smart headcloth. and he showed me a very official-looking piece of paper which certified that he was the legitimate Curator and Guardian of Sheikh Salim Chishti's mausoleum. He also told me that he had been given the post by the trustees of the monument because he was the very last surviving direct descendant of the Sheikh, so that when he died the line would end with him and he would be buried in a small plot of land near the mausoleum. Of course there was no way I could check this out, but he seemed very plausible, and as he could speak excellent English, when he offered to give me a guided tour of the mausoleum and city I was very pleased to accept. He made my visit well worthwhile. He certainly knew his stuff. While he showed me round the tomb he recited a long list of his ancestors dating back through the years to the Sheikh. He also showed me the small graveyard where they were all buried and the actual plot which had been demarcated for his final resting place. It all seemed so genuine that it was easy to believe him, and I hope it was all true and he is now resting in peace.

As there were very few visitors there that morning he also showed me the best way to get to the other main buildings that were worth seeing and gave me their histories. As I didn't have to keep referring to my guide books it made the visit that much more interesting. I think the most awe inspiring and unforgettable thing I saw was the Buland Darwaza, or the High Gateway of Victory, which is supposed to be the largest, loftiest and most stately of its kind in India, possibly in the whole world; certainly arches like the Arc de Triomphe in Paris and the Admiralty Arch in London pale in comparison with it. This triumphal gateway was erected by Akbar in 1601 to celebrate his victories in campaigns in Southern India, and white marble and red sandstone were combined to build and decorate a structure which epitomised the work and skill of the Mogul masons. From ground level a flight of about 50 steps rose up to the rectangular plinth on which the gate was built and the complete structure rose to 176 feet above ground level, dwarfing everything about it, which made it a truly wonderful sight.

I have never forgotten that visit. I have always felt that of all the sights I saw during my time in India, that deserted city was the one which had the greatest impact on me. There must be many deserted cities of that size all over the world, but to my knowledge there is no other which is not in ruins.

After paying the old man well for his hospitality and his efforts to make my visit interesting, I felt very privileged to have been able to meet him. That evening while I was waiting for the cook to finish preparing the dinner, I chatted to the bearer about Fatehpur Sikri and he said neither of them had ever seen it. They did know it was somewhere down in the Agra district, but it would have been a major operation for them to visit it. He was fascinated when I described it to him and was absolutely delighted when I told him about the old guide and the maiden's prayer ribbons still on the tomb. I don't think they had ever come across a European like me who was both willing and able to tell them about things like that, so they made the most of it.

Although I hadn't heard any more queer noises emanating from my gearbox on the road back from Agra, the next morning I decided to have a look at the oil level again and to my surprise and horror I found that it didn't register on the dip stick at all, which meant I had lost about half a gallon of oil over roughly 200 miles of motoring. This did not bode well for my 1000 mile trek back to Bagracote. The main trouble was that because private cars were not common in the country areas at that time there were very few garages and the ones that were operating were able to charge more or less what they thought the market would stand. It was a classic case of the law of supply and demand. If they had something that you needed badly then you paid their price or did without. I had found that some of their prices were really extortionate, and I didn't have any real hope of being able to buy any reasonably priced oil on the way home, but I knew that I couldn't afford large quantities of oil at their prices. What was I to do?

At first I thought I would be able to pack something into

the gap between the seal and the shaft, so I got Kancha to help me jack the car up and then support the wheels on a platform of old red bricks from a ruined wall, but when I crawled beneath it I could see that this was a useless idea. Although the hot oil crept out along the shaft quite easily, as the gap was so small it was virtually invisible. It would have been almost impossible to do anything like that in a workshop, let alone on some bricks in the middle of a dust heap. It was a complete non-starter. However, when I was gazing at the crust of dusty oil which covered the underside of the floor pan I thought that if the dust had mixed with the hot oil to make a hard crust when it cooled, if I could make it do the same on the end of the gearbox then possibly it would reduce the flow. The trouble was getting it to cool down, because it was so hot that it had only done so after it had been sprayed off by the rotation of the shaft. I knew I needed a substance which would act like oil inside the gearbox and then quickly solidify once it reached the cool air outside. The trouble was that I didn't have any idea where I was to obtain this wonderful material from - until I suddenly had a flash of inspiration. I would use butter!

At that time Indian butter was quite thick, especially the kind that was made from buffalo milk, which was rather like Stork margarine. Compared to gearbox oil it was ridiculously cheap, so I bought two pounds of this to experiment with and stuck as much as I could in the gearbox. I wouldn't have been able to do this in a modern car, but in the old Consul all I had to do was pull back the floor covering, unscrew the cover and take out the dipstick, then use it to push long, thin strips of butter down inside and then put the dipstick back in place to seal it. I then wound insulating tape around the shaft to make a ring about a quarter of an inch thick as near to the exit from the gearbox as I could get it. Then I took her out for a spin to warm the whole thing up, and it worked a treat. The butter melted as the gears rotated and then the hot fat leaked out, but when it hit the tape ring it began to congeal and pick up the road dust, and this formed itself into a crusty rotating oil seal. It was not completely oil-proof, but it was sufficient to reduce the oil leak to a slight seepage which I didn't think would interfere with the journey home provided I didn't drive too fast.

Now I knew I could settle down to enjoy the last two days of my stay. Fatehpur Sikri had made such an impression on me that I felt that any other historical buildings would pale in comparison with it, so I confined myself to visiting some of the other places which had played such important parts in the Mutiny, such as the Ridge, which is the crest of the Delhi Hills about one mile from the modern city and 60 feet in height at the highest point, from which there were such excellent panoramic views of the surrounding countryside that it became the base camp for the British forces during the final attack on the city. My first stop was at the Mutiny Memorial, an octagonal tower of red sandstone about 50 feet high which was erected in 1863 in memory of the officers and men of the Delhi Field Force, both British and Indian, who were killed in action or died of other causes between May and September 1857. Their names are recorded inside on a marble slab which made very sombre reading indeed.

Nearby was the Flagstaff Tower, which formed one of the strong points on the Ridge at the beginning of the uprising. It had a very chequered history, because on the night of May 11th 1857 it was desperately overcrowded with exhausted men, women and children who had managed to escape from the carnage inside the city and who were later evacuated to safety, after which it was abandoned and occupied by the mutineers. It was also there that the sepoys made their last stand on June 8th before they retreated and fell back behind the city walls, after which it was re-occupied by the British. I spent the rest of a very pleasant day wandering around the ruins and looking at the evidence of the British occupation that still remains.

Much as I enjoyed that, when I returned to the same area the following day I found that as I had done before I had quite unintentionally kept the best until last, rather like I had done with Fatehpur Sikri. From the time when I was a small boy I had always been fascinated with India. I had read a lot about the Mutiny, and one of the stories that had made the biggest impact on me was that of a group of British soldiers under a Lieutenant Willoughby who blew up an arsenal about six hundred yards from the Kashmir Gate to prevent it falling into the hands of the mutineers, but in order to do so deliberately blew themselves up with it as well. Miraculously, although they were blackened and singed and their uniforms were almost blasted off their bodies, several of the men survived the tremendous explosion. Yet they were not to know they would be spared, and I have always considered this to be an awe-inspiring case of devotion to duty because of their willingness to make the supreme sacrifice for the benefit of their comrades. I think that to do brave deeds in the red rage of battle is one thing, but such calculated self-sacrifice is quite another, and have often wondered if I would have been able to do such a thing in that situation.

Accordingly I was determined to try to find the site of the old magazine if anything still remained. This proved more difficult to do than I thought, until I made some enquiries and finally reached what appeared to be the site. To my disappointment there was very little to see, just some small heaps of rubble which might or might not have belonged to the original buildings. But as I stood there I experienced a feeling or aura about the place that made my spine tingle, rather like it did in the Residency at Lucknow. It was a really strange sensation which stayed with me the whole time I wandered about the place.

The rubble was spread over quite a wide area which had never been built upon, with several quite large holes in the ground. A man who passed by who could speak English told me that the local people thought that it was haunted and not a lucky place to be, and I could quite understand why. After this I felt that seeing anything else would be an anti-climax, so after wandering over it for a couple of hours I finally wished it a reluctant goodbye and returned to the guest house, where I was able to check the car and the gearbox before I had my last evening meal.

I found that I had lost some of my butter, but nothing like the amount of oil I would have used had I done nothing about it, so although my original plan had been to do the 850 miles back to Bhagalpur ferry ghat in one day on Friday and then drive on through the night to complete it if necessary, I thought discretion was the better part of valour and I would play it safe and not drive the car too hard. As a result I decided to start back the following day, Thursday morning, and follow the more direct route through Agra, Etawah and Kanpur, and spend the night in Allahabad. This would leave me all Friday to cover the final 400 miles to Bhagalpur, where I could sleep in the car and then be away on the river early the next morning.

To be on the safe side I had bought a new can of gearbox

oil to carry with me, but I still had some butter left which I intended to use, and I gave the bearer some cash to get me some more from the local bazaar so that I could pack it inside a large mouthed Thermos flask I had bought, so I was well prepared. In the evening I settled down to write a letter of thanks to Madhan's parents for their hospitality and help, without which my visit would not have been possible, expressing my gratitude to them for allowing me to use their servants during my stay, for they had made it really delightful. I told them that the food I had eaten was absolutely first class, far better than anything I would have been served in a hotel, and the servants had been so helpful and accommodating that they had made my stay a huge success and I would reward them accordingly. I closed by saying that I was very disappointed that I had been unable to meet them and thank them personally, but if they ever visited the Dooars I would love to entertain them at home and return their hospitality, and that was that. I think the two servants had really taken to us, especially to Kancha, as we had brought a bit of variety and entertainment into their lives over a period which actually would have been a bit boring for them. The next morning I congratulated the bearer on his service and the cook on the quality of his food and then gave each of them much more baksheesh than they had probably been hoping for. They appeared to be really sad that we were leaving as they waved us goodbye and we set out on the Agra road for the third and last time.

We were up early and away by 9 am, and the journey went so well that by 11 am we were within a few miles of Agra, which tempted me into thinking that it might be a lovely idea to divert and have one last look at Fatehpur Sikri while I had the chance as in all probability I would never see it again. I decided that I didn't want to tempt providence and common sense prevailed, but I need not have worried as I had to refill the gearbox with butter only once during the journey and we reached Allahabad at about 6 pm, having covered the 442 miles at an average speed of about 48 mph including stops. I had absolutely no idea where I was going to spend the night, but on the outskirts of the city I saw a policeman who gave me directions on how to find a small hotel that was used by 'Sahibs'. This turned out to be a wooden dak bungalow about a mile away which had been used by British Government officials when they visited the city on business at the time of the Raj. After partition in 1947 it had been sold by the Indian Government and bought by an Indian lady, who had updated it and converted it into a small but very comfortable guest house.

We arrived there at about 7 pm, so I was able to have a shower and change before sitting down to dinner at eight. Although it wasn't quite as good as I had got used to back in Delhi, nevertheless it was a very good substitute to a hungry man. The bed was spotlessly clean and very comfortable, so I was able to sleep like a log all night and then get up at seven the next morning ready for another day's driving.

After the dinner the previous evening I would have liked a good fried breakfast to set me up for the day, but unfortunately for some reason she didn't have any meat of any kind, so I had to fill up on a big pile of fried rice with two fried eggs perched on the top, together with toast, marmalade, fruit and coffee. This was fine when I ate it, but it left me rather hungry when I had digested it later in the day. Still I couldn't complain about the standard of her accommodation, which was very reasonably priced, so I was well rested and in a good frame of mind when I set off again.

From Allahabad it was only 18 miles to Benares, where we crossed the Ganges again and rejoined the road to Mohania, Patna and finally Mokama, the route I had traversed in the opposite direction at the beginning of my holiday. Unfortunately the roads in Bihar had not improved at all since then, as they were still covered with dust and peppered with potholes, so we didn't arrive at Mokama until 6:30 pm and then I still had another 90 miles to drive on the second-class road to Bhagalpur Ghat. This section of road was pitch black and so bad that it was gone 9 pm before we arrived, but luckily I was able to arrange my passage with the same boatman who had brought the car up. Obviously it had been a very lucrative cargo for him without too much exertion. Before Bandhna had driven off he had told him his name and how I could contact him and said that if I was back at Bhagalpur on the Friday night as planned, then he would be waiting to carry me back downstream the following day. He was true to his word. He warned me that he would like to leave as soon as possible in the morning to take advantage of the calmer air which prevailed for a couple of hours after sunrise, so I decided to buy some samosas and singarhas from a dukhan at the ghat and then sleep in the car, although this proved almost impossible due to the heat inside it and the mosquitoes outside. We spent most of the night opening and closing the windows, and as we felt that we had been almost eaten alive we were very pleased when morning came.

The ferry boat was quite large and leaf shaped, about 40 feet in length and 14 feet wide at its widest point. I couldn't see any form of loading ramp, and thinking that the car would be carried on the deck lengthwise I could not work out how we were going to get it on board. However it had been decked over at its widest point with thick planks which projected some four feet out over the water on each side, and this enabled it to be moored alongside the bank with the planks overhanging the soil and then the gap was bridged to allow the vehicle to drive straight on to the deck, where it was securely tied down broadside on. It appeared that quite large lorries could be carried in this way. At the end of the journey all the boatman had to do was moor the boat with the other side to the bank, where the weight of the vehicle tilted that side down until the overhang met the soil, when it was able to drive straight off the end and up the bank, quite a simple solution to what had seemed a difficult problem.

In the morning, as soon as we had eaten some leftover samosas and drunk the obligatory cups of hot tea from the *chah dukhan* (tea stall) I drove the car onto the platform, where it was securely tied down to rings let into the planks. Then the crew poled us out into the current so that we began to drift downstream, where it took until late afternoon to cover the first 25 miles and clear the shallows. This meant that we were unable to reach Manihari before nightfall. As there were no lights or any other navigational aids on the river, the boatman told me he would have to anchor in midstream and spend the night there. This seemed to be a bit unusual to me, but when I asked him why he didn't pull into the bank and tie up there he told me that the wild country on both sides of the river was the home of several gangs of thieves and outlaws, the dacoits, who roamed the countryside at night searching for travellers to rob. Usually they didn't worry the boatman with their normal commercial cargoes, but if they happened to notice that one of them was also carrying a car, possibly with valuables on board, they might try to hijack it if they got the chance.

Of course even if they had a boat they couldn't navigate the river at night any more than the boatman could, so we were safe in midstream, but he did ask me whether I had a *bandook,* his term for a gun. I had carried my rifle with me hidden beneath the front seat 'just in case,' so I dragged this out. When I showed him he beamed with delight and said, 'Ah, now we shall have no trouble. If anyone comes I shall quickly wake you and if you fire a couple of goolies over their heads then they will quickly run away, as they will think that you are the police'.

He was so confident about this that at about 5 pm he decided to anchor over one of the last shallow areas in the middle of the river, so that everyone could go over the side and have a good bath in the Ganges before we ate our evening meal, and in they went. At first I had my doubts about this, because further upstream where the current had been slow it seemed to be full of all kinds of unwholesome rubbish floating down from Benares, but when I saw that where they were bathing looked lovely and clean and was only chest deep, after two days of hot, dusty travel the thought of the cooling water proved to be too much for me and in I went as well, and it was absolutely lovely.

The river bed was made of grainy white sand with no vegetation or dirt in it whatsoever, and it was a real pleasure to be able to soap myself nearly all over, including my hair, before cavorting about in the water to wash it all off. It was really refreshing. If anybody had told me before I left that I would enjoy a bathe in the Ganges, because I had heard so many tales about it I would have told him that he must be out of his tiny mind, but the boatmen knew what they were doing and I can say that it was one of those completely unexpected but thoroughly enjoyable experiences which don't come along very often, but which when they do remain in the memory for ever.

After I had dried myself off and donned some clean clothes, the boatman sidled up to me rather hesitantly and said that if I would be willing to join them they would like to share their evening meal with us. Evidently under normal circumstances it was the standard procedure for them to invite their passengers to share their food when they tied up overnight, but he had never had a '*pukka Bilayati Sahib*' (genuine European gentleman) as a passenger before and he didn't know quite how I would react. Evidently they had brought enough boiled rice, vegetable curry, chapattis and fruit for all of us with them from Bhagalpur and one of the crew was heating this up over a small fire which they had lit in the small covered area at the stern where they lived and slept when they were working. He also said that he had asked Kancha about it, and he had told him that I was quite used to eating with Indians but I did carry my own plates and cutlery in the car. Kancha thought that although I would be very grateful to accept his invitation I would probably prefer to eat my dinner sitting in the car in comfort as I was not used to squatting on my haunches. It seems that after four years together he could almost read me like a book.

Of course, having had nothing substantial to eat since breakfast, I was absolutely ravenous, so his invitation had come like a gift from heaven and I accepted with thanks. Soon Kancha came back with my plate full of curry and rice, chapattis cooked in ghee and a small circular plate with a selection of hot chutneys on it which were absolutely delicious. All the others gathered in the stern to eat their meal and they had quite a party until darkness fell when the fire was doused, all the lights were put out and I was asked not to put any of the car lights on. It seemed to me to be a rather a strange thing to do, and at first I thought it was something to do with the close proximity of the dacoits, but then the boatman explained that in that area there were absolutely no artificial lights at all, so if a light was shown for any length of time it served to attract every insect for miles around, including flies, midges, moths and mosquitoes, and soon the boat would be swarming with them, much to everyone's discomfort, so it was best to manage without lights. This made a great deal of sense, so while the others slept on the deck I pushed my driving seat back and lowered the backrest so that I had quite a comfortable bed. As there were no mosquitoes over the river I was able to keep the windows open and have a really good night's sleep, and we weren't troubled by dacoits at all, thank goodness.

The next morning there was a thick mist hanging over the river, which meant that the boatmen were not able to get away as early as they had hoped to do, but after a breakfast from the leftovers from the previous evening's dinner, as soon as the rays of the morning sun had burnt it off we raised the large boulder which served as an anchor and in next to no time we were away. The two crew members poled her along with long, bamboo poles while the boatman stood at the steering oar, keeping her in the current. The anchor stones were quite interesting to see, because they were large boulders weighing about a hundredweight each which had been roughly shaped so that if they began to drag they would dig themselves into the river bed. There were five of them stored in the bow, and they all had holes bored through them so that they could be attached by lengths of chain to the manila rope anchor cables. The other ends of these were fastened to large iron rings bolted into the foredeck. Normally they only needed one for a night stop, but the others could all be used simultaneously if needed, and although one man could easily carry one to the rail and throw it overboard, it took two of them to bring it in and hoist it aboard, so they were very cumbersome things.

Because there were no sandbanks to check the current it ran very swiftly in the centre of the river, so with both crew members poling it only took us about six hours to cover the last 50 miles and we arrived in Manihari just after midday. I had checked the car and also fully buttered the gear box while we were floating down the old, green river, so all I had to do was to drive her off and up the bank to the road, settle up with the boatman and then drive the 200 miles back to Bagracote.

Regarding the boatman, I had agreed the cost of the passage with him before we left Bhagalpur, and although I knew he had probably charged me more than he would have done had I been a local, from what I had seen I didn't think that it would pay him adequately for the amount of work and effort he and his men had put in while bringing us safely down the river and also making it such a pleasure. Being a working man myself I had thought this over, so when I settled up I gave him the agreed amount and thanked him, then gave him an additional 50% as a bonus for a job well done and congratulated him on the efficient way in which they had handled the boat. You would have thought I had given him the crown jewels. He was over the moon with gratitude. I don't think it was just the money I had given him either; rather it was the fact that I had appreciated their skill and expertise and actually thanked him for his efforts that counted with him, and from his behaviour I don't think it was something that happened to him very often.

Once this was all over I was able to be on my way back to

Bagracote and it all went like a dream, because I called into the Everest Motors garage on my way through Siliguri and explained my predicament with the gearbox to Filoo, who confirmed that they should be able to import the necessary oil seals from the UK within three weeks. As there was plenty of butter still left in the box he couldn't see any reason why it shouldn't run satisfactorily until then, so I arrived back at my bungalow at about 6.30 pm very tired but very pleased that a trip which had only been arranged as a stopgap at the very last moment, had turned out to be so successful and memorable.

CHAPTER THIRTY SIX

Return to real life, and some terrible news

It was only a couple of weeks after I had returned from my trip that I realised that either my previous attack of hookworm had not been cleared up properly or I was suffering from another attack, which shook me to the core. For several months I had been able to sleep like a log, day or night, and was always hungry, but strangely I had again lost a lot of weight. Despite the fact that I had only got over the first attack just a few months before I didn't think very much about it. I suppose I put it down to lots of exercise and outside work and also living a healthy life style. It wasn't until I weighed myself when I got back that I realised that despite all the delicious food I had eaten while I was away I weighed less afterwards that I had before I went. I was very surprised when I found that I now weighed less than nine stones.

An appointment with the Dr. Babu and a couple of stool samples confirmed my suspicions. I had to have another two doses of Chenapodium Oil to kill the little devils. Possibly some of my lady readers might say, 'My, what a wonderful way to slim. Just a few weeks of the hookworm therapy and I would be as slim as a reed!', but I don't recommend it.

Remembering the discomfort and trouble I had had during my first attack, I arranged to have the first dose on the following Sunday morning so that I could at least rest between visits to the toilet. To my relief I didn't feel anything like the discomfort I had experienced the first time. It seemed to work and I soon began to regain weight. However it is possible that the medication might have been sub-standard, because only a few months later when I was home on leave I felt ill again and our local doctor prescribed a visit to the London School of Hygiene and Tropical Medicine, where they were extremely interested to find that I did have another dose of hookworm. They took great delight in treating it with a much more pleasant and efficacious drug than oil of chenapodium. It seemed almost as though they knew so much about these tropical diseases through reading books that it was a novelty when they were able to meet the culprit face to face and had a real patient to treat. They gave me preferential treatment before clearing it up completely. It was a very strange fact that Bagracote was the only place where I ever caught hookworm, and none of our family ever caught it during the other twelve years we spent living on other estates, so there must have been something on Bagracote that suited it really well.

At the end of November word had been received from the Superintendent that the company had sanctioned expenditure in the 1955 accounts for a large section of water supply piping to be replaced after it had been damaged during the monsoon. Although we were rebuilding the leaking dam I would not be on Bagracote to install the piping, but I was instructed to order the requisite lengths of pipe and fittings as quickly as possible.

Accordingly I contacted various suppliers in our area and in Calcutta, detailing our requirements for good quality, seamless, 3 inch diameter galvanised water pipe and asking them to let us have their tenders and samples of their goods as soon as possible.

Although this was the first really big tender with which I had been involved I didn't really anticipate any difficulty in obtaining the piping we required, but I hadn't reckoned on being involved with the ethics of the Indian business system and I soon had my eyes opened. Several quite competitive tenders were received and in some cases it was made known to me indirectly that there would be something in it for me if these were chosen, but in addition to an excellent one from the Bagracote shopkeeper, there was one that stood head and shoulders above the rest. The sample sent was of first-class manufacture, made of thick gauge, seamless, galvanised steel pipe, and as it could be supplied within two months and was reasonably priced, this was the one I decided on. Later on in 1955 deliveries began to arrive and I checked the first couple of consignments which were also first class, but as I was busy with the factory machinery I asked Ash to look at the other deliveries when they were made. He did this and after inspecting the fourth delivery he came and told me that it was so bad he thought I had better see it for myself, and when I did I had a shock. It was a collection of seamed piping of extremely poor quality and nothing like the sample.

Thinking that a mistake had been made and we had had another customer's goods, I contacted the supplier to come and check it with me, which he did. He was a young lad and very put out that I was finding fault with it and astonished me by saying that surely nobody expected the goods supplied to be as good as the sample sent! I explained to him that in England the sample represented the quality of the goods to be supplied for the whole of the order, so why did he bother to send it in the first place if the piping was to be nothing like it? To this he laughed and said, 'Oh, that's just for the record and so that you can show people what you are buying. Nobody expects the goods to be like the sample'. He was quite annoyed when I told him that just for the record, as far as I was concerned the goods were not up to standard so the order was cancelled and he could send his lorry and take all his piping away as soon as possible, and that's what happened. Later I told the garden shopkeeper about it and he said that the firm was noted for sharp practices. Had we continued with the order, in all probability there would have been all sorts of complications in the months ahead. Regarding his quotation, he confirmed that although he would have to charge slightly more for his goods, he would supply the correct amount of good quality piping to schedule if we gave him the order, so that's what we did and he was as good as his word.

Another rather amusing episode that occurred at this time was when I tried to learn to play bridge. Being brought up in a rural village in the 1930s and 40s, there was no electricity or mains water in any of the houses, so we had to rely on paraffin oil lamps or candles for light and the only technical entertainment we had was an old wind up gramophone and a battery powered wireless. As a result, during the long, cold winter evenings Mum, Dad, my sister Marion and I would sit in front of a blazing fire and play cards. As we took it in turn to choose which game we would play, there were very few card games I couldn't play from an early age. Whist, solo whist, bezique, brag, rummy, cribbage, Newmarket and pontoon, I loved them all. The only one I could not play was contract bridge, but I got my chance to do this in early March. A married couple from a neighbouring garden named Joe and Mandy played regularly with a couple of friends. The friends had gone on home leave, which meant that they had nobody to play with, and Joe was getting withdrawal symptoms. Talking about it at Mal club one evening he suggested that as Ash and I were unable to play, why didn't we go over to their bungalow one evening for tea, after which they could give us some lessons.

In fact playing the cards in bridge is very much like playing solo whist, so as we were both able to play that, one evening we went over to their bungalow and after a very nice tea settled down to learning the mysteries of the bidding system. I was paired with Mandy while Ash partnered Joe, who explained that the science of making your bids was to benefit yourselves, but also to learn as much as possible about the cards the other players were holding. This all seemed to be very straightforward, so we had a couple of trial hands with 'arranged' cards so that we could see why the different bids were being made but didn't actually play them. This went off so well that Joe then suggested that we should actually play the next hand with a bit of advice from our partners if needed. Although I was dealt a rather queer hand for which Mandy had to give me a bit of help when bidding, I thought it all went off very well until after we had finished, when suddenly Joe said to Mandy, 'Why did you tell Rod to bid such and such when he had such and such in his hand?'

'Well', she replied, 'he had this, that and the next thing in his hand, and I thought that that was the best bid for him to make.'

When he heard this Joe seemed to explode, and he shouted

at her, 'How many times do I have to explain to you that if you have a this and a that in your hand, you never bid such and such. I don't think you ever listen to me!'

After that there was a moment of stunned silence. Then Mandy rose quietly from her chair, threw her cards at him and said, 'Well, if you feel like that about your bloody bridge, then you can stick your cards up your XXX and play with yourself, because I am off to bed. Goodnight lads' and away she went. At this Joe gave a sickly grin and said, 'Well, I don't think we shall be getting any more cards tonight, so we had better have a drink.' So that was what the three of us did for the rest of the evening.

Later when we were going home in the car I said to Ash, 'Well, what did you think of that? If that is what bridge does to a man and his wife, then I think that it is best left alone and I think I can do without it,' to which he agreed. To the best of my knowledge neither of us ever attempted to play it again.

One of the problems we had to deal with before the beginning of the new plucking year were 936 sacks of tea waste which were the indirect result of the trouble and disruption caused by the monsoon floods, together with the record crop we had made. Despite our best efforts to maintain a seven-day plucking round and gather fine leaf, the damage done to the roads and bridges prevented us from bringing in lorryloads of casual labourers from the neighbouring villages as we normally did when we needed extra pluckers. In addition, the almost incessant rain resulted in an abnormal rate of sickness in our resident labour force, and despite the fact that we tried to get volunteers to work for several hours on the Sunday bazaar day at enhanced rates of pay, the round gradually slipped up to nine or 10 days as the conditions deteriorated and this gave us our tea waste. The tender shoots which were normally plucked on the same day each week almost doubled in size during the extra three days, and a hard stalk developed inside each stem which was impossible to separate from the rest of the shoots before manufacture. Consequently these were cut up and manufactured with the rest of the leaf, but because the resultant brownish-white fragments detracted from both the flavour and look of the finished tea, they had to be removed during the sifting process and then stored until they could be disposed of.

Normally when fine leaf was plucked the amount of stalk produced was minimal and could easily be disposed of by contaminating it with old engine oil, ashes, chemicals and other nasties and then burying it in the factory compound until it had rotted, when it could be used as fertiliser in the tea. Unfortunately this could not be done with almost 47 tons of waste, because the Indian Government Customs and Excise rules decreed that although it was completely useless to us it had a market value in the local bazaar, and as quantities were regularly dug up at night and stolen it had to be completely destroyed. We tried burning it, but because it only smouldered and refused to blaze it would have taken us a month of Sundays, so finally we decided that the only thing we could do was take it down to the Teesta and throw it into the river from the Coronation Bridge

The necessary arrangements were made and a suitable day was agreed with our local Tea Excise Officer. Twelve lorries were procured from various sources and on the appointed day they all gathered. Beginning with our three lorries the hated tea waste was checked and loaded aboard under his eagle eye to ensure that there was no skulduggery. Then a convoy was formed, and with the Tea Excise Officer and the Head Factory

Clerk riding in the leading truck and me bringing up the rear in the pickup to ensure that none of the loads diverted, we finally reached the Coronation Bridge.

I was rather surprised that the Head Factory Clerk was involved, because he was rather overweight and not inclined to do any unnecessary strenuous exercise, but he clambered out of the truck and the destruction began. Each hundredweight sack had been numbered and entered in our factory records and then loaded in sequence, so it was an easy matter for one sack to be unloaded and slit open so that it could be tipped over the bridge parapet, and then its number noted and marked as destroyed. Once we had the system operating properly it worked well and streams of waste fell into the waters below, turning them from their normal blue green into a delicate shade of brown as they were washed away into the distance.

I thought to myself that there was no way any of that would ever find its way into the local bazaar, but I was soon to find that even after four years in India, I had a lot to learn about ethics, and things rarely went as expected. Our Bagracote trucks were empty and we had started on the next batch when the Excise Inspector came up to me and said that he was satisfied with the way the operation was progressing and thanked me for attending, so as our lorries were empty and there were no complications there was no need for me to stay and supervise anything else. He added that he was quite happy to stay and see that the rest of it was destroyed, so I told our lorry drivers that they were free to drive back to the estate and once they were on their way I bade farewell to the Excise Officer and left as well.

The next day I checked our factory records and as he had certified that all the bags had been emptied and the tea waste destroyed, I thought that that was the end of the matter, and so it was except that a few days later I was chatting to one of our drivers who told me the rather surprising end of the story. Evidently he was friendly with one of the other drivers who had been there and he told him that afterwards when all the lorries except two had been unloaded, the Excise Officer and our clerk had decided that it was time for them to call it a day. After instructing the last two lorry crews to dispose of the remainder of the waste as we had been doing, they left them to it and took the rest of the empty lorries home. Then once they had disappeared the two remaining trucks carried their loads of 200 sacks into Siliguri Bazaar, where they were unloaded and the tea waste spirited away by prior arrangement, and they all went home happy.

Of course, although I was not able to say anything about it officially, this rather intrigued me, so later I asked our Factory Clerk if all the waste had been destroyed correctly and whether the Excise Officer was satisfied. Without a moment's hesitation he replied that the operation had run like clockwork and everybody was satisfied so I had nothing to worry about, and he grinned like a Cheshire cat. Well even though the stalk was quite valuable in the bazaar it was completely valueless to us, so as long as the Excise Inspector was happy that it had been destroyed then so were we. However I had a distinct suspicion that everyone from him downward had been in the scheme. If they all had made a nice little bit of money on the side then why should we worry? But it did serve to give me another small insight into the way some things were done in India.

Early in May I received a devastating item of news from home. Mum wrote and told me that Marion's husband, Peter Fox, had died in a plane crash in Scotland. By this time he was stationed at the Fleet Air Arm station at Lossiemouth and had reached the last stage of his shore-based training before he was transferred to carrier take offs and landings. From the story I heard later, on Tuesday April 26th he was flying a Hawker Sea Hawk jet fighter and strafing targets at low level in the sea off the town of Banff, a few miles east along the coast, when his aircraft developed a fault and dived into the sea. Things must have happened very quickly, because although he ejected safely before he hit the water, it seems that he was unable to free himself and was still strapped to his seat when his body was recovered several hours later. According to the letter Marion received from the Admiralty he died as a result of an aircraft accident. We will never know the exact cause, but some aircraft histories allege that the first Seahawk F1s were fitted with ailerons which had a tendency to oscillate when the aircraft was in a high-speed shallow dive, thus causing instability. To fix this problem the Hawk F2 was produced, which was fitted with power-actuated ailerons. Peter's body was buried in the Royal Naval cemetery in Lossiemouth.

Of course this shocked me to the core, because Jan had written and told me how much in love they were and both Mum and Dad thought he was wonderful, so I was looking forward to getting acquainted with him when I got home. Having been obsessed with planes ever since I was a small boy and almost joining the Royal Navy in order to join the FAA when I was called to do my national service, I thought it was wonderful to have a pilot in the family. For Peter to enter it and then be so tragically snatched away after only sixteen months was absolutely heart rending. God knows how poor Marion must have felt, but I do know that Mum and Dad felt his loss very deeply and were hit especially hard by two strange coincidences. On the morning of the day they heard of his death, Dad had been cleaning out the roof gutters at the back of the house when he discovered the body of a dead sparrow. It had been building a nest and had brought in some long horsehairs, but for some reason it had lost control of them so that they had wrapped themselves around its throat. In its struggles to free itself it had been strangled and was hanging from the end of them. Of course, Dad being a countryman and never having seen anything like that before brought its body down to show Mum, and according to her he said 'Well, that's one little soul that won't fly again'.

Also that day the postman had delivered a package to them from Marion and Peter. The last time they had visited home they had wished to thank Mum and Dad for all the help they had given them and had ordered a framed print of a painting by Sir Peter Scott to be delivered for them after they had returned to Lossiemouth. By a strange quirk of fate it depicted geese coming in to land on a lake against a lovely sunset sky and was entitled 'The Last Flight'. It was later that day that they got the tragic news from Marion that Peter was dead.

These two happenings affected them deeply, but the picture hung above the mantelpiece for many years until Dad left the old house and it came into our possession. However, when we asked Marion whether she would like us to send it to her she declined, and as it only had sad memories for us we didn't wish to keep it either, so although it was a lovely print we disposed of it.

CHAPTER THIRTY SEVEN

Home leave I - homeward bound

The last few weeks before I began my home leave passed like a dream. It was almost unbelievable to think that the time was almost upon me after so many years and that the countdown had begun, and it was not until I was actually told that I could make the necessary arrangements to book my passage that the reality struck me. In one way it seemed as though it was only a few days before that I had disembarked in Bombay. Where had the years gone? I could only imagine how the four years had dragged by for Jan and my Mum. Despite all our letters it seemed to me that we would be meeting once more almost as strangers. Mum had said that they would be happy for me to live at home with them while I was on leave, but I could only hope that Jan's feelings hadn't changed.

For my furlough, Goodrickes paid for either a standard air flight home or a first-class passage by boat. My six-month-long leave began the day I left the estate and flew down to Calcutta, where it would take two or three working days to obtain my Final Income Tax Release Certificates, without which I would not have been allowed to leave the country. Although I was quite keen on getting home, I still felt very jaded from my second bout of hookworm and also believed I would benefit from having a period by myself to unwind from the pressures of life in tea before I did so. I decided that if possible I would take my time and see a little of Europe along the way.

In our newspaper I had read an advertisement stating that the Italian Lloyd Triestino shipping company ran a regular Far Eastern passenger liner service from Italy via India to Hong Kong and return, and at regular intervals their luxury liner the *Victoria* sailed from Bombay to Genoa, calling in at Karachi, Aden, Suez, Port Said and Naples along the way. As there seemed to be an excellent rail service between Genoa and London I thought this would be ideal, and I made my plans accordingly. She was scheduled to sail from Bombay on Monday August 8th, so I decided to fly down from Saugaon on Wednesday the 3rd, which left me two working days in which to get my Final Release Certificate from the Central IT office and then fly over to Bombay. The only fly in the ointment was Kancha. When I told him I was going on home leave he became very morose and moody, as though he had something on his mind, so I was not surprised when he came up to me a few days later and asked if he could speak to me about my leave. Of course I agreed and asked him what was worrying him. He told me that he knew I had been receiving letters from a Mem Sahib all the time I had been in India, and he asked if this meant I would marry her while I was on leave and bring her back to India. Thinking nothing of this I replied that I had known Jan for a long time and that if things went as I hoped and she agreed to marry me, I would bring her back with me, whereupon he dropped a bombshell and replied that in that case he wouldn't be able to work for me when I came back.

Naturally I was absolutely amazed at this, because he had always seemed very happy working for me, so I asked him what was wrong, and very self-consciously he began to explain. Evidently he had been talking to some of the older bearers whom he usually met when he went to Mal bazaar on a Sunday and they had told him that although many of the Sahibs were fine when they were single, once they brought a wife back with them she took over in the bungalow and made the servants' lives unbearable. They said she usually made unreasonable demands to 'Clean this! Polish that! Mend something else!' while at the same time making them account for every anna of the housekeeping money after they had come back from the bazaar. He was very afraid at the thought of working for Jan and was worried that he wouldn't be able to cope.

As soon as I heard this my heart leapt, and I put him at his ease with a smile. 'Look Kancha,' I said, 'all Mem Sahibs are different exactly the same way as all the Sahibs are and one thing is certain. If I marry a girl and bring her back with me she definitely won't be like that, because if she was I wouldn't be able to live with her either. Don't believe everything the old men say to you as they are probably just having a bit of fun. If I do bring a wife back, why don't you give her a chance and work for us for a few weeks and then you can make up your mind whether you like her or not? I think you would, but if you didn't then I would allow you to leave with the best of references. In the meantime, what I would like you to do is have your holiday while I am away, for which I will pay you a retainer, and then we will reconsider the situation when I come back. How about it?'

At that his face lit up as though he had lost an anna and found a rupee. With that settled and him happy, all I had to do was confirm the arrangements I had already made with Bill Milne. Because his family still lived on Zurrantee, Bill had agreed to allow Kancha and the pani walla to live in a spare house there while I was away, so I also left some cash with him so that he could pay them their monthly pay as arranged. Once this was done, all that remained for me to do was arrange for the pickup to take them and their gear back to Zurrantee and pack my few remaining things.

Lionel was very helpful, and said he would allow me to garage the Consul in a spare shed near the factory and run it on a regular basis to keep it working satisfactorily. Because I was a bit short of ready cash to pay my outstanding bills, I sold my Mauser rifle to a local shopkeeper for 600 rupees, although what he was going to shoot with it goodness only knows. Probably he was only going to use it as a status symbol, because anyone less like a hunter was hard to imagine, but he had a licence and he had the cash so it was not up to me to ask why so I demonstrated just how accurate the weapon was and accepted his money with thanks, then handed him his certificate of sale and he carried it proudly away as happy as a sandboy. On Sunday I went up to Sam Sing and returned the cine projector that Martin Hawes had lent me. Once I had cleared my debts, it didn't take me long to pack the rest of my gear in my tin trunks and give them to the Stores Clerk for safe keeping until I returned.

At last I was ready to go. I said my goodbyes to everyone on the Tuesday evening and early next morning, August 3rd, I drove the Consul down to the airfield to catch the early morning passenger flight. Both Kancha and the pani walla came with me, and as we waited in the early morning light I looked around and thought just how much I had come to love this part of India. We had had some very heavy monsoon storms during the previous few days, but that morning dawned cool and clear with a beautiful view of the mountains, almost as though Mother Nature was giving me the best send off she could. It was an experience I have never forgotten. We could never be sure exactly what time the flight would come in. As the other fourteen passengers and I hung around chatting, the Jamair loading labourers carried out the sacks and tea chests which would make up the rest of the load and stacked them in a tidy pile at the edge of the gravelled hard-standing area, while the *gai wallas* chased their cows off the runway, and then we were ready.

A few minutes later we heard the faintest of engine sounds over the river, which enabled us to pick up the slowly-moving speck over the distant Siliguri forest. When she came roaring in over the Saugaon bungalow on her approach, reality really struck me and I knew the time had come. I was on my way at last.

Soon after the plane taxied in, Ash came along from his bungalow to see me off and we chatted as the 24 passengers disembarked. After that it took only a matter of minutes for the aircraft's seating to be altered and her return freight to be loaded aboard, and then it was time to go. Although I had only known Ash for just over a year, we really got on very well together and had become good friends, so I was genuinely sorry to be saying farewell to him and Kancha. The consolation was that if things went as planned at home I would be back in due course, so that cheered me up.

Luckily I didn't have long to wait before the aircrew came out of the Jamair office after their cup of tea and I followed them aboard. However, after they had waved us off and we banked back round over the Teesta river, I glimpsed what was left of VT-DGO below and the Saugaon bungalow in the distance and realised just how much I had become attached to them. I wondered whether I would ever see them again; as it turned out, I never did.

Except for several bouts of very severe clear air turbulence which threw the old aircraft about all over the sky above the River Ganges, the flight down was quite uneventful, but when we descended at Dum Dum two hours later the difference in temperature between Bagracote and Calcutta was absolutely amazing. With the temperature in the low nineties and the humidity in excess of 90 per cent as well, it was like walking into a steam bath. The one hour journey into town in the rattly old Jamair airport bus was absolute purgatory and left me in a bath of sweat, so I was extraordinarily relieved when we finally reached the air-conditioned comfort of the Grand Hotel at about 10 am. Normally when we visited Calcutta on our own business our finances did not run to enjoying this measure of comfort and I stayed at one of the smaller, cheaper hotels, but when we were travelling through on company business Goodrickes paid the bill, so I made the most of it.

Although Goodrickes had no direct links with Messrs Duncan Brothers and our gardens and staff were completely separate, they were our agents in Calcutta and attended to all our affairs in India. As my time was limited and I had to visit the Income Tax Office, I went and paid the customary courtesy visit to their office in Netaji Subhas Road to thank them for their help in making my leave arrangements and to find out what I needed to do to obtain my income tax certificate. To my relief I was told that arrangements had been made for me to present myself at the Central Tax Office at 2 pm that afternoon, when I would see one of the Senior Tax Officers, who would check my annual tax payment details. I had these with me and as they were all in order DBs thought he would be able to authorise my clearance at that time and then I would be able to collect my Final Income Tax Release Certificate the following day and that would settle the matter. Of course I had forgotten that life in India was never as straightforward as that. When I presented myself at the office that afternoon, I was told that the officer who was to have seen me had been unexpectedly called away on business and nobody knew when he was likely to return, so I could either go away and come back the next morning or I could wait in the office in the hope that he would come back. Well I knew I was tight for time, and although I did have two more days in which to obtain the certificate I would not be allowed to leave the country without the clearance certificate, so I decided I would wait it out for as long as possible in the hope that he would come back. I knew that it was futile to create a scene and that discretion was the better part of valour, so I explained my predicament to the Head Clerk and said I would appreciate his help in solving my problem. I asked if he could give me a seat somewhere where I could wait until someone could see me. He was completely perplexed by this attitude, because most people knowing how the system worked would have come back the next day, but he gave me a chair in the corner of the office and I settled down to watch them all work.

The office was like a hothouse, with vibrating fans whirling round overhead and disturbing the dust on the piles of documents and papers which the thirty clerks were working on. Occasionally one would shout for a messenger and a uniformed man would come in and take away a pile only to replace it with another, and I marvelled that people could work their lives away in conditions like that. I had no real idea what they were actually doing to the papers as they did very little writing, but probably they were checking figures and totals etc and ensuring that all the returns were correct. I suppose most of them felt that they were extremely lucky to have a well-paid government job in Calcutta despite the working conditions, because most of them seemed happy enough.

As I watched them, the minutes seemed to drag by into hours until finally the heat, the monotonous hubbub in the office and the fact that I thought I was sickening for a cold took effect and I fell fast asleep until 3.30 when I opened my eyes and heard a messenger telling me that Sri. Majumdar had returned to the office and if I would like to follow him he would take me there. When I was ushered into his sanctuary I found a very fresh looking, uniformed Bengali gentleman sitting at his desk, which made me think he had never been near the office during the heat of the day, but at least I was being seen and when we got down to business he proved to be very helpful and accommodating. He was very efficient and after checking through my papers and asking me a few questions about my leave, he said he could see no reason why I could not have my certificate without any further delay. He was as good as his word. By 5 pm I was on my way back to the Grand with my precious paper, and the rest of my time was my own.

The only thing I really wanted to do in the way of shopping was to buy a new shirt and tie for when I arrived in the UK. Jan had written to me that both she and Mum would try to come up to Dover to meet me off the boat train when I arrived and as I knew that the journey home would take nearly three weeks, I realised that I would have very few clean clothes left by that time, so thought that if I packed the shirt and tie in the bottom of my suitcase I would be well prepared when the time came. The only drawback was that I had no idea what the well-dressed tea planter going on home leave was wearing that year, so the next day I decided to take the plunge and bought a very snazzy grey shirt with a white paisley-design tie which I thought was very smart. I could only hope that Jan would think so too, as I really wanted to make a good first impression.

Once I had done this I had nothing else to do but wait until Monday, so as it was so hot outside and I had definitely developed a cold, I spent most of the next two days relaxing and resting in the hotel's air conditioned lounge. On the Sunday I decided to go to the cinema in the evening. The Lighthouse was just round the corner from the Grand so I could have gone to the afternoon performance, but I was in no hurry. Luckily I decided to sit down in the air-conditioned reception area and read a newspaper before I got ready.

I hadn't been there very long when I heard an Indian voice saying, 'Well, well, and here is Mr Brown on his way back to the UK'. When I looked up it turned out to be Durga Roy, an old friend of Wee Mac's whom I had got to know during our shikar outings and our visits to Siliguri. He owned the T&I petrol station on the road up to Darjeeling and his office was always open for visitors when we were passing that way, as he usually had something to eat and a cool drink for any of his friends who cared to stop. He had been in Calcutta for a few days on business and was at a loose end until he flew up to Bagdogra the following morning, so when I suggested that he could accompany me to the cinema he jumped at the idea. I was only too grateful for a bit of company, especially as Durga knew where we could get good, genuine drinks at very reasonable prices, so later that evening off we went.

Unfortunately the film was *The Caine Mutiny*, which dealt with a mutiny aboard a US Navy destroyer during WW II when the captain lost his nerve as the ship was almost sunk during a hurricane and some of his officers took command. It was a tremendous film full of action and special effects and the wave and storm effects were so realistic that halfway through the film Durga got up in a hell of a hurry, mumbling something like, 'Sorry, I've got to go' and shot out. I had noticed that he had been squirming a bit in his seat, but he was away for several minutes so I went out to look for him and was surprised when he told me he had been seasick. He had never experienced waves like that before, and when they showed the violent motion of the ship it all became too much for him until finally he had to leave.

Luckily the last part of the picture dealt with the subsequent courts martial as some of his officers were charged with mutiny, and as there was very little film of the storm in it he was able to enjoy it to the end. Afterwards he had recovered enough to take me to a small club he knew where we enjoyed an excellent curry dinner accompanied by Scotch whiskies, which because of import restrictions imposed by the National Government were very difficult to get at that time, so I had a lovely last evening in Calcutta, all thanks to Durga.

Departure day, August 8th, dawned bright and sunny and we parted that morning with the hope that we would meet again when I returned in 1956. Then, as the *Victoria* was not sailing until the afternoon I took the early morning Indian Airlines flight to Bombay so that I would not have to spend the night there. For this service they used Douglas DC4

Skymasters, the four-engined big brother of the faithful old Dakota. It left Dum Dum at about 6 am and as it had a cruising speed of 280 mph, the 1200 mile flight across only took just over four hours and I had plenty of time to take a taxi from Santa Cruz airport to the docks, where I arrived soon after midday.

The flight could have been very comfortable and enjoyable, but the sniffles that had begun in the Tax Inspector's office had developed into a very severe head cold and with the plane cruising at 14,000 feet the altitude played havoc with my nostrils and sinuses, so that after a period of quite intense pain I became completely blocked up. It was so bad that when I landed I was stone deaf. I took a taxi to the docks, where the passengers were already boarding when I arrived at the ship, and as I only had two medium-sized suitcases and a shoulder bag as luggage I was soon on board and being shown to a very nice, well appointed single cabin with a porthole. She was fully air conditioned, and as I was travelling first class I had a three-foot-wide bed, a wardrobe and a chest of drawers, together with a small private bathroom which contained a sink, a toilet and a shower. They were overall perhaps the best-equipped liners between Europe and the East.

By this time it was early afternoon, so I had a cold buffet lunch in the dining room, then went up onto the top deck to watch all the last-minute preparations prior to departure. While leaning over the rail I started chatting to a young Indian girl who happened to be standing beside me. She too had come over from Calcutta, and as she had lost her father she was travelling to England in the hope of starting a new life there. She intended sending for her mother once she was settled. Unfortunately she was travelling second class, and as the first and second-class passengers were not allowed to mix once the vessel was at sea, we didn't see very much of each other on the voyage. However, over the years we kept in touch. She did make a success of her life in London and she did send for her mother. The friendship we began then still continues.

We sailed at about 3 pm. As we pulled out from the docks into the open sea, the afternoon sun illuminated the city and a local beauty spot the Malabar Gardens, so I got an absolutely superb view of the whole area which was much better than the one I had been treated to when I arrived, almost as though Bombay was saying 'Sorry to see you go. Come back and see me again some time' and I was almost sorry to be leaving. The first leg of the journey home was the 600 miles to Karachi, which we reached the next evening. We stayed until the following day to discharge cargo and take on passengers, then it was a 1700 mile leg to Aden where we were able to go ashore to visit the market in the Crater area and do a bit of sight-seeing. Because the *Victoria* was anchored out in the Crater harbour itself, I was able to see her full beauty from a distance for the first time, and I fell in love with her straight away because she looked really beautiful. At a tonnage of 11,695 gross tons, she was only just over half the size of the old *Strathaird,* which weighed in at 22,544 gross tons, but whereas the *Strathaird* had quite angular lines and looked very rugged and reliable the *Victoria* was completely streamlined and graceful. With her white and blue paintwork surmounted by a yellow and blue funnel she looked more like a millionaire's pleasure cruiser than a working liner, but the big difference came was in the number of passengers carried. As a passenger liner pure and simple, the *Strathaird* carried a total of 1166 passengers, of which roughly 900 were first class and the rest

tourists. Because the *Victoria* carried freight as well, her passenger capacity was only 286 first-class and 181 second-class passengers, and this was really evident in the standard of service her passengers received. Fully air-conditioned and with private or shared facilities in all cabins, she was magnificently equipped, and as each class had its own lounge, veranda, card room and writing room, she and her sister ships earned an envied reputation for fine accommodation, excellent food and attentive service.

As the company sales blurb put it, 'On board it is as if you were staying at a Riviera hotel. In this small but complete floating city, passengers will have the opportunity of spending their days absolutely free of care, without any need to forgo their most cherished habits' (whatever they were), but they were not far wrong. She was only just over a year old, having been completed in Trieste in 1953, so all the facilities on her were very new. In my opinion Lloyd Triestino were to be congratulated on producing one of the finest and most stylish, elegant, graceful and beautiful vessels ever to sail the oceans of the world.

After the noises on board the *Strathaird* she was also an exceedingly quiet ship, and even the bow wave seemed to glide by with an almost imperceptible hiss. The one thing I did dislike about her were her Fiat diesel engines, because whenever she was at sea there was a constant vibration on every deck. These engines were absolutely enormous, with the cylinder head nuts being some three feet in diameter and the connecting rods stretching up through three decks. Later in the voyage I went on a guided tour of the ship which included a visit to the engine room, and when I saw them working I realised why there was a small vibration everywhere on board.

However we soon got used to this, and they must have been very efficient because she cruised at 20 knots, and we had a really smooth passage during the next 1600 miles up the Red Sea from Aden to Suez, which we reached on August 18th.

Here the ship anchored out in the Gulf. As she had to wait for several hours for her slot in the next northbound convoy to Port Said, the company had arranged an optional trip for passengers to visit the pyramids and the Sphinx at Cairo, and I thought this was too good a chance to miss. Local tenders were waiting to ferry us across to the dock, where minibuses had been arranged to take us the hundred or so miles to the pyramid complex. They were not air conditioned and by the time we caught sight of the pyramids our clothes were like wet rags, but as we walked over the baking hot sand to get closer to these ancient wonders we couldn't have cared less. They were absolutely awe inspiring. No photographs can illustrate their sheer size and the dimensions of the blocks that were used to build them and the thought that was continually in our minds was, 'How on earth did labourers build edifices of this size and complexity with virtually their bare hands and brute strength, without the aid of any real construction equipment at all?'

When I got close to the Sphinx and saw the damage Napoleon's artillery had done to its face I got the feeling that we had a lot to learn from the builders of the ancient world. Of course the interiors of the pyramids were not open to tourists in those days and all we could do was wander around outside and drink in the atmosphere, but as we continued our trip north to catch the *Victoria* at Port Said that afternoon, we were all very impressed and subdued by the visit, and I felt very privileged to have had the opportunity to see them.

When we reached Port Said we found the ship waiting for us and ready to sail, so we were absolutely delighted to regain the air-conditioned comfort of our floating hotel. From then on it was like a delightful 1100 mile cruise through the Mediterranean until the next land we reached, which was the toe of Italy. It was a beautiful, summer evening when we sailed through the Strait of Messina, which at the narrowest point is only about five miles wide, and although the sun had set the light was quite clear and we had a superb view of the country on both sides as we passed through.

It was about 200 miles from there to our next stop, Naples, and I think the Captain had deliberately timed our passage so that we would pass by the island of Stromboli with its active volcano at some time in the late evening. We had had a good view of Mount Etna on Sicily, some 50 miles away, as we had skirted the toe of the mainland, but as it wasn't active at that time it looked just like a normal mountain and didn't hold our interest for very long. However Stromboli was totally different. Situated about 80 miles north of Messina in the Tyrrhenian Sea, although it has a permanent population of several hundred people it also has a volcano which is permanently active with minor eruptions which are visible from many miles out at sea, and these have given the island its nickname 'The Lighthouse of the Mediterranean'. An officer who joined us on deck told us that the same pattern of eruptions has been maintained for thousands of years, in which explosions occur in the summit craters with mild to moderate eruptions of incandescent volcanic 'bombs' at intervals ranging from a few minutes to several hours. These usually result in the ejection of ash, molten, incandescent lava and fiery solids up to a height of several hundred metres that last for several seconds, and he said that with good weather and excellent visibility we should get a good view as we sailed by, so we waited with eager anticipation for the entertainment.

Our course took us straight towards it. As darkness fell we could see a crimson point of light away above the northern horizon, but after watching it for a while it got boring so we went down to dinner. When we came on deck again at 9 pm we could just make out the smudge of the island in the darkness about 20 miles away and the light had grown into a glowing cauldron hanging in the sky, from which gouts of fiery, molten lava and flame would erupt into the air every few minutes. The nearer we got to the island the more spectacular this natural firework display became. Evidently the Captain believed in giving his passengers their money's worth, because he took the ship in to within a mile from the north western side of the cone as we passed by and then illuminated the walls of the crater with his searchlights, which gave us all an absolutely superb view. The summit of Stromboli stands 3034 feet above sea level, but as it actually rises over 6500 feet above the sea bed its sides and underwater sea cliffs must descend almost vertically for thousands of feet, so he must have known what he was doing. Probably he had done this many times before and the ship must have been in no danger, but I don't think the captain of a British liner would have taken the risk.

In fact this was one of the biggest differences I found after sailing in both the *Strathaird* and the *Victoria*. On the *Strathaird*, although the Captain and the First Officer had their own tables in the dining room at which only selected passengers were seated, they were usually conspicuous by their absence and were only present when things were going really well or there was something special on. Entertaining and looking after the passengers was left to the younger officers and we assumed that the Captain and First officer were usually away sailing the ship, which was always reassuring to know. The ship was very sports orientated, with deck tennis, deck quoits and table tennis competitions being organised by the Entertainments Officer throughout the voyage, while 'keep fit' classes took place every morning.

On the *Victoria* it was very different. Both the senior officers usually ate at their respective tables most evenings and were very sociable and made themselves known to many of the other passengers during the course of the voyage. They entered into the spirit of the entertainments and dances in the evenings and presumably their attitude was that they had a skilled team of officers beneath them whose responsibility it was to run the ship, while their jobs were to oversee them all and make sure that the passengers were happy and it seemed to work. As far as I know there were no organised sports competitions during our voyage, but despite the fact that there seemed to be a very happy and carefree 'Mediterranean' atmosphere everywhere on board, she was spotlessly clean and run in a very seamanlike manner and I can't remember anybody complaining about anything on that trip.

It took about thirty minutes to skirt the cliffs of Stromboli, then once we had lost sight of the fiery crater it was quickly swallowed up in the darkness and we all went to our cabins for our last night's sleep before we reached Naples. At about 6 am I awoke from a deep sleep with the feeling that something was different and I lay listening for several moments until I realised that the ever present vibrations had stopped, so I hopped out of bed and rushed on deck, where I was greeted by the most magnificent sight. We had moored out in the bay and the waterfront and city of Naples were spread out before us in a panorama of multi-coloured lights which spread back to the slopes of Vesuvius in the distance. As many of the ships in the harbour were illuminated with various coloured lights as the stevedores worked, it seemed the city was giving me a very special display to welcome me home.

We appeared to be moored to gigantic buoys, and as we had been told that we would spend two whole days in Naples while some passengers disembarked and freight was unloaded, it looked as though we would go in and dock the next morning, so after enjoying the free show for a few minutes I went back to bed. Unfortunately the excitement was too much for me and I didn't enjoy much sleep as my mind revolved round the rest of the journey and what would be waiting for me when I got home, so I rose quite early the next morning.

Because of the time it would take to unload the cargo, the company had arranged two optional full day tours for those passengers who were sailing on to Genoa, where the voyage officially ended. The first day was a trip to the crater of Vesuvius, followed by a tour of the ruins of Pompeii and then a visit to a cameo factory, while the second was a boat trip across the bay to the Isle of Capri to see Gracie Field's home and the Blue Grotto and then on to Sorrento and the invasion beaches of Salerno. For me these were two trips not to be missed, and although we were unable to see the sights in the same manner that today's tourists would do so, for me they were absolutely breathtaking. Because we were not officially disembarking we did not have to go through customs, so the next morning we passed through the passport control office in a group and then drove the six miles to the volcano in a couple of old ex-military buses. Once there they parked at the base of the cone, where we transferred to some old Jeeps which carried us up a rough road to a parking place about 800 feet below the summit, and from there we had to walk. This entailed a scramble up a rough zig-zag path until we reached the rim of the crater. After the pyrotechnics we had seen on Stromboli, when we stood and gazed down into its dirty blackness it seemed to me to be a bit of an anti climax, as it looked like the inside of a gigantic, almost dead, smelly garden bonfire.

Vesuvius' last proper eruption took place on March 18th 1944 when three villages were destroyed. Since then it had remained dormant, and when I saw it the only activity to be seen was plumes of steam rising from vents in the bottom of the crater accompanied by waves of intense heat and a vile chemical smell. In retrospect I am very glad I visited it, especially as it was this sleeping giant which had completely destroyed Pompeii, the place we were to visit later, but I think I preferred the view of Stromboli I had seen the night before. Unfortunately, just as I had done in Egypt, I forgot to take my cine camera with me, so I'm afraid I was unable to record this visit for posterity.

Back at the buses we ate our picnic lunch, then in the afternoon we visited the remains of Pompeii. As at that time the modern excavations there were in their infancy, we were only able to visit a small area which had been cleared, but even this was enough to show us what a wonderful place it must have been in its heyday and just how much of it was still waiting to be discovered. At that time it was thought the victims had been killed by being suffocated by the noxious gases and volcanic ash which filled the atmosphere and that their bodies had been completely smothered by the thick layer of volcanic ash that fell later. Inside these natural coffins they gradually decomposed until a unique void was made in the identical form of the original body. When they were rediscovered in the late 19th century it was realised that if these shells were completely filled with fine plaster, exact replicas of the victims could be made, complete in every detail. When I saw them in the museum later they were so lifelike that they made a big impression on me.

Since then this theory has been changed, because many more have been discovered, together with the skeletons of people who had sheltered inside buildings and had not been suffocated. Research has found that in all probability, before they were covered with their blanket of hot ash they were all killed by exposure to a cloud of fast-moving superheated gases and steam which was sufficient to cause instant death, even though they were sheltering inside buildings, very similar to the 400° C pyroclastic flow which moved at a speed of at least 400 mph and took so many lives during the Mount St. Helens eruption in 1980.

It is strange to think that when I visited the site in 1955 we were about the only tourists there, whereas it was estimated that in 2008 about 2.8 million people visited it. How times have changed.

To complete our trip, after drinking a very refreshing cup of tea in a nearby restaurant, we drove a few miles to a local cameo factory where we found about 50 men grinding away at the shells from which the cameos were made. The heat, noise and the clouds of grinding dust made the conditions absolutely unbearable and as there was not a dust mask or extraction system anywhere in sight, I dread to think what the insides of their lungs were like. I can't imagine many of them lasted very far into old age.

As an engineer I was quite interested to see how they ground away the outer surfaces of the shells to make the designs and decorations and then mount them. Although I bought a very nice table lamp made from a conch shell, I wasn't really interested in the sets of jewellery they had for sale. Because Italy had suffered very badly during the war and was very poor at that time, they were ridiculously cheap, and I could have bought a complete matching set of a necklace, pendant, brooch, ring and a pair of earrings for about five pounds, but because Mum had kept a really beautiful cameo brooch in a box in my bedroom at home for many years and had never worn it, I thought they were very dated and completely out of fashion and nobody ever wore them any more. It was only after I had reached home and told Jan about them that she explained to me that they were all the fashion at that time and I realised just what a chance I had missed.

The following day was our trip along the coast south of Naples. After I had washed and dressed myself before going down to breakfast, I was sitting on the edge of my bed with my head between my legs tying up my shoelaces, when suddenly there was a tremendous report in my right ear quickly followed by another in my left one. For a moment I thought I had heard gunshots. Then to my surprise I realised that I was hearing all the shipboard noises I had missed when I had compared the *Victoria* with the *Strathaird*. Suddenly I could hear the voices of the crew, the thumps and bumps around the ship and the lapping of the water, and realised the *Victoria* was not as quiet a ship as I had thought. Soon I realised that my Indian cold had clogged up my sinuses so much that, unknown to me, I had been stone deaf for the whole of the voyage until they had cleared themselves and I could hear normally once more.

Goodness knows how much of the conversations I had missed when I had been chatting to other passengers during the voyage. They must have thought I was a little abnormal.

After breakfast really comfortable coaches had been laid on to carry us to the pretty little town of Sorrento 30 miles away, where a boat would be ready to take us on a trip along the edge of the Bay of Naples to the Isle of Capri, and then on to the town of Salerno, where our coaches would be waiting to take us back to the *Victoria*. It was a beautiful sunny Mediterranean summer morning as we followed the main coastal highway that switchbacked along the coast in the small area of flat land sandwiched between the sea and the mountains. Each time we travelled around a small bay and then reached the tip of another headland we were treated to another superb view of Vesuvius across the bright blue water of the bay.

Sorrento was a small town of about 8000 inhabitants built on the 150-foot-high cliffs at the southern extremity of the bay, and from there ferry boats provided services to Naples and many of the ports along this stretch of the coast. Most of the houses were painted or lime washed white. As we walked from the coach terminus through the town the dazzle of the glaring sun reflecting off them was absolutely blinding, and I wondered why they had not painted them in pretty pastel shades as people in many other Mediterranean villages had done. Possibly it was done to keep them cool. From a distance across the bay the white town snuggled down on the top of its cliffs looked really picturesque, but that morning the glare gave me quite a severe headache, something I am not normally prone to, and I was really glad when we reached the harbour and found our cruise boat waiting for us.

She was quite a large vessel with plenty of room to

accommodate our 150 passengers with no difficulty, and to our surprise a lovely Italian buffet lunch had also been laid ready for us which consisted of huge amounts of cheeses, hams, sausages, hot crusty bread, butter and salads, together with bottles of red and white wine. Then while the Captain gave us an excellent guided tour right round the southern side of the bay, then round Capri with its Blue Grotto and Gracie Field's villa and finally across the Gulf of Salerno to the town itself, we sat beneath the awning on the top deck and stuffed ourselves while we admired the views as they were pointed out to us. However for me the best was still to come. I was particularly interested in visiting the town of Salerno and the adjacent beaches because they had featured prominently in the BBC news broadcasts only twelve years before. During World War II the first invasion of Axis home territory began on the night of July 9th 1943 when 181,000 men of the Allied armies invaded Sicily. It took 38 days of heavy fighting before the Italian and German troops defending the island finally retreated and were then evacuated and escaped back to the Italian mainland across the Straits of Messina.

On July 25th Benito Mussolini was stripped of his supreme power by the Fascist Grand Council of Italy, who passed it on to King Victor Emmanuel, and under his leadership Marshall Badoglio formed a new Government and immediately began negotiating with the Allies in an effort to surrender and then change sides. He had hoped that Italy would then be allowed to fight against Germany, but the Allies would not agree to this and it was not until September 3rd that Italy surrendered unconditionally and her army stopped fighting. Once this was accomplished the Allies were divided as to how best to exploit their victory, but finally it was decided that the British forces should invade southern Italy across the Straits of Messina and also launch a sea-borne landing near the strategic port of Taranto on the heel of Italy, while a combined American and Allied force would land on the beaches at Salerno. By doing this it was hoped that the three-pronged attack would prevent the German army from forming a credible line of defence across Italy out of the isolated German units which had been sent in to bolster up the Italian resistance before its surrender.

Salerno was chosen as the site for the invasion because it was the nearest suitable spot to Naples that was within the range of Allied fighter aircraft flying from bases in Sicily, and the Allied planners anticipated that it would force the German Army to make a rapid withdrawal back to Rome and beyond before General Kesselring, the German C-in-C, could organise an effective defensive line, but they were wrong. On the night of September 8th/9th 1943, the news of the Italian capitulation was broadcast to the troops of the invasion force, who were on their way to the Salerno beaches, so they didn't anticipate very much resistance from the defenders, but although they were able to land on the beaches virtually unopposed, they did not anticipate the ability of Kesselring to construct a formidable defence out of virtually nothing. Although all the Allied landings in the Gulf of Salerno established themselves without much opposition, their first attempts to push inland through the mountains behind Salerno were repelled by devastating German fire. The local German commander launched such a deadly counter-attack that he almost drove the Allied forces back into the sea, but at the last moment the drive ran out of steam, the front held and reinforcements poured into the beachhead once more. As long as this held, Kesselring could not ignore the steady advance of the 8th Army from the foot of

Italy, and after a 10-day crisis for the Allies the Germans were forced to begin a planned withdrawal to a new defensive line on the Volturno river south of Rome and the British were able to enter Naples on October 1st.

Of course in 1955 this was still very fresh in my memory, so while most of our group visited the shops in the centre of the town, I spent an unforgettable three hours walking the beaches and the cliffs imagining how it must have been for the lads who had fought and died there. Seeing the mountains rising behind the town, I realised how difficult it must have been for them to break through against an army that was firing down on them, and this was something that was to be repeated from the monastery of Monte Cassino when they tried to break through the Gustav Line later in the campaign. However as I looked down on the scene below, with the beaches bathed in the afternoon sun and the blue water sparkling across the bay, I had great difficulty in visualising the horror and carnage that must have ensued during those ten critical days before the Germans were forced to retreat.

CHAPTER THIRTY EIGHT

Another memorable breakfast, and home again

When we returned to the *Victoria* she was almost ready to leave harbour for the last part of our voyage, the 400-mile hop from Naples to her home port of Genoa, and within an hour we had weighed anchor and were on our way. Because she had discharged a large portion of her cargo and most of her passengers in Naples, she was a very quiet ship that evening and as there was no organised entertainment arranged, some of us took our drinks onto the promenade deck after dinner and watched the brilliantly-lit Italian coast sliding by a few miles away. As she was considerably lighter she must have sailed much faster than her normal 20 knots, as the journey only took about 16 hours and at 9 am the next morning we were home, safe and sound in Genoa harbour

By this time I was completely ready to disembark. Because I was a transit passenger and intended leaving on the evening train for Paris, in the Customs Hall I was able to join a special queue which fast-tracked us through the customs procedure. However as I waited my turn to open my cases, my attention was drawn to a row which had erupted in the section that was reserved for Italian nationals only. The man in question was a middle-aged doctor or scientist who had been working abroad, and in his numerous items of baggage he had a beautifully-polished wooden case which he said contained a microscope he had bought in Aden. The customs man wanted him to open it so that he could check the contents for himself, so he was very annoyed when the doctor said he could not find the key to unlock it, and as he and his wife got more and more flustered because the key could not be found, the official and his superiors became increasingly suspicious and unhelpful. They insisted that it had to be opened. Very soon a group of irate passengers had gathered round supporting the doctor, while increasing numbers of officials came to support their colleagues. In next to no time a full-scale row had broken out as both sides lost their tempers, and it was absolutely chaotic as they berated each other in Italian at the tops of their voices. For a while I thought they would come to blows, but suddenly with absolutely no warning, the little doctor went berserk. At that time various items of fire fighting equipment such as small hand axes and buckets of sand and water were fixed to the walls in case of emergencies, and without more ado he broke through his ring of friends, ran over to the wall and came back with an axe in his hand. I thought he was going to use it to clout the customs officer, but instead of this he laid into his wooden box as though he was smashing up wood to make a fire. Bits and pieces flew off it and he wasn't content until he had completely destroyed the outer case and the mangled remains of his microscope were sitting completely exposed on its base amidst the wreckage. Then he threw down his axe. 'There' he shouted, 'I told you it was a microscope.' For a few moments there was a stunned silence as everyone realised what he had done, then the customs man quietly picked up his piece of chalk and carefully marked a big 'X' on the one bit of case that remained intact. Without another word he turned round and walked away, at which the crowd dispersed and the little doctor broke down in tears. I had always been told that the Italians were a very volatile and excitable people, but I had never considered that they were as bad as that. I thought that if this case had occurred in England in all probability we would have said, 'Well, I can't find the key at the moment, so take it into safe custody and when I do find the key I will come back later with someone to open it and collect it then', and that would have been the end of it. As they say, 'You live and learn'.

After this things returned to normal. Once I had passed safely through passport control and customs, I took a taxi down to the railway station to check my train times and ticket and then left my two cases in the left luggage office so that I could collect them that evening, so the rest of the day was my own. My train to Paris was scheduled to leave at 7.30 pm, so I took a seat on a coach trip which combined a tour of the city in the morning then lunch, followed by an afternoon tour of the Italian Riviera. Genoa was once a typical Italian city with many ancient monuments, but it was so badly damaged during the war that several large sections of the city and the port area had to be almost completely rebuilt and as a result it became Italy's largest port and the Mediterranean's busiest, while it was also the first in that area to build modern container facilities. Consequently it was a bit of a disappointment to me as a sightseeing tourist, but once we had travelled down the coastal road and reached the small sea side towns of Rapallo, Porto Fino and Santa Margherita Ligure everything changed completely. Clustered on the small stretches of flat land between the mountains and the sea they were lovely, small towns with a real 'chocolate box' appearance.

It was the view out to sea that amazed me the most. Since the war business practice had changed completely. Instead of locating a business in one country and paying taxes, the real tycoons had realised that if they bought a boat large enough to accommodate everything they needed, modern communications had improved so much that they could travel from place to place without being resident in any one country and having to pay taxes. They could still control their empires while living on board. At the same time, if the weather got bad or they fancied a break they could still hop ashore and stay as tourists without any questions being asked. As a result the shallow waters just offshore were a mass of yachts and larger craft - I don't think I had ever seen so much money tied up in one place before.

The largest and most impressive of all these vessels was the *Christina*, which was owned by Aristotle Onassis, the Greek shipping magnate. He had made his immense fortune after the war by various means and the ship had originally been a Canadian navy frigate named HMCS *Stormont*, which he bought for $34,000 and then spent $4 million to convert her into a luxurious yacht and renamed her *Christina* after his daughter. From the shore she looked immense, 325 feet long with a helicopter platform on the promenade deck to top things off. With her gleaming white hull and superstructure and her streamlined yellow funnel she looked like a fairy palace floating on the blue water.

Subsequently the ship had a very chequered career, because later she was the home of Onassis' mistress, Maria Callas, as well as his second wife, Jackie Kennedy, and at various times she was one of the most famous society venues of the time, with numerous celebrities such as Marilyn Monroe, Frank Sinatra, John F. Kennedy and Winston Churchill amongst the people who enjoyed a good time on board. After his death in 1975 Onassis left her to his daughter, who then gave her to the Greek Government to use as a presidential yacht, but she was allowed to decay until 1998 when she was bought by another Greek ship owner who undertook another intensive refurbishment and renamed her the *Christina O*. The last I heard of her was in 2006 when she was available for charter at about 50,000 euros per day. Possibly this is a sad end for such a beautiful ship, but in a way I am rather glad that she is still in active service, because so many of the beautiful liners that I saw or sailed on have gone to the 'great scrap yard in the sky' during the past 60 years and they seemed to have much more grace and mystique than the gigantic 'block of flats' appearance of today's cruise liners.

Later that afternoon I returned to the railway station and reclaimed my luggage, then after a meal in the station restaurant I boarded the train and we left at exactly 7.30 pm. It was only an overnight journey from Genoa to Paris, so I decided not to book a sleeper birth and made do with a first class seat instead. As I was rather tired after my day's excursions I managed to sleep most of the way. About the only time I was disturbed was when we reached Domodossola, on the border between Italy and Switzerland, where they checked my passport, presumably in order to make sure that I had left the country as promised, but after that nobody seemed to bother and we reached Paris early next morning.

Other than the fact that I had decided to stay in Paris as

long as my money lasted, I had made no other arrangements and didn't know what to expect, but I had met a young American lad about the same age as myself on the train ('My name is Benny, but call me Ben'), who was also going to stop over and he advised me that the best place to go to for value for money was to a *pension*, a French boarding house where one could get a room only. Consequently we took a taxi and finished up at the Hotel Bleu, which was within walking distance of the Gare du Nord from where the boat train departed for England each morning. We were able to get accommodation on a room-only basis at very reasonable rates. From what I could gather Ben was a art student who had dropped out of university in America and was now travelling round Europe visiting all the ancient ruins and art galleries on a shoestring before going back to America to take up a job in his father's law firm. As he had travelled round most of Europe he only had to 'do' Paris and London before it was time to go home.

My room was quite simple and old fashioned but very clean and nice and was furnished with a large single bed, wardrobe, dressing table, cupboard and a wash basin. The bathroom containing the shower and toilet were a few yards away along the corridor and as I was in no hurry to see Paris, I decided to have a rest, then count my money and plan my stay. Under the Indian income tax laws, after I had paid my tax each month what was left was divided into three equal portions. One was reckoned to be what I needed to spend in order to live in India, the second was deemed to be my Indian savings in Rupees, which had to remain in India until I retired, while I was allowed to transfer the third portion home as my savings in the UK. As I knew I would need this when I went on home leave I had made some transfers over the last few months. However

I had been told that although my holiday pay would be paid to me from the day I left Bagracote, this would not be paid into my bank account until the end of the month and as I had not been able to save as much as I would have liked to, I didn't want to use this until I got home. Luckily I did have some sterling notes that I had got from a fellow planter who was short of rupees to pay a bill one day, and once I had deducted the cost of my train fare home and my hotel bill, I decided that I had enough left for me to stay for three days if I had one proper cooked meal each day, which was virtually what I had got used to in India. If I did this I would be able to buy cold groceries such as bread, ham, butter, cheese, biscuits, jam and fruit from the local market and keep them in my room, and these would enable me to eat whenever I was hungry.

Accordingly I walked to the Gare du Nord and booked a seat on the *Flèche d'Or* for the morning of Monday August 25th, then sent a telegram to Jan telling her of my plan, after which I visited the local market and bought my supplies and was then ready for a spot of sightseeing. The *Flèche d'Or* was the French railways section of a luxury boat train service which linked Paris with Calais, where passengers took the ferry to Dover and then joined the Southern Railways *Golden Arrow* for the rest of the journey to Victoria station in London. Originally it had been an 'all first class' Pullman system, but when it reopened after the war, ordinary first and third-class were added and the ferry was modified to allow other classes of passengers, but it was still a first-class service and I was going home in style.

I suppose because it was so near and its history had been involved with ours for so many years I had always been fascinated by Paris, but my main reason in visiting it on the way home was that I wanted to see one of the many jazz clubs that had sprung up since the war on the Left Bank. During the past ten years Paris had become the mecca for traditional New Orleans jazz in Europe, partly through the legacy left by the American armed forces, but also because of the influence of French jazzmen such as Sidney Bechet, Django Reinhardt and Stephan Grapelli, who played much of their jazz in the city, and I felt this was my one chance to visit one in the hope of hearing some really good live music. Luckily when I talked to Ben later in the morning he told me that he too was interested in traditional jazz, so that afternoon we went out together to do a bit of detective work to find out where to go.

Initially, owing to the fact that neither of us could speak French fluently, we didn't have much success, until we met a couple of young girl students from Paris University who were trying to sell some of their rag week magazines. As soon as they approached us we realised that their English was a lot better than our French, so when they told us they loved jazz and were regular visitors to some of the jazz clubs, we asked them whether they would be willing to take us that evening. We really didn't think they would, so we were quite surprised when they said they would be quite happy to take us there. However they still had quite a pile of magazines to sell and wouldn't be able to spare any time until they had done so. Well this didn't present any difficulty to Ben and myself. To their joy we said that if they would go with us that night we would sell their magazines in double-quick time. Taking a pile each we approached all and sundry, but especially anybody who looked like a tourist, and speaking in English we pointed out what interesting keepsakes these would be to remind them of their stay in Paris. This seemed to work, because in a couple of hours we had sold them all, much to the two girls' delight. True to their word they met us that evening at the local metro station and we had a wonderful evening at the Caveau de La Huchette.

Having been opened just after the war, this was one of the oldest and best-known jazz clubs in Paris, where both Sidney Bechet and Lionel Hampton had performed. For a few francs we were admitted and descended a stone staircase to the cellar, which was a small room where there was sufficient space to accommodate a small bar where we could buy quite reasonably priced drinks. There was a seven-piece traditional New Orleans band and room for about 100 listeners. From the way we were packed in there must have been at least twice that number there, but that only seemed to heighten the atmosphere and increase the enjoyment of the music, because although we had never heard of any of the musicians before, their interpretations of the old New Orleans jazz favourites that were popular at that time were out of this world, and we were all extremely disappointed when the 1 am closing time came. The one thing I did notice compared with the clubs in London was that the French audience became much more excited and involved with the music. In the London jazz club where I had listened to the Humphrey Lyttelton band play before I went out to India, the listeners enjoyed the music without actually becoming involved, whereas the French audience seemed to become part of the music rather as they did in New Orleans.

The last item the band played was Sidney Bechet's famous street march 'In the streets of Antibes', for which the clarinettist exchanged his clarinet for a soprano sax in true Bechet style. By the time they finally reached the last chorus the crowd was stomping round and round the room in time to the music, which was a truly memorable experience.

Finally it was time for us to make our way up the steps into the chill of the Parisian morning, after which the two girls led us back to the local metro station, where we all thanked each other and said goodnight. Then we went on our way and they went theirs and we never saw each other again. It was one of those chance happenings that occur quite unexpectedly now and again which can never be repeated, but thanks to those girls it was an absolutely unforgettable experience and one I don't think that we could have arranged on our own.

Although this experience was the real highlight of my visit, there were two other incidents that occurred which are worth recording. One happened the next morning when I asked a French policeman to direct me to one of the tourist spots I wished to see and he didn't seem to understand a word I was saying. Having listened to a lot of French being spoken since I had arrived, I thought my schoolboy French was flowing freely and not too badly at all, but the silly fellow persisted in misinterpreting everything I said and looked at me as though I was a bit off my rocker, until finally he raised his eyes to the sky, gave a Gallic shrug of his shoulders and walked off. Well I thought that this was extremely ill mannered of him and it annoyed me, but I couldn't do anything about it so I looked around until I found someone who could speak English who showed me the way. It was only later that I realised what an absolute fool I had made of myself, when it suddenly struck me that instead of speaking to him in French, I had been conversing fluently with him in Hindi! No wonder the poor man didn't have the slightest idea what I was asking him. In all probability if I had spoken to him in English he would have understood, but I had got so used to conversing with the workers in India that it didn't cross my mind that he wouldn't understand my French, so really for a western-looking man to be speaking some intelligible language, he must have thought I was a refugee from the Russian steppes or something. I bet he told a fine tale when he got back to his wife that evening.

The other incident occurred when I had my hot midday meal that day. My plan of buying cold food to eat in the hotel had worked well, as I always had a well-stocked bag of food in my wardrobe whenever I felt hungry, but after sightseeing that morning I realised that I hadn't had a proper curry since I had left India and it was almost as though I was having withdrawal symptoms. I had noticed a very authentic looking Indian restaurant not far from the Hotel Bleu, so I decided to have my lunch there and then go back to the hotel and sleep it off afterwards, little thinking what was about to happen. It was lovely and cool inside and once the waitress had shown me to my table I had no difficulty in ordering some of my favourite dishes, but when it came to a drink this was much more difficult as both the beer and cider were extremely expensive. Finally I asked her what the workers seated at the front of the restaurant were drinking. It turned out that this was 'vin de pays', or vin ordinaire, a wine of undistinguished quality which was cheap enough for everyday quaffing. They all seemed to be enjoying it, so I ordered a litre carafe. To my surprise, when my curry was served I found it very much hotter than most of the food I had ever had in India and it just about blew the top of my head off. Although I was given plenty of rice and cool chutneys, these were not enough for me to be able to eat it properly and I soon found that after every two or three spoonfuls I had to cool my mouth off with wine. In fact it was so hot that I soon realised that before very long it would be very difficult for me to eat very much of it at all, but I did not have enough money to waste it and buy something else so I decided to mix all the rice and curry together and then eat five mouthfuls between slugs of wine in the hope that this would last until the end.

Unfortunately the waitress had to bring me another half litre to enable me to finish the curry off. This seemed to work, because once the inside of my mouth became numb with the effects of both the curry and the wine I got on fine, and other than feeling a bit merry and bright I was perfectly all right as long as I was sitting down. Unfortunately when the waitress brought me my bill and I stood up to pay her, everything started to rotate. When I withdrew a handful of money from my trouser pocket I dropped it all over the floor, which meant she had to scrabble around to collect it for me so that I could hold it out for her to take what she required to pay the bill. After this she took my arm and escorted me to the street door, where I took out what must have been quite a large note as a tip, as she seemed absolutely overcome with joy when I gave it to her.

I walked out into the street and felt as though a red-hot hammer had hit me. The afternoon sun was beating down and the combined effect of the sun, the curry and the wine meant I was as hot outside as I was inside, and my brain just gave up. I just had enough sense left to realise that if I turned right and kept on walking, the hotel was about 400 yards away on my right hand side, so I staggered away and kept going, but it seemed an eternity until I finally saw its blue-painted facade through my bleary eyes. Once inside I tottered up to my room, took my shoes off and collapsed on the bed, only to find that the moment I shut my eyes the bed started swinging backwards and forwards like a ship in a gale, an action that left me with a terrible feeling of nausea inside. I could only counter this by opening them again.

After drinking 1.5 litres of red wine I must have been suffering from an attack of alcoholic poisoning, because after a while as the ship slowed down, the last thing I remember was looking at my watch, which showed 2.30 pm, and then I must have gone into a drunken stupor. The queer thing was that I didn't vomit, nor did I get up to visit the bathroom.

When I woke up at 7 am the next morning it seemed as though I had an army of little men beating the inside of my head with hammers. At first my mouth tasted like the bottom of a parrot's cage and I felt like death warmed up, but other than that I felt fine, so once I had drunk several glasses of water and eaten a couple of ham sandwiches I felt like a new man. The only lasting legacy I had from that curry was that I developed an intense dislike for red wine. It is only in recent years that I have overcome my aversion and been able to drink it in moderation, although to my shame I prefer it to be extremely sweet or diluted with lemonade or apple juice. Shame! Shame!

Once my brain had recovered and I had chased the little men with their hammers away, I realised that it was Monday August 25th and I was due to be at the station at 10 am, so it was very fortunate that I had woken up when I did and was able to make it to the Gare du Nord in plenty of time to take my seat. In comparison with flying, normal train travel holds very little attraction for me, and as the journey to Calais was completely without incident and my stomach was still quite queasy, I slept most of the way to try to build myself up for the ferry journey across.

As it turned out it was a beautiful morning with a bright

sun, blue skies and a gently rolling swell, just the right kind of day to return home on, and I was really looking forward to reaching Dover to discover whether anybody had been able to come down to meet me.

I had one extremely important decision to make. My snazzy grey shirt and white Paisley tie still nestled in the bottom of my suitcase in their original packaging. I had to decide whether to change into them before I had my breakfast with the second sitting or whether to eat first and change later, but when I went down to the restaurant I found it so crowded that I decided on the first option. I had plenty of time to get ready and as I left the changing room I admired myself in the mirror and thought I looked very much like a swell planter coming home from India on leave, so what could go wrong? Little did I realise that my trip to India that had started with a memorable breakfast on board a ship all those years before was destined to end in a similar fashion, although not in exactly in the same way.

As I entered the restaurant and took my seat at a table a young steward was clearing the ones nearby, and as he wished me good morning he said that as soon as he had cleared the table he was doing he would return and take my order for breakfast. To do this he had to pass behind me. As he hurried by with his tray loaded high with dirty crockery and cutlery, several tea cups and dirty plates slipped from a pile, hit me on the head and shoulders and deposited quite a lot of cold tea slops, bacon bits, fried bread and other juicy delicacies all over my new finery and into my lap.

I lost my rag! For a few seconds I sat in a cold rage, absolutely speechless as the reality of what had happened sank in, then, realising that my carefully-made plans were all completely ruined, in a fury I burst out and said, 'Jesus Christ, what in the hell do you think you are doing? This was all new, and look at all the mess you've made'.

'Oh, sorry Guvnor' he replied 'We'll soon put that right' and he began gathering up the rubbish and scraps on a spare plate and rubbing all the grease, egg, tea and coffee stains off with a dirty dish cloth, thus making the mess even worse.

'Do you know' I went on 'I'm meeting someone special at Dover and can you guess how far I've carried these bloody things with me just so that I could look decent when I got here? 6000 miles, all the way from bloody Calcutta!'

He didn't turn a hair. 'Oh, sorry Sir' he said 'I can't say I've ever heard of it. Still, we can't have you meeting somebody like that, all dirty like, so it's up to me to clean you up isn't it and if you come with me we'll put you through the wash and have you all spruced up in no time.'

With that he marched me off into the galley kitchens, where my clothes were all machine-washed, dried and ironed until they looked like new again. While this was being done I washed in a sink, then sat in front of one of the stoves in my underclothes and ate a slap-up free breakfast off a tray, so when I finally dressed again I looked just as smart and beautiful as I had before the whole incident had started. Nevertheless it was still a very memorable breakfast to end my adventures in India.

Once we were approaching the harbour I took my suitcases and went up on the foredeck where I could get a good view of the dock, but there were so many people there waiting to meet us that no matter how hard I strained my eyes it was impossible for me to identify anyone that looked like Jan or Mum. During the preceding years I had often thought what it would be like and what my feelings would be when I got home once more, so it was with a sense of uncertainty and unease, mixed with excitement at the thought that I might soon be seeing my loved ones again, that I walked down the gangway on to British soil once more after 1681 days away.

I wondered where they had all gone to. Although I was 22 years old when I went I had been a late developer and at that time I was still an inexperienced and callow youth, but now I felt that my work, experiences and responsibilities had helped me develop into a responsible adult ready to face whatever the future held. I loved life in India and wanted to return, but I also knew that I loved Jan. I had six months in which to get to know her again and plan my future, even though I realised that this might not be quite what I would have liked. Still this was all in the future.

Then I heard some well-remembered voices shouting out, 'Rod, Rod, Cooee Rod!' and all my doubts and worries slipped away. I hurried over to the crowd and into the arms of the people I loved most in the world. Jan and Mum seemed little different to how I remembered them and my sister Marion had come with them as well, so it was a triple reunion. As I hugged and kissed them I must have been the happiest person in the world.

At that time Marion was still trying to recover from Peter's tragic death and was staying with a cousin of ours in Broadstairs, so Jan and my mum had travelled up from Stroud by train on the previous day and spent the night with them. Then in the morning Marion had arranged to borrow a car and driver from a friend of hers so that they could welcome me in and they arrived in good time to meet the boat. After that we spent the night in Broadstairs before returned to Coaley the next day. I don't think we stopped talking excitedly for the whole of the period, except when we were asleep in bed. It was even better than I had ever imagined.

But what happened about the new shirt and tie, I hear you ask? Was Jan suitably impressed? Well I don't know whether they thought I would come back weather beaten and tanned like an Indian Stewart Grainger, but in fact I had never got very sun-tanned because 300 inches of monsoon rain out of a leaden grey sky every year had put paid to that, and through my two attacks of hookworm I had lost about two and a half stones in weight, so I weighed only just over nine stones when I came home. As a result my face looked quite gaunt and pallid, my clothes hung on me like a scarecrow and as Jan told me lovingly afterwards, with the grey shirt and white tie taking what little colour I had out of my thin and scraggy face, she thought that as came off the boat I looked like a survivor walking out of Belsen. Such is life!

So I arrived home, and I suppose this is the end of the story of my life as a bachelor in India, but now I feel that I have only told half a tale. As must be evident from some of the out-of-context incidents I described earlier, I did marry Jan and she went back to India with me and we stayed there until 1967. During these twelve years both our children, Vivian, our son, and Janita, our daughter, were born in Darjeeling Hospital. Their stories alone would raise the eyebrows of many of today's 'mothers to be', so I intend to tell these and many more in volume two of the story of our lives in India, if time permits. This one has taken so much longer to complete than I had anticipated that this may not come to pass, but by using the experience I have gained while writing this one I hope things may go much better. So if you enjoyed reading this, we can only wait and see.